Judicial Law-Making in European Constitutional Courts

This book analyses the specificity of the law-making activity of European constitutional courts. The main hypothesis is that currently constitutional courts are positive legislators whose position in the system of State organs needs to be redefined.

The book covers the analysis of the law-making activity of four constitutional courts in Western countries: Germany, Italy, Spain, and France; and six constitutional courts in Central–East European countries: Poland, Hungary, the Czech Republic, Slovak Republic, Latvia, and Bulgaria; as well as two international courts: the European Court of Human Rights (ECtHR) and the Court of Justice of the European Union (CJEU). The work thus identifies the mutual interactions between national constitutional courts and international tribunals in terms of their law-making activity. The chosen countries include constitutional courts which have been recently captured by populist governments and subordinated to political powers. Therefore, one of the purposes of the book is to identify the change in the law-making activity of those courts and to compare it with the activity of constitutional courts from countries in which democracy is not viewed as being under threat. Written by national experts, each chapter addresses a series of set questions allowing accessible and meaningful comparison.

The book will be a valuable resource for students, academics, and policy-makers working in the areas of constitutional law and politics.

Monika Florczak-Wątor is Professor in the Constitutional Law Department of Jagiellonian University in Krakow, Poland, and the Head of the Centre for Interdisciplinary Constitutional Studies.

Comparative Constitutional Change

Series editors:

Xenophon Contiades is Professor of Public Law, Panteion University, Athens, Greece and Managing Director, Centre for European Constitutional Law, Athens, Greece.

Thomas Fleiner is Emeritus Professor of Law at the University of Fribourg, Switzerland. He teaches and researches in the areas of Federalism, Rule of Law, Multicultural State; Comparative Administrative and Constitutional Law; Political Theory and Philosophy; Swiss Constitutional and Administrative Law; and Legislative Drafting. He has published widely in these and related areas.

Alkmene Fotiadou is Research Associate at the Centre for European Constitutional Law, Athens.

Richard Albert is Professor of Law at the University of Texas at Austin.

Comparative Constitutional Change has developed into a distinct field of constitutional law. It encompasses the study of constitutions through the way they change and covers a wide scope of topics and methodologies. Books in this series include work on developments in the functions of the constitution, the organization of powers and the protection of rights, as well as research that focuses on formal amendment rules and the relation between constituent and constituted power. The series includes comparative approaches along with books that focus on single jurisdictions, and brings together research monographs and edited collections which allow the expression of different schools of thought. While the focus is primarily on law, where relevant the series may also include political science, historical, philosophical and empirical approaches that explore constitutional change.

Also in the series:

Courts, Politics and Constitutional Law
Judicialization of Politics and Politicization of the Judiciary
Edited by Martin Belov

Judicial Law-Making in European Constitutional Courts
Edited by Monika Florczak-Wątor

For more information about this series, please visit: www.routledge.com/Comparative-Constitutional-Change/book-series/COMPCONST

Judicial Law-Making in European Constitutional Courts

Edited by
Monika Florczak-Wątor

Routledge
Taylor & Francis Group
LONDON AND NEW YORK

First published 2020
by Routledge
2 Park Square, Milton Park, Abingdon, Oxon OX14 4RN

and by Routledge
605 Third Avenue, New York, NY 10017

Routledge is an imprint of the Taylor & Francis Group, an informa business

First issued in paperback 2021

This book has been prepared as part of the research project financed by the Polish National Science Centre (Decision No. 2015/18/E/HS5/00353).

British Library Cataloguing-in-Publication Data
A catalogue record for this book is available from the British Library

Library of Congress Cataloging-in-Publication Data
A catalog record has been requested for this book

ISBN: 978-0-367-90075-5 (hbk)
ISBN: 978-1-032-18799-0 (pbk)
ISBN: 978-1-003-02244-2 (ebk)

DOI: 10.4324/9781003022442

The open access license fee of the book was funded by the Priority Research Area Society of the Future under the programme "Excellence Initiative – Research University" at the Jagiellonian University in Krakow.

Contents

Figure

Contributors

Belov, Martin – University of Sofia, Bulgaria

Czarny, Piotr – Jagiellonian University in Cracow, Poland

Ferrer Martín de Vidales, Covadonga – Complutense University of Madrid, Spain

Florczak-Wątor, Monika – Jagiellonian University in Cracow, Poland

Kawczyńska, Monika – Jagiellonian University in Cracow, Poland

Malíř, Jan – Institute of State and Law, Czech Academy of Sciences, Czech Republic

Mouchette, Julien – University of Reims Champagne Ardenne, France

Naleziński, Bogumił – Pedagogical University of Cracow, Poland

Ondřejková, Jana – Charles University in Prague, Czech Republic

Palazzo, Nausica –University of Trento, Italy

Pozsár-Szentmiklósy, Zoltán – ELTE Eötvös Loránd University, Hungary

Rodiņa, Anita - University of Latvia, Latvia

Spale, Alla – Constitutional Court of the Republic of Latvia

Steuer, Max – Comenius University in Bratislava, Slovak Republic

Štiavnický, Ján – Constitutional Court of the Slovak Republic

Tsekov, Aleksandar – University of Sofia, Bulgaria

Weber, Ruth – Humboldt University of Berlin, Germany

Wojtyczek, Krzysztof – European Court of Human Rights, Jagiellonian University in Cracow, Poland

Introduction

Monika Florczak-Wątor

Do constitutional courts (CCs) create the law or do they just apply it? Does the interpretation of the Constitution in the process of analysing the constitutionality of the law have a creative or purely reconstructive nature? Can the CC develop, correct, and supplement the law or should it limit itself only to the assessment of compliance with the patterns of control specified in the application? These are questions that have been raised in the literature for years and have not been answered exhaustively. Although CCs currently exist in most European States, the question regarding the extent of their judicial activities and their optimal position in the structure of States organized on the basis of the separation of powers still remains open.[1] A significant number of active CCs raises an additional important question: Is it possible to analyse previously mentioned problems in terms of comparative law in order to discuss specific (and if so, which) typical assumptions (phenomena or tendencies), or are there such significant divergences that CCs should be analysed separately?

The aim of this book is to analyse and describe the specificity of law-making for selected European CCs. Our understanding of the notion of law-making, which is the key to our research, is very broad. It includes the repeal, modification, and supplementation of the law by CCs within the scope – and as a consequence – of the examination of the compliance of the law with the Constitution. The above-mentioned concept of law-making is applied through the creative interpretation of law, including the interpretation of law in accordance with the Constitution and in a manner that is friendly to European Union (EU) law and international law, as well as through adjudication on constitutionality of law combined with the determination of the extent of the declared unconstitutionality and the legal consequences of the CC judgements. Moreover, CCs have normative competence

1 See e.g. Wojciech Sadurski, *Rights Before Courts. A Study of Constitutional Courts in Postcommunist States of Central and Eastern Europe* (Springer 2008); Andrew Harding & Peter Leyland (eds.), *Constitutional Courts: A Comparative Study* (Wildy, Simmonds & Hill Publishing 2009); Victor Ferreres Comella, *Constitutional Courts and Democratic Values. A European Perspective* (Yale University Press 2009); Alec Stone Sweet, 'Constitutional Courts' in Michel Rosenfeld & András Sajó (eds.), *The Oxford Handbook of Comparative Constitutional Law* (Oxford University Press 2012) 816, 817–825.

DOI: 10.4324/9781003022442-1

sensu stricto as they are entitled to issue internal rules concerning the organization of CCs, in particular with regard to procedural issues. The initial research hypothesis is the assumption that the CCs determine the shape of the law, not only by repealing unconstitutional norms from it, but also by modifying and supplementing those norms that remain in the legal order after the announcement of the ruling on their conformity with the Constitution or their partial unconstitutionality. Therefore, the judicial review would seem to position itself between law-making and law-application, while the CC is not only a negative but also a positive law-maker,[2] which requires a redefinition of its position within the system.[3] This is because, in our opinion, Hans Kelsen's description of CCs being linked to the term 'negative law-maker'[4] does not reflect the essence of the changes which a ruling on the unconstitutionality of the law involves. This is due to the finding that, at present, the effect of such a judgement increasingly relates not to the repeal of a law, but to an amendment of normative content of the reviewed provision. The constitutionality of a law is examined at the level of legal norms and these are not always *expressis verbis* articulated in the wording of the legal provision. Often the provisions are not contested in their entirety, but only to a certain extent or in terms of a specific meaning, and therefore, if they are found to be unconstitutional, they lose their binding force only to a certain extent. Such a derogation is usually not expressed in the wording of a statute which, as such, does not change. Reconstruction of the normative content of a statute after issuing CC ruling declaring the partial unconstitutionality of the statute often leads to the conclusion that this content has not been reduced, but, on the contrary, extended to cover issues that have been previously excluded from the scope of the relevant regulation.

In our research, the results of which we present in this book, we analyse twelve CCs, ten of which are national CCs operating in European States that have adopted the model of the centralized control of the constitutionality of law, and the other two are international courts protecting the legal orders created at the

2 See Allan R. Brewer-Carías, *Constitutional Courts as Positive Legislators. A Comparative Law Study* (Cambridge University Press 2011); Anna Gamper, 'Constitutional Courts and Judicial Law-Making: Why Democratic Legitimacy Matters' (2015) 4 *Cambridge Journal of International and Comparative Law* 423, 424–434; Stone Sweet (n 1) 827–828.

3 As Alec Stone Sweet indicated: 'constitutional courts ought to be conceptualised as specialised legislative organs, and constitutional review ought to be understood as one stage in the elaboration of statutes'. Alec Stone Sweet, *Governing with Judges* (Oxford University Press 2000) 61. Referring to this opinion, Wojciech Sadurski added: 'This seems quite obvious – although not to many legal scholars who often prefer to perceive constitutional courts as judicial organs; following the legal fiction propounded by the courts themselves, they tend to situate them within the judicial branch within the general tri-partite scheme of separation of powers'. Sadurski (n 1) 87.

4 See Hans Kelsen, *Allgemeine Staatslehre* (J Springer 1925) 229–231; Hans Kelsen, 'Wesen und Entwicklung der Staatsgerichtsbarkeit' in Vereinigung der Deutschen Staatsrechtslehrer (ed.), *Veröffentlichungen der Vereinigung der Deutschen Staatsrechtslehrer,* vol 5 (De Gruyter 1929) 30–32; Friedrich Koja, *Hans Kelsen order Die Reinheit der Rechtslehre* (Böhlau Verlag Wien 1988) 131–133.

European level. Within the first group, the analysis takes into account both the CCs established in Western European countries just after the Second World War (Germany, Italy, Spain, and France), as well as CCs established in Central and Eastern European countries after the fall of communism, including the Visegrad countries (Poland, Hungary, the Czech Republic, and the Slovak Republic), the Baltic States (Latvia), and the Balkan States (Bulgaria). Therefore, we have considered those countries that have a tradition of CCs having functioned in a stable democracy dating back several decades, as well as those in which CCs are relatively young institutions that are still building their authority and real constitutional position. We have also included in our research those countries in which the CC system is currently in a constitutional crisis and in which the law-making of the CCs is beginning to threaten democracy and the rule of law.[5]

In addition to the national CCs, as already mentioned, we have analysed two international courts operating within the structures of European integration; namely, the European Court of Human Rights (ECtHR) and the Court of Justice of the European Union (CJEU). The inclusion of these courts in the category of CCs may seem controversial, since until now the concept of the CC has referred to the national courts that protect the supremacy of the Constitution and that have the competence to review the constitutionality of the law. Although neither the Council of Europe nor the EU are federal States, the constituent documents (the European Convention on Human Rights (ECHR) and the EU Treaties) perform a similar function in these organizations to those of national constitutions within State organizations.[6] These two international courts protect the standards arising from these documents and, likewise, perform functions similar to those performed by national CCs. Furthermore, in countries where traditional CCs have found themselves in crisis (Poland and Hungary), the role of the guardian of constitutional standards has been taken over precisely by the above-mentioned international courts. This is perfectly illustrated by the situation in Poland, where the number of legal questions and constitutional complaints filed with the CC has declined dramatically during the last three years,[7] while the number of complaints

5 On the constitutional crisis in Poland see: Piotr Radziewicz & Piotr Tuleja (eds.), *Konstytucyjny spór o granice zmian organizacji i zasad działania Trybunału Konstytucyjnego: czerwiec 2015 – marzec 2016* (Wolters Kluwer Polska 2017); Wojciech Sadurski, *Poland's Constitutional Breakdown* (Oxford University Press 2019). On the constitutional crisis in Hungary see Peter Wilkin, *Hungary's Crisis of Democracy: The Road to Serfdom* (Lexington Books 2016).

6 See Francis Jacobs, 'Is the Court of Justice of the European Communities a Constitutional Court?' in Deirdre Curtin, Daniel O'Keeffe (eds.), *Constitutional Adjudication in European Community and National Law* (Butterworth Dublin 1992) 25, 25; Anthony Arnull, 'A Constitutional Court for Europe?' (2003–2004) CYELS (*Cambridge Yearbook of European Legal Studies*) 2; Bo Vesterdorf, 'A Constitutional Court for the EU?', IJCL (*International Journal of Constitutional Law*) (2006) 4, 607, 607; Lukas Bauer, *Der Europäische Gerichtshof als Verfassungsgericht?* (Nomos 2008) 160–161.

7 See the Report of the Stefan Batory Foundation Legal Experts Group 'Functioning of the Constitutional Court 2014–2017' available in Polish at http://www.batory.org.pl/upload/files/Programy%20operacyjne/Forum%20Idei/Funkcjonowanie%20Try

on constitutional matters submitted by citizens to the ECtHR and the corresponding preliminary questions referred by the courts to the CJEU have increased. Since the allegation of a breach of constitutional standards cannot be formally raised before such international bodies, it is transformed into an allegation of a violation of the ECHR or EU standards. However, the same standards are still at stake as regards, for instance, non-discrimination, the protection of fundamental rights and freedoms, the independence of the judiciary and the separation of powers. Therefore, there is no doubt that in those States where the CC is being marginalized or is even actually disappearing, the CCs' role is being taken over by international courts, which are the guardians of European standards developed on the basis of constitutional standards common to the Member States associated with the given organization.

Each chapter of this collection of studies is devoted to one specific CC. These chapters have a similar structure and take into account similar research problems. The concluding comments concerning the law-making activities of all CCs covered by the research are included in the last chapter. The authors of particular chapters are all researchers from the countries of the CCs whose law-making activity they have analysed. First, they present the legal basis for the functioning of a respective CC, the evolution of its constitutional position, its competencies, as well as the social trust it enjoys and the social acceptability of its rulings. Subsequently, the individual chapters present the issue of law-making of the particular CC, referring to specific examples from rulings in which both constitutional law-making and statutory law-making were considered for the national CCs functioning in the individual countries. In both cases, the aim was to demonstrate how CCs modify or supplement constitutional and statutory provisions by applying various methods of interpretation, and how, when a ruling declares unconstitutionality, it can result in large and quality-diversified changes in the content of the examined provision. The authors of the individual chapters also mention specific examples of CC decisions containing a law-making component, as well as the consequences of these decisions for the applicable legal order. The specific chapters also present the reactions of various State authorities, particularly the courts, to the law-making activity of the CCs, as well as the position of the legal science in this respect. It is worth noting that the judicial activism of the CCs in many countries has been, and continues to be, the main cause of conflicts with other courts, especially the Supreme Courts.[8] The studies contained in this collection

bunalu%20Konstytucyjnego.pdf (30 November 2019). The synthesis of this report is available in English at http://www.batory.org.pl/upload/files/Programy%20operacyjne/Forum%20Idei/Functioning%20of%20the%20Constitutional%20Tribunal%202014.pdf (30 November 2019).

8 See e.g. Leszek Garlicki, 'Constitutional Courts Versus Supreme Courts' (2007) 5 *International Journal of Constitutional* 44, 44–68; Law Rafał Mańko, '"War of Courts" as a Clash of Legal Cultures: Rethinking the Conflict between the Polish Constitutional Tribunal and the Supreme Court Over "Interpretive Judgments"' in Michael Hein, Antonia Geisler, Siri Hummel (eds.) *Law, Politics, and the Constitution: New Perspectives from Legal and Political Theory* (Peter Lang, 2014) 79, 79–94.

also demonstrate the mutual inspirations of the CCs regarding the development and supplementation of the law. This is also an important element of their law-making activity. The sources of inspiration for CCs are not only the rulings of the CCs operating in other countries, but also the judgements of the above-mentioned international European courts, which undoubtedly contributed to the harmonization of European standards with regard to the protection of human rights and systemic matters. Yet, both the ECtHR and the CJEU benefit from European constitutional traditions, which the conventional CCs largely create and develop in their rulings. The problem of these interactions between the constitutional and national courts, which is frequently described in the literature before referring to the concept of judicial dialogue, is discussed in greater detail in some of the chapters.

In order to address the issue of the CCs' law-making in relation to more European countries, it was necessary to significantly limit the size of particular chapters. Therefore, many specific problems have only been signalled or briefly elaborated (without going into detail). Moreover, we do not consider further some theoretical problems that are directly connected with the topic of our research, such as the issue of legitimacy of CCs,[9] since our aim was mainly the analysis, description and systematic categorization of different law-making techniques applied in the case-law of European CCs. We hope the results of our research will enrich the discussion on these theoretical issues with new relevant findings.

This book has been prepared as part of the research project entitled 'Specificity of Constitutional Courts law-making and its limits,' which was financed by the Polish National Science Centre (Decision No. 2015/18/E/HS5/00353).

9 On the issue of legitimacy of CCs see e.g. Wojciech Sadurski (ed.), *Constitutional Justice, East and West: Democratic Legitimacy and Constitutional Courts in Post-Communist Europe in a Comparative Perspective* (Kluwer Law International 2003); Kim Lane Scheppele, 'Democracy by Judiciary (Or Why Courts Can Sometimes Be More Democratic than Parliaments)' in Wojciech Sadurski, Martin Krygier & Adam Czarnota (eds.), *Rethinking the Rule of Law in Post Communist Europe: Part Legacies, Institutional, and Constitutional Discourses* (Central European University Press 2005) 25, 25–60; Sadurski (n 1) 27–63; Gamper (n 2) 436–440; Rosenfeld & Sajó (n 1) 828–829.

Part I

Western European Constitutional Courts

1 The French Constitutional Council as a law-maker: from dialogue with the legislator to the rewriting of the law

Julien Mouchette

The concept of the Constitutional Court as a 'negative legislator,' formulated by Hans Kelsen,[1] is well known to jurists. In the Kelsenian model, the Constitutional Court exercises a power of censorship of the law by annulling unconstitutional law. In this way, it exercises a legislative function, but only a 'negative' function: it undoes the law without being able to make it. Georges Vedel, President of the French Constitutional Council (CC), once declared that 'the CC has the right to use erasers, not to use pencils.'[2] In other words, the CC does not participate in the drafting of a bill and simply acts as a 'negative legislator,' a role described by the dyad 'annulment/rejection.'

Today, however, in countries governed by the rule of law, constitutional courts influence the legislative process as to the content, and also the procedure. The difference in nature between legislative and judicial functions seems to be overshadowed by the activity of the Constitutional Court. Undoubtedly, the Kelsenian proposition of the negative legislator is simply no longer appropriate as a description of the current function of constitutional courts.[3] Indeed, it rules on the effects over time of an invalidation of the law, as well as on its material scope. It sets out in directives the manner in which a law is to be interpreted and applied. Sometimes it provides a legal framework for future action by the legislator. Therefore, the Council intervenes in the optimization of the legislative process. By its very nature, the constitutionality review generates an intervention, sometimes a far-reaching one, in the exercise of the legislative function.

The French Constitutional Council (CC) is consistent with this observation. The existence of an *ex ante* constitutionality review necessarily has an impact, upstream, on the law-making process. This phenomenon can only be reinforced by the implementation of an *ex post* constitutionality review (*QPC*) in 2008. On its own initiative, the CC has developed methods to escape the constraints of this dyad, 'annulment/rejection.' It is concerned to 'save' the law from annulment.

1 Hans Kelsen, 'La garantie juridictionnelle de la Constitution' (1928) *RDP* (*Revue du droit public*) 252.

2 Georges Vedel quoted by Robert Badinter, 'Du côté du Conseil constitutionnel' (2002) *RFDA* (*Revue française de droit administratif*) 208.

3 Christian Behrendt, *Le juge constitutionnel, un législateur-cadre positif* (Bruxelles Paris Bruylant LGDJ, 2006) 537.

DOI: 10.4324/9781003022442-2

However, very often these methods lead it to the verge of rewriting the law. But the question here is about the intensity of this influence.

The purpose of our study is to present these methods and to show how the Council's normative function is expressed and how it relates to the normative function of the legislator and government authority from a practical point of view. Indeed, the introduction of a constitutionality review in France in 1958 strengthened the authority of the Constitution and gave rise to case law with important consequences on the way in which the legislator makes law. However, not all laws are subject to such control; some have been excluded by the CC itself.

1 Exclusion of certain laws from constitutional review

In accordance with Article 61 of the Constitution, Institutional Acts before their promulgation and Rules of the assemblies (National Assembly, Senate, Congress, High Court) before their enforcement are automatically forwarded to the CC, which decides on their conformity with the Constitution within one month (a period that may be reduced to eight days in cases of emergency, at the request of the Government). Apart from this systematic control, which is mandatory, only ordinary laws passed by Parliament can be referred to the Council a priori and a posteriori in order for it to verify their conformity with the Constitution.[4] Indeed, the CC has declared itself incompetent with regard to constitutional laws and laws adopted by referendum.

First, with regard to constitutional amendment, the question of their control was raised in the late 1980s. In a political context marked by the constitutional revisions involved in strengthening European integration, the doctrine has occasioned a lengthy debate on the question of a possible review of the constitutionality of constitutional laws, following a Council decision of 2 September 1992 on the Treaty on European Union known as the Maastricht Treaty.[5] By this decision, the Council established the principle of its jurisdiction over constitutional laws and then specified the points on which its control could, if necessary, focus. While the limits on the periods for revision do not permit a substantive examination, the limit on the republican form of government implies that the Council must control the very content of the constitutional laws adopted. The extent of its control here depends on its conception of the 'republican form': is it 'only' to block the return of the monarchy or, in a broader and riskier approach, to sanction

4 In addition to the statutory laws, it is worth adding the special case of so-called 'country laws' (*lois de pays*), which are legislative norms adopted by the deliberative assembly of New Caledonia on the basis of Article 77 of the Constitution.

5 Decision 92–312, of 2 September 1992, § 19. Everything started from the phrase 'under the condition'. In this decision, the Council ruled that 'the constituent power is sovereign under the condition, on the one hand, that there are limitations on the periods during which a revision of the Constitution cannot be initiated or continued, which result from Articles 7, 16, and 89 paragraph 4 of the constitutional text, and, on the other hand, that the requirements of the fifth paragraph of Article 89, which stipulate that the republican form of government cannot be revised, are respected'.

any constitutional law that aims to call into question respect for certain values or principles deemed consubstantial with the republican form (secularism, solidarity, separation of powers, etc.)? However, whatever the approach adopted, the question of the Council's legitimacy to censor the revision of the constitutional text by the authors of the Constitution comes into sharp focus here. In order to avoid the awkward position in which this alternative would place it, the Council resolved to renounce such control by declaring itself incompetent in a decision of 26 March 2003.[6] At the source of this decision were some senators who contested the amendment of Article 1 of the Constitution by the addition of a reference indicating that the organization of the Republic is 'decentralized.' In their view, this reference directly challenged a principle enshrined in the same article according to which the Republic is 'one and indivisible.' This was a highly political issue that could only embarrass the members of the Council. Indeed, it should have determined whether the 'republican form' implied a unitary organization of the Republic or whether decentralization was compatible with the republican form. The difficulty that this posed to the members of the Council can be seen in the speed of its response. Only eight days after being referred to it, the Council declared that it 'does not have the power to rule on a constitutional review under Article 61, Article 89 or any other provision of the Constitution.'[7] However, the debate in France on the control of constitutional laws is not definitively over. Indeed, the contentious immunity of these laws is still being discussed by academic authors in the light of developments in European law,[8] and in particular of the model of what exists abroad.

Second, with regard to referendum laws – that is, laws adopted by the people through referendums – the CC decided not to control them, regardless of their purpose. This solution results from its decision of 6 November 1962 concerning the law of 28 October 1962 amending the method of electing the President of the Republic.[9] This solution has since been confirmed by the Council in its decision of 23 September 1992.[10] The lack of constitutionality review of the referendum law is due to the fact that it is the 'direct expression' of the sovereign, the people. These two decisions of 1962 and 1992 introduced a hierarchy giving referendum law a pre-eminent place over parliamentary law. It was in its 1992 decision that the Council clarified its reasoning. In 1962 the law submitted to the referendum was a constitutional law. However, the referendum law of 1992 was not a

6 Decision 2003–469 DC, of 26 March 2003 on the constitutional amendment of the decentralized organization of the Republic.

7 Decision 2003–469 DC, *a.m.*, § 2.

8 See Philippe Blachèr, 'Le contrôle par le Conseil constitutionnel des lois constitutionnelles' (2016) *RDP* 545; Joel Andriantsimbazovina & Helene Gaudin 'Contrôle de constitutionnalité des lois constitutionnelles et droit européen: débat sur une nouvelle piste' (2009) 27 *Cahiers du Conseil constitutionnel* 52.

9 This was one of the decisions that raised the most virulent criticism of the CC, with the then President of the Senate, Gaston Monnerville, going so far as to state that 'the CC had just committed suicide' (*Le Monde*, 8 November 1962).

10 Decision 92–313 DC of 23 September 1992, *a.m.*

constitutional law, but an ordinary law adopted by referendum. The Council therefore distinguished between national sovereignty according to the modes of expression. Parliamentary laws are subject to control because they may not respect the will of the sovereign people: a question that, by definition, does not arise for referendum laws, since the people express their will without intermediaries. The distinction between the people as legislator and the people as sovereign did not convince the Council. This position is motivated by a lack of legitimacy to examine the legislative work of the sovereign people. Already heavily criticized for its examination of the work of the people's representatives, the Council declined to provoke strong popular protests.[11] This decision was extended to the field of post-clearance control by a *QPC* decision of 25 April 2014.[12]

In summary, the Council only reviews laws – statutory or institutional acts – adopted by Parliament, and not those adopted by the French people following a referendum, which constitute a direct expression of national sovereignty. If we can observe a 'dialogue' between the Council and Parliament, then it must be said that the sovereign people, as legislators, escape this dialogue, possibly for the better.

2 The Council's methods of influence on the law-making process

2.1 The Council's recommendations to correct or complete the law

Unlike the Council of State, which has an advisory function, the CC, contrary to its name, does not exercise any advisory functions. However, within its litigation function, the Council may recommend to the legislature that it adopt a new provision in accordance with the Constitution or that it take into account its indications or interpretations in the future. The particularity of these counsels here is that if the legislator does not comply with them, it accepts the risk of being censored. Is this really still advice?

This is what doctrine has sometimes called *le contrôle à double détente* – two-pronged control.[13] The method is simple. First, the Council declares certain provisions of a law

11 Dominique Rousseau, Pierre-Yves Gahdoun & Julien Bonnet, *Droit du contentieux constitutionnel* (Paris LGDJ 206) 157.

12 Decision 2014–392 *QPC* of 25 April 2014. Despite its coherent logic, this position is hampered by the constitutional revision of 4 August 1995, which broadened the scope of the legislative referendum under Article 11 of the Constitution to include 'any draft law on reforms relating to the nation's economic or social policy and the public services that contribute to it'. During the debates, the constituents deliberately rejected an amendment organizing a prior check on the constitutionality of the referendum bill on the grounds that its adoption would make the revision lose all relevance. Therefore, the interest of the revision – extending the scope of referendum laws – is clearly to build a legislative space free from any control and, in particular, from the control of the constitutional judge. Since this revision, a government, uncertain of the constitutionality of its plans, can therefore avoid both Parliament and the CC by legislating directly by referendum.

13 Guillaume Drago, *Contentieux constitutionnel français* (France University Press PUF 2009) 412.

to be unconstitutional, which makes it impossible for it to be promulgated. In doing so, it explains why these articles of law are unconstitutional but also explains how parliamentarians must ensure that these provisions of the law are in conformity with the Constitution. Second, Parliament decides to legislate again on the issue that has been censored by the CC. Moreover, the reviewed statute may, at the request of the President of the Republic, be discussed again by Parliament, for example, in order to draw conclusions from a decision of the Constitutional Court.[14] The parliamentarians' freedom of discrimination is then severely restricted, because if the CC is again so minded, it will be able to verify whether the Parliament has followed its 'recommendations.' If this is not the case, the Council will again annul the provisions, which will be deemed unconstitutional. This control is permitted by Article 61 of the Constitution, which in fact does not prohibit the possibility of referring the matter twice to the Council before the Act is promulgated.[15] Only the presidential decree promulgating the Act concludes the legislative procedure and in principle prohibits any preventive control of its conformity with the Constitution.

Here, in addition to the legal and symbolic weight of the power to repeal the law at the judge's disposal, there is also the corrective scope of his office. Thus, for example, in a decision of 29 December 1983,[16] the Council ruled against the provisions of a law concerning the procedures for carrying out a search for tax reasons, considering that the law grants exorbitant powers to the tax authorities and thus undermines personal security, the inviolability of the home, and respect for private life. But at the same time, the CC indicates to parliamentarians in which direction the text of the law should be corrected. In particular, the judicial judge must be able to review the merits of the tax administration's investigations, specifically that the judge be present during searches. A year later, a new law was again submitted to the CC, which organized tax searches. It noted that the legislator had rewritten the law in accordance with the 'explicit requirements' of the previous decision.[17] Therefore, not surprisingly, it ruled that the new wording of the law was in line with the Constitution. While the position here is not open to question in terms of the law and respect for the guarantees attached to freedoms, it must be admitted that the CC here 'held the pen of Parliament.'[18]

14 Article 10, paragraph 2 of the 1958 Constitution.

15 The CC, which had to review a law resulting from a new deliberation by Parliament, at the request of the President of the Republic, on a text that had been partially censored, considered that, 'in this case, it was not a question of voting for a new law, but of the intervention, in the current legislative procedure, of a complementary phase resulting from the constitutionality review'. Consequently, the constitutionality review is presented by the CC itself as a phase of the legislative procedure, insofar as this procedure is only perfect from the moment the law is promulgated (Decision 85–197 DC, of 23 August 1985).

16 Decision 83–164 DC, of 29 December 1983.

17 Decision 84–184 DC, of 29 December 1984.

18 Xavier Vandendriessche, 'Loi immigration et asile, une Nouvelle Occasion Manquée?' (2018) *AJDA* (*Actualité Juridique Droit Administratif*) 2234.

This dialogue with the legislator can now result from the combination of *ex ante* and *ex post* controls. A provision that is censored in the framework of a *QPC* is rectified by a law, which will then be referred to the Council, either immediately after its adoption or possibly once it has entered into force. More than ever, the Council is therefore called upon to provide the legislator with instructions for use.

The amendment of Article L 512–1 relating to the conditions under which the Administrative Court rules on an appeal against a requirement to leave French territory notified to a detained foreigner (hereinafter *OQTF*) illustrates this dialogue. Before the amendment of the Article, the legislator had allowed the foreigner in detention a total period of five days to file his appeal against the requirement to leave French territory and the judge to rule on it. In a *QPC* decision of 1 June 2018,[19] the Council ruled that the legislator had not struck a balanced conciliation here between the right to an effective judicial remedy and the objective of avoiding the placement of the foreigner in administrative detention at the end of his sentence. The legislator drew the consequences from this decision by amending the Act two months later.[20] It now provides that, when it appears, during the proceedings, that the detained foreigner is likely to be released before the judge rules, the administrative authority shall inform the president of the administrative tribunal or the designated magistrate who decides on the appeal against the *OQTF*, within eight days of the court being informed by the administration. Having been alerted to this amendment to the Act, the Council, in the context of 'two-pronged control,' welcomed the amendment, in its decision of 6 September 2018.[21]

The legislator is also sometimes invited by the CC not to correct but to amend a legislative provision by adopting another provision, sometimes by setting a time limit for it.[22] The Council must still declare the norm in conformity with the Constitution, but enjoins the legislator to intervene to correct the law before it becomes unconstitutional, and attaches a 'decision of appeal to the legislator' to it.[23]

For example, the Council ruled that the provisions of the Orientation and Programming for Justice Act relating to local jurisdiction were in conformity with the Constitution. However, on that occasion, it also specified in paragraph 15 of its decision of 29 August 2002 that, 'on the date on which the CC decides on the law referred to it, the legislator has not adopted any provision relating to the status of members of local courts; that, consequently, in the silence of the law on the

19 Decision 2018–709 *QPC*, of 1 June 2018.

20 Act No. 2018–778 of 10 September 2018 for controlled immigration, effective asylum, and successful integration.

21 Decision 2018–770 DC, of 6 September 2018.

22 The examples given are taken from Jean-Luc Warsmann's article 'La place du Conseil constitutionnel dans les institutions de la Ve République' in *Cahiers du Conseil constitutionnel*, series 2009 (50th anniversary symposium, 3 November 2009), URL: conseil-constitutionnel.fr/nouveaux-cahiers-du-conseil-constitutionnel/la-place-du-conseil-constitutionnel-dans-les-institutions-de-la-ve-republique#_ftn16.

23 Dominique Rousseau, *La justice constitutionnelle en Europe* (Paris Montchrestien 1998) 104.

entry into force of its Title II, local courts may be set up only once a law setting the conditions for appointment and the status of their members has been enacted.'[24] In this paragraph, the CC invited the legislator to adopt a law on the conditions for the appointment and status of local judges, which the legislator did six months later.[25]

This decision by the CC is not only an invitation to take over the legislative work, as in the previous decisions mentioned. It is also an indication of the forms that future legislative provisions will have to take in order to be in conformity with the Constitution. Indeed, the CC specified that 'this law must include appropriate guarantees to satisfy the principle of independence, which is inseparable from the exercise of judicial functions and the capacity requirements arising from Article 6 of the 1789 Declaration.' It was on the basis of these capacity requirements stemming from Article 6 of the Declaration of the Rights of Man and of the Citizen that the CC, its attention subsequently drawn to the Institutional Act on Local Judges, censored a provision allowing a person who had performed functions involving responsibilities in the administrative, economic or social field to become a local judge.[26]

There are several examples in constitutional case law of this second form of dialogue, which consists in formulating normative indications on the future provisions that the legislator would like to adopt in a matter. Some authors see it here as a manifestation of a 'close dialogue'[27] between the Council and Parliament.[28] But how can we see it as a dialogue, when the Council has the power of the final word? On the other hand, this is the case with the modulation of the effects over time of the decision, which allows the CC 'both to set the date of repeal and to postpone its effects in time and to provide for the questioning of the effects that the provision produced before the intervention of this declaration.'[29] In other words, it is divided into two variants: the postponement of the date of entry into force and the modulation of the temporal effects of the decision. They both relate to positive action by the Constitutional Court in that the former can change the general scheme of the law and the latter can increase the pressure on the legislator to change the state of existing law.

2.2 The formal rectification of a legislative provision 'by consequence'

The CC may rule that the entire text is not in conformity with the Constitution or that the law contains unconstitutional provisions that are inseparable from the rest

24 Decision 2002–461 DC, of 29 August 2002.
25 Institutional Act No. 2003–153 of 26 February 2003 on local judges.
26 Decision 2003–466 DC, of 20 February 2003.
27 Georges Bergougnous, 'Le Conseil constitutionnel et le législateur' (2013) 38 *Nouveaux cahiers du Conseil constitutionnel* (le Conseil constitutionnel et le Parlement). URL: conseil-constitutionnel.fr/nouveaux-cahiers-du-conseil-constitutionnel/le-conseil-constitutionnel-et-le-legislateur.
28 Warsmann (n 22).
29 Decision 2010–108 *QPC*, of 25 March 2011, § 5; Decision 2010–110 *QPC*, of 25 March 2011, § 8.

of the law. In both cases, under Article 22 of the Organic Ordinance, the entire law cannot be promulgated. However, decisions of total nonconformity are uncommon, which is not surprising.[30] The Council is proceeding cautiously. Only about ten decisions of total nonconformity have been adopted. Some were for procedural reasons,[31] others for substantive reasons.[32] In these two situations, the legislator was compelled to resume examination of the law and adopt a text in accordance with the directives sought by the CC. However, as we have seen before, the new amended text is not immune to a second referral, although in practice the CC has never censored the amended text a second time.

Most often, declarations of unconstitutionality concern only a part of the law, a few provisions. Under Article 23 (1) of the Ordinance of 7 November 1958, the President of the Republic may either promulgate the law without the censored provision(s) (more frequently) or request a new discussion from the Chambers.[33] In addition, he may, in accordance with Article 23 of the Ordinance, have new provisions substituted for unconstitutional provisions.[34]

However, there is a particular case where the CC may have to reclassify the title of a law after partial censorship of the law. Since 2007, the CC has itself participated in the implementation of its decisions on partial unconstitutionality by coordinating and rectifying certain statutory provisions kept in the legal system, in order to ensure that the text is legible. This is called the 'rectification of the law by consequence.'[35] Already in 2007, the CC had rectified the title of the law referred to it as a result of the declaration of unconstitutionality of one of its provisions.[36] After it was established that one of the provisions of the referred bill was unconstitutional, changing the spirit of the bill, it decided 'accordingly' to change its title. Subsequently, it proceeded for the first time to rectify a statutory provision as a consequence in the context of the constitutionality review of organic laws.[37] It has since been transposed into the constitutionality review of statutes,[38] as well as the priority preliminary ruling on constitutionality (*QPC*).[39]

30 Jean-Marie Garrigou-Lagrange, 'Les partenaires du Conseil constitutionnel ou de la fonction interpellatrice des juges' (1986) *RDP* 664.
31 Decision 79–110 DC, of 24 December 1979.
32 Decision 81–132 DC, of 16 January 1982.
33 Ordinance No. 58–1067 of 7 November 1958, constituting the Institutional Act on the CC.
34 It is a choice of the President of the Republic, which is not free in the sense that it requires a countersignature. This provision of Article 23 (1) is to be read in conjunction with Article 10 (2) of the Constitution (possibility of requesting a new deliberation). In 1985, the CC considered that this new reading procedure of Article 23 (1) was only one of the modalities of the second deliberation of Article 10. Therefore, for the CC, these two procedures are equivalent.
35 See Maxime Charité, 'Quand le Conseil constitutionnel réécrit la loi. À propos de la rectification d'une disposition législative par voie de conséquence' (2018) *AJDA* 261.
36 Decision 2007–546 DC, of 25 January 2007.
37 Decision 2007–559 DC, of 6 December 2007.
38 Decision 2009–588 DC, of 6 August 2009.
39 Decision 2012–250 *QPC*, of 8 June 2012.

These corrections do not concern the substance, but only the form of the bill. To date, the Council has not used this litigation technique to remedy material mistakes made by the legislator. These corrections are therefore limited in scope. The rewriting of one or more statutory provisions is done solely in order to ensure coordination and readability of the provisions retained in the legal system.[40] Otherwise, they would be tantamount to a manifestation of an authentic power to make the law, or even to replace the legislator with the CC. However, as soon as it became necessary, the Council issued a reminder that it does not have the power to make changes to the law. Thus, for example, in a decision of 6 August 2009, before which the Accounts Settlement and Management Report Act for 2008 was submitted, it recalled that it was not its responsibility 'to make the corrections to the Settlement Act requested by the applicants.'[41]

When it rectifies 'by consequence,' the Council corrects only formal errors of the legislator – editorial clumsiness or the consequences on the drafting of the law of a decision of unconstitutionality. For example, in its decision of 6 August 2009, it declared a provision of the law unconstitutional as the legislator referred to the wrong paragraph of an article of the Labour Code. It went on to say 'accordingly' that the words in the law that referred to the wrong article must be replaced by the words referring to the right article. Another example is found in its *QPC* decision of 8 June 2012, in which a comma that the Council decided to delete was replaced with 'and.'[42]

2.3 Attempts to remake the law: 'reservations of interpretation'

Among the techniques developed by the Council to avoid the stark alternative between censorship and conformity, it is worth focusing on the so-called 'interpretation reservations' technique. This allows the Council to declare a provision to be in conformity with the Constitution provided that it is interpreted or applied in the manner it indicates. This technique makes it possible to validate a provision, which, without this reservation, could or should be censored.[43] Through this technique, the Council 'frames and supervises the conditions for implementing the law, thus completing the intervention of the legislator.'[44]

Throughout case law, three types of interpretative reservations have been observed: neutralising reservations, which eliminate possible interpretations that would be contrary to the Constitution; directive reservations, which include a prescription for the legislator or a State authority responsible for the application of the law; and constructive reservations, when the Council adds to the law to bring it into

40 Michel Verpeaux, *La QPC* (Paris Hachette 2013) 118.

41 Decision 2009–585 DC, of 6 August 2009, § 7.

42 Decision 2012–250 *QPC*, of 8 June 2012.

43 See Alexandre Viala, *Les réserves d'interprétation dans la jurisprudence du Conseil constitutionnel* (Paris LGDJ 1999) 336.

44 Bertrand Mathieu, 'Le Conseil constitutionnel "législateur positif". Ou la question des interventions du Juge Constitutionnel Français dans l'exercice de la fonction législative' (2010) *RID comp.* (*Revue internationale de droit comparé*) 520.

conformity with the Constitution. It should be noted that in its comments on its decisions, the CC only partially uses this classification. Moreover, as we can see, these constructive reservations are also neutralising in nature: classifications must be assessed flexibly, since the different categories of reservations can, in reality, overlap.

The CC's first recourse to the interpretation reserve technique took place in 1959 in a decision on the rules of procedure of the National Assembly.[45] The 1980s saw a rapid rise in interpretation reservations due to political changeovers and the legal crisis. The technique has developed, especially since the decisions on the security and freedom law of 20 January 1981[46] and on the law on press companies of 11 October 1984.[47]

In practice, these reservations are of great importance. They appear in about a quarter of the decisions and often settle very important points of law. Moreover, they allow the CC not to be locked into a binary choice between censoring the law or rejecting the appeal. The interpretation reservation is the expression of the general power of interpretation that is included in the constitutionality review operation. It constitutes a 'rescue' procedure, which makes it possible not to censure a legal provision that hypothetically could or should be censored.

It is a technique with many advantages when the control exercised by the CC is an *ex ante* review – which means abstract (i.e. independent of any concrete dispute). The CC's attention is drawn to a law that has several possible applications. It must therefore identify, in order to prohibit them, those law enforcement scenarios that are subject to constitutional requirements. This is a work of anticipation; the reservation of interpretation contributes to better legal certainty insofar as it settles upstream questions of application of the law, which are of a constitutional nature; on the political level, the technique of reservations makes it possible to avoid too brutal a conflict with the Government and with the majority of Parliament, which voted for the law, while giving satisfaction to the members who oppose it. For example, with regard to the personalized autonomy allowance, a social assistance benefit distributed by local authorities, the law gave a Commission a decision-making role in an area that concerns the free administration of local authorities. The legislator had remained unclear about the composition of the Commission, indicating only that the Commission was 'notably' composed of general councillors. The Council issued a reservation that 'in particular' meant 'majority,' in accordance with the parliamentary debates.[48]

However, some observers may have found the power of interpretation given to the CC in this way exorbitant. The criticism mainly concerns the so-called 'constructive' reservations, i.e. those in which the Council adds to the law to bring it into line with the Constitution. These types of reservations are no longer an expression of the general power of interpretation that is included in the constitutionality review process. In this type of reservation, the Council '[adds] to the text what it lacks to be in conformity,

45 Decision 59–2 DC, of 24 June 1959.
46 Decision 80–127 DC, of 20 January 1981.
47 Decision 84–181 DC, of 11 October 1984.
48 Decision 2001–447 DC, of 18 July 2001.

under the guise of interpreting it.'[49] The positive nature of this technique is obvious, given that the reservations of interpretation are 'at the limit of rewriting'[50] the law.

However, and this is the problem, the Council sometimes rewrites the law by adopting one of these interpretative reservations in a way that is contrary to the legislator's intentions.

One of the most obvious examples of this is the Council's decision on the Civil Solidarity Pact Act.[51] In this Act, the legislator created the Civil Solidarity Civil Partnership (PACS), which is defined as an agreement between two natural persons of full age, of different sex or of the same sex wishing to organize their life together. Very close to the features of marriage, this contract was an initiative of the government towards people of the same sex so that they could organize their lives together. However, at no time in the Act is there any mention of a couple's life as a condition for such a convention. In this respect, PACS thus comes closer to a pact of common interest between two people, regardless of their sex. The signing of this pact therefore consisted, at least, of two people pooling goods for the purpose of a community of life, regardless of whether or not sexual relations existed. In this decision, the Council redefined the text as establishing a contract for a community of life, in particular and implicitly, in sexual terms, which was obviously not part of the voted text or the parliamentary debates.[52] In this way, the CC has rewritten many of provisions of the Act, which can hardly be applied without reference to the Council's decision.

However, according to Article 62, paragraph 3, of the Constitution, 'no appeal shall emanate from the decisions of the CC. They shall be binding on public authorities and on all administrative authorities and all courts.' This authority focuses on the operative part of the Council's decisions as well as on the 'grounds that provide the necessary support and constitute the very basis for them.' Reservations are the necessary support for a decision taken in the context of an abstract constitutionality review (i.e. *ex ante*) by the Council. When the Simplification of Law Act was reviewed in 2004, the Council stated that its decisions have the force of res judicata, but also the force of res interpretata. Reservations are meaningful only if they guide the resolution of disputes arising subsequently from the interpretation or application of the law. Therefore, the judge or law enforcement authority must be mindful that, if the Council had not made such a reservation on a legislative provision, that provision could not have been promulgated. The reservation is therefore incorporated into the law.

However, by making a reservation, the CC allows a provision to escape into the legal field, which, if interpreted differently from the way in which it has done, is not in conformity with the Constitution. It is then the recipient of the reservation

49 Louis Favoreu, *La décision de constitutionnalité*, quoted by G. Drago, *Contentieux constitutionnel français*, (Paris PUF 1998) 419.

50 Jean Gicquel, *Droit constitutionnel et institutions politiques* (Paris Montchrestien 2002) 599.

51 Decision 99–419 DC, of 9 November 1999.

52 See the Council's official commentary on the decision 99–419 DC, of 9 November 1999.

(judge, supervisory authority, etc.) who becomes in a way the depository of respect for the Constitution. The central administrative authorities, first and foremost the Prime Minister and members of the government, respect and faithfully reproduce the reservations of the Constitutional Court regarding the interpretation of the law, in particular in the law enforcement circulars. Whether in its advisory or contentious configurations, the Council of State expressly applies the interpretative reservations expressed by the CC. The Court of Cassation tends to do the same and is ex officio responsible for this means of cassation.

Reservations are an appropriate instrument for *ex ante* control because they make it possible to condition the application of a law that has not yet entered into force in a manner that conforms to the Constitution without undermining its promulgation. The question is therefore whether these interpretative reservations are also well suited to *ex post* control. Indeed, in this case, their effects would disturb legal certainty by challenging already well-established interpretations or jurisprudential or administrative practices.[53]

Certainly, this control technique makes it possible to extend the protection of the rights and freedoms of the litigant and all those in the same situation. It also avoids statutory censorship. The CC has transposed to the *QPC* the technique of interpretative reservations used in the context of *ex ante* control. It did so for the first time in the 18 June 2010 decision on the employer's inexcusable fault.[54] It then ruled that Article L 452–3 of the Social Security Code cannot prevent victims from claiming compensation from the employer before the social security courts for all the damage not covered by Book IV of the Social Security Code. This reservation was immediately applicable to all cases not definitively decided on the date of the Council's decision.

From the point of view of parliamentarians, the decisions of the CC, through invitations to adopt other provisions, through restrictions imposed on the legislator for the adoption of future texts or through the classification of provisions in the normative hierarchy, can sometimes be perceived as an interference in the exercise of legislative authority.

3 The deepening of the Council's control of the law: towards control of the appropriateness of the law?

We have seen that the CC participates in the legislative process, but would this not sometimes amount to a direct participation in the political determination of the law? Some of the legislator's choices are undoubtedly based on political affiliations. This is particularly the case when it chooses among several objectives of general interest and among several means to achieve them. In principle, the political motives for legislative activity do not fall within the jurisdiction of the CC. The risk is that political bias in legislative activity may lead the CC to engage directly in

53 Olivier Dord, 'La QPC et le Parlement: une bienveillance réciproque' (2013) 38 *Les Nouveaux Cahiers du Conseil constitutionnel* 31.

54 Decision 2010–8 QPC, of 18 June 2010.

the legislative function. Everyone agrees on the undecidable nature of what is or is not appropriate, and many therefore consider that elected representatives have, in the final analysis, more democratic legitimacy than constitutional judges to decide on objectives of general interest and the modalities for satisfying them.[55]

Moreover, the CC recalls in its decisions, as soon as necessary, that 'the Constitution does not confer on the CC a general power of discretion and decision identical to that of Parliament.'[56] In a famous *obiter dictum*, the Council emphasized that the law passed by Parliament expresses the general will only in accordance with the Constitution;[57] hence, its control is marked by prudence, and it refrains from judging the legislator's intention. In this sense, it does not have the discretion of Parliament exercising its legislative function. Nor is it its responsibility, in its own estimation, to replace the legislator: 'in the context of this task (to rule on the conformity with the Constitution of the laws referred to it for examination), it is not for the CC to substitute its own assessment for that of the legislator.'[58] The Council therefore considers that it is not its place to review the legislator's assessment of the general interest insofar as this assessment is always based on political allegiances.

However, as Bastien François rightly observes, 'its decisions frequently contradict such *petitio principis*.'[59] Indeed, in decision after decision, the Council has deepened its constitutionality review of laws to the point of giving it a considerable influence in certain areas (in particular in the tax field).[60] This deepening is observed first by the emergence of a control of the 'manifest error of assessment' (*erreur manifeste d'appréciation*) and, second, by the implementation of the principle of proportionality. There is even an explicit control of political motives in a decision of 29 December 2012, which we will see on p. 25.

3.1 The review of manifest error of assessment

The review of manifest error of assessment appears for the first time in the decision of 18 January 1982 as a means of reviewing the legislator's assessment of the facts, circumstances or situations on which the laws are based. In this decision, it ruled that 'the legislator's assessment of the need for nationalisations decided by the law under consideration by the CC cannot, in the absence of a manifest error, be recused.'[61] The logic here is as follows: the Council refuses to control the purposes pursued by the legislator, but it exercises limited control over the means used to achieve them. Since that decision, this control method has been used regularly. For example, it was used to verify the legislator's assessment of the

55 Rousseau, Gahdoun & Bonnet (n 11) 310.

56 In particular: Decision 74–54 DC, of 15 January 1975, § 1; Decision 80–127 DC, of 20 January 1981, §12; Decision 86–218 DC, of 18 November 1986, § 10.

57 Decision 85–197, of 23 August 1985, § 27.

58 Decision 80–127 DC, of 20 January 1981, *a.m.*, § 13.

59 Bastien François, *Misère de la Ve République: essai* (Paris Denoël 2001) 120.

60 See Martin Collet, *L'impôt confisqué* (Paris Odile Jacob 2014).

61 Decision 81–132 DC, of 16 January 1982, § 20.

seriousness and necessity of the penalties in relation to the offences in question,[62] on the infringement of the principle of equality by setting a different age limit for different groups of officials,[63] or on the evaluation of health expenditure.[64]

The CC argues that it respects the legislator's discretionary assessment of the choice of means, even if it considers them irrelevant, as long as they are not manifestly inappropriate. At this stage, some authors, notably Louis Favoreu, consider that the control of manifest error of assessment and, more broadly, that of proportionality, far from allowing the Council to penetrate the area of appropriateness – control of political motives – preserves the freedom of decision and the discretionary power of the legislator.[65] In their view, this review is limited to matters where the imprecision of the constitutional text deprives the Council of the basis for a thorough review and consequently leaves a wide margin of discretion to the legislator. Moreover, they argue that this control is necessarily limited: the error is sanctioned only if it is 'manifest' or 'excessive.' There is no question of punishing simple mistakes. For example, the Council admits that the legislator may have been responsible for making errors in the delimitation of certain electoral divisions, but points out that 'it is not for the Council to determine whether the electoral divisions have been delimited as equitably as possible.'[66] It sanctions only manifest errors of assessment. However, the control of manifest error has sometimes reached such an intensity that the idea that its control would be limited in principle is unconvincing. The constitutionality review of the demographic gap between the constituencies for the elections to the Congress of New Caledonia provides a 'caricatured' illustration.[67] In two decisions of 8 August 1985 and 23 August 1985,[68] the CC reviewed a 1985 law that organized the division of New Caledonia's territory into four regions and promoted the representation of the Canaque[69] regions in the regional Assembly to the disadvantage of the Noumea region, which was the most populous but also the fiefdom of the Caldoches.[70] Each elected representative in Noumea had to represent 2.13 times more people, which makes the election in this region more difficult. In its 8 August decision, the Council ruled that political representation need not necessarily be proportional

62 Decision 84–176 DC, of 25 July 1984.
63 Decision 85–179 DC, of 1 September 1984.
64 Decision 2004–508 DC, of 16 December 2004.
65 Louis Favoreu, 'Le Droit Constitutionnel Jurisprudentiel' (1986) *RDP* 436.
66 Decision 86–218 DC, of 18 November 1986, *a.m.*, § 10.
67 François (n 60) 123.
68 Decision 85–196 DC, of 8 August 1985, *a.m.*; Decision 85–197 DC, of 23 August 1985 *a.m.*
69 The Kanak (French spelling until 1984: Canaque) are the indigenous Melanesian inhabitants of New Caledonia, an overseas collectivity of France in the southwest Pacific.
70 Caldoche is the name given to European inhabitants of New Caledonia, mostly native-born French settlers. The formal name by which to refer to this particular population is Caledonians, short for the formal New Caledonians, but this self-appellation technically includes all inhabitants of the New Caledonian archipelago, not just the Caldoche.

to population. According to the Council, the legislator is free to follow, in addition to a demographic criterion, imperatives of general interest. However, the Council ruled the law unconstitutional because it considers that 'these considerations can only be applied to a limited extent, which in this case has clearly been exceeded.'[71] After this decision, the President of the Republic requested a second vote to take into account the Council's censorship. Consequently, the legislator increased the number of elected representatives in Noumea from 18 to 21. The Council, to which the change was once again referred, ruled that the inequality here was in accordance with the Constitution. In other words, there was a manifest error of assessment by the legislator when the Noumea region had a representative for 4,728 inhabitants, but not when this figure was reduced to 4,052 inhabitants. The inequality is still patently glaring. The Council noted the persistence of the legislator, but it must be admitted that the first censorship was not based on any objective element.

Thus, this control is not limited to areas where constitutional texts are imprecise, but is used by the Council very widely, sometimes even to control only the necessity of a legislative provision. Even if the Council denies it, the review of the manifest error of assessment leads it in some cases to substitute its assessment and decision for that of the legislator.

As such, the control of manifest error is a concept often misunderstood by parliamentarians, who wonder how national representation can commit manifest or excessive errors of assessment. To dodge this accusation, the Council has, in recent years, avoided using the term 'manifest error,' which is somewhat 'derogatory' with regard to parliamentarians.[72] However, the expression has not completely disappeared from the Council's decisions;[73] most often, it has turned into a proportionality control or, more accurately, control of what is 'manifestly disproportionate.'[74]

3.2 *The implementation of the principle of proportionality*

The principle of proportionality was first used by the Council in its decision of 28 July 1989 on the Law on the Security and Transparency of the Financial Market. In this decision, the control of proportionality has served to provide a basis for a constructive interpretation that makes it possible to establish the constitutionality of the provision under review; thus, in the event of multiple sanctions, 'the principle of proportionality implies that the total amount of any sanctions imposed does not exceed the highest amount of one of the sanctions incurred.'[75] This control has all the advantages of manifest error without the disadvantages, namely: 'to avoid censorship while indicating to the legislator that it could not go further in infringing a principle; and, in the event of censorship, to inform Parliament that

71 Decision 85–196 DC, *a.m.*, § 16.

72 Rousseau, Gahdoun & Bonnet (n 11) 30.

73 Decision 2010–29/37 QPC, of 22 September 2010.

74 Georges Bergougnous, 'Le Conseil constitutionnel et le légilateur', 38 *Les Nouveaux Cahiers du Conseil constitutionnel* (*NCCC*).

75 Decision 89–260 DC, of 28 July 1989, § 22.

it will admit the constitutionality of a "less excessive" infringement.'[76] The principle of proportionality can be used differently and for different reasons by the CC. Clearly, this type of control allows it to ensure that the standard enacted complies with all the constitutional requirements imposed on the legislator. In this circumstance, the Council does not replace the legislator in determining which solution should be adopted, but sets limits, a minimum and a maximum, that delimit the legislator's scope of action.[77] In the second circumstance, the principle of proportionality is an express constitutional requirement, being linked to a particular constitutional principle. This is the case, for instance, of the principle of equality or the right of property. In all these cases, the reference to the principle of proportionality is only one aspect of the classic operation of comparing a legislative rule with a constitutional principle.[78]

However, there is another hypothesis in which the CC refers to the principle of proportionality to assess the internal coherence of the law. In this circumstance, the Council shall verify that the means chosen are not manifestly disproportionate to the objectives pursued. It is in such cases that the CC engages in a more direct intervention in the very process of law-making.[79] The positive nature of this control is particularly illustrated by the application in tax matters of the principle of equality enshrined in Articles 3 and 6 of the Declaration of the Rights of Man and of the Citizen.

Until the end of the 1990s, the CC confined itself to a 'not very operational'[80] interpretation of the principle of equality in tax matters. According to this interpretation, the legislator may, on the one hand, treat taxpayers in different situations with regard to the very purpose of the tax differently and, on the other hand, treat taxpayers who nevertheless have the same contributory powers differently if the general interest so warrants. However, as Martin Collet clearly shows in his book *L'impôt confisqué*, in the tax field, the law is intended to take into account the differences in economic, social, family, and other circumstances between taxpayers. These differences are many. The Council does not consider itself entitled to be overly prescriptive about the legislator's choice to

76 See Xavier Philippe, *Le contrôle de proportionnalité dans les jurisprudences constitutionnelle et administrative* (Paris Economica-PUAM 1990); Valerie Goesel-Le Bihan, 'Le contrôle de proportionnalité dans la jurisprudence du Conseil constitutionnel: figures récentes' (2007) *RFDC* 270; Jean-Baptiste Duclerq, *Les mutations du contrôle de proportionnalité dans la jurisprudence du Conseil constitutionnel* (Paris LGDJ 2015).

77 Where such conciliation cannot be carried out *in abstracto* and *ex ante*, the Council refers to the law enforcement judge the task of carrying it out (see 94–352 DC, in the case of police measures requiring the reconciliation of the protection of public order and individual freedoms); Bertrand Mathieu, 'Le Conseil constitutionnel "législateur positif" ou la question des interventions du juge constitutionnel français dans l'exercice de la fonction législative' (2010) 62 *RID comp.* 518.

78 See Rousseau, Gadhoun & Bonnet (n 11) 305, 310.

79 See Bertrand Mathieu & Michel Verpeaux, *Contentieux constitutionnel des droits fondamentaux* (Paris LGDJ 2002).

80 Collet (n 60) 33.

take into account one difference in situation rather than another in order to justify a difference in treatment. In addition, the Council always rules that the legislator pursues an objective of general interest when it grants a particular tax regime to a category of taxpayers. Since the 2000s, the Council has changed its interpretation of the principle of equality in tax matters. It has developed a particularly intense proportionality control in this field, sometimes called 'tax rationality review.'[81] According to a now classic formula, the Council considers that it is up to the legislator to determine the 'contributory capacity' of the taxpayers he intends to tax, by basing his assessment on 'objective and rational criteria according to the objectives he has in view,' in order to avoid a 'characterised breach of the principle of equality vis-a-vis public encumbrances.'[82] In other words, this jurisprudence requires the legislator to adopt tax measures that must be consistent with the objective intended to guide it and also with the mechanisms that it modifies.

This way of proceeding is particularly noticeable in its decision of 29 December 2008.[83] In this decision, the CC censured the mechanism adopted by the legislator concerning the so-called 'carbon tax.' The legislator's aim was simple (Nicolas Sarkozy's campaign promise): to set up a tax system that would significantly reduce greenhouse gas emissions in order to combat global warming. This objective was to be achieved by introducing a tax on the consumption of energy products offered for sale and intended for use as fuel, so that businesses, households, and administrations would have an incentive to reduce their emissions. However, the legislator has come up against the interests of companies. To avoid angering anyone, it has multiplied the derogations to the point that, in the end, as the CC points out, '93% of industrial carbon dioxide emissions [...] would have been totally exempt from the carbon tax.'[84] To censure this tax measure, it essentially relies on two arguments: the first is violation of the principle of equality; the second is an application of the principle of tax rationality. It considers that as soon as a very large part of the activities emitting greenhouse gases and carbon dioxide are not subject to a contribution (exemption), the law goes against the objective of combating global warming. The Council examines here not only the conformity of the law with requirements laid down in the Constitution but also the internal coherence of the law. Here, however, the Council has not yet decided on the relevance of the political reasons for the tax bills. It was just cancelling – at the end of an already rather audacious piece of jurisprudence – the tax mechanisms deemed inconsistent with the purpose assigned to them by the law.

In a decision of 29 December 2012, the CC went further.[85] It substituted its own vision of the general interest for that retained by Parliament; this decision has given rise to much criticism in the specialist press and from jurists. For instance,

81 Ibid., 37.
82 Decision 2007–555 DC, of 16 August 2007, § 20. Recently: Decision 2018–755 QPC, of 15 January 2019, § 4; Decision 2019–793 QPC of 28 June 2019, § 5.
83 Decision 2009–599 DC, 29 December 2009.
84 Decision 2009–599 DC, *a.m.*, § 83.
85 Decision 2012–662 DC, of 29 December 2012.

Martin Collet wrote an article in the national daily newspaper *Le Monde* entitled: 'Are the "sages" doing too much?'[86] In this decision, the Council made an unprecedented series of annulments. In the 2013 Finance Act, the legislator planned to increase the rate of several taxes aimed at hitting, though timidly and at marginal rates, the incomes of the richest. However, the Council has ruled that many provisions are unconstitutional because they are considered inconsistent – which is not true, as a reading of the text shows – and implements a proportionality control, which leads it above all to control political motives.

In its decision, it ruled that taxing certain incomes (those from a supplementary pension plan,[87] in this case) at 75.34% was a disproportionate violation of the principle of equality before public encumbrances, while maintaining a 68.34% rate was still permissible.[88] The Council was making an unprecedented interpretation here. What justified this seven-point difference? What legal and economic reasoning did the Council use to produce this figure? The appropriateness of the Council's decision is all the more obvious. Embroiled in the debate on the confiscatory nature of taxation, the Council agreed with the supporters of limiting taxes on the richest; however, this decision above all made a socialist conception of taxes impossible. It applied this reasoning to other tax measures aimed at raising the marginal rates that can affect the highest share of income.

And finally, in its decision of 29 December 2012, the CC went well beyond such a control of the consistency of the law: it unhesitatingly substituted its own vision of the general interest for that adopted by Parliament. By annulling the extension of a tax exemption for inheritances in Corsica, on the grounds that it was not based on any 'legitimate motive,'[89] it granted itself the power to decide a political question: that of the advisability of maintaining a tax advantage.

In doing so, the CC went deeper into the substance of political decision-making. The CC's analysis then became more subject to political criticism or, as in this case, to criticism of the validity of the economic analysis to which the Council referred in order to carry out this check on the consistency of the law.[90] Whether the CC considered Parliament's assessment unconstitutional or confirmed the distinctions introduced by the legislator does not change anything. Since objective answers cannot be given to questions concerning the criteria of different situations or the nature of the reasons of general interest, we have here what looks very similar to a control of the appropriateness of the choices made by the legislator. The CC has granted itself the sovereign power to substitute its opinion for that of Parliament, even though there is nothing to suggest that its opinion is more objective or better founded than that of parliamentarians. This type of decision also led a former member of the Council, François Luchaire, to write that, in this

86 Martin Collet, 'Les sages en font-ils trop?', column, *Le Monde*, January 3, 2013.

87 This refers to a mechanism for so-called super-complementary pensions, financed by businesses to increase the value of the pensions for certain employees by giving them pensions supplementary to those coming out of retirement funds.

88 Decision 2012–662 DC, of 29 December 2012, *a.m.*, § 81.

89 Decision 2012–662 DC, of 29 December 2012, *a.m* , § 133.

90 Mathieu (n 44) 519.

matter, 'Parliament's assessment is replaced by that of the CC.'[91] In his column in the daily newspaper, Martin Collet concluded with a warning in the form of a question: 'Judicial activism, you say?'[92]

By fulfilling its role as a negative legislator, the CC is sometimes called upon to exercise a normative function in competition with that of the legislator. Attempts to rewrite the law are still the subject of much criticism from doctrine and political circles. There is 'a difference between the legislative and judicial functions that the "hunger" of judicial bodies tends to confuse.' Although its role as guardian of the Constitution is generally accepted by the public authorities and, increasingly, by public opinion, it would be wrong to assert that its normative function is also accepted. The normative function is undoubtedly problematic. The introduction of the *ex post* control procedure of the law in 2008 strengthened the role of the Constitutional Council as a defender of freedoms. This has increased its legitimacy in the eyes of the public. In particular, it allows itself to take decisions that it did not take before. As Martin Collet rightly points out, at each normative decision, 'The Constitutional Council tests its legitimacy.'[93] In conclusion, it is not a question of whether the Council has the competence to correct the law or to deepen its control on political grounds, but rather whether it has the legitimacy to do so – a classical but unresolved question.[94]

91 François (n 60) 122.
92 Collet (n 86).
93 Ibid.
94 See L. Favoreu, 'La légitimité du juge constitutionnel' (1994) 46 *RID comp.*; H. Roussillon, 'Le Conseil constitutionnel: une légitimité contestée'. In *La légitimité des juges* (Toulouse PUT 1 Capitole 2004); L. Garlicki, 'La légitimité du contrôle de constitutionnalité: problèmes anciens c/développements récents' (2009/2) 78 *RFDC* (*Revue française de droit constitutionnel*) 227; G. Drago, B. François & N. Molfessis, *La de la jurisprudence du Conseil constitutionnel* (Paris Economica 1999).

2 Law-making activity of the German Federal Constitutional Court

A case-law study

Ruth Weber

Law-making as a judicial activity? At first glance, such a notion seems contradictory. But a closer look at the constitutional court's task reveals that the distinction is more delicate: to put it more abstractly, constitutional courts' law-making activity could be seen to antagonize democracy and the rule of law. The *raison d'être* of a constitutional court is to preserve the rule of law through its jurisdictional activity while ensuring that the principles of democracy are upheld. Current Federal Constitutional judge Gabriele Britz describes the constitutional court's task in this context as follows: 'A constitutional court may not shy away from naming violations of the Constitution and from objecting to them, even in a well-functioning democratic state under the rule of law.'[1] This is the first indication of the German Federal Constitutional Court's (FCC's or the Court's) self-perception. At the same time, it assists an understanding of the law-making activity of this Court, which is of the utmost importance within the German legal system.

While the Court does not establish legal norms such as regulations or statutes, it still develops law at both the constitutional and sub-constitutional levels. Based on this understanding, the question arises as to how the FCC actually proceeds when it identifies and objects to violations of the Constitution. What fundamental conditions influence this decision-making process? On that basis, when does a decision surpass the realms of mere application and amount to a law-making activity?

To answer these questions, this chapter is divided into three main headings. Firstly, the Court's historical, institutional, and organizational setting is outlined. The second heading presents important stages of the law-making activity in the FCC's case law. Third and finally, the Court's style of reasoning and its legal cultural setting in the context of its law-making activities are assessed.

1 Historical, institutional, and organizational setting

Through the Basic Law (*Grundgesetz*) of 1949, the Federal Republic of Germany established a new institution by creating the FCC. The Court took up its work in 1951 and has been located in Karlsruhe, the so-called residence of the law, ever

1 Gabriele Britz, 'Contribution' in *Role of Constitutional Courts in Upholding and Applying Constitutional Principles* (Constitutional Court of Georgia vol. I 2018) 47, 48.

DOI: 10.4324/9781003022442-3

since. The addition of the FCC to the Basic Law was a response to the failure of the Weimar Constitution and the National Socialist government's abuse of the law.[2] The political culture in Germany after 1945 favoured the strengthening of judicial review. After the failure of the pluralistic party state of Weimar, it was the law and the judiciary that were trusted to restore order. The FCC was part of this new framework and represented the 'guardian' of the new Constitution.[3] With this, the Court stood for the hope that the rule of law would prosper.

The FCC took up this role *ab initio* and gradually acquired a powerful and decisive position. Right from the beginning, it increasingly expanded its power. By the 1950s, the Court had already extended, through its case law, its material scope of review, positioning itself as a leading constitutional body. Thus, the Court acquired a decisive role in the internal jurisdictional order, not only by virtue of the Basic Law, but also owing to its own mode of action.

This is also reflected in the fact that the Court is highly accepted by society and enjoys great trust. In the Federal Republic, 'going to Karlsruhe'[4] is shorthand for the enforceability of each individual's fundamental rights vis-à-vis the State. The FCC is regarded as the 'citizens' court par excellence.'[5] It is held in high esteem by German society – especially in comparison with the trust afforded to other constitutional bodies.[6]

Although the Court's status and functions are partly determined by the Basic Law,[7] it does not regulate the Court's status as a constitutional body. The Court is mentioned in the section on jurisdiction (Articles 92 to 104 of the Basic Law), thereby underlining its judicial function. Further, the Basic Law does not provide any rules for its internal organization. The introduction of the Federal

2 Understanding the emergence of the FCC only as a response to Germany's Nazi past, however, does not reflect its complexity. See Michaela Hailbronner, 'Rethinking the Rise of German Constitutional Court' (2014) I CON 626 et seq., who focuses on value formalism from a legal-cultural perspective. See also Anuscheh Farahat, 'Das Bundesverfassungsgericht' in Armin von Bogdandy, Christoph Grabenwarter & Peter M Huber (eds.), *Handbuch Ius Publicum Europaeum* (CF Müller vol. VI 2016) § 98, marg. 1–5.

3 On the debates within the Weimar *Staatsrechtslehre* (Weimar constitutional law doctrine) see Hans Kelsen, *Wer soll der Hüter der Verfassung sein?* (Rothschild 1931); Carl Schmitt, *Der Hüter der Verfassung* (Mohr 1931); for a comprehensive analysis see Oliver Lembcke, *Hüter der Verfassung* (Mohr Siebeck 2007) 15; Michael Stolleis, *Geschichte des öffentlichen Rechts in Deutschland* (CH Beck vol. IV 2012) 145.

4 See e.g. Rolf Lamprecht, *Ich gehe bis nach Karlsruhe* (DVA 2011).

5 Jutta Limbach, 'Wirkungen der Rechtsprechung des Bundesverfassungsgerichts' in Peter Hanau, Friedrich Heither & Jürgen Kühling (eds.), *Richterliches Arbeitsrecht* (CH Beck 1999) 344 ('Bürgergericht par excellence').

6 Hans Vorländer & André Brodocz, 'Das Vertrauen in das Bundesverfassungsgericht' in Hans Vorländer (ed.), *Die Deutungsmacht der Verfassungsgerichtsbarkeit* (VS Verlag für Sozialwissenschaften 2006) 259; Werner J Patzelt, 'Warum verachten die Deutschen ihr Parlament und lieben ihr Verfassungsgericht?' (2005) Zeitschrift für Parlamentsfragen 517; Uwe Kranenpohl, *Hinter dem Schleier des Beratungsgeheimnisses* (VS Verlag für Sozialwissenschaften 2010) 400 et seq.

7 See in particular Art. 92 to 94, 99, 100, 115g and 115h BL.

Constitutional Court Act (*Bundesverfassungsgerichtsgesetz*) in 1951 was therefore preceded by fierce deliberations.[8]

Another controversy that arose when the Court was initially established was the debate around whether a legal qualification requirement for its judges should be introduced.[9] Finally, however, it was decided that judges must not be younger than 40 years of age, must be eligible for election to the *Bundestag*, and must hold general qualifications for judicial office. This latter condition is particularly important because it requires legal training up to the Second State Examination in Law.[10] In addition, at least three out of eight judges of a senate must have previously been judges at one of the highest federal courts.[11]

The *Bundestag* and the *Bundesrat* each elect half of the sixteen Court judges.[12] Since 2015, the *Bundestag's* Election Committee has no longer been responsible for the election of judges; instead, following the Election Committee's proposal, the plenum of the *Bundestag* votes on the proposed candidate using hidden voting cards without any debate.[13] The proposed candidate must be elected by a two-thirds majority. The maximum term of office for judges is twelve years; re-election is not possible.[14]

In practice, the political parties sharing the responsibilities of government in the federal State and the States (*Länder*) agree on the election of judges before the judge elections in the *Bundesrat* and the *Bundestag*. Formerly, Christian Democrats and Social Democrats had the right to propose four judges in one senate, which was intended to ensure a political balance within the senates. At present, the smaller coalition parties (Greens and Liberals) also have the right to make proposals after consultation.[15] The requirement of a two-thirds majority in the election, the comparatively long duration of the position, and the fact that re-election is excluded are intended to ensure the political independence of judges. In addition, there are far-reaching incompatibility provisions that exclude any other political or professional activity apart from positions as university professors.[16] An empirical study of the voting behaviour of constitutional judges when rendering their decisions has shown that those nominated by the same political camp behave, in part, similarly in terms of their votes. Proximity to a party can thus influence judicial

8 See Farahat (n 2) marg. 7.
9 Ibid., marg. 8.
10 § 3 para. 1 and 2 FCCA.
11 Art. 94 para. 1 sentence 1 BL, § 2 para. 3 FCCA.
12 Art. 94 para. 1 sentence 2 BL, §§ 5 to 7 FCCA.
13 German Federal Law Gazette, Part I (2015) 973.
14 § 4 FCCA.
15 Uwe Kischel, 'Amt, Unbefangenheit und Wahl der Bundesverfassungsrichter', in Josef Isensee & Paul Kirchhof (eds.), *Handbuch des Staatsrechts der Bundesrepublik Deutschland* (CF Müller vol. III[3] 2005) § 69, marg. 21 et seq.; Michaela Hailbronner & Stefan Martini, 'The German Federal Constitutional Court' in András Jakab, Arthur Dyevre & Giulio Itzcovich (eds.), *Comparative Constitutional Reasoning* (Cambridge University Press 2017), 365 et seq., who describe the selection process as 'not particularly transparent'.
16 Art. 94 para. 1 sentence 3 BL and § 3 para. 4 FCCA.

decision-making behaviour as a background factor, but only as one among several other factors.[17]

Being appointed as a judge at the FCC is regarded as the undisputed culmination of a legal career.[18] However, the various legal professions are not equally represented. Over time, the majority of judges have been professors of law. In addition, due to legal requirements, a large number of former judges of the highest federal courts are represented. They are meant to have great procedural experience.[19] This is supplemented by a more scientific, 'dogmatic' understanding of the law that characterizes those judges who are law professors. Against this background, there is a kind of 'division of labour' between these two professional groups at the Court.[20] Occasionally, politicians have held and still hold the office of a FCC judge. Attorneys, however, are rarely represented at the Court.

2 Important stages of the law-making activity in the Federal Constitutional Court's case law

The following analysis of the case law of the Court with regard to its law-making activity highlights the Court's practice: the early emancipatory decisions of the 1950s are particularly interesting (heading 2.1). After that, some of the decisions that have led to controversial political and societal discussions are presented (heading 2.2). A further aspect is the activity of the Court with regard to the creation of new fundamental rights (heading 2.3). Subsequently, the instructions to the legislature and their influence on sub-constitutional law are examined (heading 2.4). Finally, further aspects of the relationship between the Court and the legislature complement the presentation (heading 2.5).

2.1 Early self-definition in the 1950s: emancipatory decisions at the Federal Constitutional Court

The FCC rendered its first decision three weeks before the Court's official opening ceremony on 28 September 1951. The Court granted an interlocutory injunction, which provisionally suspended a referendum on the foundation of a southwest state, entailing the restructuring of the states of Baden, Württemberg-Baden, and Württemberg-Hohenzollern. With the Court's final decision in this case, subsequent to the interlocutory injunction, the Court confirmed the validity of the restructuring law.[21]

17 Benjamin Engst et al., 'Zum Einfluss der Parteinähe auf das Abstimmungsverhalten der Bundesverfassungsrichter – eine quantitative Untersuchung' (2017) *JZ* 816, 822, 824.

18 Kranenpohl (n 6) 456 et seq.

19 Kranenpohl (n 6) 203.

20 Ibid., 205.

21 BVerfGE 1, 1 [provisional suspension] and BVerfGE 1, 14 [final decision] – Südweststaat (Southwest State).

As an initial observation, the format of this decision alone makes it remarkable, as the thirty-nine guiding principles preceding the operative part extend over five printed pages. Articulating the judgement in the strictest of tones, on the one hand, the Court goes beyond the concrete subject matter of the decision and, on the other, it makes significant statements of self-definition, right at the beginning of the Court's decision-making activity. These statements concern, for example, the reformulation of the principle of equality, as well as the scope of the Court's own authority.

In the following years, the FCC displayed self-confidence towards its own role through various statements; namely, through its expert opinions and its so-called status memorandum (*Statusdenkschrift*). These statements went beyond the realms of pure judicial decision-making practice. Initially, the Court was authorized to issue expert opinions.[22] Accordingly, certain federal bodies could obtain a legal opinion from the FCC. In practice, however, only two expert opinions were obtained in total.[23]

An example of this activity is an expert opinion requested by Federal President Theodor Heuss. It was technically resolved by the withdrawal of the application. Nevertheless, the FCC published an opinion, stating: 'However, an institutional Constitutional Court that is exclusively called upon to adjudicate constitutional law cannot be measured with the same degree as an ordinary civil or criminal court, especially if it is endowed with the diversity of competences as the Federal Constitutional Court. Even where it decides on violated rights or alleged obligations, it is less in the service of subjective prosecution than in the service of objective preservation of constitutional law.'[24]

In this document, the Court outlines its early self-image by considering itself as holding a special position as the 'preserver of constitutional law.' However, the Court itself subsequently proposed deleting the legal provision according to which it was to be entrusted with the function of issuing expert opinions. In its own words, this was 'a task alien to the nature of the Constitutional Court' with there being a 'danger of a reduction in the reputation of the Court.'[25] In 1956, the possibility of requesting expert opinions was eventually removed because the actual task of the judiciary was meant to be about ruling on disputes and not about providing more or less non-binding expert opinions.[26]

In its adolescence, the FCC exceptionally issued a statement – the so-called status memorandum from 1952 – claiming the status of a constitutional body for

22 § 97 FCCA old version.

23 BVerfGE 1, 76 – Steuerverwaltung (Tax Agencies) and BVerfGE 3, 407 – Baugutachten (Construction Project).

24 BVerfGE 2, 79 <86> – Plenargutachten *Heuss* (Plenary Opinion *Heuss*).

25 Cited after Willi Geiger, 'Zur Reform des Bundesverfassungsgerichts', in Theodor Maunz (ed.), *Vom Bonner Grundgesetz zur gesamtdeutschen Verfassung* (Isar-Verlag 1956) 211, 216.

26 See law of 21 July 1956 (German Federal Law Gazette, Part I (1956) 662) and Bundestag Document 2/2388, 4.

itself. With this memorandum, the Court highlighted its desire to be more than just a court; namely, a self-governing constitutional body 'endowed with the highest authority.'[27] Thus, achieving institutional independence from the Federal Ministry of Justice was an important step in the early emancipation of the FCC, which from then on has acted 'at eye level with the legislature.'[28]

In the 1950s, the FCC also laid the foundation for its future jurisprudence by providing a broad understanding of what should be viewed as constitutional law. Its jurisprudence in the field of fundamental rights in particular set the tone for the Court's character as the protector of individuals' rights.[29]

The best-known decisions are the *Elfes* decision of 1957[30] and the *Lüth* decision of 1958.[31] In the *Elfes* decision, the Court derived, from the fundamental right to general freedom of action, that citizens could challenge the constitutionality of every legal provision restricting freedom by way of a constitutional complaint (*Verfassungsbeschwerde*). The formal and substantial constitutionality of the infringed provision was then reviewed. Only one year later, the FCC pronounced one of its most famous decisions with the *Lüth* decision, simultaneously repositioning itself and gaining more power.[32] According to the *Lüth* decision, the Basic Law represents an objective order of values and fundamental rights that permeate all areas of law. With this decision, the FCC also had to deal with Germany's Nazi past. The lawsuit had its origins in a call for boycotts pronounced by Hamburg Senate Director Erich Lüth. With his call for boycotts, Erich Lüth objected to a film by a director who had made his career in Nazi Germany. As the FCC understood the Basic Law as a set of values and the freedom of expression as one of its central components, it came to the conclusion that the prohibition of the call for boycotts was not compatible with the Basic Law. Fundamental rights thus also have an impact on private law, which means that individuals are indirectly bound by fundamental rights. The fundamental rights were thus granted a far-reaching effect and the legal order was 'constitutionalized' as a whole.

The constitutional judges themselves consider the *Lüth* and *Elfes* decisions to be milestones of the 1950s with regard to their effect on the meaning and establishment of their constitutional jurisdiction.[33] This demonstrates that in the early years of the Court, its own activism led to its outstanding position in the Federal Republic of Germany.

27 Richard Thoma & Gerhard Leibholz, *Die Rechtsstellung des Bundesverfassungsgerichts* (CF Müller 1953) 3.
28 Farahat (n 2) marg. 13.
29 Dieter Grimm, 'The role of fundamental rights after sixty-five years of constitutional jurisprudence in Germany' (2015) I CON 21 et seq.
30 BVerfGE 6, 32 – *Elfes*.
31 BVerfGE 7, 198 – *Lüth*.
32 Matthias Jestaedt, 'Phänomen Bundesverfassungsgericht' in Matthias Jestaedt et al. (eds.), *Das entgrenzte Gericht* (Suhrkamp 2011) 93.
33 Uwe Kranenpohl, 'Die Bedeutung von Interpretationsmethoden und Dogmatik in der Entscheidungspraxis des Bundesverfassungsgerichts' (2009) 48 Der Staat 385 et seq.

2.2 The Federal Constitutional Court and political neutrality: a complex issue

The FCC had thus gained increasing authority in its early years and was considered to be largely free from political influence. After several Conservative governments and a grand coalition in the 1960s, the Social Democratic Party won the government majority for the first time in 1969 and formed a coalition with the Liberal Democratic Party. From this moment onwards, the FCC, with the majority of judges aligned with the Christian Democratic Party, ruled against several legislative projects introduced by the Social Democrats and the Liberals. In 1975, the Court took an important decision on abortion. Following a change in the law, punishment was precluded for abortion within the first three months of pregnancy. The FCC declared that this exemption from punishment was unconstitutional because it violated the protection of life.[34] In the same way, it opposed a change in the military service law according to which it should be possible to refuse military service without stating the reasons for doing so by simply invoking the Basic Law.[35] These decisions were heavily criticized and the FCC was accused of having decided based on party lines.[36]

In the following years, critics repeatedly accused the Court of not being politically neutral.[37] Such criticism came at different times from different political camps. In the 1990s, for example, the Conservatives accused the Court of lacking neutrality: on one occasion, the scope of religious freedom was reviewed. The Court ruled that Christian crosses in classrooms were not mandatory. According to the Court's decision, this violated the gentle balance required by the Basic Law between freedom of religion and parental education.[38] A decision on the freedom of opinion and expression was subject to similarly strong controversy. The Court held that the reproduction of Kurt Tucholsky's statement 'Soldiers are murderers' was covered by freedom of expression and thus did not constitute a criminal offence.[39]

Current FCC decisions, in the context of politically controversial questions, show that it can certainly be seen as an important actor in society's development. Take, for example, the Court's decision following a constitutional complaint on the so-called third sex.[40] Here, it was not the legislature that took action, for instance by amending the Civil Status Act, but the FCC, which declared that the Civil Status Act violated the general right of personality and the principle of equality by requiring the gender to be registered without allowing for a further positive entry other than male or female.

34 BVerfGE 39, 1 – Schwangerschaftsabbruch I (Abortion I).
35 BVerfGE 48, 127 – Wehrpflichtnovelle (Military Service Amendment).
36 Farahat (n 2) marg. 18–19.
37 Christoph Schönberger, 'Anmerkungen zu Karlsruhe' in Matthias Jestaedt et al. (eds.), *Das entgrenzte Gericht* (Suhrkamp 2011) 9–76.
38 BVerfGE 93, 1 – Kruzifix (Crucifix).
39 BVerfGE 93, 266 – 'Soldaten sind Mörder' ('Soldiers Are Murderers').
40 BVerfGE 147, 1 – Geschlechtsidentität (Gender Identity).

If the Court was praised for its openness in this decision, only one week later these former partisans expressed criticism of a further decision. In this case, the Court rejected a constitutional complaint because the party's rights were not at risk and they thus did not require legal protection. Therefore, the Court decided not to hear the case on the substance of the issue. The complainant brought an action against an administrative refusal to change his/her name and civil status under the Transsexuals Act.[41] The FCC considered it to be constitutionally obvious that the prerequisite proof of two expert opinions for the proposed changes was compatible, in particular, with the general right of personality.

The fact that such different decisions were taken in such a short time shows that the Court does not simply follow a political line and take unilateral decisions accordingly. As a matter of fact, the Court can already avoid a decision on the merits – as happened in the proceedings on transsexual law – by strictly applying the admissibility criteria. In the decision on gender identity, however, it declared the law unconstitutional, but left the legal consequences to the legislature. The decision stated that the legislature had several possibilities, including deciding against any gender entry under personal status law or creating the possibility for the persons concerned to choose a uniform positive designation of gender that is neither male nor female. The option of a further gender entry can – the Court says – be developed in different ways by law.[42]

Surprisingly, one FCC ruling was not ultimately pursued in respect of a similarly controversial social question. After the *Bundestag* had introduced the law on 'marriage for all,'[43] that is, the possibility for same-sex couples to marry (quite surprisingly, shortly before the parliamentary summer break in 2017), the State of Bavaria initially announced that it would take action against this law before the FCC because of an alleged infringement of the right to family and marriage. In 2018, however, the State government announced that it did not intend to take such action, as the expert opinions it had obtained were unlikely to provide sufficient evidence for the proceedings to be successful.[44] This indicates that not every political problem concerning constitutional law will be finally dealt with by the Court. Yet, arguments on the constitutionality of statutes are often omnipresent in the public debates about legislative amendments.

Irrespective of where one stands with regard to the actual claims made in the individual cases mentioned, these decisions clearly show that the FCC in its function as guardian of the Constitution is not an apolitical court. This already became clear in the early decisions of the Court in the 1950s, the implications of which are still relevant today. Both then and now, the Court has positioned itself between the judiciary as a supreme court and as the controller of the legislature, as a

41 BVerfGE, decision of the Second Chamber of the First Senate of 17 October 2017 – 1 BvR 747/17, www.bverfg.de.

42 BVerfGE 147, 1 <30, marg. 65>.

43 *German Federal Law Gazette*, Part I (2017), 2787.

44 Lisa Schnell, 'Bayern verzichtet auf Klage gegen die Ehe für alle', Süddeutsche Zeitung, 6 March 2017 (https://www.sueddeutsche.de/bayern/justiz-bayern-verzichtet-auf-klage-gegen-die-ehe-fuer-alle-1.3894363, 9 November 2019)

constitutional body whose status is derived directly from the Basic Law and which necessarily acts politically.[45]

2.3 Creation of new fundamental rights: constitutional law-making

The important role of the FCC in the legal system of the Federal Republic of Germany has remained unchanged to this day. The Court has a very high reputation within German society, largely due to the possibility of being able to make individual constitutional complaints.[46] Although this requires a subjective infringement of a fundamental right, this remedy promotes the 'constitutionalization' of the objective legal order as a whole.

There is a wide range of different proceedings before the FCC. Almost 97% of all proceedings are constitutional complaints. This procedure was initially only set out in the Federal Constitutional Court Act. It was not until 1969 that it was incorporated into Article 93 paragraph 1 No. 4a of the Basic Law. This legal remedy is symbolic of the FCC as a court that serves the individual legal protection of citizens and is described as its 'core resource.'[47] The high number of proceedings is mainly due to the fact that the procedure is open to everyone. Additionally, legal representation is not even necessary. In contrast, the circle of petitioners in the other proceedings is limited, which also shows that their sparsity does not necessarily correlate with their significance.[48]

A constitutional complaint may be filed by anyone who believes that one of his or her fundamental rights has been infringed by public authorities.[49] The admissibility requirements for a constitutional complaint are high. The majority of complaints fail either because they do not substantiate a violation of a fundamental right or because they do not meet the strict subsidiarity requirements. To review these admissibility criteria, a procedure was introduced in order to rationalize the decision-making process of the Court.

In the beginning, there were only two formations in which judges met: on the one hand, the standard formation of two senates with eight judges each; on the other hand, a plenum of both senates, which, however, plays almost no role in practice. Eventually, it turned out that a large number of constitutional complaints would already have failed because they did not meet the admissibility criteria. It therefore proved impracticable to decide all these proceedings in the senates. This is why the so-called chamber procedure was introduced, according to which constitutional complaints[50] and concrete reviews of norms[51] could also be decided in a chamber of three judges.

45 Farahat (n 2) marg. 37–38.
46 On social acceptance of the FCC see p. 29, especially n 6.
47 Farahat (n 2) marg. 50 et seq.
48 Further procedures are abstract (Art. 93 para. 1 No. 2 BL) and concrete norm controls (Art. 100 BL), federal-state, organ and other constitutional disputes at federal and State level (see Art. 93 para. 1 BL).
49 Art. 93 para. 1 No. 4a BL, supplemented by §§ 90 et seq. FCCA.
50 § 93b-d FCCA.
51 § 81a FCCA.

In order to relieve the pressure from the senates of the Court, these chambers are allowed to reject constitutional complaints via a unanimous decision on the grounds of a lack of prospects for success. As the Federal Constitutional Court Act offers the possibility to refrain from disclosing a formal justification in these cases, the vast majority of these decisions do not incorporate reasons.[52] Furthermore, the chambers are authorized to grant complaints, which are obviously justified on the basis of clear constitutional case law on this issue.

The function of an individual petition by means of a constitutional complaint is not only to protect individual rights, but also to uphold the objective constitutional order. The citizen is thereby mobilized as the constitutional centrepiece for the enforcement of fundamental rights.[53] This is clearly stated in one of the first FCC decisions – the *Elfes* decision of 1957.[54] It represents the beginning of the far-reaching jurisdiction of the Court on the general freedom of action according to Article 2 paragraph 1 of the Basic Law. Since then, this Article has served as a 'catch-all fundamental right' (*Auffanggrundrecht*), thus making it possible to also challenge violations of regulations concerning legislative procedures or competences – that is, the formal constitutionality of incorrect laws – by invoking fundamental rights.

Through this broad understanding of the scope of protection of the general freedom of action, the FCC furthers the influence of constitutional law on the entire legal system. In addition, the Court has combined different fundamental rights, or defined the scope of certain fundamental rights in various places, in such a way as to create 'new' fundamental rights. Examples include the right to informational self-determination,[55] the right to guarantee the confidentiality and integrity of information technology systems,[56] and the guarantee of a minimum subsistence level.[57]

2.4 Instructions to the legislature: influence on sub-constitutional law

The protection of the objective constitutional order is expressed by the fact that the authority of res judicata does not remain between the parties to the dispute, but exceeds them and binds the constitutional bodies of the federal State and the States, as well as all courts and public authorities.[58] The binding effect of its own decisions is very widely understood by the FCC and corresponds with the fundamental authority of the Court as the highest instance interpreting the Constitution.[59] Furthermore, the Federal Constitutional Court Act stipulates that decisions

52 § 93d para. 1 sentence 2 FCCA.
53 Farahat (n 2) marg. 54.
54 See p. 33, BVerfGE 6, 32 – *Elfes*.
55 BVerfGE 65, 1 – Volkszählung (Census)
56 BVerfGE 120, 274 – Online-Durchsuchung (Online Search).
57 BVerfGE 125, 175 – Hartz IV.
58 § 31 para. 1 FCCA.
59 See heading 3.1 on the operative part of the decision and in detail: Helmuth Schulze-Fielitz, 'Wirkung und Befolgung verfassungsgerichtlicher Entscheidungen' in Peter Badura & Horst Dreier (eds.), *Festschrift 50 Jahre Bundesverfassungsgericht* (Mohr Siebeck vol. 1 2001) 388 et seq.

on the control of norms shall have the force of law. The decisions shall be published in the *Federal Law Gazette*.[60] This clearly shows the general and universal binding character of these decisions. The FCC can also use interim injunctions[61] for the effective implementation of its decisions and issue enforcement orders for its own decisions.[62] The Court makes excessive use of this second option in order to be certain that its own decisions will be enforced.

Section 31 of the Federal Constitutional Court Act enables the Court to declare the invalidity of a law with binding effect *erga omnes*. In the event of a declaration of invalidity, the FCC has adopted detailed transitional provisions in a number of decisions. These are particularly prominent examples of the law-making activity of the Court. In this context, the decision on abortion – already mentioned because of its political controversy – and the decision on the Asylum Seekers' Benefits Act are especially instructive.

The FCC has twice decided on the criminal treatment of abortion. In its first decision in 1975, the Court had ruled that the amendment to the law, which provided for a regulation on time limits, was null and void. The Court decided that abortion remained punishable; however, not according to the strict previous legal regulation, but in a modified form.[63] In the second 1993 decision on abortion, the Court again annulled the offending legislation. The reasons of the decision are preceded by an operative part of almost six printed pages. In this part of the decision, the Court establishes a detailed transitional arrangement, which provides for the organization and content of a new consultation system for pregnant women.

The following passage from the decision itself illustrates how the Court perceives its relationship with the legislature:

> It is the legislature's task to specify the nature and scope of protection. The constitution prescribes that protection must be the goal, but provides no details on the form it must take. Nevertheless, the legislature must comply with the ban on inadequate protection [...], which means it is subject to constitutional oversight. What is necessary is an appropriate level of protection – taking into account potentially conflicting legal interests. The decisive issue is whether the protection, as such, is effective. The measures adopted by the legislature must be sufficient for appropriate and effective protection and also be based on careful investigation of the facts and on reasonable prognoses.[64]

60 § 31 para. 2 FCCA.
61 § 32 FCCA
62 § 35 FCCA.
63 Also see p. 34, BVerfGE 39, 1 – Schwangerschaftsabbruch I (Abortion I).
64 BVerfGE 88, 203, 254 – Schwangerschaftsabbruch II [Abortion II], cited after Christian Bumke & Andreas Voßkuhle, *German Constitutional Law* (Oxford University Press 2019) marg. 210.

Even if the Court expressly states that the Basic Law 'provides no details' on the nature and scope of the protection, it has clearly set the direction in its detailed transitional arrangement. In addition, the legislature subsequently adopted most of these provisions directly.[65]

The second example in this context concerns a 2012 decision on the Asylum Seekers' Benefits Act.[66] In this decision, the Court annulled the amount of cash benefits under this law. The previous cash benefits were based on flat rates that had not been harmonized since 1993. Therefore, the Court considered a transitional arrangement to be necessary. In the reasons for the decision, it comprehensively explains why precise transitional arrangements are needed. Accordingly, a further application of the unconstitutional provisions was not acceptable because of the existential significance of basic benefits. The fundamental vital needs of the beneficiaries were to be met at the time when they arose.[67] Moreover, the Court stated that it could not foresee the legislature introducing a new regulation – despite an announcement to the contrary. In the Court's eyes, there was 'an inevitable need for a uniform, abstract, and general provision'[68] on the amount of cash benefits. The Court also explains the considerations that led it to the concrete transitional arrangement and emphasizes: 'This transitional arrangement does not replace the decision of the legislature. The latter has a constitutional duty to take a decision of its own, consistent with the requirements of the Basic Law as to how and by which amount the minimum existence of the group of individuals affected by the provisions declared unconstitutional may be guaranteed in the future.'[69]

This shows that the wording of the decision clearly seeks to give the legislature considerable leeway, which is, however, limited in practice by the concrete proposal of a transitional arrangement. Both examples illustrate that even in decisions originating from completely different fields of law, the FCC submits detailed proposals for the correction of unconstitutionality to the legislature.

Furthermore, in addition to the declaration of invalidity, the Court often makes use of the so-called declaration of unconstitutionality (*Verfassungswidrigkeitserklärung*): it states in the operative part of the decision that a certain provision is unconstitutional, but can order its temporary continuation if the immediate invalidity of the provision would unintentionally harm the public interest. With this, the Court then continues to make an appeal to the legislature to regulate the entire matter anew.

One example of this procedure is the decision on preventive detention, in which the FCC reasoned:

> In view of the encroachment upon fundamental rights associated with preventive detention [...] it is necessary to create a transitional arrangement for

65 Peter Lerche, 'Das Bundesverfassungsgericht als Notgesetzgeber, insbesondere im Blick auf das Recht des Schwangerschaftsabbruchs', in Meinhard Heinze & Jochem Schmitt (eds.), *Festschrift für Wolfgang Gitter* (Chmielorz 1995) 509 et seq.

66 BVerfGE 132, 134 – Asylbewerberleistungsgesetz (Asylum Seekers Benefits Act).

67 BVerfGE 132, 134 <174, marg. 99>.

68 Ibid.

69 BVerfGE 132, 134 <175, marg. 101>.

> the period until there is a detailed statutory reform; this transitional arrangement must admittedly permit the existing provisions to continue in effect, to avoid a legal vacuum, and the pending review proceedings to be continued [...], but must ensure that minimum constitutional requirements are complied with. During the period when the current provisions continue in effect, therefore, the existing provisions must be applied subject to the conditions set out [...] [in] the operative part of the judgment.[70]

Again, we see the FCC ordering transitional arrangements in the operative part of the decision. In some cases, however, the rules that the FCC considers unconstitutional continue to apply until a deadline is reached that is set by the Court for the legislature. This represents – in addition to the transitional arrangements – a further possibility to call upon the legislature to create a statute in accordance with the Basic Law.

2.5 The relationship between the Federal Constitutional Court and the legislature: further aspects

These stages in the development of the FCC's jurisdiction reveal that the law-making activity of the Court is a finely nuanced dialogue. Transitional arrangements, for instance, seem to be largely accepted by the legislature but, in their subtle differentiation, appear to be a characteristic feature of a potentially conflict-prone relationship. Especially regarding the final acceptance of the decision, four aspects can be added to the aforementioned lines of jurisdiction that prove the influence of the FCC on the legislature.

Firstly, it is generally disputed as to whether the legislature can re-enact exactly the same provision after the FCC has declared a provision null and void.[71] While this question causes various theoretical democratic problems, the legislature generally follows the decisions of the FCC.

Secondly, the FCC has set requirements for the legislative methodology itself in various decisions. A well-known example of this is the decision on the question of whether the amount of the standard benefit paid to secure the livelihood of adults according to the provisions of the social law is compatible with the Basic Law:[72]

> The Court declared itself competent to examine 'whether the legislature has covered and described the goal to ensure an existence that is in line with human dignity [...], whether within its margin of appreciation it has selected a calculation procedure that is fundamentally suited to an assessment of the

70 BVerfGE 128, 326 – Sicherungsverwahrung II (Preventive Detention II) <404, marg. 171>.

71 See for a more detailed examination Mehrdad Payandeh, *Judikative Rechtserzeugung* (Mohr Siebeck 2017) 405 et seq.

72 BVerfGE 125, 175 – Hartz IV.

> subsistence minimum, whether, in essence, it has completely and correctly ascertained the necessary facts and, finally, whether it kept within the bounds of what is justifiable in all calculation steps with a comprehensible set of figures within this selected procedure and its structural principles [...] [and that in] order to facilitate this constitutional review, there is an obligation for the legislature to disclose the methods and calculations used to determine the subsistence minimum in the legislative procedure.'[73]

This decision clearly shows that the FCC goes beyond examining the constitutionality of a law in purely substantive terms but imposes requirements on the legislative procedure. As can be seen from the quoted passage, the legislature must observe certain principles and, in particular, it must 'disclose the methods and calculations.' With this requirement, the FCC indirectly furthers law-making by imposing requirements on the legislative procedure.

Thirdly, the Court can decide that a provision is not unconstitutional if it can be interpreted in a way that ensures its conformity with the Constitution. The FCC illustrates the requirement for this method of interpretation with regard to the legislature as follows:

> Respect for the legislative power [...] mandates that, within the limits of the constitution, the maximum amount of the legislature's intent must be preserved. It therefore requires an interpretation in conformity with the constitution, to the extent that this can be achieved within the wording of the law and while preserving the goal, which the legislature, in principle, desired to achieve.[74]

The principle of interpretation in conformity with the Constitution is thus an example of the interaction between the FCC and the legislature, while highlighting the scope and limitations of judicial interpretation. As this quotation shows, the key premise of the Court is to preserve 'the maximum amount of the legislature's intent.' According to this understanding, interpretation in conformity with the Constitution shall be used to promote legislative goals, limited only by the wording of the rule.

Fourthly, when examining the constitutionality of a law, the Court regularly applies the principle of proportionality. For its examination, the Court applies a four-step test.[75] The first step consists of determining the purpose of the law and whether this purpose is compatible with the Basic Law (1). The next two steps are to examine whether the specific statutory rule is suitable (2) and necessary to achieve this purpose (3). Lastly, the proportionality of the rule is questioned (4); that is, whether the benefits of the purpose pursued overweigh the limitation of the fundamental right. This subtle differentiation in the review of laws enables the

73 BVerfGE 125, 175 <143–144>.

74 BVerfGE 86, 288 <320> – § 57a StGB (§ 57a German Criminal Code), translation cited after Bumke & Voßkuhle (n 64) marg. 162.

75 For a detailed explanation see Grimm (n 29) 19 et seq. and Hailbronner & Martini (n 15) 387.

Court to finely nuance its control of the legislature. According to former FCC judge Dieter Grimm, '[d]ue to the principle of proportionality, the legislature has much less leeway than before the principle was applied to statutes.'[76]

All these highlights show the diversity in which law-making activities take place. The passages from the decisions reveal that the FCC explicitly reflects and thus shapes its relationship with the legislature.

3 Dimensions of the law-making activity

The law-making activity of the FCC is a multi-layered phenomenon, enabling self-determination of its position not only, but first and foremost, vis-à-vis the legislature. To further explain this, two essential points must be understood: on the one hand, there is the Court's style of reasoning; that is, at which points in the decision-making process the Court carries out its law-making activity (heading 3.1). On the other hand, it is essential to examine the legal cultural background and its connection to the law-making activity (heading 3.2).

3.1 The Federal Constitutional Court's law-making activity through the lens of its style of reasoning

When analysing the FCC's law-making activity through the lens of the Court's style of reasoning, it is, firstly, important to examine the structure of judicial decisions. While the operative part of the decision concerns the part of the provided decision with a binding legal effect, the Court's paradigmatic technique of 'scale building' (*Maßstabsbildung*) takes place in the reasons of the decision and reveals the self-positioning of the Court.

The operative part of the decision is provided at the beginning of the decision and is indicated by the heading 'decision formula' (*Entscheidungsformel*). It is only preceded by the guiding principles (*Leitsätze*) and the caption of the decision. In most cases, the operative part consists of one to two sentences that set out the legal consequences of the decision. It is often related to the reasons of the decision, because the reasons can be and are used as an aid for interpreting the operative part. For example, in the case of a declaration of compatibility with the stipulation that the controlled norms must be interpreted in conformity with the Constitution,[77] the Court uses the formula of the reference to compatibility with the Basic Law 'in the interpretation evident from the reasons.'[78] In these cases, according to the case law of the FCC itself, not only the operative part of the decision but also the 'supporting reasons' of the decision are legally binding.[79]

76 Grimm (n 29) 20.

77 For this type of decision statement see heading 2.5.

78 German version: 'in der aus den Gründen ersichtlichen Auslegung', on the interdependency of operative part and reasons see Hans Lechner & Rüdiger Zuck, *Bundesverfassungsgerichtsgesetz* (CH Beck vol. VIII 2019) § 30, marg. 8 et seq.

79 See the above-mentioned first decision of the Court, BVerfGE 1, 14 <37> – Southwest State. Another example of this is BVerfGE 40, 88 – Führerschein (Driving

Within the reasons of the decision, the substance of the relevant constitutional norms is thoroughly displayed in the so-called scale sections (*Maßstabsteile*).[80] In this part, the FCC explicitly refers to its own precedents. This elaborate way of interpreting the Constitution leads to transparency. In the internal editorial work of the Court, the focus of judicial activity seems to lie in the formulation of these parts: they are meant to be intensively discussed within the deliberations of the decision. Their final wording is precisely coordinated and – according to the judges – often differs significantly from the reporting judge's first version.[81] In the same way, the possibility for judges to announce dissenting opinions[82] makes the decision-making process transparent and allows conclusions to be drawn about the culture of deliberation. They convey the image of a court whose deliberative process does not always result in a unanimous decision.

The FCC's decisions are considered to be comprehensive and complex, which, while producing generally transparent decisions, makes it difficult for the wider public to understand their ramifications. Accordingly, guiding principles precede the most important decisions to improve comprehensibility and readability. The guiding principles are proposed by the reporting judge and discussed within the senate. They allow certain points to be accentuated and thus to influence the reception of the decision. In a certain sense, they can be read as an abstract of the decision and thus stand symbolically for the doctrinal nature of the reasoning style at the FCC.[83]

The characteristic feature of the reasoning style of the decisions is their focus on so-called dogmatics (*Dogmatik*), which can be understood as a doctrinal approach that uses concepts from legal science as well as the Court's own decisions for the development of new jurisprudential lines. This is shown by the fact that there are a high number of quotations within the scale sections, in particular from the Court's own case law. It can thus be inferred that the dogmatic approach correlates with the high discursivity of the deliberations. This finds its expression within the reasons for the decision in the formation of constitutional scales.[84] This form of presentation markets the deliberative culture and presents the decision as the 'consensual result of an open and deliberative exchange of exclusively legal arguments.'[85] This way of proceeding certainly is one element behind the social acceptance of the Court. By exposing its deliberative culture and orienting itself

Licence). Within this decision, the binding effect is founded on the self-perception as 'authoritative interpreter and guardian of the constitution' (93 et seq.).

80 Oliver Lepsius, 'Die maßstabsetzende Gewalt' in Matthias Jestaedt et al. (eds.), *Das entgrenzte Gericht* (Suhrkamp 2011) 168 et seq.; Hailbronner & Martini (n 15) 367 translate the expression as 'overall standards'.

81 Ruth Weber, *Der Begründungsstil von Conseil constitutionnel und Bundesverfassungsgericht* (Mohr Siebeck 2019) 280 et seq.

82 § 30 para. 2 FCCA permits the inclusion of dissenting opinions and the communication of proportions of votes.

83 On the use of guiding principles at the FCC and as a stylistic feature of German courts in general, see Weber (n 81) 67 et seq.

84 Weber (n 81) 130 et seq., 317 et seq.

85 Farahat (n 2) marg. 89.

towards dogmatic concepts of law, the Court strengthens its external image as a transparent court oriented towards the 'best' legal solution. Accordingly, this also strengthens the acceptance of its law-making activity.

3.2 Law-making activity as an expression of German legal culture

The image of the FCC conveyed by its style of reasoning thus appears to be an important source of authority. However, this aspect has not lacked criticism. Constitutional scholarship accuses the Court of blurring the distinction between law-making and the application of law through its self-confident establishment of constitutional standards. As has been shown, the FCC gives detailed instructions to the legislature in some decisions and is innovative in the development of new dogmatic concepts. At the same time, the question arises as to whether this strategy is successful; that is, whether, in practice, the Court also receives recognition for the perceivable consensus upon which its decisions are founded. Such perceptions enhance the general acceptance and trust placed in these decisions, which further emanates from the respective legal culture.

Generally, the strong position of the Constitution as a whole is an expression of the German legal culture, which is often described as 'constitutionalist' or is even designated as 'constitutional patriotism.'[86] The importance of the law as a means for resolving conflicts and as a common medium of communication goes back to the Holy Roman Empire.[87] Subsequently, the idea of the rule of law prevailed in the nineteenth century and a State order, which protected citizens not only against each other but also against State interference emerged.[88] With the foundation of the Federal Republic of Germany and the creation of the FCC, the legal culture developed into a 'constitutional' legal culture, which requires 'thinking from the constitution.'[89]

Constitutional scholarship plays an important role for the German legal culture. By orienting itself towards a dogmatic decision style, the scholarship supplements and spreads the effects of FCC decisions. The term 'Federal Constitutional Court positivism' is used to describe the Court's dominant role.[90] In this context, the main task of scholarship is to conceptualize and critically reflect national jurisprudence, especially in view of the Europeanization and internationalization of law.[91]

The FCC judges also acknowledge the importance of scholarship. From their own perspective, among the various addressees of the Court's decisions, not only

86 Jan-Werner Müller, *Verfassungspatriotismus* (Suhrkamp 2010); also see Weber (n 81) 249.
87 Etienne François, 'Das Bundesverfassungsgericht und die deutsche Rechtskultur' in Michael Stolleis (ed.), *Herzkammern der Republik* (CH Beck 2011) 54 et seq.
88 Kranenpohl (n 6) 403.
89 Jestaedt (n 32) 87.
90 Bernhard Schlink, 'Die Entthronung der Staatsrechtswissenschaft durch die Verfassungsgerichtsbarkeit' (1989) 28 Der Staat 162: 'Bundesverfassungsgerichtspositivismus'.
91 Weber (n 81) 319 et seq.

the general public or those involved in the proceedings, but especially constitutional scholarship is of the utmost importance.[92] In addition to ensuring general social acceptance, it seems to be particularly important to the Court to maintain and shape the exchange with the constitutional law doctrine. With its decisions, the Court seeks to refer to doctrinal concepts, to adopt positions which support its own arguments and to converge them into broad lines of jurisprudence. In the broader context of law-making activity, this shows that the approach of the FCC is embedded in a long-established culture of constitutional discourse.

4 Summary and outlook

Due to the strong influence of the Constitution on the entire German legal system, so-called 'constitutionalization,' the outstanding role of the FCC appears to be somewhat self-evident. However, this fails to fully explain the phenomenon of its law-making activity. As has been outlined, the early decisions of the 1950s show that the Court itself was decisively involved in establishing its own authority. The recurring debates about the politicization of the Court regarding important societal questions show that the Court has repeatedly been criticized and will continue to be in the future. With its ambition of being a citizens' court for every individual and the guardian of the constitutional legal order as a whole, the Court has great influence in terms of shaping the constitutional law. At the same time, it affects sub-constitutional law through transitional and interim arrangements. To ensure this, its toolbox consists of, in particular, a differentiated legal technique and a transparent style of reasoning.

The FCC always seems to be eager to gain acceptance from the general public as well as from the political sphere. In a recent article, the current President of the FCC, Andreas Voßkuhle, names three factors that, in his opinion, promote this acceptance: firstly, 'the content of the relevant decisions, the persuasiveness of its reasoning, and feasibility regarding its consequences', secondly, 'the willingness on the part of constitutional court justices to foster understanding among the general public regarding the functioning of their court and the overarching themes and precepts set out in their case-law,' and thirdly, 'based thereon, confidence of the people and politicians in the independence, integrity and professional competence of justices serving at the constitutional court, as well as confidence in their work'.[93] In response to the question posed at the beginning of this chapter, the way in which the FCC proceeds, especially when it comes to its law-making activity, is a multi-layered and finely nuanced proceeding, which requires the (self-) critical reflection of all the players involved.

92 Kranenpohl (n 6) 312, where the testimony of a judge states: 'The media do not read every ramification of the decision, but jurisprudence does. Whether or not we are convincing depends on the reasons given. With good justifications, we also shape the legal debate and thus a large part of the legal world'.

93 Andreas Voßkuhle, *Constitutional Court: The Dilemma of Law and Politics* (2019) 64 *Osteuropa-Recht* 481.

3 Law-making power of the Constitutional Court of Italy

Nausica Palazzo

Where exactly the Italian Constitutional Court (CC) stands on the metric of power is not fixed. The Court's positioning within the frame of government has significantly shifted throughout the years. It has been largely dependent on factors such as the stability of the executive branch, and the availability on the part of the judiciary to cooperate in aligning the legal framework with the newly introduced constitutional values. However, acknowledging such a shifting reality does not prevent some tentative conclusions being drawn. What is especially warranted is the observation that, overall, the attitude of the Court has been marked by activism and a willingness to incisively intervene in the face of persistent legislative inertia.[1]

1 A primer on the Court's functions

The CC is the gatekeeper of the Constitution. To this end, the judicial review of laws is the key function it performs.

The Italian constitutional review model is centralized, a posteriori (or repressive) – in the sense that judicial scrutiny is carried out over laws and acts having the force of law (legislative decrees and law decrees) *after* their enactment,[2] – and hybrid with respect to access (which includes both *incidenter* and *principaliter* proceedings for lodging constitutional petitions with the Court).[3] Furthermore, as to the types and effects of decisions, the Court can deliver: (1) cassation decisions, striking down laws

1 On which see Roberto Pinardi, 'Brevi note sull'"effettività" delle tecniche decisionali elaborate dalla Corte costituzionale allo scopo di ovviare all'inerzia legislativa', in Roberto Bin et al. (eds.), *'Effettività' e 'seguito' delle tecniche decisorie della Corte costituzionale* (ESI 2006) 327.

2 A notable exception to the general *a posteriori* model is the scrutiny over the statutes of ordinary regions. Pursuant to the Constitution, as amended in 1999 and 2001, ordinary regions should enact a statute mainly dealing with the frame of government of the region, the electoral law, popular referendum, and the fundamental principles of the organization and functioning of the region. The scrutiny over these statutes is preventative since it operates when the statute is not yet come into effect. See Roberto Bin, Giovanni Pitruzzella, *Diritto Costituzionale* (Giappichelli 2017) 423–425.

3 Lucio Pegoraro, 'Giustizia costituzionale' in Giuseppe Morbidelli et al., *Diritto pubblico comparato* (Giappichelli 2016) 547, 559–561.

DOI: 10.4324/9781003022442-4

with retrospective effects (amounting to an annulment rather than the mere abrogation of the law); and (2) interpretative decisions, in which it provides an interpretation of laws aligned with the Constitution and deletes alternative constructions that run counter to the letter or spirit of the Constitution. Annulment decisions yield *erga omnes* effects in the sense that they are generally binding under Article 136.1 of the Constitution. By contrast, judgements of dismissal only produce *inter partes* effects, and thus only bind the parties.

In addition to carrying out the judicial review of laws, the Court can:

- resolve disputes between the State and regions and between 'constitutional powers' – that is, branches of the government, such as parliament, the judiciary, the President of the Republic etc.
- rule on the impeachment of the President of the Republic, and
- rule on the admissibility of a popular referendum under Article 75 of the Constitution.

2 The law-making activity of the Constitutional Court at the sub-constitutional level

Despite the Court carrying out numerous functions, there is little doubt that its key function is the judicial review of laws.[4] This function is narrower and more specific compared to the general function of ensuring compliance with the Constitution, often referred to as 'constitutional adjudication' or 'constitutional justice.' The latter includes all the instances in which a constitutional court (or supreme court, or ordinary judges, depending on the model of constitutional adjudication) ensures compliance with the Constitution, for example, by scrutinizing the admissibility of a popular referendum or the constitutionality of the actions of institutional actors.[5] Within the category of the judicial review of laws, *incidenter* proceedings have largely remained central. A decrease in their incidence was only noted in the aftermath of the 2001 constitutional reform on the reallocation of competences between the State and regions. This reform forced the Court to deal with a significant docket of *principaliter* challenges in order to clarify the scope of their respective competences.[6]

4 Franco Modugno, 'Corte costituzionale e potere legislativo' in Paolo Barile et al. (eds.), *Corte costituzionale e sviluppo della forma di governo in Italia* (Il Mulino 1982) 19.

5 Justin Orlando Frosini, 'Constitutional Justice' in Giuseppe F Ferrari (ed.), *Introduction to Italian Public Law* (Giuffré 2008) 183, 184.

6 For instance, it was noted that in the period from 1996 to 2005, the annual rate of *incidenter* proceedings fell from 87.64% to 65.15% as a result of an increasing incidence of *principaliter* challenges. See Annibale Marini, *La giustizia costituzionale nel 2005*, Conferenza stampa del Presidente Annibale Marini del 9 febbraio 2006 (20 July 2019), www.issirfa.cnr.it/la-giustizia-costituzionale-nel-2005-conferenza-stampa-del-presidente-annibale-marini-9-2-2006.html.

The judicial review can be seen as a form of cooperation with the legislative function entrusted to parliament. While it raises concerns in terms of the separation of powers, these concerns are attenuated if one considers that the full implementation of the Constitution is a complex task that requires multiple contributions from different actors. This view, however, is less tenable where overt conflicts between the Court and parliament arise.[7]

Conflicts can be commonplace if one considers some relevant features of the Italian constitutional adjudication model and its operation in practice. These features include the deliberate vagueness and general nature of several constitutional provisions, the frequent reference to meta-principles and values guiding constitutional adjudication that are rooted in the meta-normative level of moral and political thinking, and the inclusion of social goals in constitutional provisions (such as 'social function,' 'general interest,' and 'equitable social relations') that afford the legislature ample leeway as to the means for achieving them.[8] When combined, these elements illustrate how blurred the boundaries can be between constitutional adjudication and the law-making power of parliament. They all increase the likelihood that, through constitutional adjudication, justices can encroach upon the sphere of the powers of parliament.

To assess the likelihood of such an encroachment, it is first necessary to distinguish between the different functions the Court can have when carrying out the judicial review of laws. Based on a famous classification proposed by former Justice Zagrebelsky, the functions of the CC can be: (1) non-legislative, (2) legislative, and (3) co-legislative.[9]

(1) The non-legislative function materializes in judgements through which the Court acts as an external guarantor of the constitutionality of legislation. In these cases, the Court merely eradicates rules that are considered as unconstitutional, in accordance with the famous Kelsenian view pursuant to which constitutional courts act as a 'negative legislator.' A negative legislator is one that only strikes down unconstitutional rules without intruding into the prerogative of legislatures to create new rules.

In the Italian context, the type of decision that best reflects this attitude is a judgement of acceptance. When such a decision is delivered, the Court merely strikes down a provision without replacing it with alternative rules or interpretations. A further example concerns judgements of pure dismissal, whereby the Court dismisses the case on the merits of the question of unconstitutionality. As previously argued, the effects of these decisions are *inter partes*, as they only bind the parties to the controversy. In this sense, the Court only rejects the question *as raised* by the remitting judge (without this entailing that different motives or a different reasoning could lead to a future declaration of unconstitutionality).

However, the set of decisions under (1) hardly captures the great variety of the decisions that the Court delivers.

7 See Modugno (n 4) 45.
8 Ibid., 47.
9 Gustavo Zagrebelsky, 'La Corte costituzionale e il legislatore,' in Barile et al. (n 4) 103.

(2) The most recurring examples of the CC's legislative function relate to self-executing decisions that do not necessitate cooperation from other institutional actors to interpret and implement the Constitution.

These decisions, often referred to as 'law decisions' (*sentenze legge*),[10] include interpretative judgements of acceptance (*sentenze interpretative di accoglimento*), additive judgements (*sentenze additive*), substitutive judgements (*sentenze sostitutive*), and manipulative judgements in general. These decisions arise out of strong judicial activism, despite yielding different effects, and impacting on the law-making activity of the Court in different ways.

A clarification is necessary in this regard. When speaking of the CC's legislative function, this work does not refer to a legislative function *sensu stricto* consisting of the CC establishing legal norms such as regulations or statutes. It refers to two further meanings; namely, the capacity of the Court to adopt (and even impose) one of the meanings within the spectrum of possible ones that the text offers, and the judicial development of the law that results in meanings that are not inferable from the text of the statute; that is, meanings that are beyond the law.[11] The first scenario is subsumed under what German legal scholarship calls *gesetzesimmanente rechtsfortbildung*, to the extent that the construction put forward is 'immanent' in the statute, while the second is labelled as *gesetzesübersteigende rechtsfortbildung*, to the extent that a construction that goes 'beyond' the statute is adopted.[12] I will parse out both types of decisions under headings 2.1. and 2.2.

(3) Ultimately, there is a peculiar co-legislative function whereby the Court engages, with varying degrees of intensity, with the law-making process. In any such context, the pathway leading to the creation of legislative rules goes well beyond standard legislative proceedings (whereby a qualified actor presents a bill, which is then discussed and approved by both chambers).[13] Rather, this process plays out as a collaborative or conflictual interchange between the CC and the so-called majoritarian *continuum*, which includes the majority party in parliament and its projection into the Council of Ministers.

The Court is petitioned both *ex post*, when the opponents of legislative reforms recur to strategic constitutional litigation to strike down or undermine such reforms, and *ex ante*, when the Court autonomously initiates a dialogue with the

10 Ibid., 105.

11 Frank L Schäfer, 'Judge-made Law beyond the Civil Code', in Jan von Hein et al., *Relationship between the Legislature and the Judiciary: Contributions to the 6th Seoul-Freiburg Law Faculties Symposium* (Nomos Verlag 2017), 89, 90–91 and accompanying notes to text 4–5.

12 Karl Larenz, *Methodenlehre der Rechtswissenschaft* (Springer 1991) 366.

13 When referring to standard proceedings, one should necessarily include acts having the force of law. The reality of the law-making activity shows an increasing incidence of law decrees and legislative decrees for the production of the law. Yet, this consideration is relatively irrelevant to the distinction I am trying to make between the formalistic 'standard law-making process' and the wider context that includes both the formalistic law-making process and the plethora of impulses, warnings and reprimands that allow the CC to de facto participate in the law-making process.

majoritarian *continuum*.[14] Especially, the Court's role in triggering legal reforms in controversial social, political, and economic areas is plain for all to see. The key tool whereby it does so is referred to as guideline ruling (sentenza indirizzo).[15]

In the next three sections I will analyse the law-making activity of the Court; namely, the Court's judicial development of the law within the text, the judicial development of the law beyond the text, and its co-legislative functions at the sub-constitutional level.

2.1 Legislative function: judicial development of the law within the text

In the early stages of its operation, the Court was more inclined to interact with ordinary judges or 'gate guards,' as they were called, who soon became its privileged counterparts. This dialogue was made possible by the Court's development of a set of so-called interpretative decisions, and saw the Court initially imposing its interpretation of laws on courts, later giving way to the Court of Cassation developing the law in action, free from interference.

The set of decisions that can be ascribed to the category of the judicial development of the law within the text (or *gesetzesimmanente rechtsfortbildung*) is somewhat less controversial in that the interpretation put forwards by the Court is still grounded in the text. What is problematic, however, is the curtailment of the prerogative of ordinary courts to interpret the law without external interference (so-called horizontal independence).[16] Constitutional decisions mandating or prohibiting a certain interpretation differ from the run-of-the-mill interpretative activities of ordinary courts, which have no such power to impose interpretative norms derived from rules on other judicial actors. Pursuant to the principle of vertical independence applying to the judiciary, ordinary judges are not bound by interpretations provided by other equal- or higher-ranking judges. This principle is so deeply rooted that it is even inaccurate to speak of 'ranks,' as each judge can potentially tell what the law is in a definitive manner.

Interpretative decisions of the CC can either be acceptance or dismissal judgements. In the case of dismissal judgements, the Court, as with any other dismissal, holds that the provision is not unconstitutional (while these decisions always fall short of arguing in the affirmative that the provision 'is' constitutional). In ordinary dismissals, the conclusion is that the provision, as interpreted by the remitting judge, is not unconstitutional. By contrast, when the Court delivers an interpretative dismissal

14 Zagrebelsky (n 9) 104.

15 Ibid., 105.

16 Vertical independence refers to the prerogative of each and any judge to interpret the law without interference from other judges. Horizontal independence, by contrast, refers to the prerogative to interpret the law without interference from other powers, especially the legislative or executive power. While in Italy, the CC is aptly considered a *super partes* body that cannot be ascribed to any of the branches of government; the principles of horizontal independence, to achieve its fullest potential, should shield judges from any interference, including that exerted by the CC.

judgement, it stresses that while the interpretation put forwards by the remitting judge is actually unconstitutional (norm A), there is a second, overlooked interpretation that would comply with the Constitution (norm B). In so doing, the Court basically deletes a specific meaning (norm A) from the range of possible meanings by soliciting[17] judges to adopt the meaning that is compatible with the Constitution (norm B).

By contrast, when interpretative judgements of acceptance are issued, the Court argues that although several meanings are available, some of which are in accordance with the Constitution (norm A or B), the ordinary courts have insisted on adopting a meaning which is not compatible with the Constitution (norm C). The fact that the law in action or the 'living law' (*diritto vivente*) is not constitutionally compliant – since the judges have insisted on adopting the 'wrong' interpretation – 'forces' the Court to declare the deviant meaning as unconstitutional.[18] The process whereby the CC does it is a 'double judgement': in the first instance, the Court dismisses the question, arguing that a constitutionally compliant meaning is possible; then, in the face of persistent reluctance on the part of the judiciary to apply this norm, it reacts by striking down the unconstitutional meaning.[19]

Interpretative judgements of acceptance have been fairly controversial ever since they were introduced. They often gave rise to arm wrestling between the CC and the Supreme Court (*Corte di Cassazione*). The struggle revolved around which institution had the final say when it came to interpreting the law. Notably, the Supreme Court has the power to ensure uniformity in the interpretation of the law, while the CC has the duty to ensure that interpretations comply with the Constitution. That is to say, both actors, each in their own capacity, contribute to creating the law in action.[20] Yet, common sense dictates that just as the Supreme Court does not impose the proper interpretation of the Constitution on the CC, the latter should not impose the proper interpretation of the law on the former.[21]

17 The effects of the interpretative judgements of dismissal on ordinary judges are debated. On the one side are those who argue that these decisions yield affirmative effects, in the sense that the remitting judge is bound by the interpretation considered by the Court as compatible with the Constitution. On the other side are those who contend that the remitting judge is only bound not to apply the 'wrong' norm; that is, the norm that was held to be unconstitutional. In this sense, these judgments would merely yield negative effects on remitting judges who, except for censured norms, remain free to infer alternative meanings that are compatible with the Constitution. See Fabrizio Cassella, 'Le sentenze interpretative di rigetto della Corte costituzionale: la loro efficacia nei giudizi successive e il limite del diritto vivente (a proposito di Corte cost. n. 372/1994)' (1995) Responsabilità Civile e Previdenziale.

18 Frosini (n 5).

19 Judgements of this kind usually read: 'the law is unconstitutional *if* and *to the extent to which* one infers the norm X from it'. See Antonio Ruggeri & Antonino Spadaro, *Lineamenti di giustizia costituzionale* (Giappichelli 2014) 163.

20 Law no 134/2001 explicitly acknowledges that all law 'practitioners', including the CC, contribute to the creation of the law.

21 Corte costituzionale 231/1986, of 31 October 1986.

The longest and harshest conflict revolved around the maximum length of precautionary measures under the Code of Criminal Procedure.[22] On that occasion, the justices put forwards an interpretation with the effect of capping the unfettered length of precautionary measures,[23] while the Court of Cassation kept adopting an interpretation to the contrary. At the outset, the CC issued an interpretative judgement of dismissal, arguing that a constitutionally compliant interpretation was possible. Faced with many further questions of unconstitutionality, the Court laconically rejected each of them.[24] Yet, when the Supreme Court itself raised a constitutional challenge in its plenary composition (*Sezioni Unite*), the CC resolved to step back by arguing that, in the meantime, the opposite interpretation by the Supreme Court had 'become' the law in action (i.e. it became sufficiently constant and widespread to amount to *diritto vivente*) and, as such, it was worthy of deference.[25]

2.2 *Legislative function: judicial development of the law beyond the text*

The set of decisions falling under the umbrella of the judicial development of the law beyond the text (or *gesetzesübersteigende rechtsfortbildung*) shed light on the incisive role that the CC can play in shaping the law. These decisions include judgements of partial acceptance, additive judgements, and substitutive judgements. They are labelled as 'manipulative judgements' as they manipulate the text of the law. An increasing rate of manipulative judgements was noted compared to judgements of full acceptance.[26] This illustrates the increasing incidence of the law-making activity of the Court, especially in its most 'extreme' form.

In the ambit of judgements of partial acceptance, the Court declares a rule unconstitutional 'to the extent it reads X.' Thus, while judgements of full acceptance consist of a wholesale cassation of a rule, judgements of partial acceptance involve deleting single words or passages within the impugned rule. The removal of words or passages can have material effects on the meaning of a rule and, in this sense, it potentially results in a powerful creative effect. Case on point is the bold use of these techniques in the context of the abrogative referendum where the promoters exploited the creative potential in deleting single words or even punctuation to reach a certain outcome.

22 The question was a complex one and concerned the applicability of art 304 para 6 of the Code of Criminal Procedure for the maximum length of precautionary measures, even when the proceeding resets following an annulment decision by the Supreme Court. Pursuant to the letter of the law (art 303 para 2, Code of Criminal Procedure), it seems that the maximum length of such measures resets as well. Yet, the CC insisted that the interpretation that is mostly compatible with the Constitution requires avoiding this anomalous outcome.

23 Corte costituzionale 292/1998, of 7 July 1998.

24 Corte costituzionale orders 249/1999, 214/2000, 529/2000.

25 Corte costituzionale 299/2005, of 7 July 2005.

26 Ruggeri & Spadaro (n 19) 168.

However, there is no principled approach to discerning whether a judgement of partial acceptance can be ascribed to the Court's legislative function. An assessment always needs to be made regarding what the consequences are of erasing words or passages from the rule. Only when the decision leads to new normative prescriptions, principles, or goals to be pursued, will it be ascribed to the category of partial acceptance.[27]

Major examples of judgements of partial acceptance are Decision No. 90/1970 and No. 11/1979.[28] The Court was called on to scrutinize the Consolidated Law on Public Security, requiring that notice be given by promoters to the police for rallies in a public space. The existing framework set forth criminal sanctions for both promoters and persons taking part in such rallies if notice to the public authorities was lacking. In two subsequent decisions, the Court first decriminalized the conduct of persons other than the promoters who were unaware that such notice was lacking, and then of all persons other than the promoters, including those who were aware that the notice was lacking.

Substitutive judgements hold the unconstitutionality of a rule 'to the extent it reads "X" rather than "Y".' Through this kind of manipulative decision, the Court replaces an unconstitutional passage with a new one aligned with the Constitution. I shall provide an illustrative example in this regard. In Decision No. 215/1987, the CC held that the 1971 law dealing with the accommodation of disabled persons in the education system was unconstitutional. The controversy arose as the duty to accommodate disabled children only applied to compulsory school, which at the time comprised primary and secondary schooling. By contrast, when it came to the high school system and institutes of higher education (such as universities), it only read 'the attendance of disabled persons in high school shall be *facilitated*.'[29] The Court found the law to be unconstitutional for the duty set forth by it was too vague and replaced 'facilitated' with 'ensured.'

In additive judgements, the Court declares unconstitutional a provision Y 'since it lacks the sentence or word X.'[30] Additive judgements are thus delivered as a reaction to legislative omissions. In Decision No. 144/1983, the Court declared unconstitutional Article 156 of the Civil Code as it set forth a difference in treatment between spouses divorced by mutual consent and spouses divorced based upon a judicial order.[31] The petitioner was a mother, lamenting that the divorced father was not paying for child support. She thus invoked Article 156 of the Civil Code to request a temporary seizure of the father's assets. However, the rule only applied to divorced spouses who had separated based upon a judicial decision, and they had not. Therefore, the civil judge raised the question of constitutionality. The CC held

27 Zagrebelsky (n 9) 107.
28 Corte costituzionale 90/1970, of 3 June 1970 and 11/1979, of 4 May 1979.
29 Art 28 para 3 of Law 118/1971.
30 Franco Modugno & Paolo Carnevale, 'Sentenze additive, "soluzione obbligata" e declaratoria di inammissibilità per mancata indicazione del "verso" della richiesta di addizione' (1990) Giurisprudenza costituzionale 519; Carlo Lavagna, 'Sulle sentenze additive della Corte costituzionale' (1969) Giurisprudenza italiana 152.
31 Corte costituzionale 144/1983, of 12 June 1986.

that the provision of the Civil Code was unconstitutional as it did not contain the words 'and spouses divorced by mutual consent'.

Additive judgements can be distinguished between those: (1) adding guarantees/services; and those (2) adding legal principles. Additive decisions under (1) are those decisions where the result is directly inferable from the Constitution.[32] Guarantees are added in the context of decisions concerning civil rights, while services are added when social assistance and welfare benefits are at stake.

An example of a decision that involves adding a 'guarantee' is the one provided above, where the Court equated the treatment of divorced spouses, regardless of the way in which the divorce was obtained. Unlike guarantees, decisions adding services pose special problems in the light of the financial burden they impose on the legislature. In the earlier stages of its operation, the Court seemed to largely overlook the financial consequences of its judgements, especially those levelling up affirmative entitlements for excluded categories. This practice reached its peak in 1994, where the Court issued a judgement levelling up pensions, which caused an enormous increase in expenditure (30,000 billion lire, roughly 15 million euros).[33] Thereafter, the Court became more sensitized to financial concerns. In particular, the opposite trend of levelling down entitlements has been noted in recent years.[34]

Additive decisions under (2), as argued, add a mere principle. With these innovative decisions, the Court has found a way to still weigh in on cases where a solution is not directly inferable from the Constitution. In so doing, it refrains from creating rules that are not unequivocally derivable from the Constitution, while it identifies a guiding principle. In such cases, there are several concrete means through which the principle can be implemented and each of them is virtually compatible with the Constitution. As a consequence, it is the exclusive province of the legislature to choose the concrete means through which to implement the principle identified by the Court. One such example relates to the decision through which the Court added the principle under which fathers should enjoy the same rights as mothers to maternity (in this case paternity) benefits.[35] Yet, since the decision was not cost free, the justices left it to the legislature to define the most appropriate mechanism to implement the equality principle in this policy area.

32 Vezio Crisafulli, 'La Corte costituzionale ha vent'anni, Giurispudenza costituzionale' in Nicola Occhiocupo (ed.), *La Corte costituzionale tra norma giuridica e realtà sociale. Bilancio di vent'anni di attività* (Il Mulino 1978) 84. Prominent scholars argued that this conviction that a certain solution is directly inferable from the Constitution is just wishful thinking, since this inference only exists in the 'minds of judges'. See Leopoldo Elia, 'Le sentenze additive e la più recente giurisprudenza della Corte costituzionale (ottobre '81-luglio '85)', in Amorosini et al., *Scritti in onore di Crisafulli* (Cedam 1985) 313.

33 Corte costituzionale 240/1994, of 10 June 1994 (deposited).

34 Ruggeri & Spadaro (n 19) 171; Filippo Donati, 'Le ripercussioni delle pronunce giurisdizionali sull'equilibrio di bilancio', in Franco Bassanini & Stefano Merlini (eds.), *Crisi fiscale e indirizzo politico* (Il Mulino 1995) 585; Enrico Grosso, *Sentenze costituzionali di spesa che non costino* (Giappichelli 1991).

35 Corte costituzionale 385/2005, of 11 October 2005.

2.3 Co-legislative function

As argued, the Court can be petitioned *ex post*, when the opponents of legislative reforms resort to strategic litigation to challenge legal rules, and *ex ante*, when the Court autonomously triggers a dialogue with the majoritarian *continuum* to create new rules.

Former Justice Gustavo Zagrebelsky provides an example of the former by considering the statement made by Hon. Quilleri in the debate surrounding the legality of the broadcasting regime. There, Hon. Quilleri placed the emphasis on the need to shift the axis of the opposition to the regime from parliamentary debates to challenges before the CC.[36] However, it is to be noted that strategic litigation has a much less relevant role in Italy than it has in North American jurisdictions. In particular, it is not commonplace for citizens or advocacy groups to resort to strategic litigation before the CC (as would be the case in the United States). The privileged terrain for policy battles is political not judicial, and politicians are the natural target of advocacy actions.

On the other hand, there are countless examples of *ex ante* Court interventions. For illustrative purposes, we can consider the decisions on abortion rights rebuking the overly broad criminalization of abortion services, even in situations where women's health was put in jeopardy; on the confidentiality of judicial investigations; on the due compensation under a compulsory purchase procedure (expropriation); and on public broadcasting services. For all of the above examples, the Court seemed to take the old legal regime as a pretext to trigger a process leading to its wholesale replacement with a new one that was more aligned with constitutional values.[37]

The most illustrative types of decisions falling under the umbrella of the co-legislative function are exhortative judgements.[38] When this type of decision is issued, it results in a dismissal of the constitutional challenge. Yet, the CC, in the motivation of the judgement, urges the legislature to amend the legal framework, sending out a warning that if the legislature fails to act within a reasonable time the law will be struck down.

For instance, in Decision No. 212 of 1986, the Court urged parliament to introduce public hearings in tax courts to comply with Article 101 of the Constitution enshrining the right to a fair trial.

A recent decision provides a valuable example of how nuanced the exhortation of the Court became over the years. The context in which it was delivered is worth recalling, as the delicate policy choices surrounding the legality of assisted suicide were intertwined with the touching story of a popular public figure. Fabo, a famous DJ, became quadriplegic following a car accident and, after a long convalescence, decided to end his life in a private clinic in Switzerland where assisted suicide was permitted. A member of the Italian Radical Party, Marco Cappato, who advocated in favour of legalizing assisted suicide, went with him to

36 Zagrebelsky (n 9) 104.

37 Paolo Franceschi & Gustavo Zagrebelsky, 'Il colegislatore e il Parlamento' (1981) 1 *Quaderni costituzionali* 162.

38 Roberto Pinardi, *La Corte, i giudici e il legislatore. Il problema degli effetti temporali delle sentenze d'incostituzionalità* (Giuffré 1993).

Switzerland and then turned himself in to the police for having provided material assistance to DJ Fabo to enable his death by suicide.[39]

The case went to the CC. Yet, surprisingly, the Court 'decided not to decide'[40] and delayed the judgement to September 2019 through a procedural order to allow the legislature to think the issue through.[41] However, in so doing, the justices put language to the effect that the criminal provision could be held unconstitutional in the absence of parliament's intervention. In their reasoning, it emerged that the criminal provision prohibiting and sanctioning assisted suicide was not unequivocally unconstitutional. The legislature, at the time when it passed the law in the 1930s, could not foresee medical advancements. Especially, it could not foresee the possibility that futile medical treatments could be carried out and that patients with a terminally ill condition who were still able to express their will could seek the assistance of a third person in committing suicide. Since the decision touches upon the heart of delicate policy choices involving death, life, and self-determination, the Court concluded that it was preferable to delay the decision.

This new type of decision was labelled as a decision of 'foreseen unconstitutionality,' which, on the one hand, avoids legislative gaps flowing from a declaration of unconstitutionality and, on the other hand, avoids an exhortative judgement that recognizes but does not declare unconstitutionality.[42] The latter type of decision would bring injustice as it exposes the claimant to criminal sanctions, despite an acknowledgement of the unconstitutionality of the law. This decision is thus a reasonable compromise between preserving legislative discretion and protecting civil rights.

3 The law-making activity of the Constitutional Court at the constitutional level

Manipulative judgements have been the privileged tool through which the CC has established new norms at the constitutional level. The creative activity of the

39 'The Cappato Trial Step by Step', Associazione Luca Coscioni (4 July 2019) www.associazionelucacoscioni.it/the-cappato-trial-step-by-step/.

40 Antonio Ruggeri, 'Pilato alla Consulta: decide di non decidere, perlomeno per ora … (a margine di un comunicato sul caso Cappato)' (2018) *Consulta online*, No. 3, 568.

41 Corte costituzionale order 207/2018. See the numerous essays on the Issue No. 2 of 2019 in the *BioLaw Journal*, especially: Federico G Pizzetti, 'L'ordinanza n. 207/2018 della Corte costituzionale, pronunciata nel corso del "Caso Cappato", e il diritto del paziente che rifiuta le cure salvavita a evitare un'agonia lenta e non dignitosa'; Maria E Bucalo & Giuseppe Giaimo, 'Le sollecitazioni delle Corti e l'inerzia del legislatore in tema di suicidio assistito. Un confronto tra Italia e Inghilterra'. See also Marco Bignami, 'Il caso Cappato alla Corte costituzionale: un'ordinanza ad incostituzionalità differita', Questione Giustizia, 23 November 2018; Ugo Adamo, 'La Corte è 'attendista' … "facendo leva sui propri poteri di gestione del processo costituzionale". Nota a Corte cost., ord. n. 207 del 2018' (2018), *Forum quaderni costituzionali*, No. 11, 3.

42 Cristiano Cupelli, 'Sindacato costituzionale e discrezionalità legislativa. Le prospettive penalistiche nella Relazione del Presidente Lattanzi sulla giurisprudenza costituzionale del 2018', Diritto Penale Contemporaneo, 27 March 2019 (10 July 2019) https://www.penalecontemporaneo.it/d/6579-sindacato-costituzionale-e-discrezionalita-legislativa.

Court at this level worked in three main directions: (1) an expansion of the procedural rules of constitutional proceedings and interpretations thereof; (2) an active shaping of the powers of constitutional actors; and (3) an active redrawing of the hierarchy of legal sources at the constitutional level.

I will analyse each scenario and then focus my attention on the scenario under (3), as it offers a valuable snapshot of the breadth of the law-making activity of the Court at the constitutional level.

3.1 Expansion of the procedural rules

There are many examples of expansions of the procedural rules dealing with access to the Court and the types of justiciable issues. In a controversial decision, the justices conferred the power to raise constitutional challenges upon the Court of Auditors, despite this power not being inferable from the law.[43] A second decision concerned the power to 'shift' the question of admissibility of an abrogative referendum from the old to the new discipline in cases where the legislator has abrogated the old one, pending the judgement of admissibility. This decision was made based on the assumption that the legislator had often replaced the previous law to obstruct referendums.[44] The consequence of the judgement has been to widely expand the possibility for intervention in situations that have not been envisaged by the legislature.

In general terms, the Court has consistently interpreted the notion of 'constitutional power' in a liberal and broad sense, thereby conferring the legal standing to bring constitutional challenges vis-à-vis conflicts of power upon a larger number of actors. Again, these decisions have had the effect of opening the gates of constitutional justice to organs or institutions not envisaged by the law. For instance, in Decision No. 68/1978, the Court recognized the promoters of an abrogative referendum as having just such a legal standing.

3.2 expansion of the powers of the constitutional actors

Italy's participation in the European Union (EU) has had significant effects on its domestic legal system. Faced with the issue of the compatibility of domestic rules with European law, the Court introduced important innovations that impacted on the scope of the powers of ordinary judges. A major innovation consisted in conferring upon ordinary judges the power to temporarily set aside laws that were incompatible with self-executing European legal sources such as European regulations.

43 Stefano Rodotà, 'La Corte, la politica, l'organizzazione sociale' in Paolo Barile et al. (n 4) 339.

44 Corte costituzionale 16/1978, of 2 February 1978, on which *see* Carlo Mezzanotte, 'La Corte costituzionale: esperienze e prospettive' in Giuliano Amato, Antonio Baldassarre, Angelo A Cervatti, *Attualità e attuazione della Costituzione* (Laterza 1979) 149. In this regard, the author speaks of a 'made-up' prerogative that finds no linchpin whatsoever within existing laws.

In the famous *Granital* judgement, the CC clarified that the EU and Italian legal system were two different and separate orders (by adopting a dualistic approach).[45] The practical consequence of the alleged separation is that in cases where a conflict arises between the domestic rules and the self-executing European rules, the domestic rule is not invalid, abrogated, nor modified.[46] When EU law comes into play, the domestic rules are merely set aside as if they were dormant.

Thus, the Court has de facto introduced a diffused system of judicial review whereby ordinary judges can scrutinize the compatibility of domestic laws with European law and, when an incompatibility is detected, they can temporarily set aside the domestic rules.[47]

3.3 active redrawing of the hierarchy of sources at the constitutional level

An incisive law-making activity resulted in an active redrawing of the hierarchy of sources and of what, in Italian constitutional law, goes by the name of a 'parameter.' A parameter is a set of constitutional or quasi-constitutional rules invoked before the Court to assess whether the law is compatible with the Constitution or not. Questions of constitutionality always require the remitting judge to point to law X (the object),[48] the constitutional rules that are considered as having been violated (the parameter), and the reasons for the alleged incompatibility.

The CC has extended the parameter so as to include legal sources other than the Constitution and constitutional laws. Especially in recent years, it has considered the European Convention on Human Rights (ECHR) to be an 'interposed norm' (***parametro interposto***) of intermediate rank, whose violation (only) indirectly entails a violation of the Constitution.[49]

Reference is made to the twin judgements of 2007,[50] where it clarified the position of the ECHR in the hierarchy of sources. Following the 2001 constitutional amendments, parliament, in carrying out its legislative power, shall act within the limits of international obligations and EU law. Given this constitutional

45 The dualistic approach or separation theory postulates that the two legal systems are distinct. It differs from monist systems in that the latter recognize the international legal system as integral to the domestic system and, as such, it is directly applicable. Such a system is, for instance, in force in the Netherlands. Giuseppe F Ferrari, *Le libertà. Profili comparatistici* (Giappichelli 2011).

46 A thus-framed approach, arguing for the invalidation of the domestic rule, was advocated for by the Court of Justice in the famous *Simmenthal* Judgment in Case 106/77, *Amministrazione delle Finanze dello Stato v Simmenthal SpA*, of 9 March 1978.

47 Ruggeri & Spadaro (n 19) 169.

48 Under art 134 para 1 of the Constitution, 'The Constitutional Court shall decide on disputes involving the constitutional legitimacy of laws and acts having the force of law, passed by the state and the Regions.'

49 An example of interposed rules is the Delegation Act when it comes down to assessing the constitutionality of delegated decrees. Since these decrees depend on the former, through which parliament delegates legislative power to the government, a violation of the Delegating Act indirectly entails a violation of the Constitution, and precisely of art 76, which regulates the relationship between these two sources of law.

50 Corte costituzionale 348/2007, of 22 October 2007, and 349/2007, of 22 October 2007.

limit, the Court reasoned that the ECHR was to qualify as an interposed norm and hence as a quasi-constitutional rule.[51] As such, on the one hand, the ECHR should comply with the Constitution, and on the other hand, ordinary laws and acts having the force of law should comply with the ECHR.

The same applies to other international agreements executed by Italy,[52] although from the reasoning of the Court, an intention to recognize the special force of the ECHR emerges due to the substantive, human-rights-centred content of the treaty.

A second illustrative example for this category is the introduction of a further layer at the constitutional level: super-constitutional norms, which cannot be violated by any source, including European law. This constitutional core is described as the sum of 'the fundamental principles of the legal systems and human rights.'[53] Such a notion is strictly connected to the doctrine of so-called counterlimits. Under this doctrine, self-executing European rules are directly applicable to the domestic legal system unless they violate these supreme principles. In case of a violation, Italy would only be left with the option of striking down the law incorporating the founding treaties of the EU, and thus of leaving the EU.

Starting from the *Frontini* judgement,[54] the Court made it clear that the limitations to sovereignty imposed by the Constitution (under Article 11) can never entail the unfettered power of European institutions to impinge upon the core of Italy's constitutional system. In other words, alongside the diffused system of judicial review (which allows each judge to scrutinize the compatibility of domestic rules with EU law), the power of the CC to assess EU law against the core values of the constitutional order remains intact.[55]

While the doctrine has remained on the books for decades, lately the Court has threatened to trigger the counterlimits in the context of a proceeding concerning VAT fraud – the famous *Taricco* case.[56] The Court of Justice of the European Union (CJEU), upon the request of a preliminary reference, noted that the limitation period for VAT frauds and for tax frauds in general had resulted in impunity in many instances and, as such, was against EU law.[57]

51 Some authors define the Convention as a sub-constitutional norm. See Luca Mezzetti & Francesca Polacchini, 'Primacy of Supranational Law and Primacy of the Constitution in the Italian Legal System' in Luca Mezzetti et al., *International Constitutional Law* (Giappichelli 2015) 141, 164. However, I stipulate that they are 'quasi-constitutional' norms as the term is more specific and able to clarify the intermediate position of these rules, as they exist halfway between the Constitution and ordinary laws. By contrast, by sub-constitutional rules, one usually refers to all rules placed under the Constitution in the hierarchy of sources.

52 The ICC, with decision no. 7/2013, struck down a provision of the Criminal Code as being in violation of the United Nations Convention on the Rights of the Child and the European Convention on the Exercise of Children's Rights, which were both ratified by Italy.

53 Corte costituzionale 1146/1988, of 15 December 1988.

54 Corte costituzionale 183/1973, of 18 December 1973.

55 Luigi Daniele, *Diritto dell'Unione Europea* (Giuffré 2018) 328.

56 Case 105/14, of 8 September 2015 [*Taricco I*].

57 In particular, the limitation periods run against art 325 of the TFEU to the extent to which this provision requires states to 'counter illegal activities affecting the financial

The decision was not met with favour by the Italian CC, as this interpretation ran counter to a fundamental principle governing criminal law; that is, the principle of legality. The principle requires the State to punish crimes pursuant to rules that have already been enacted at the time of the offence.[58] By contrast, the *Taricco* decision entailed a regrettable change in the rules of the game that resulted in a prejudicial impact on the accused person. The Court thus asked the CJEU to clarify its stance to avoid the (otherwise necessary) triggering of the counterlimits.[59] In a second much-awaited judgement (*Taricco II*),[60] the CJEU seemed to scale down its previous position and take a conciliatory approach to the issue. It stressed that the principle stated in *Taricco I* did not apply to offences committed before the CJEU's judgement had been made, and used language to the effect that the principle of legality was integral to the common constitutional traditions of Member States as protected under Article 49 of the EU Charter.[61]

Despite this, in a subsequent judgement, the CC rejected the '*Taricco* rule' altogether as not sufficiently clear, and as incompatible with the principle of certainty.[62] Yet, the Court, in reaching this conclusion, did not activate the counterlimits, implying that the same conclusion concerning the vagueness of the rule would have been reached by the CJEU itself.[63]

Thus, the constitutional landscape is much more complex than it used to be at the time when the Constitution was enacted. The Court played a pivotal role in innovating it by adding new layers and making the picture much more complex than it used to be. These innovation processes were especially triggered by the increasing relevance of human rights treaties and by the (not-so-conciliatory) dialogue with the CJEU.

5 An ancient dilemma: judicial self-restraint, or activism, that is the question

All jurisdictions somehow grappled with the dilemma of whether judicial self-restraint should be preferred over judicial activism or vice versa. Reference is

interests of the European Union through effective deterrent measures' and to 'take the same measures to counter fraud affecting the financial interests of the European Union as they take to counter fraud affecting their own interests'. Case 105/14, *Taricco I*.

58 Francesco Viganò, 'Le parole e i silenzi. Osservazioni sull'ordinanza n. 24/2017 della Corte costituzionale sul caso Taricco', *Diritto Penale Contemporaneo*, 27 March 2017 (3 July 2019) https://www.penalecontemporaneo.it/d/5305-le-parole-e-i-silenzi-osservazioni-sullordinanza-n-242017-della-corte-costituzionale-sul-caso-taric.

59 Corte costituzionale order no 24/2017 (requesting a preliminary reference to the CJEU).

60 Case 42/17, of 5 December 2017 (*Taricco II*).

61 Chiara Amalfitano & Oreste Pollicino, 'Two Courts, two Languages? The Taricco Saga Ends on a Worrying Note', *Verfassungsblog*, 5 June 2018 (3 July 2019) https://verfassungsblog.de/two-courts-two-languages-the-taricco-saga-ends-on-a-worrying-note/.

62 Corte costituzionale 115/2018, of 10 April 2018.

63 Amalfitano & Pollicino (n 61).

especially made to the United States, where rather obsessive attention is paid to the topic both in law school classrooms and in legal-philosophical scholarship.

This is not to say that other jurisdictions are immune from the problem nor that they are insensitive to the issue. Article 28 of Law No. 87/1953 (Rules on the Establishment and Functioning of the Constitutional Court) states that: 'The judicial review of laws and acts having the force of law can never entail political evaluations nor a scrutiny on the use of Parliament's discretionary powers.' This clause illustrates that Italy too has always been faced, ever since the establishment of the Court, with the issue of balancing judicial activism and judicial self-restraint.

Yet, obvious structural differences between systems of constitutional justice advise against civil law jurisdictions relying too much and uncritically on the North American debate. Among these structural differences is the predilection for the collaborative principle over a rigid principle of the separation of powers in Italy, and the existence of an ad hoc body, unlike systems adopting a diffused judicial review system where a fear of 'juristocracy' more reasonably arises.[64] By distributing the power of judicial reviews across the whole judiciary, judicial reviews in the United States end up being seen as a struggle between equal-ranking branches of government, each one pitted against the other.[65]

By contrast, many structural devices in Italy aim to avoid the CC being seen as a 'party' to the struggle.[66] First is the positioning of the Court in the frame of government. In this sense, it important to note that the Court is not integrated within the judiciary. It is an ad hoc, external *super partes* body that is 'only' entrusted with the function of protecting the constitutional order. Second, features such as the concealment of dissenting opinions contribute to an image of the Court as a non-partisan body, entrusted with the task of 'objectively' ascertaining compliance or otherwise with constitutional values.

In addition, when political scientists attempt to assess whether the Court has a majoritarian or countermajoritarian role, they often rely on foreign, especially American, literature in defining complex notions of 'activism,' 'self-restraint,' 'majoritarian,' and 'countermajoritarian.'[67] Drawing on these works, they take the number of decisions that have struck down laws as the key variable in assessing such a role.

I briefly analyse an illustrative work drawn from the political science literature to show the dangers of this type of uncritical comparison. The text explains that the

64 Ran Hirschl, *Towards Juristocracy. The Origins and Consequences of the New Constitutionalism* (Harvard University Press 2004).

65 See Pasquale Costanzo, 'Legislatore e Corte costituzionale: Uno sguardo d'insieme sulla giurisprudenza costituzionale in materia di discrezionalità legislativa dopo cinquant'anni di attività' (20 July 2019) http://www.giurcost.org/studi/CostanzoLanzarote.htm#_ftn1.

66 Gustavo Zagrebelsky & Valeria Marcenò, *Giustizia costituzionale. Oggetti Procedimenti Decisioni* (Il Mulino 2018) 43 et seq.

67 See the extended references to Dahl, Bickel and Shapiro contained in Patrizia Pederzoli, *La Corte costituzionale* (Il Mulino 2008) c 5.

'independent variable' in assessing the positioning of the Court on the metric of power is the political system: the weaker the political system, the stronger the CC and vice versa.[68] The index used to assess whether the Court is more active is the number of judgements of acceptance. Based on this index, it has been noted that when the political system takes a majoritarian turn, the Court tends to prefer self-restraint.[69] This can be attributed to the fact that the Court is warier of acting in situations where its counterpart (the legislature) has stronger political leverage.[70]

Yet, I argue that this index hardly aligns with the notion of activism adopted by Italian jurists, and thus is not suitable for assessing the majoritarian or counter-majoritarian role of the Court.[71] There is a significant difference between the notion of activism in North America and the same notion in Italy. 'Activism' in the United States has a political connotation, referring to which institutional actor 'wins' – whether it is the Court by striking down the law or the legislature by getting to keep its laws intact.

By contrast, in Italy, activism has a legal-constitutional connotation in the sense that it is not understood solely in win/lose terms but could be seen as: (1) a departure from the letter of the law (legal aspect); or (2) a departure from the result that the Constitution commands (constitutional aspect). In this sense, it is not concerned with the result but with the 'process' that leads to reaching a result. I have described the legal aspect above by analysing the set of manipulative decisions. Let me provide an example of a scenario under (2). The key factor in assessing the activism of the US Supreme Court is the number of decisions that are taken to strike down laws. By contrast, in Italy, even a decision that constitutes a political victory for the legislature – as would be the case with an exhortative decision that 'acknowledges' without 'declaring' the unconstitutionality of the law – can be read as a form of activism.

68 Ibid., 253. See also Alec Stone Sweet, *Governing with Judges: Constitutional Politics in Europe* (Oxford University Press 2000). Again, I contend that American political scientist Stone Sweet over-relies on US notions and concepts in carrying out his work on Europe.

69 In the decade from 1996 to 2006, following the shift from a proportionality to a majority electoral system, a decline in the number of declarations of unconstitutionality was registered. See Pederzoli (n67) 259.

70 Similar observations were put forward by American scholar Samuel Bickel, who coined the term 'countermajoritarian difficulty'. His theory also boils down to the conclusion that in times of consociativism, the Court is more aggressive, while when majoritarian governments are formed, it is warier of acting. Alexander M Bickel, *The Least Dangerous Branch: The Supreme Court at the Bar of Politics* (Miriam Rose Books 1962).

71 Pederzoli (n 67). The author, in conducting quantitative research on the level of activism of the Court from 1996 to 2006, considers the number of decisions striking down laws as the key index. See ibid. 208. The same index is adopted by Elisa Rebessi and Francesco Zucchini in assessing whether the Court acts as a countermajoritarian power. See Elisa Rebessi & Francesco Zucchini, 'The role of the Italian Constitutional Court in the policy agenda: persistence and change between the First and Second Republic' (2018), 48 Italian Pol Science Rev/Rivista Italiana di Scienza Politica, Special Issue No. 3 (Policy Agendas in Italy) 289–305.

Hence, one should not be as much concerned with the political aspects of the decision but with a departure or otherwise from the solution that the Constitution commands. This is an important theoretical clarification that hints at the limits associated with current quantitative analyses. It casts doubt on the reliability of methodological approaches to examining the role of the Court in the field of political science and, in turn, on the results achieved thereby.

This methodological premise clarifies why, in expounding the role of the Court, I will focus my attention on legal scholarship and the constitutional case law without referring to the relevant literature in political science.

5.1 An activist Court? A theoretical analysis of constitutional scholarship and a case law analysis

In assessing whether the Court has played an active role, it is paramount that we first identify its relationship with the legislature, especially in terms of the justiciability of political questions. I will start off by saying that the very same reasons outlined in the previous section run against applying notions borrowed from foreign experiences.[72] Reference is especially made to the political question of the doctrine – a doctrine outlined in *Baker*,[73] whereby the US Supreme Court identified ambits that cannot be scrutinized by courts.

Starting from Judgement No. 28/1957, the Italian CC recognized that the legislature enjoys discretion when constitutional rules do not command any specific solution/mechanism for their implementation.[74] Other reasons include the need to avoid a legislative gap caused by a declaration of unconstitutionality endangering further situations of unconstitutionality.

Yet, the Court changed its mind as to the type of decisions through which legislative discretion should be ascertained. While in the first two decades of operation it delivered judgements of dismissal,[75] it then moved on to issue (procedural) orders of inadmissibility.[76] The issue is not merely formalistic, as only judgements of dismissal entail proper scrutiny over whether the case warrants legislative discretion. When the Court delivers judgements of dismissal, it means that the question has passed the admissibility muster and that, only after a thorough assessment, can it reject the question as not founded. In this sense, the earlier praxis resembled the margin of appreciation doctrine in force at the

72 In particular, the US doctrine is the by-product of a rigid understanding of the separation of powers that is not traceable in the Italian system. Costanzo (n 65).

73 *Baker v. Carr* (1962) 369 US 186. On the various versions of the doctrine see Fritz Scharpf, 'Judicial Review and the Political Question: a Functional Analysis' (1966) 75 Yale LJ 517; Laurence H Tribe, *American Constitutional Law*, Vol. I (Foundation Press 2000) 96.

74 Corte costituzionale 28/1957, of 22 January 1957.

75 See, e.g., Corte costituzionale 175/1971, of 5 July 1971 (on the non-justiciability of the use of amnesty by parliament, despite the records demonstrating parliament anomalously frequently resorting to it).

76 See Costanzo (n 65).

European Court of Human Rights (ECtHR) level much more so than the US political question doctrine of non-justiciability. At the outset, the Court, while acknowledging the existence of a margin of discretion, continued policing the use of the margin with a view to reacting to abuses of this discretion. This approach clearly emerges from the reasoning of earlier judgements:

> The Court considers the question as not founded. It is very true that the Legislator, even in the context of criminal procedures [...] must live up to a standard of reasonableness and comply with the Constitution: yet, it can hardly be said that in the law under scrutiny it went beyond the limits within which its discretion can be exercised.[77]

The Court then abandoned this approach and started issuing orders of inadmissibility where the policy decision at stake required discretion, without policing the 'use' of discretion. An example from the 1970s concerns a case where the Court was called on to introduce a general provision on the civil liability of civil servants, allegedly inferable from Article 103 of the Constitution, to fix the confusing legal framework concerning their civil liability. On that occasion, the Court laconically declared the question 'inadmissible' on the grounds that it was not a genuine complaint on the unconstitutionality of a provision. Rather, it was a request to make the delicate policy evaluations surrounding the introduction of a 'new' law that are the exclusive province of the legislature.[78]

A compromise between the full non-justiciability and justiciability of claims involving the exercise of discretionary powers was later reached and it resulted in the creation of additive decisions where the Court only set forth a 'principle,' leaving the definition of the means through which to fulfil it to the legislature.[79] In any such cases, the Court acknowledges the existence of a margin of discretion, without giving up on its function of steering future legislative action in the direction that is mostly compatible with the Constitution. Furthermore, in the 1990s, the Court restarted issuing, along with inadmissibility orders, judgements of dismissal.[80]

The Court reduced the scope of political questions in another way. In several manipulative decisions, it rejected assertions to the effect that a margin should be warranted, and it imposed a specific solution on the grounds that it was commanded by the Constitution. Consider the *rime obbligate* doctrine. The term *rime obbligate* stands for 'prescribed verses' of the statute. This doctrine, elaborated by prominent constitutionalist Vezio Crisafulli,[81] is a self-imposed standard for when the Court can react to legislative omissions (through additive judgements),

77 Corte costituzionale 172/1972, of 5 December 1972.
78 Corte costituzionale 102/1977, of 24 May 1977.
79 See, e.g. Corte costituzionale 215/1987, of 3 June 1987.
80 Paolo Zicchittu, 'La Corte costituzionale di fronte alle "zone franche"', Forum Quaderni Costituzionali, 18 May 2018, 7 (12 July 2019) http://www.forumcostituzionale.it/wordpress/?p=10718.
81 See Crisafulli (n 32).

allowing an intervention only when the Constitution requires it.[82] These decisions show that even omissions are justiciable and that legislative discretion cannot shield the legislature when the Constitution commands a specific result.

The reduced scope of the discretionary powers of parliament contributed to seeing the Court as more inclined towards judicial activism than towards self-restraint. Starting in the 1970s, scholars noted the increasing incidence of 'substitution' (*supplenza*)[83]; namely, the CC's attitude of taking on the duty of aligning the legal framework in the face of a failure of the legislature to do so. This duty was mainly carried out through manipulative decisions such as additive decisions.

An inherent feature of 'substitution' is its temporary nature – so the theory goes. This substitutive power would be doomed to failure in normal situations where the legislature finally 'takes the reins' and starts fulfilling its duty of aligning the legal framework with constitutional imperatives.

Despite other scholars challenging this attitude as a form of encroachment on the legislative power that, among other things, results in a ripple effect whereby the legislature becomes unwilling to act,[84] the phenomenon is still widely acknowledged. In accordance with substitution theory, the legislature is to blame for the ongoing activism of the Court. Put differently, there still is a parliamentary reluctance to reform the legal system in ways that are more compatible with the Constitution, and thus there is a need to compensate for its poor performance. This poor performance results in transferring controversial policy decisions from the legislature to courts in order to preserve the political balance, or when there is a lack of consensus on the part of legislatures.[85]

Yet, Professor Rodotà aptly notes how illusory the belief is that one can put the brakes on judicial activism, even when the legislature is willing to fulfil its constitutional duties. This is because the Court is unlikely to switch back to a state where it only uses the powers expressly conferred on it by the Constitution and renounces the arsenal of mechanisms it has forged throughout the years to compensate for legislative inaction. He thus reframes the issue not so much as one of substitution but rather as one of the (irreversible) 'redistribution' of powers within the constitutional framework.[86]

This stance holds especially true if one considers that manipulative judgements are on the rise, while judgements of full acceptance are on the decline.[87] Put differently, there is a trend towards the growing familiarity of the Court with this set of nuanced mechanisms to shape the law and a reduced incidence of decisions where it acts as a negative legislator. The trend reinforces the idea of a linear

82 Frosini (n 5) 205.
83 Stefano Rodotà, 'La "svolta" politica della Corte costituzionale' (1970) 1 Politica del diritto 41.
84 Modugno (n 4) 121.
85 *Ex multis* see Massimo Luciani, 'Funzioni e responsabilità della giurisdizione. Una vicenda italiana (e non solo)' (2012) 3 Rivista AIC 1, 3.
86 Zagrebelsky (n 9) 99.
87 Ibid., sec 2.2.

progression towards 'more' power and of the predictable reluctance of the Court to give up the manoeuvrability it has gained throughout the years.

It is worth recalling that activism does not necessarily derive from using a specific type of decision. It is more often the result of decisions that strongly intrude on the law-making activity of parliament and of the Council of Ministers, regardless of the substantive result that has been achieved: in this sense, they can also emerge from orders of inadmissibility or judgements of dismissal.

I shall provide a recent example in this regard. It concerns an order of inadmissibility (which is a de facto judgement of dismissal, if one considers the articulate reasoning with which the claim is rejected).[88] The Court has always deferred the resolution of disputes arising throughout the legislative process to the chambers, for example, amendments, voting procedures etc.[89] For the first time, in Order No. 17/2019, it acknowledged that the autonomy of parliament did not shield its members from all forms of possible behaviour. Particularly, it does not shield acts aimed at curtailing the 'constitutional function' of single Members of Parliament (MPs).[90] This constitutional function boils down to a prerogative to discuss the content of bills, to propose amendments and, ultimately, to vote for or against bills.

For Italy, this is a dramatic innovation, since for the first time the Court has acknowledged that single MPs are a 'constitutional power.'[91] As such, they have the standing to bring constitutional challenges to resolve conflicts between branches of government when other actors curtail their constitutionally attributed powers.[92]

The Court declares the claim inadmissible, and thus does not satisfy the claimant's request. Yet, much ink has been spilled to justify the recognition of MPs'

88 Raffaele Manfrellotti, '"Quindici uomini sulla cassa del morto": questione di fiducia e funzioni costituzionali del Parlamento (ord. n. 17/2019)' (2019) Forum di Quaderni costituzionali, No. 3, 1.
89 This doctrine goes by the name of *autodichia*.
90 Massimo Cavino, 'La necessità formale di uno statuto dell'opposizione' (2019) Federalismi, No. 4; Nicola Lupo, 'Un'ordinanza compromissoria, ma che pone le basi per un procedimento legislativo più rispettoso della Costituzione' (2019) Federalismi, No. 4; Valerio Onida, 'La Corte e i conflitti interni al Parlamento: l'ordinanza n. 17 del 2019' (2019) Federalismi, No. 4.
91 By contrast, the legal standing to bring constitutional challenges in the name of parliament was only recognized for MPs in key positions such as the President of the Senate and the President of the Chamber of Deputies, or for groups such as parliamentary commissions or groups. See Bin & Pitruzzella (n 12) 495.
92 In the case under scrutiny, 37 MPs of the Democratic Party, the main opposition party, lamented that the government had deprived parliament of any possibility to debate and amend the 2019 Budget Law through the following: a 'maxi-amendment' to the law, and a motion of confidence. A maxi-amendment is a despicable technique through which the government, to tackle filibustering, includes all the articles of the bill in a 'gigantic' amendment, and entrenches it through a motion of confidence. A motion of confidence is an ultimatum whereby the government says, 'either you approve the amendment, or I fall'.

legal standing. There is little doubt that this inadmissibility decision is the result of strong judicial activism.

The theory of the redistribution of power proved especially accurate in the last two decades when the Court got involved, in one way or another, in all the most sensitive ethical issues to remedy legislative inertia or to fix illiberal regulations. Among these controversial issues one should especially mention end-of-life decisions, same-sex marriage, and artificial insemination. In the decision on same-sex marriage, while falling short of recognizing the right to same-sex marriage, the Court acknowledged that gay couples are social formations protected under Article 2 of the Constitution.[93] As such, they are worthy of protection through legal benefits. This decision, combined with the *Oliari* judgement of the ECtHR,[94] urging Italy to create a 'legal framework' that was open to same-sex couples, led to the introduction of civil unions in 2016.

Then, in reviewing the law prohibiting heterologous fertilization for sterile and unfertile persons,[95] the Court struck down the provision on the grounds that it violated the principle of equality, and the inviolable freedoms and right to family life of these persons. The reasoning of the justices reflects the shifting balance that a 'more activist' Court struck between legislative discretion and constitutional justice: '[These questions] touch at the heart of sensitive ethical issues, with respect to which the duty to balance competitive interests [...] primarily rests with the legislature. Yet, the way the duty is carried out is justiciable with a view to ascertaining whether a reasonable balance between competing interests and values was reached.'[96]

Besides sensitive ethical issues, the Court also intervened in key ambits related to the frame of government. The scrutiny of electoral laws is likely the most emblematic example of the linear progression towards an expansion of the Court's law-making activity in this area. While in the past it has been wary of acting in situations involving electoral laws, in recent times, the applicable electoral laws were actively shaped and indeed written by the Court. Consider Decision No. 1/2014, where it held the Electoral Law No. 270/2005

93 Corte costituzionale 138/2010, of 14 April 2010. See also Corte di Cassazione (civil division I) 9801/2005, of 10 May 2005. On which see Marco Gattuso, 'La Corte costituzionale sul matrimonio tra persone dello stesso sesso', *Articolo 29* (10 July 2019) http://www.articolo29.it/dottrina/la-corte-costituzionale-sul-matrimonio-tra-persone-dello-stesso-sesso-di-marco-gattuso/.

94 ECtHR, Appl nos 18766/11 and 36030/11 (*Oliari and Others v. Italy*), of 21 July 2015, at 159 [*Oliari*]. The Court noted that Italy only allowed these couples to enter into cohabitation agreements that did not provide for the core needs of stable and committed same-sex couples, and that these agreements were not a response to their lack of recognition, since all cohabiting couples, including flatmates, were eligible to enter into them. *Oliari,* at 169.

95 Heterologous fertilization refers to the assisted fertilization of women's ova with donor sperm.

96 Corte costituzionale 162/2014, of 9 April 2014, para. 5. On which see Carlo Casonato, 'La fecondazione eterologa e la ragionevolezza della Corte', *Confronti costituzionali,* 17 June 2014; Paolo Veronesi, 'La legge sulla procreazione assistita perde un altro "pilastro": illegittimo il divieto assoluto di fecondazione eterologa', *Forum di Quaderni costituzionali,* 5 March 2015.

unconstitutional, and Decision No. 35/2017, which partially struck down Electoral Law No. 52/2015, the so-called *Italicum*. Notably, the wide discretion the Court has shown in carrying out its scrutiny engendered deep uncertainty regarding the fate of any future electoral reform and drew criticism.[97]

For instance, the first electoral law provided for a proportionality system, complemented by the provision of a majority bonus system in favour of the winning party. In the controversial Decision No. 1/2014, the Court struck down the majority bonus on the grounds that the absence of a minimum threshold to trigger the bonus was running roughshod over the constitutional right to vote (and its corollary of the required equal weight of each vote).[98]

Importantly, in order to decide the case, it made an interpretative stretch to set aside the procedural requirement of 'relevance'; that is, the requirement according to which parties can only raise a constitutional question when they are personally affected by the impugned law and when the constitutional challenge, on the one hand, and the claim lodged with the ordinary court, on the other, are distinguishable.[99] This will allow the CC to decide whether the latter can only be decided after the resolution of the constitutional question and, hence, whether it is relevant. Yet, in the case of electoral laws, it is not possible to argue that someone is personally affected, nor is it possible to distinguish the constitutional question (does the electoral law violate the constitutional right to vote?) from the claim lodged with the ordinary court (again, does the electoral law violate the constitutional right to vote?).

Despite this, the Court concluded that the relevance requirement was fulfilled, and it argued, through strong policy-based arguments, for a need to extend its reach to 'free zones'; that is, ambits that would not be justiciable under the current constitutional doctrine.[100]

This power was hardly inferable from the law. On several occasions, scholars and legislatures voiced the need to reform the Constitution to eliminate free zones

97 Alessio Rauti, 'Il giudizio preventivo di costituzionalità sulle leggi elettorali di Camera e Senato' (2016) 6 *Federalismi* 1, 1–2.

98 Nausica Palazzo, 'Constitutional Developments in Armenia: New Electoral System, (B)old Party System' (2017) 9 Const L Rev (Bilingual Journal of the Constitutional Court of Georgia) 24.

99 Adele Anzon Demmig, 'Accesso al giudizio di costituzionalità e intervento "creativo" della corte costituzionale' (2014) 2 Rivista AIC 1; Andrea Morrone, 'Exit porcellum', Forumcostituzionale, 15 February 2014 1; Nicola Zanon, 'La seconda giovinezza dell'art. 67 Cost.', *Forumcostituzionale,* 5 March 2014 1; Giovanni Serges, 'Spunti di giustizia cost. a margine della declaratoria di illegittimità della legge elettorale' (2014) 1 Rivista AIC 1.

100 See 'Dibattito sulla sentenza della Corte costituzionale n. 1 del 2014 dichiarativa dell'incostituzionalità di talune disposizioni della l. n. 270 del 2005' (2014) Giurisprudenza Costituzionale, No. 1, 629; Adele Anzon Demmig, 'Un tentativo coraggioso ma improprio per far valere l'incostituzionalità della legge per le elezioni politiche (e per coprire una "zona franca" del giudizio di costituzionalità)' (2013) Nomos, No. 1, 1; Enrico Grosso, 'Riformare la legge elettorale per via giudiziaria? Un'indebita richiesta di 'supplenza' alla Corte Costituzionale, di fronte all'ennesima disfatta della politica' (2013) 4 Rivista AIC 1.

(especially those shielding electoral laws).[101] Lately, former President of the Council Matteo Renzi submitted constitutional amendments to the popular vote, introducing, among others, a form of preventative judgement on electoral laws.[102] This is to say that, despite the Court working around free zones, their existence was so widely acknowledged that a constitutional reform was still considered necessary.

6 Taking stock of the past and looking at the future

The Italian CC has certainly lived up to its role as the guardian of the Constitution. Unlike the Albertine Statute, the Constitution, as interpreted by the Court, (thus far) has certainly prevented authoritarian drifts. In recent times, when an unprecedented 'bi-populist government'[103] came to power, the Court took this role quite seriously. In this sense, what is emblematic is the decision conferring legal standing upon MPs to resist government attempts at curbing their prerogatives within the legislative process.[104] This decision, acting in tandem with the President of the Republic's statement urging the government to respect such prerogatives, demonstrates how both guardians are awake and vigilant.[105]

The linear progression of the Court towards an expansion of its powers clearly emerges from the analysis. In the earliest stages of operation, it focused its attention on aligning the legal framework with the Constitution, especially relating to illiberal laws passed during the Fascist era. In so doing, it used a twofold strategy: (1) a declaration of admissibility by striking down unconstitutional laws altogether; and (2) interpretative judgements,[106] with respect to which the principal interlocutors were ordinary judges (the gate guard).

101 Marco Croce, 'Sull'opportunità dell'introduzione di un ricorso diretto e preventivo di costituzionalità sulla legge elettorale' in Andrea Cardone (ed.), *Le proposte di riforma della Costituzione* (ESI 2014) 289; Virginia Messerini, 'La materia elettorale' in Roberto Romboli (ed.), *L'accesso alla giustizia costituzionale. Caratteri, limiti, prospettive di un modello* (ESI 2006) 553.

102 Art 13 para 1, Constitutional Bill No 1429/2015. On which see: F. Dal Canto, 'Qualche osservazione sulla proposta di introduzione del ricorso preventivo di costituzionalità avverso le leggi elettorali' (2015) 1 Osservatorio sulle fonti 1, 1–5.

103 Fulco Lanchaster, 'I custodi della costituzione e la loro azione parallela (2018) 3 Nomos 1, 2.

104 Ibid., sec 5.1.

105 Lately, the President of the Republic, Giorgio Mattarella, made a non-ordinary promulgation of the law on the right to self-defence. In the face of the reduced trust in parliament, instead of vetoing the law, it promulgated it while stressing the potential grounds for the unconstitutionality of the law. According to Prof. Alessandro Morelli, it thereby sent a message to justices and law practitioners that the law should be either brought before the CC or interpreted in a manner consistent with the Constitution (especially the part of the law publicized as allowing persons to punish trespassers). Alessandro Morelli, 'La promulgazione "abrogante" della legge sulla legittima difesa e la fiducia del Presidente', *lacostituzione.info*, 28 April 2019 (10 June 2019) http://www.lacostituzione.info/index.php/2019/04/28/la-promulgazione-abrogante-della-legge-sulla-legittima-difesa-e-la-fiducia-del-presidente/.

106 Besides interpretative judgments, one could further recall the threshold requirement to interpret the impugned law in a manner consistent with the Constitution. This

This was the phase in which the Court successfully injected constitutional values into the legal system and acquired sufficient prestige and authority to push the boundaries of constitutional justice one step further.

In the 1970s, the Court was strong enough to redirect attention onto the legislator and to become a countervailing power. In this sense, this phase saw a politicization of constitutional justice stemming from two factors: the creation of a sophisticated set of manipulative decisions and the increasing political cost of decisions (taken in highly controversial policy areas). At the end of the 1980s, its efficiency increased because of amendments to procedural rules and due to it its ability to function as a trigger for major legal innovation processes.[107]

At the turn of the century, its ability to weigh in on controversial areas of social policy and institutional relevance reached its peak. A major example of the former are decisions concerning end-of-life decisions, artificial insemination, and same-sex marriage, and the chief example of the latter relates to the decisions shaping electoral systems.

Surely, Italy is in stormy times. Looking at the 2019 European elections, it seems obvious that the alternative to the current government coalition is a far-right government led by the League Party, a national-populist party with an overt xenophobic ideology. This is not the proper venue to address all the changes our frame of government and State risk undergoing should such a government take office. But I will say that it is clear that a dangerous climate of intolerance is spreading across the country, often under the auspices of far-right factions. A second cause for concern are the clumsy attempts to curb the principle of responsible government made by the bipopulist government that led the country from June 2018 to September 2019.[108]

In this context, it is not only desirable but also necessary that the Court retains its role as guardian of the Constitution and reacts to (both conscious and unconscious) attempts at deviating from it. While judicial activism poses several theoretical problems, in these situations, it is reassuring to know that the guardian of the Constitution is very much awake and ready to preserve civil rights and the rule of law in the country.

requirement, called *interpretazione costitutionalmente orientata* or *conforme a costituzione*, was introduced through the Court's case law and soon became a threshold requirement that, if not fulfilled, led the Court to declare the question inadmissible.

107 Alfonso Celotto (n 2) 125. The author lists the principal reforms that are anticipated or have been pushed forwards by the Court, and among these are the new Code of Civil Procedure, the pension system, the privatization of civil servants' apparatus, and administrative decentralization.

108 For an analysis of the marginalization of the role of parliament see ibid. sec 5.1, and accompanying notes to text 90–91. For the constitutional 'abomination' known as 'the government contract' (i.e. the 'contract' detailing the common policy interests of both populist parties) that the government pledged it would strictly adhere to while in office, see: R Bin, 'Il "contratto di governo" e il rischio di una grave crisi costituzionale', *lacostituzione.info,* 16 May 2018 (10 July 2019) https://www.lacostituzione.info/index.php/2018/05/16/il-contratto-di-governo-e-il-rischio-di-una-grave-crisi-costituzionale/.

4 The Spanish Constitutional Court as a law-maker

Functioning and practice

Covadonga Ferrer Martín de Vidales

In Spain, as in other democratic countries, the CC holds the essential function of safeguarding the Constitution and interpreting it, also ensuring that the rest of the legal system complies with the Constitution. It can be said that its role and existence is essential for a democratic Spanish State.

During its forty years of existence, the CC has contributed to the configuration of Spain's democracy, helping to legally pacify complex conflicts, granting the conditions for the effective enjoyment of rights and freedoms, and for the development of Spain's decentralized model for the State. This has to do not just with carrying out the classic negative legislator's function of expelling unconstitutional norms, but also of performing a creative role, especially through its interpretative judgements. It can be said, therefore, that the assessment of the role performed by the Court over these years has been positive, although some problems and tensions have also arisen, as we will examine in this chapter.

1 General characteristics and powers

The CC is regulated in Part IX of the Constitution (Articles 159 to 165), which closes the part of the Constitution dedicated to regulating the constitutional organizational structure.[1] This location emphasizes the CC's function as the body that guarantees the entire constitutional order. It is completely separated from the judicial power (regulated in Part VI), thus proving the option for a model of concentrated constitutional justice[2] – with also some elements of the diffuse model.[3] The constitutional provisions are

1 Which shows the importance placed on granting a constitutional jurisdiction. Javier García Roca, *La experiencia de veinticinco años de jurisdicción constitucional en España* (Porrúa 2009) 2. Some analysis in English can be found in Víctor Ferreres Comella, *The Constitution of Spain. A Contextual Analysis* (Hart Publishing 2013) 215–234; Maria José Falcón y Tella et al., *Case Law in Roman, Anglosaxon and Continental Law* (Brill Academic Publishers 2011) 64 et seq.; Enrique Guillén López, 'Judicial Review in Spain: The Constitutional Court' (2018) 41 *Loyola of Los Angeles Law Review* 529.
2 Guillén López (n 1) 531–532.
3 Since questions on the constitutionality of laws can be brought before the CC when such issues arise in a case pending before a judicial body. See Art. 163 SC. Ignacio

DOI: 10.4324/9781003022442-5

further developed by an organic statute, the *Ley Orgánica 2/1979 del Tribunal Constitucional* (hereafter, the LOTC).[4]

The Court is a *constitutional body*, which the Constitution configures as one of the essential bodies for the shaping of the State model.[5] It is independent from the other constitutional bodies[6] but, at the same time, is also called on to establish relations with other constitutional bodies; in particular with the legislative power, which the CC must not substitute for, thus making an effort in terms of *self-restraint*.[7]

The CC is also a *judicial body*. Despite being separated from judicial power and often having to resolve politically relevant disputes, the Court is a tribunal as it consists of twelve totally independent judges (*Magistrados*), it can only act at the request of the legitimated parties and it follows jurisdictional procedures for the adoption of legally binding decisions subject to law.[8]

And it is the supreme interpreter of the Constitution and the so-called block of constitutionality (*bloque de constitucionalidad*),[9] but not the only one. All the public authorities are subject to the Constitution (Article 9.1 SC) and, therefore, they can all interpret it. However, as the supreme interpreter, the Court's interpretation binds the rest of the public authorities,[10] ensuring from this position that all the norms and acts that conform the legal order respect the Constitution.[11]

Torres Muro, 'Sinopsis artículo 161' in *Constitución Española. Índice sistemático* (Congreso de los Diputados 2003). Retrieved on 8 March 2019 from www.congreso.es; Enrique García De Enterría, *La Constitución como norma y el Tribunal Constitucional* (Cuarta ed.) (Thomson-Civitas 2006) 72.

4 An English version can be found on the Court's website, www.tribunalconstitucional.es.

5 Manuel Medina Guerrero, 'Artículo 1', in Juan Luis Requejo Pagés (Coord.), *Comentarios a la Ley Orgánica del Tribunal Constitucional* (Tribunal Constitucional-BOE 2001) 69, 70.

6 Since it establishes the rules governing its own functioning and organization (Article 2.2 LOTC), draws up its own budget (second additional provision in the LOTC), and is subject only to the Constitution and its organic law (Article 1.1 LOTC).

7 The CC has recognized that the legislator creates law freely within the framework offered by the Constitution and that the Court's competence is only to guarantee that this framework is not exceeded. Judgement of the CC (hereinafter, STC) 209/1987, of 22 December 1987, Para. 3. The CC cannot, in an abstract way, determine which interpretation is the most appropriate, relevant or convenient. STC 227/1988, of 29 November 1988, Para. 13. Neither can the CC assess the opportunity or merits of the election made by the legislator. STC 142/1993, of 22 April 1993, Para. 9. For more information, see Javier Salas, 'El Tribunal Constitucional español y su competencia desde la perspectiva de la forma de Gobierno: sus relaciones con los poderes legislativo, ejecutivo y judicial' (1982) 6 *Revista Española de Derecho Constitucional* 141, 147 et seq.; Javier Pérez Royo, *Tribunal Constitucional y división de poderes* (Tecnos 1988) 72 et seq.; Medina Guerrero (n 5) 82–84. All the CC's judgements can be found on the Court's website: https://hj.tribunalconstitucional.es/es.

8 STC 9/1981, of 31 March 1981, Para. 1.

9 This block includes the norms referred to in Article 28.1 of the LOTC: laws enacted within the framework of the Constitution for the purpose of delimiting the powers of the State and the individual autonomous communities or of regulating or harmonising the exercise of their powers.

10 STC 1/1981, of 26 January 1981, Para. 2.

11 STC 163/2011, of 2 November 2011, Para. 3.

The Constitution assigns the CC precise powers to carry out its function (Article 161.1.d SC). These powers can only be exercised according to the requisites established in the framework of the proceedings laid down in the Constitution and the LOTC, and they can be extended by the Constitution or by the organic legislator.[12] The main function of the CC is the control of the constitutionality of the legislation. Only the CC can carry out this a posteriori and abstract control by holding a legislative provision to be invalid and expelling it from the legal order.[13] This control can also be carried out through the constitutional questions (*cuestión de inconstitucionalidad*) submitted by ordinary judges.[14]

Through the use of these powers, the CC has been able to interpret Spain's Constitution and the essential principles of a democratic State governed by the rule of law, also ensuring that the legal system respects both. And, as we will examine in the following pages, it has carried out this important role not only in a negative way, but also by exercising a creative role.

2 The CC as a law-maker

The Spanish CC, as stated previously, is the supreme interpreter of Spain's Constitution (Article 1 LOTC),[15] guaranteeing its primacy (Article 27 LOTC). Its main function is to carry out an abstract control over the constitutionality of the law. Most of the doctrine explains the system by emphasising its origins in Kelsen's classical definition of a 'negative legislator,' understanding that with abstract control the Court is not creating any new laws, but is limiting itself to declaring, with *erga omnes* effects, what is already implicitly contained in the Constitution.[16] On the contrary, some authors consider that when the Court fulfils its function as the judge on the constitutionality of the laws, it is participating in the legislative

12 Ramón Punset Blanco, 'Artículo 2' in Juan Luis Requejo Pagés (Coord.), *Comentarios a la Ley Orgánica del Tribunal Constitucional* (Tribunal Constitucional-BOE 2001) 89, 91–92; Pedro Ibáñez Buil, 'Artículo 59' in Juan José González Rivas (Dir.-Coord.), *Comentarios a la Ley Orgánica del Tribunal Constitucional* (La Ley 2010) 620, 621–622. Thus, for example, the LOTC has given the CC the authority to settle controversies between various constitutional bodies (*conflictos entre órganos constitucionales*, Articles 2.d, 59.1 and 73 to 75 LOTC). Other organic laws have also granted other competences to the CC. For example, the LOREG (Act on Electoral Law), whose Art. 42.3 regulate the complaints against the proclamation of candidates. With regard to these specific complaints, see María Garrote de Marcos, 'El recurso de Amparo electoral' in Alejandro Villanueva Turnes (Coord.), *El Tribunal Constitucional Español: una visión actualizada del supremo intérprete de la Constitución* (Tébar Flores 2018) 157.

13 Ferreres Comella (n 1) 219–220.

14 Article 163 SC.

15 See, for example, STC 78/1984, of 9 July 1984, Para. 4.

16 Medina Guerrero (n 5) 72–73.

function and acting as a 'positive legislator' that not only adds content to the Constitution but also to other legal regulations.[17]

Taking into account its current configuration and practical development, it can be said that the CC carries out law-making activity through its interpretative function, specifying not only the content of the Constitution's provisions but also of the other legal norms, interpreting their content according to the current cultural and social reality, and integrating the possible omissions of the legislator in some cases.[18] There is a tendency to carry out innovative and expansive interpretations rather than literal interpretations. However, it must be emphasized that this law-making activity or creative role must be differentiated from what we understand as 'statute-making' activity; that is, the Court makes a constructive interpretation of norms, constructs principles and, in this way, participates in the establishment of superior rules of law. It creates norms, rules, and principles that adhere to those of constitutional rank. But it does not create any new laws; it only makes explicit what is already contained in the constitutional provisions.[19] The Court does not act as a legislator creating abstract norms, since there is no legislative initiative nor any procedure that allows for the participation of majorities or minorities; in sum, none of the elements that characterize the legislator. It fulfils a law-making activity different from that of the legislator, as Rubio Llorente emphasizes, as it does not obey opportunity reasons and it is not free but provides a mere declaration of a pre-existent law.[20] Therefore, its definition as a 'positive' or 'negative' legislator is not adequate.[21]

2.1 The development of the law: a constructive interpretation of statutes in accordance with the Constitution

The CC can interpret the content of provisions both at constitutional and at sub-constitutional level with constructive patterns creating constitutional principles. Its role, therefore, is not just circumscribed to expelling from the legal order norms that contravene the Constitution through a merely declarative resolution with *ex tunc* effects. Through the technique of interpretation of the norms according to

17 Francisco Fernández Segado, 'El Tribunal Constitucional Español como legislador positivo' (2011) 15 *Revista Pensamiento Constitucional* 128, 131–132; Antonio Luis Martínez Pujalte, 'Spanish Legal System: Between Statutory Legal Systems and Case Law' (2018) 1 *Studia Iuridica Lublinensia*, 157, 160; Allan R. Brewer-Carias, 'General Report on CCs as positive legislators in Comparative Law', *XVIII International Congress of Comparative Law of the International Academy of Comparative Law*, George Washington University Law School, Washington, 27 July 2010, 1–2.

18 As the supreme interpreter, the CC can clarify the meaning of the Constitution's provisions, integrate them where they are not explicit (making them emerge), or interpret them constructively. García Roca (n 1) 16.

19 Ibid., 16–22.

20 Francisco Rubio Llorente, 'La jurisdicción constitucional como forma de creación de Derecho' (1988) 22 *Revista Española de Derecho Constitucional* 9, 38.

21 Neither is its definition as a 'commissioner' of the constituent power. The CC is a constitutional body subject thereon. García Roca (n 1) 21.

the Constitution, and the principle of their conservation, the CC takes into account the consequences that its judgements can have for the community and that, on many occasions, certain elements of the provisions need to be 'saved' or 'maintained' to preserve legal certainty.[22]

The CC has at its disposal different types of judgements to achieve the aforementioned purpose, like interpretative judgements, which give to the norm an interpretation according to or in conformity with the Constitution; or judgements of mere unconstitutionality, when the unconstitutionality derives from an omission by the legislator, inviting it to resolve the problem.[23]

However, the Court has pointed out that 'it is not a legislator and all that can be asked of this Court is a declaration on whether or not the precepts can be deemed to comply with the Constitution.'[24] Therefore, the Court makes clear that its function is not that of the legislator, because to interpret is not the same as to legislate. Through its interpretative function, the Court creates law, but not abstract norms like the legislator does.

Regarding the elements that reflect the law-making activity of the CC, they appear in the dispositive part of the judgement as well as in the reasoning that supports it. The dispositive part is short and concise, since it is preceded by the reasoning for the ruling. For example, in Judgement 22/1981, the Court declared that the fifth additional provision of the Statute of Workers was unconstitutional if 'interpreted as a norm that establishes the incapacity to work at sixty-nine years and in a direct and unconditioned way the cessation of the employment relationship at that age.'[25]

In summary, it can be said that the CC's judgements are a type of law-making activity and that, due to their *erga omnes* effects, can be practically identified with norms – obviously, maintaining the clear differences in respect to them. Therefore, as they are universally binding, they are published in the Official Journal for maximum dissemination.

22 Therefore, the link between unconstitutionality and nullity is not always necessary. STC 45/1989, of 20 February 1989, Para. 11. Ignacio Torres Muro, 'Sinopsis artículo 164' in *Constitución Española. Índice sistemático* (Congreso de los Diputados 2003). Retrieved on 8 March 2019 from www.congreso.es.

23 Other type of judgements are additive, where the Court adds to the precept the content that has been omitted; reconstructive or substitutive, where part of the normative content of the precept is substituted for another; and reductive, which reduce the cases to which the precept is applicable or the legal consequences that are derived from it. Torres Muro, 'Sinopsis artículo 164', 2003. An analysis of the different types of interpretative judgements in Francisco Javier Díaz Revorio, *Las sentencias interpretativas del Tribunal Constitucional* (Lex Nova 2001); Leo Brust, 'The interpretation according to the constitution and the manipulative sentences' (2009) 2 *Rev. direito GV* [online] 134, 135–136.

24 SSTC 5/1981, of 13 February 1981, Para. 6; 77/1985, of 27 June 1985, Para. 4; 16/1996, of 1 February 1996, Para. 6.

25 STC 22/1981, of 2 July 1981, ruling.

2.1.1 The development of the law at constitutional level

Interpretation is usually necessary for any constitutional text due to the open and general character of many of the provisions,[26] as well as to the need for adaptation that the same evolution of reality may require, since the Constitution is not only a normative text but a 'living constitution.'[27]

In the case of Spain, the huge effort needed to reach agreement with regard to Spain's Constitution in 1978 must be taken into account. Consequently, some provisions were not clearly defined, being interpreted subsequently by the CC. One of its first tasks was to ensure the supremacy of the Constitution and its own role as its supreme interpreter and guarantor, thus acting against the attempts to weaken Spain's new democracy by devaluating the Constitution itself.[28] The Court clearly stated that the Constitution was not a simple programmatic declaration but the supreme normative statute of Spain's legal system and, as such, binding to all.[29]

The CC has also contributed to the implementation and explanation of the principles and values which determine the democratic character of the State. Article 1.1 of the SC provides that 'Spain is hereby established as a social and democratic State, subject to the rule of law, which advocates freedom, justice, equality, and political pluralism as the highest values of its legal system.' The Court indicates that this formula transcends the whole legal order and, therefore, other rules contained in the Constitution must be interpreted in the light of this formula.[30] Through Article 1.1, the superior values of Spain's legal system are positivized (freedom, equality, justice, and political pluralism) and understood by the CC as central.

The other two fundamental principles describing the character of the Spanish State stem from the formula provided in Article 1.1 of the SC:[31] the principles of a democratic and social state.[32] These principles inspire Spain's Constitution and the CC uses them when it needs to substantiate a decision, but no decision is based directly on them. For example, the CC's case law is not referred directly to the formula of a 'social State.' Rather, it is focused on

26 This is not a defect of the Constitution. Uno Lõhmus, 'The application of different techniques of interpretation of the Constitution as a factor of development thereof', in Venice Commission, *Conference on the 'Role of the CC in the maintenance of the stability and development of the Constitution'*, Moscow, 25 February 2004, CDL-JU (2004) 031, 3.

27 As the Canadian Privy Council already noted in the so-called *Persons* case. *Edwards v. Canada* (Attorney General), 1929 CanLII 438 (UK JCPC), 9.

28 Guillén López (n 1) 541.

29 SSTC 16/1982, of 28 April 1982, Para. 1; 80/1982, of 20 December 1982, Para. 1.

30 Teresa Freixes Sanjuan & Jose Carlos Remotti Carbonell, 'Los valores y principios en la interpretación constitucional' (1992) 35 *Revista Española de Derecho Constitucional* 97, 108–109. Based on this clause, the Court has required the reasoning of judicial decisions (STC 55/1987, of 13 May 1987, Para. 1) and has imposed their binding enforcement (STC 67/1984, of 7 June 1984, Para. 2).

31 Freixes Sanjuan & Remotti Carbonell (n30) 103.

32 Javier Perez Royo, *Curso de Derecho Constitucional* (Marcial Pons 2003) 204.

the incidence of the formula on the Spanish legal order, on the action of public powers and citizens, and on what is legitimate, or not, to deduce from it.[33] In Judgement 81/1982, the Court uses this formula as a basic element of the mechanism that must be used to restore equality between male and female social security personnel with regard to overtime payments for working during holidays.[34]

Another area in which the Court has developed a major role is that related to the construction of the regional State (*Estado autonómico*).[35] It has been forced to fulfil this role due to a lack of political compromise and that has had an undeniably corrosive effect on the institution.[36] Title VIII was one part of the Constitution where the achievement of political compromises was more complex. Therefore, the SC designed only the principles and framework within which the construction of the regional State could be carried out.[37] The CC has had to define this regional State, in particular with respect to the scope of the self-government principle of autonomous communities,[38] regarding which the Court has emphasized that it is a limited power, it is not sovereign, and it cannot be opposed to the unity principle enshrined in the Constitution.[39] Therefore, it can never consist of a right to self-determination as a right to foster and accomplish unilateral secession, as the Court has recently noted.[40] Despite this limitation, the Court recognizes that this right to self-determination is a political aspiration that can be defended within the constitutional framework.[41]

Finally, the Spanish CC has interpreted certain constitutional principles by taking into account the changes that have resulted from the social and cultural evolution; changes that, obviously, when drafting the constitutional text, were not in the mind of the constituent. One of the most outstanding examples is Judgement 198/2012, which adjudicated the action of unconstitutionality against Law 13/2005, which amended the Civil Code allowing for same-sex marriage. In particular, the Court addressed the possible unconstitutionality of Article 32 of the SC,[42] which recognizes the right of men and women 'to marry with full legal

33 Javier Pérez Royo, 'La doctrina del Tribunal Constitucional sobre el Estado social' (1984) 10 *Revista Española de Derecho Constitucional* 157, 172–180.

34 STC 81/1982, of 21 December 1982, Para. 3.

35 Regarding the CC's role in the configuration of the regional State, see Germán Fernández Farreres, *La contribución del Tribunal Constitucional al Estado Autonómico* (Iustel 2005).

36 Francisco Pérez de los Cobos Orihuel, 'El papel del Tribunal Constitucional en el Estado Autonómico' (2017) 40 *Teoría y Realidad Constitucional* pp. 369, 369–372.

37 The SC establishes that there is only one State, the Spanish Nation, characterized by its 'indissoluble unity' but, at the same time, it recognizes and guarantees 'the right to self-government of the nationalities and regions' (Article 2 SC).

38 See STC 4/1981, of 2 February 1981, Para. 3.

39 Ibid.

40 SSTC 114/2017, of 17 October 2017, Para. 2 b) and 127/2017, of 8 September 2017, Para. 5 c). The 'right of self-determination' as a 'right to decide' is not recognized in the Constitution. STC 42/2014, of 25 March 2014, Para. 3 b).

41 Pérez de los Cobos Orihuel (n36) 378. To this respect see STC 42/2014, of 25 March 2014, Para. 4 c).

42 STC 198/2012, of 6 November 2012, Para. 6.

equality.' As the CC points out, it is clear that in 1978, when the Constitution was drafted, the constituent was not discussing same-sex marriage but the regulation of the institution of marriage; which does not mean that it implicitly accepted same-sex marriage, or that it excluded this possibility. Strictly and literally interpreted, says the CC, Article 32 only identifies the holders of the right to marry, not the other spouse. From this point, the Court takes another step in its interpretation and brings up the idea of the Constitution as a 'living tree' and of the progressive interpretation of the Constitution to allow for its adjustment to fit the current reality.[43] This progressive interpretation according to which 'we are able to build up legal culture, to the extent that the law is treated as a social phenomenon that is linked to the reality in which it is implemented.' The Court cannot ignore social reality. Taking these considerations into account, the CC understands that the legislator develops the institution of marriage in accordance with Spain's legal culture, without making it unrecognizable for Spanish society. The option chosen by the legislator, consequently, lies within the margin of appreciation acknowledged by Article 32 of the SC. In summary, the Court declared that the legislator had opted from among the different available options, and chosen an option that respects the fundamental text.[44]

In conclusion, the CC has not focused only on preserving the determined contents, but it has also provided the criteria and principles for the promotion of the values and rights that are constitutionally protected, as well as the numerous contributions to the idea and defence of the democratic State.[45]

2.1.2 The development of the law at sub-constitutional level

The Constitution's character as the supreme norm implies that the other norms and acts must respect and be interpreted according to it. At the sub-constitutional level, therefore, the CC influences legal regulations as it can decide over the constitutionality or unconstitutionality of a law – or part of it – and, consequently, declare it valid or invalid.

The SC only contemplates the expulsion of the unconstitutional law from the legal order (Article 164.2 SC).[46] The legislator, however, links unconstitutionality with the nullity with *ex tunc* effects (Article 39.1 LOTC).[47] That said, the Court has modulated the effects of these provisions and has taken into account the need

43 The Court expressly cites the Judgement *Privy Council, Edwards c. Attorney General for Canada* of 1930, recovered by the Supreme Court of Canada in its judgement on same-sex marriage. Para. 9.

44 Para. 9 and 11.

45 García Roca (n 1) 22–26.

46 Ángel J. Gómez Montoro, 'Artículo 39' in Juan Luis Requejo Pagés (Coord.), *Comentarios a la Ley Orgánica del Tribunal Constitucional* (Tribunal Constitucional-BOE 2001) 578, 583; Ignacio De la Cueva Aleu, 'Artículo 39' in Juan José González Rivas (Dir.-Coord.), *Comentarios a la Ley Orgánica del Tribunal Constitucional* (La Ley 2010) 437, 438–439.

47 Ibid. The only limit is the effect of *res judicata,* with the exceptions contemplated in Article 40 LOTC.

to maintain certain elements of the law on certain occasions for legal certainty issues and in order to safeguard other constitutionally significant rights and values.[48] Consequently, on determined cases, unconstitutionality and nullity are separated, and both of them are separated from the *ex tunc* effects.[49]

Therefore, the CC can rule that the legal norm has become invalid with *ex tunc, ex nunc* or *pro future* effects. In order to do so, the Court has at its disposal a wide range of types of judgements. Nonetheless, the general rule remains that of unconstitutionality/nullity/effects *ex tunc*, being necessary to motivate any departures from it.[50]

Consequently, through its function as the supreme interpreter, the CC can influence the adoption of legal norms or their content, although it cannot directly act as a legislator. When it declares the nullity of the legal norm as consequence of its unconstitutionality, the Court usually explains, in the dispositive part of the judgement, the cause or causes for the unconstitutionality; directions that must be considered as a type of orientation so that the legislator takes them into account in future reforms of the law.[51] For example, Judgement 166/1998 declared the unconstitutionality and nullity of the subsection 'and assets in general' of Article 154.2 of the Law Governing Local Tax Offices, with the scope indicated in Paragraph 15 of the Judgement, where the Court explains that the privilege of unseizability of the 'assets in general' of local entities cannot comprise the patrimonial assets that are not connected to a public use or service, since it does not respect the right to effective judicial protection.[52] The legislator took these directions into account by excluding these patrimonial assets of the aforementioned privilege.[53]

In other cases, the Court considers that it is better to save the constitutionality of the provision, although it cannot maintain the entire normative content since part of it is unconstitutional.[54] Through interpretative judgements, the CC can modify the scope of the provision, avoiding the unconstitutionality effect without

48 De la Cueva Aleu (n 46) 438–439.

49 Interpretation adopted since STC 45/1989, of 20 February 1989, Para. 11. Therefore, the Court can extend the limits of retroactivity to other cases not contemplated in Article 40.1 of the LOTC. Torres Muro recommends to include these exceptions in the LOTC. Ignacio Torres Muro, 'Tribunal Constitucional: composición y funciones', in Teresa Freixes Sanjuán y Juan Carlos Gavara de Cara, *Repensar la constitución. Ideas para una reforma de la Constitución de 1978: reforma y comunicación dialógica. Parte primera* (CEPC, BOE 2016) 173, 186. From there on, the ordinary judges are the ones that must determine if the process has finished through a judgement having the force of res judicata, or if the unconstitutionality of the law has an impact on the validity of the act whose revision is intended. Ángel J. Gómez Montoro, 'Artículo 40' in Juan Luis Requejo Pagés (Coord.), *Comentarios a la Ley Orgánica del Tribunal Constitucional* (Tribunal Constitucional-BOE 2001) 608, 615–616, 622–623.

50 Ricardo Alonso García, 'El Tribunal Constitucional y la eficacia temporal de sus Sentencias anulatorias' (1989) 119 *Revista de Administración Pública* 255, 263–264.

51 Gómez Montoro (n 46) 589.

52 STC 166/1998, of 15 July 1998, Para. 15.

53 See current Art. 173.2 TRLRH.

54 Díaz Revorio (n 22) 53–57.

provoking a legal lacuna or impeding the positive effects or constitutionally necessary effects that the provision can produce. This technique is used to respect both the reviewed law and the will of the legislator.[55] For example, in Judgement 115/1987, the CC addressed the possible unconstitutionality of the second paragraph of Article 26.2 of the Organic Law 7/1985 on the rights and freedoms of foreigners in Spain and their social integration. According to this Article, the government authority agreeing to the arrest of an alien 'shall address to the investigating judge of the place in which the alien has been arrested, within a period of 72 hours, "*interesando*",[56] the internment at his disposal in detention centres.' The Court, recognizing the ambiguity of the terms used by the legislator, noted that the precepts can only be declared invalid when their incompatibility with the Constitution is unquestionable, thus rendering it impossible to carry out an interpretation.[57] The Court points out that it is clear that the will of the legislator is to eliminate the previous situation of total governmental availability over the freedom of aliens pending expulsion, demanding the judicial intervention once the 72-hour deadline passes. Therefore, in conformity with the Constitution, the Court explains that the term '*interesando*' must be understood as equivalent to a request from the judge for the authorization to extend the internment beyond the 72-hour term,[58] providing the terms under which the precept must be interpreted in order to be considered respectful to the Constitution.

These types of judgements (unconstitutionality without nullity) are especially frequent when the legal norm infringes the equality principle, usually due to the exclusion of determined individuals. The most respectful solution with regard to the legislator would be to declare the unconstitutionality and defer the efficacy of the nullity, invoking the legislator to correct the unconstitutionality as soon as possible. But this solution poses the problem of maintaining the unconstitutional norm in the legal order.[59] For this reason, the CC usually extends the application of the norm to those that have been excluded. For example, in Judgement 103/1983, the Court declared the unconstitutionality of the term 'the widow' in order to extend to the widowers of the female workers affiliated with the social security system the right to a pension under the same conditions as female holders.[60] These are the so-called manipulative judgements,[61] and they have been criticized for going beyond the Court's power.[62]

55 Gómez Montoro (n 46) 588–589; Brewer-Carias (n 17) 7.
56 The exact term that is used does not exist in English, so it has been considered convenient to leave the Spanish word that, as examined, was ambiguous and led the CC to have to clarify its meaning.
57 STC 115/1987, of 7 July 1987, Para. 1.
58 Ibid.
59 Gómez Montoro (n 46) 599.
60 STC 103/1983, of 22 November 1983, ruling.
61 That can be reductive, additive or substitutive. Díaz Revorio (n 22) 26–27.
62 As in the examined judgement, where Magistrate Jerónimo Arozamena's dissenting opinion indicates that the adaptation of the social security system to the demands of the Constitution was a 'task that corresponds to the Government and the *Cortes Generales* [the Parliament]'.

Last, besides *ratio decidendi*, in some judgements the CC includes *obiter dicta*, for example, when addressing the constitutional or *informing* principles.[63] A recent example can be found in Judgement 42/2014;[64] the first time the Court addressed the Catalan sovereignty process and the 'right to decide'. Once the Court had established that the nature of the consultations contemplated by Resolution 5/X of the Catalonian parliament were related to a referendum, other arguments pertaining to how the resolution was unconstitutional were unnecessary for the ruling, despite the Court having made several assertions about them, assertions that, as Eduard Roig points out, can be considered *obiter dicta*, and that leave 'open the possibility of the State to make a pact for a consultation as a way of implementing the "right to decide."'[65]

2.2 *The 'creative' interpretation of the law*

It is clear that, currently, the CC performs a creative role, searching for an interpretation in conformity with the Constitution and examining the will of the legislator whenever possible. And, of course, it bears in mind that the interpretation must be carried out by taking the social and cultural reality into consideration.

The Court recognizes that interpretative judgements are 'legitimate means in the hands of the Court'[66] but are subject to limits,[67] as an interpretation cannot lead to the understanding that the provision says the opposite or says something substantially different to what it actually says.[68] Hence, the Court can establish the meaning or the sense of the text of the legal precept and decide that it is in conformity with the Constitution, but it cannot deduce or reconstruct the mandate that it contains.[69] Therefore, the use of an interpretation is inappropriate when the unconstitutionality of the law is not eliminated.[70] The Court adds that it must exhaust the possibilities for interpretation, declaring unconstitutionality only in those cases where it is unquestionable that there is no interpretation that can save the finding of unconstitutionality.[71]

Even when several interpretations are feasible, the one that adjusts to the Constitution must prevail. The principle of interpretation according to the Constitution is justified because the Constitution is 'one of the interpretative elements that must be considered in any task of legal hermeneutic, in particular when using the systematic and teleological interpretation,' since the citizens and the public authorities are

63 Javier Martínez-Torrón, *Religion and Law in Spain* (2nd edition) (Wolters Kluwer 2018) §6, Para. 92.
64 STC 42/2014, of 25 March 2014.
65 Eduard Roig i Molés, 'The catalan sovereignty process and the Spanish CC. An analysis of reciprocal impacts' (2017) 54 *Revista catalana de dret public* 24, 32–33.
66 STC 5/1981, of 13 February 1981, Para. 6.
67 STC 42/1981, of 22 December 1981, Para. 6.
68 Ibid.
69 STC 11/1981, of 8 April 1981, Para. 4.
70 STC 196/1996, of 28 November 1996, Para. 4.
71 STC 4/1981, of 2 February 1981, Para. 1.

subject to the Constitution, which compels an interpretation of the legal norms according to it.[72]

References to this principle of interpretation according to the Constitution can be found in the case law of the CC, which uses it in order to preserve the will of the legislator, as in Judgement 115/1987 (already examined) where the Court points out that this is the interpretation that is the most consistent with the global context of the law.[73]

In the case of legislative omissions, especially in the area of fundamental rights, the CC resorts to the analogy and to the general principles of law[74] in order to fill the technical lacunas provoked by the legislator's inactivity.[75] For example, in Judgement 36/1982, concerning a complaint (*recurso de amparo*) against the prohibition of a demonstration, where the Court inferred the necessary rule from the constitutional principles, applying the Constitution *per saltum* due to the lack of regulation of the right of assembly.[76] The Court has notwithstanding, established clear limits to analogy. For example, it is incompatible with the principle of legality in criminal proceedings,[77] or its use to restrict rights.[78]

3 The relations between the CC, and the judges, and tribunals of the judicial power

Resolutions that declare the unconstitutionality of a law have *erga omnes* effects. Therefore, the doctrine of the CC binds the courts and tribunals of the ordinary judiciary and has prevalence over their case law,[79] which shall be understood as being corrected by the doctrine of the Court.[80]

When a legal norm is declared unconstitutional and null, it is expelled from the legal order and, therefore, the relevant case law also disappears. The case law regarding legal norms or provisions that have not been adjudicated by the Court

72 STC 77/1985, of 27 June 1985, Para. 4.
73 STC 115/1987, of 7 July 1987, Para. 1.
74 To which we have already made reference to under heading 2.1.1. The CC makes use of them, in general, as interpretative means – rather than as integrative ones. Francisco Javier Ezquiaga Ganuzas, *La argumentación en la justicia constitucional española* (IVAP 1978) 46.
75 Using, therefore, the two methods par excellence to fill lacuna cases. Ezquiaga Ganuzas (n 75) 46.
76 Ángela Figueruelo Burrieza, 'La incidencia positiva del Tribunal Constitucional en el Poder legislativo' (1993) 81 *Revista de Estudios Políticos (Nueva Época)* 47, 68.
77 STC 75/1984, of 27 June 1984, Para. 5–6. Ezquiaga Ganuzas (n 75) 56–57.
78 STC 45/1983, of 25 May 1983, Para. 4. Ezquiaga Ganuzas (n 75) 58.
79 Eugeni Gay Montalvo, 'El diálogo del Tribunal Constitucional Español con la doctrina de otros Tribunales' in E. Ferrer Mac-Gregor, A. Herrera García (Coords.), *Diálogo Jurisprudencial en Derechos Humanos. Entre Tribunales Constitucionales y Cortes Internacionales* (Tirant lo Blanch 2013) 243, 247.
80 The infringement of the case law of the CC by the judicial bodies is one of the cases in which an *amparo* appeal can be grounded. See STC 155/2009, of 25 June 2009, Para. 2.

will be corrected by the more general linkage to the constitutional doctrine, as Article 5.1 LOPJ establishes.[81]

This doctrine is the one established with regard to constitutional provisions and the interpretation of laws.[82] If the CC declares that a certain interpretation of the legal norm is unconstitutional, the ordinary judiciary is negatively bound by the Court's judgement and can choose any possible interpretation provided that it is different to the one excluded by the Court. For example, Judgement 22/1981, where the Court declared the unconstitutionality of the fifth additional provision of the Statue of Workers if 'interpreted as a norm that establishes the incapacity to work at sixty-nine years and in a direct and unconditioned way the cessation of the employment relationship at that age.'[83] If the Court declares that there is an interpretation in conformity with the Constitution, the ordinary judiciary is positively bound and must interpret the legal norm in the sense established by the Court.[84] For example, Judgement 178/1985, where the Court declared that Article 1355 of the LEC (Code of Civil Procedure) is constitutional if it is interpreted as an entitlement for the judge to adopt, in a reasoned manner, the measure for the restriction of liberty in order to protect the assets of the bankrupt.[85]

The case law of the CC and the interpretations established in its different types of judgements can, consequently, influence the case law of ordinary courts. For example, the interpretation of a fundamental right can determine the scope of the laws that develop it, which may in turn imply the amendment of the case law of the ordinary courts with regard to such laws.[86] For example, the CC had interpreted Article 17 of the SC and the exigencies that stem from it regarding pre-trial detention, by pointing out that 'it is a measure of prudential and exceptional nature that, in no case, can this be transformed into an anticipated deprivation of liberty,'[87] with pre-trial detention only being justified in its adoption when legitimate constitutional purposes need to be reached.[88] This interpretation has influenced the way in which criminal court judges understand Articles 503 and 504 of the LECrim (Code of Criminal Procedure). For example, Order No. 516/2019 of the Second Section of the Provincial Court of Valencia makes express reference to this CC judgement and the need for the prudential measure to be addressed for the achievement of any of the purposes that the constitutional doctrine associates with pre-trial detention.[89]

81 Ignacio De la Cueva Aleu, 'Artículo 40' in Juan José González Rivas (Dir.-Coord.), *Comentarios a la Ley Orgánica del Tribunal Constitucional* (La Ley 2010) 456, 466.
82 Gómez Montoro (n 49) 628.
83 STC 22/1981, of 2 July 1981, Para. 8 and ruling.
84 Gómez Montoro (n 49) 597.
85 STC 178/1985, of 19 December 1985, Para. 2.
86 Gómez Montoro (n 49) 629.
87 STC 191/2004, of 2 November 2004, Para. 4.
88 For example, if there is a risk of reoffending. Ibid.
89 Order of the Second Section of the Provincial Court of Valencia 516/2019, of 17 May 2019, Para. 3.

In practice, how the ordinary courts and tribunals do not always respect the doctrine of the CC has been criticized, although these cases are exceptional. The main tensions have occurred with relation to the Court's decisions rendered in *amparo* appeals,[90] which reflect the difficulty of establishing the distinction between constitutional and ordinary jurisdictions.[91] For instance, in Judgement 63/2005, the Court addressed the question of the interruption of the prescription of crimes and offences, adopting an interpretation that ran counter to the dominant case law of the Supreme Court and of the Spanish criminal courts. While the Supreme Court interpreted the criminal procedure as being 'directed against the responsible person' when a suit or a complaint was filed by the offended or by the prosecution, interrupting the prescription, the CC held that this was not enough and that criminal proceedings begin only when the competent criminal court formally opens a criminal procedure.[92] The prosecutors and the Supreme Court decided not to apply this new doctrine[93] and, as we will examine later, the legislator amended the Criminal Code in 2010 in a direction that basically endorsed the Supreme Court's position.[94]

Another well-known and paradigmatic example of the tension between the CC and the Supreme Court is the so-called *Preysler* case, where the CC did not limit itself to overruling the decision of the Supreme Court, and return the case for a new decision, but affirmed the opinion of the Court of Appeals of Barcelona and awarded the plaintiff EUR 60,101.21 in order to re-establish the violated personal right and to not delay the final decision of the case.[95] The Supreme Court expressed its strong disagreement with this decision.[96]

What happened, however, in 2004, was highly improper, as García Roca points out.[97] The Civil Chamber of the Supreme Court sentenced eleven CC magistrates for civil non-contractual liability on the grounds that their decision rejecting an *amparo* appeal had been negligent.[98] The CC magistrates fielded, in turn, an

90 Ferreres Comella (n 1) 230.

91 They cannot be considered as 'different and uncommunicated worlds'. SSTC 111/1993, of 25 March 1993, Para 5; 50/1984, of 5 April 1984, Para. 3. And the CC must carry out an exercise of *self-restraint* and avoid becoming another court of justice that reviews the decisions of the other bodies. STC 92/2008, of 21 June 2008, Para. 8.

92 For more information, see José Manuel Chozas Alonso, 'Cuándo se interrumpe la prescripción en el ámbito procesal penal? Un nuevo enfrentamiento entre el Tribunal Constitucional y el Tribunal Supremo' (2005) 2 *Foro: Revista de ciencias jurídicas y sociales* 201.

93 Instruction 5/2005 issued by the Prosecution Office and Judgement of the Supreme Court 331/2006, of 24 March 2006.

94 Ferreres Comella (n 1) 231.

95 Since this was the second occasion the Supreme Court had adjudicated the case, not taking into account the previous STC 115/2000. STC 186/2001, of 17 September 2001, Para. 9. Pablo Salvador Coderch et al., 'Freedom of Speech and Power Struggles between Courts. Defamation, Privacy and Freedom of Speech in the Cases Decided by the First Chamber of the Supreme Court between 1998 and 2000 (I)' (2001) 3 *In Dret* 1, 10.

96 Ferreres Comella (n 1) 231. García Roca (n 1) 110.

97 Ibid.

98 Judgement of the Supreme Court 51/2004, of 23 January 2004.

amparo appeal against the decision, declaring the Supreme Court's decision null for violating the right to effective judicial protection.[99]

4 The CC and the legislator

As is well known, the legislator enjoys a great margin of appreciation for normative configuration and its laws have a presumption of constitutionality.[100] The main source of tension, therefore, is the CC's power to strike down laws. The Court tries, in this respect, to exercise *self-restraint* in order to avoid substituting for the legislator.[101] Therefore, when addressing the possible interpretation of a norm or part of it, the Court tries to take into account the legislator's will. Thus, we can find decisions where the Court has declared unconstitutionality without nullity. For instance, in Judgement 236/2007, the Court rejected declaring only the nullity of part of the challenged provision as 'it would entail a clear modification of the law's intention.' The Court emphasized that it was not within its competence to decide on a specific option – it was an issue related with foreign persons' rights – as its decision must be confined to stating whether or not the option chosen by the legislator is in conformity with the Constitution.[102]

The cases are even more problematic when the CC indicates to the legislator how the law should be in order to be compatible with the Constitution. This was the case, for example, for Judgement 53/1985, which was criticized by dissenting opinions, like the one issued by Magistrate Jerónimo Arozamena.[103] However, the issue in these cases is that the unconstitutionality derives from an infringement of the protection mandates that arise from certain constitutional provisions, in particular, the ones derived from the fundamental rights. The constitutional judge cannot invade the sphere that belongs to the legislator, but the Court can underline which protection requirements do lead to the unconstitutionality of the law.[104]

The CC can also decide on legal lacuna cases; that is, when the breach of the Constitution derives from the inactivity of the legislator when there is a constitutional mandate to issue norms to implement constitutional provisions.[105] In some cases, the lacuna can be covered through hermeneutic techniques. In others, this would not be possible due to the same limits of constitutional interpretation, for example, that it is not possible to concretize a mandate because the necessary rule cannot be deduced from the constitutional principles.[106] Therefore,

99 STC 133/2013, of 5 June 2013, Para. 8.
100 García Roca (n 1) 31; Pérez Royo (n 7) 78–79.
101 SSTC 5/1981, of 13 February 1981, Para. 6; 77/1985, of 27 June 1985, Para. 4; 16/1996, of 1 February 1996, Para. 6.
102 STC 236/2007, of 7 November 2007, Para. 17.
103 STC 53/1985, of 11 April 1985, dissenting opinion issued by Magistrate D. Jerónimo Arozamena Sierra.
104 Gómez Montoro (n 46) 592.
105 STC 24/1982, of 13 May 1982, Para. 3.
106 Figueruelo Burrieza (n 77) 69.

the lacuna can be addressed when the constitutional mandate can be concretized, giving immediate efficacy to the constitutional provision and using an analogy to overcome the obstacles that legal reservation implies.[107] Unconstitutionality will be declared when the omission cannot be overcome. In these cases, the Court can resort to several options: give recommendations to the legislator, use manipulative sentences, declare partial unconstitutionality in those cases relating to the infringement of the principle of equality, or declare unconstitutionality without nullity.[108] For instance, in Judgement 45/1989 (*IRPF*) the Court declared the unconstitutionality of the legal precept since it did not contemplate the possibility of a separate imposition for the members of the family unit, but it could not annul it since it was part of a legal system whose complete accommodation to the Constitution could not be reached through the sole annulment thereof. The Court indicated that it was the legislator who must carry out the pertinent reforms.[109]

The CC can also decide to give time to the legislator to correct the unconstitutionality, deferring the efficacy of nullity during a determined period,[110] when the immediate declaration of nullity could lead to serious damage. For instance, in Judgement 195/1998, nullity effects were deferred 'to the moment in which the Autonomous Community adopts the pertinent provision with which the *Marismas de Santoña* will be declared a natural protected area,' since the immediate nullity could cause environmental vulnerability in the area 'with serious damages and disturbances to the general interests at stake.'[111] These are cases where a flaw in territorial competence[112] had been detected and, therefore, the distortion that the maintenance of the unconstitutional provision provokes is less pronounced.[113]

In sum, as García Roca emphasizes, it is necessary that there is a fluid dialogue between the CC and the legislator. This dialogue has been reasonable in certain areas, such as those relating to fundamental rights.[114] For example, despite the public criticism that Judgement 53/1985 with regard to the partial decriminalization of abortion received, the parliament changed the law accordingly.[115] On other occasions the legislator did not follow the Court's decision, like Judgement 63/2005 already examined.

107 Ibid.
108 Ibid. 70–71.
109 STC 45/1989, of 20 February 1989, Para. 11.
110 De la Cueva Aleu (n 46) 449.
111 STC 195/1998, of 1 October 1998, Para. 5.
112 The delimitation of the natural park had been carried out through state law when the competence belonged to the autonomous community.
113 De la Cueva Aleu (n 46) 449.
114 García Roca (n 1) 32–33.
115 Ferreres Comella (n 1) 228.

5 Final considerations

After forty years of functioning, it can be said that law-making activity of the Court is positively evaluated. In general, legal scholars make a positive assessment,[116] emphasizing the role played by the Court during the first years of Spain's democracy, but also its contribution over these years to the legal pacification of complex conflicts.[117] However, some tensions and problems have occurred. For example, its role as the supreme interpreter of the Constitution has, on certain occasions, gone beyond what was desirable, and the Court has been put in the spotlight, with the risk of its perception by society being that of another protagonist in the political game.[118] The Court has acquired protagonism due to the lack of dialogue and consensus between political actors.[119] One of the most criticized judgements, in this respect, was the one on the Statute of Autonomy of Cataluña.[120] As Roberto Blanco points out, the political parties were responsible for forcing the Court to enter into a political battle that seriously affected the Court's reputation.[121] The Court has seen itself involved in this problem again, due to the secessionist process of Cataluña, since it has had to adjudicate numerous challenges against laws and resolutions of the Catalonian parliament proclaiming, for example, the sovereignty of the people of Catalonia or the right to 'self-determination.' Undoubtedly, the CC is faced with a political problem. However, the lack of political answers and the challenges to the adopted decisions have transferred the conflict to the Court. The Court has been put at the centre of the political dispute. Nonetheless, on this occasion, the Court has recovered its reputation as an impartial body, trying to resolve the issues in a short timeframe alongside exercising *self-restraint*.[122] The Court has noted that it cannot solve the dispute and that the public authorities, including the local ones, 'are the ones entrusted with resolving any matters arising in this field, through dialogue and cooperation.'[123]

Another problem that is usually highlighted is the workload of the Court. Although the Court has tried to keep on reducing the number of pending issues and the time necessary to adjudicate the laws whose constitutionality is challenged, some decisions are still adopted with an excessive delay: between three and five years for *amparo* appeals, and even ten years in constitutional challenges and some

116 García Roca (n 1) 4; Pablo Pérez Tremps, *Sistema de Justicia Constitucional* (Civitas-Thomson Reuters 2016) 189; Roberto L. Blanco Valdés, *Luz tras las tinieblas. Vindicación de la España Constitucional* (Alianza Editorial 2018) 183.

117 Blanco Valdés (n 118) 184.

118 Ibid., 193.

119 Díaz Revorio (n 22) 30.

120 STC 31/2010, of 28 June 2010. This resolution opened a serious gap up between the Court and the Catalonian authorities. Josep Maria Castellà Andreu, 'Tribunal Constitucional y proceso secesionista catalán: respuestas jurídico-constitucionales a un conflicto político-constitucional' (2016) 37 *Teoría y Realidad Constitucional* 561, 561–565.

121 Blanco Valdés (n 118) 183.

122 Castellà Andreu (n 122) 590.

123 STC 42/2014, of 25 March 2014, Para. 4.

constitutional conflicts.[124] These delays affect the legitimacy of the institution since, as Pérez Tremps points out, they weaken the Court's role as a guarantor of rights and an arbiter of conflicts.[125] In fact, citizens' trust has declined in the past few years with respect to institutions, including the Court, which, in a report carried out between April 2015 and July 2016, did not reach the 'pass' score.[126]

Last, it must also be noted that despite the CC usually making reference to the ECtHR and the CJEU case law, the LOTC does not contain any mention of the possible conflict between the EU law and the Constitution; neither does it mention the ECtHR and its case law, notwithstanding the undeniable Europeanization of the legal order and the concurrence of jurisdictions and declarations. Therefore, as García Roca emphasizes, it is necessary to establish mechanisms to solve the conflicts between legal norms, in particular the ones relating to the recognition and guarantee of fundamental rights, and thus facilitate the dialogue between the CC, the ECtHR, and the CJEU.[127]

In any case, despite the problems that can be detected and that need to be corrected, there is no doubt that the existence of the Court is essential for the democratic Spanish State and for ensuring the supremacy of the Constitution, pacifying the conflicts that, if it were not for its interpretations, could not be solved at the political level.[128]

124 Pablo Pérez Tremps (n 118) 194. For instance, the action of unconstitutionality brought before the CC on 16 October 2009 against certain provisions of the Law of the Catalonian Parliament 12/2009 was adjudicated on 11 April 2019, STC 51/2019.

125 Pérez Tremps (n 118) 165.

126 Marta Romero, '¿Cuál es el alcance del descrétido institucional?', *eldiario.es*, 15 April 2018.

127 García Roca (n 1) 118 et seq. With respect to this dialogue, see Javier García Roca, 'El diálogo entre el Tribunal Europeo de Derechos Humanos, los Tribunales Constitucionales y otros órganos jurisdiccionales en el espacio convencional europeo', in Eduardo Ferrer Mac-Gregor, Alfonso Herrera García (eds.), *Diálogo Jurisprudencial en Derechos Humanos. Entre Tribunales Constitucionales y Cortes Internacionales* (Tirant lo Blanch 2013) 219.

128 Blanco Valdés (n 118) 187.

Part II

Central and Eastern European Constitutional Courts

5 The Constitutional Court of the Republic of Bulgaria as a law-maker

Martin Belov and Aleksandar Tsekov

1 Legal status of the Constitutional Court of the Republic of Bulgaria

Both the Constitutional Court (CC) and constitutional control are among the great novelties introduced by the 1991 Constitution. Until 1991, neither centralized control for constitutionality concentrated in the Supreme Court, CC or constitutional council, nor diffuse control for constitutionality accomplished by all courts, existed in the Bulgarian constitutional order. There have been some suggestions in legal theory for the establishment of constitutional control during the Tarnovo Constitution (1879–1947), but they remained isolated opinions.

Thus, the provision of control for constitutionality became possible only after the fall of the Berlin Wall in 1989. In fact, it became not only possible, but even inevitable, due to several reasons. First, all Central and Eastern European states have adopted a centralized model for constitutional control structured around the CC. The Bulgarian constitutional legislator joined this common trend. Indeed, the 1991 Bulgarian Constitution was the first entirely new post-communist constitution adopted in Central and Eastern Europe. However, the trend in favour of the establishment of centralized control for constitutionality accomplished by a CC was already visible. Second, this type of control for constitutionality was already well established in most of the Western and Southern European countries. This is particularly true for Italy whose model has been chosen as the main prototype for shaping the Bulgarian CC. Third, the founding fathers and mothers of the 1991 Constitution were generally aware of the fact that control for constitutionality is a cornerstone of the principle of rule of law, which they enshrined in the constitutional axiology of the current Bulgarian Constitution.

The choice of the European model of control for constitutionality has been predetermined by several factors. Bulgaria traditionally belongs to the continental legal system. The intellectual influence of legal realism is nominal to non-existent, in sharp contrast to Kelsenian normativism and legal positivism. The institutional influence of the US constitutional model is meagre. Moreover, the Bulgarian constitutional legislator has deliberately chosen, as models for legal transplantation of constitutional control, the Italian and to a lesser extent the Spanish, German, and Austrian Constitutions. Indeed, there are many differences among these four

DOI: 10.4324/9781003022442-6

models but also one main common feature. They provide a concentrated model for constitutional control centralized in a CC.

The Bulgarian CC has been established by virtue of the 1991 Constitution and the CC Act, which was adopted in the same year. The CC is an independent state institution. It is coequal with the other central state institutions – the Parliament, the Council of Ministers, the President, the Supreme Court of Cassation, the Supreme Administrative Court, the State Prosecutor General, and the Ombudsman.

The 1991 Constitution allocates the CC outside of the judicial power. Thus, the Bulgarian CC is institutionally independent from the judicial power institutions. Moreover, there is no formal and institutional hierarchy between the CC, the Supreme Court of Cassation, and the Supreme Administrative Court. This is also due to the fact that the decisions of the two Supreme Courts cannot be appealed (e.g. by virtue of a constitutional complaint) in front of the CC. In other words, all Bulgarian courts, including the Supreme Court of Cassation and the Supreme Administrative Court, must obey and follow the decisions of the CC. This is due to the fact that they are not only binding for them but also superior sources of law.

The Bulgarian CC is composed of 12 judges. One third are elected by the National Assembly, one third by the general assembly of the Supreme Court of Cassation and the Supreme Administrative Court, and one third are appointed by the President of the Republic. Indeed, the judges of the CC are supposed to be fully neutral and impartial. There is a system of safeguards for their neutrality and impartiality, e.g. the requirement for professional and ethical qualities, independence from the constituent institutions, high salaries, immunity, irremovability, etc. However, the 1991 Constitution entrenches internal checks and balances in the composition of the CC, which aim at preventing its transformation into a biased institution. The most important of them is the separation of the patronage power[1] for appointment or election of CC judges among the President, the Parliament, and the two supreme courts.

Another safeguard is the mismatch between the terms of office of the CC judges. The CC is a permanent institution, whereas the judges possess nine years non-renewable term of office. However, their terms of office do not expire simultaneously. Each three years, the term of office of one third of the judges expires and they are replaced by new judges. This replacement is done on the basis of a formula according to which if two judges are to be elected by the President, one by the Parliament, and one by the supreme courts, then after three years it is the Parliament which elects two of them, and in six years this number applies to the quota of the supreme courts, while the other two institutions elect one judge each. Hence, there is a rotation of the number of judges, which can be elected or appointed by the three constitutive institutions.

The Bulgarian CC possesses numerous important competences. The most important and widely used among them is the posterior control for constitutionality and compliance with the international and EU law of the acts of the Parliament.

1 See Martin Belov, *Constitutional Law of the Republic of Bulgaria* (Kluwer 2019).

The CC can control the compliance also of the parliamentary regulations and the decrees of the President with the Constitution, but this is rarely the case. Moreover, the CC accomplishes preventive control for the compliance of the international treaties with the Bulgarian Constitution.

Hence, the institutional centre of the CC's competences is the control for compliance with the normative hierarchy of the Bulgarian legal order. The control for compliance of the acts of Parliament with the 1991 Constitution is the most frequently used competence of the Court. It should be noted, however, that frequently the CC is approached to control simultaneously the compliance of the acts of Parliament with both the Constitution and the international treaties.

The Bulgarian CC possesses the relatively rare, in comparative perspective, competence for abstract interpretation of the Constitution. This allows the Court to function as de facto constitutional legislator, accomplishing virtual amendment of the 1991 Constitution by virtue of constitutional interpretation. The Court frequently uses teleological (purposive) interpretation and broadens or narrows the scope of constitutional concepts thus implicitly accomplishing constitutional policy-making.

Furthermore, the CC possesses competences for defence of the constitutional order. It can pronounce the impeachment of the President or Vice President of the Republic due to high treason or violation of the Constitution. It can also declare political parties as unconstitutional if they aim at violent ascent to power or are based on ethnicity, race or religion. The CC controls also the legality of parliamentary and presidential elections.

The CC is also vested with the power to resolve conflicts for competences regarding the horizontal and vertical separation of powers. It can resolve such competence disputes between the Parliament, the Council of Ministers, and the President of the Republic, as well as between the Council of Ministers and the municipal councils. However, there is a very limited number of cases related to these two competences. Especially, the case law on the resolution of conflicts for competences between the Council of Ministers and the municipal councils is rather scarce. These cases are initiated by the municipal councils and most of them are declared inadmissible by the CC.

It is remarkable that the Bulgarian CC is among the rather rare cases of constitutional jurisdictions which cannot be approached directly by the citizen. This means that the 1991 Constitution does not provide for a direct constitutional complaint. There are only three indirect ways the citizens may approach the CC. First, they may approach the national Ombudsman, who can then initiate a case for defence of constitutionally proclaimed human rights infringed by an act of Parliament. Second, they can defend the same type of rights against infringement by the act of Parliament via the Supreme Bar Council. These two procedures are in fact indirect constitutional complaints. They are slow and dependent on the discretion of the Ombudsman or the Supreme Bar Council.

The third option is to raise claims for unconstitutionality during a pending case in front of a regular or specialized court, which can then approach the Supreme Court of Cassation or the Supreme Administrative Court with the demand that they shall approach the CC. In fact, this is not a constitutional complaint because the initiator (the parties to the pending law suit) does not possess the formalized right to claim unconstitutionality. They are entirely dependent on the decisions of several institutions. Thus, their path to the CC is a very remote one.

The CC can be approached by various state institutions. Some of them have the general competence to approach the Court with regard to all of its competences (with a few exceptions, which are expressly limited to concrete institutions). The general competence to approach the CC belongs to one-fifth of the MPs, the President, the Council of Ministers, the Supreme Court of Cassation, the Supreme Administrative Court, and the State Prosecutor General.

Furthermore, there are institutions which can approach the CC with regard to a specific and particular competence. It has already been mentioned that the municipal councils may initiate procedures for resolution of competence conflicts with the Council of Ministers. The Ombudsman and the Supreme Bar Council may approach the CC with the claim for declaration of unconstitutionality of acts of Parliament infringing constitutionally proclaimed human rights.

The decisions of the CC are published in the State Gazette (the Official Journal of the state). They enter into force three days after their publication. It has to be emphasized that this procedure is similar to the procedure for publication and entering into force of the acts of Parliament. It is an indicator of proximity of the effects of the acts of Parliament and the CC's decisions for declaration of unconstitutionality of acts of Parliament.

2 The Constitutional Court as a negative legislator

The law-making activity of the CCs is manifested in two main directions: a negative function of repealing certain acts, and a positive function of creating or amending legal acts. The Bulgarian CC makes no exception in this respect.

The negative function is manifested in the activity of the CC as a body, competent to repeal both ordinary legislative acts (negative statutory legislator) and unconstitutional constitutional amendments[2] (negative constitutional legislator).

2.1 The Constitutional Court as a negative statutory legislator

Is it possible to define the Bulgarian CC as a negative legislator? The Constitution provides that any act found to be unconstitutional *shall cease to apply* as of the date

2 For the concept of unconstitutional constitutional amendments, see e.g. Yaniv Roznai, 'Unconstitutional Constitutional Amendments – The Migration and Success of a Constitutional Idea' (2013) 61(3) *American Journal of Comparative Law* 657; Yaniv Roznai, *Unconstitutional Constitutional Amendments: The Limits of Amendment Powers* (Oxford University Press 2017); Gábor Halmai, 'Unconstitutional Constitutional Amendments: Constitutional Courts as Guardians of the Constitution?' (2012) 19(2) *Constellations* 182; Aharon Barak, 'Unconstitutional Constitutional Amendments' (2011) 44 *Israel Law Review* 321; Otto Pfersmann, 'Unconstitutional Constitutional Amendments: A Normativist Approach' (2012) 67(1) *Zeitschrift für öffentliches Recht* 81.

on which the ruling shall come into force (Art. 151, para. 2) and any part of a law, which is not ruled unconstitutional, *shall remain in force* (Art. 151, para. 3). In the 1990s, the doctrine raised the question of the meaning of the phrase 'shall cease to apply.'[3] The CC provides an answer to this question. Decision No. 22 of the CC of 31 October 1995 on constitutional case No. 25/95 sets out (particularly in its reasoning) that the phrase 'shall cease to apply' contains a prohibition on the application of the law in the future. The CC considers this prohibition as 'unconditional, imperative, and permanent.' According to the CC, as a consequence of this prohibition, the declared unconstitutional act of Parliament ceases to be valid law and thus to have any regulatory force. In the Court's view, this conclusion is also supported by the provision of Art. 151, para. 3 of the Constitution, according to which, 'any part of a law which is not declared unconstitutional shall remain in force.' The CC considers that 'by an argument to the contrary,' that the part of the law, which is unconstitutional, loses its effect, which means that it ceases to exist in the future.

The CC's decision, which declares an act of Parliament to be unconstitutional is equal to revoking the act of Parliament by the National Assembly itself (Art. 84, para. 1 of the Constitution). The repeal of an act of Parliament by the National Assembly and the annulment of an act of Parliament by declaring it unconstitutional by a decision of the CC both lead to the same consequences – the suspension of the future validity of the act of Parliament. Hence, an act of Parliament can be repealed not only by the National Assembly but also by the CC when it is unconstitutional.

2.2 The Constitutional Court as a negative constitutional legislator

Many CCs control the conformity of constitutional amendments, adopted in the form of constitutional laws with the Constitution. In theory, such control is permissible in legal systems providing a distinction within the formal constitutional law (hierarchical distinction of formal constitutional law)[4] or so-called 'constitutional polymorphism.'[5] This means that the power of constitutional revision is limited and the constituent power has provided for different procedures for the creation (or abolition) of formal constitutional law, and sometimes there are explicit prohibitions on the abrogation of certain norms. The distinction within the formal constitutional law has two manifestations. The first one is the hard constitutional core according to which certain elements of the Constitution

3 Zhivko Stalev, Neno Nenovski. *The Constitutional Court and the legal force of its decisions* (Sibi 1996) 9 (*in Bulgarian*); Boris Spassov, 'Variations on Theme from the Constitution (Art. 151, sec. 2)' (1997) 2, 27 (*in Bulgarian*).

4 Louis Favoreu et al., *Droit constitutionnel* (Dalloz 2005) 107–110; Xavier Magnon, 'Quelques maux encore à propos des lois de révision constitutionnelle: limites, contrôle, efficacité, caractère opératoire et existence' (2004) 59 *Revue française de droit constitutionnel*, 595.

5 See Pfersmann, (n 2) 81.

cannot be amended.[6] The second one is the flexible constitutional core that allows all constitutional provision to be amended, but not in the same way.[7]

In this context, the constitutionality of constitutional norms, and in particular, the existence of an 'unconstitutional constitutional amendment' are discussed. The possibility of such a change is a result of the 'new constitutional normativity,'[8] which imposes limits on constitutional revision. The potential for 'unconstitutional constitutional amendments' allows the CC to control whether the institutions competent to amend the constitution have respected the imposed constraints and especially the procedural or substantive limits for constitutional change. The distinction between different normative levels within the general framework of formal constitutional law serves as a basis for the exercise of constitutional control over constitutional revision. Thus, certain constitutional norms (those enjoying additional protection) serve as a standard and criterion for controlling other, inferior constitutional norms.[9] Through the constitutional review of a constitutional amendment, the CC is functioning as a constituent body. It controls another constituent body with competence to amend the constitution whether it exceeds its competence or not, and does not act as a primary constituent power.[10] Constitutional control of constitutional amendments is a subject of debate, both in academic circles and in the practice of increasing the number of CCs.[11] The Bulgarian CC is among those which, in principle, accepts its competence to exercise such control and even has the opportunity to repeal constitutional amendments as unconstitutional.

The Bulgarian Constitution of 12 July 1991 is characterized by a distinction within the formal constitutional law. All constitutional provisions can be amended, however not in the same way. Chapter IX of the Constitution provides for two different revision procedures depending on the subject matter of the constitutional amendment.[12] The principle distinction between the two main procedures for

6 e.g. Art. 79, al. 3 of the German constitution, Art. 139 of the Italian constitution, Art. 89, al. 5 of the French constitution.

7 e.g. Art. 44–46 of the Austrian Federal Constitutional Law, Art. 166–169 of the Spanish constitution, Art. 153–163 of the Bulgarian constitution.

8 Claude Klein, 'Le contrôle des lois constitutionnelles. Introduction à une problématique moderne' (2009) 27 *Les Cahiers du Conseil constitutionnel* 9.

9 Pfersmann, (n 2) p. 103.

10 E. J. Sieyès. *Qu'est-ce que le Tiers état?* (Flammarion 1988); Carl Schmitt, *Théorie de la constitution* (Presses Universitaires de France 1993); Olivier Beaud, 'Maastricht et la théorie constitutionnelle. La nécessaire et inévitable distinction entre le pouvoir constituant et le pouvoir de révision constitutionnelle' (1993) Les petites affiches 31 mars et 2 avril, (n 39) et (n 40), 14, 7; Claude Klein, *Théorie et pratique du pouvoir constituant*, (Presses Universitaires de France 1996), 217; Arnaud Le Pillouer, 'Le pouvoir constituant originaire et le pouvoir constituant derivé: à propos de l'émergence d'une distinction conceptuelle' (2005–2006) 25–26 Revue d'histoire des facultés de droit et science politique, 123.

11 See Kemal Gözler, *Judicial Review of Constitutional Amendments: A Comparative Study*, (Ekin Press 2008); See Roznai (n 2).

12 See Belov (n 1); Evgeni Tanchev, Martin Belov, 'The Bulgarian Constitutional Order, Supranational Constitutionalism and European Governance' in Albi A., Bardutzky S. (eds.) *National Constitutions in European and Global Governance: Democracy, Rights, the Rule of Law* (T.M.C. Asser Press 2019) 1133.

constitutional amendment is provided by Art. 153. According to this article, the National Assembly (NA) is competent to amend all provisions of the 1991 Constitution with the exception of the provisions which fall within the competences of the Grand National Assembly (GNA).

The Bulgarian Constitution does not explicitly provide for the possibility of judicial review of the constitutional amendments. Nevertheless, the CC has adopted a decision devoted especially to this issue.[13] The Court accepts that a constitutional amendment adopted by the National Assembly is subject to a check for compliance with the Constitution by the CC. The Court has to verify that the procedure for constitutional amendment has been duly observed. More precisely, the Court is allowed to control the compliance of the constitutional amendment with the separation of the competences between the NA and the GNA.

In 2003, the CC adopted the principle stance that control on the act for amendment of the Constitution is admissible. Later on, in 2006, the Court has been approached with the demand to check the constitutionality of a constitutional amendment adopted by the NA, according to which, the Chairman of the Supreme Court of Cassation, the Chairman of the Supreme Administrative Court, and the State Prosecutor General shall be dismissed from office by the President of the Republic on proposal of a quarter of the Members of the NA adopted by a two-thirds majority. The CC has declared this amendment to be unconstitutional.[14]

The Bulgarian CC plays an increasingly active role in both statutory and constitutional law-making. In that regard, the traditional dichotomy between 'legislating' and 'judging' is being blurred. Nevertheless, there are several limitations in this law-making activity of the CC. The Court is limited because it: (1) pronounces on an act adopted by another institution; (2) pronounces on the initiative of another institution; and (3) is obliged to provide motives to its decisions. Altogether these circumstances make a distinction between the NA and the CC in their functioning as positive legislators. The judge's discretion in deciding the case is important. However, the CC's judges cannot create, on a discretionary and political basis, legal rules with a content that has been freely elaborated.

Currently, the Bulgarian CC can no longer be perceived and conceptualized only as a 'negative legislator' as the idea of constitutional review has been initially conceived in the early twentieth century. The constitutional adjudication has progressively evolved. However, in some cases, more than being assistants to the legislator, the constitutional jurisdiction has just substituted for it, assuming the role of 'positive legislator'[15] by issuing alternative legislatives rules. The gradual development of this alternative positive legislative competence acquired by the CCs raises many issues and may be perceived as problematic.

13 Case 22/2002, of 10 April 2003.

14 Case 6/2006, of 13 September 2006.

15 Allan Randolph Brewer-Carías, 'CCs as Positive Legislators' in K. Brown & D. Snyder (ed.) *General Reports of the XVIIIth Congress of the International Academy of Comparative Law/Rapports Généraux du XVIIIème Congrès de l'Académie Internationale de Droit Comparé* (Springer 2012) 549.

3 The Constitutional Court as an alternative positive legislator

It is important to briefly clarify the concept of interpretation. The distinction between legal norm and legal text is of particular importance in law. The norm is the meaning(s) of the text, i.e. deontic modality, denoting that something is mandatory, forbidden or permitted. The linguistic formulations that constitute a natural language always have a certain degree of indeterminacy. This indeterminacy results from the vague and/or polysemic nature of words that go into the composition of utterances. This is especially true of the way constitutional texts are formulated. The degree of this indeterminacy is an open question. It is quite possible that different texts (linguistic formulations) contain a single rule or one single text contains multiple norms. Often, the legal rules are even deliberately formulated in vague and indeterminate terms so as to leave a greater margin of appreciation for their application. Interpretation, in the sense used here, means the purely cognitive activity of determining the content of a normative text.[16]

Interpretation as an analysis and extraction of the meaning can only identify the entire spectrum of possible norms (meanings) in the prescriptive text. Once interpretation has defined the array of discretion of the judge due to the semantic indeterminacy and vagueness of legal texts, the Court has to make a choice among different possible outcomes and to state how it uses its discretion to resolve the case. This operation can be defined as specification.[17] The Court has to provide arguments in order to justify this choice. In this context, it may be assumed that an argument aimed at justifying an outcome, which does not fall inside the range of possible meanings established by interpretation, is incorrect. All other outcomes are in this sense 'correct.'

It is worth mentioning here that the Bulgarian CC explicitly rejects the possibility of acting as a positive legislator. It tries to not replace 'the content of the interpretative power – to clarify the exact meaning of a particular constitutional provision – and to not turn the court into an advisory body or an instance acting as positive legislator, which is clearly outside its powers.'[18]

However, the methods of interpretation that are traditionally available to courts, and explored by theory, frequently do not have epistemological but rather volitional nature. This means that interpretation is not always used for cognitive analysis of the meaning of a set of prescriptive propositions but rather is used instrumentally for implication of meaning. The notion of interpretation often refers to the judicial competence to decide otherwise than the text requires.[19] Let us take as an example the 'teleological' or 'purposive' interpretation as favoured in

16 Otto Pfersmann, 'Le sophisme onomastique: changer au lieu de connaître. L'interprétation de la Constitution', in F. Mélin-Soucramanien (ed.), *L'interprétation constitutionnelle* (Dalloz 2005) 33; Arthur Dyèvre, 'Comprendre et analyser l'activité décisionnelle des cours et des tribunaux: l'intérêt de la distinction entre interprétation et concrétisation' (2010) 4 *Jus Politicum*, 7.

17 See Dyèvre (n 16) 11.

18 Case 7/2005, of 1 September 2005.

19 See Pfersmann (n 16) 33–60.

the doctrine by Aharon Barak[20] and frequently practised by the Bulgarian CC. According to the Court:[21]

> while interpreting constitutional provisions, the CC inevitably examines and establishes the actual will of their original creators. This guarantees legal stability and the rule of law, and protects the fundamental constitutional ideas and values. At the same time, this approach is not incompatible with an evolutionary, teleological interpretation, when the same ideas and values must be protected in a fundamentally changed social context. In order to maximize its positive effect, the Constitution must be seen not as a 'fossilized' phenomenon, but as a living organism. The abandonment of old interpretations and the adoption of new views on the content of individual constitutional norms is permissible in the practice of the CC.

In this case the Court accomplishes its reasoning in three steps and only the first one constitutes an interpretation in the sense which has been described on p. 98.

The first step comprises the analysis of the text's meaning. During the second step the 'purpose' of the required behaviour is explored. The third step determines whether the realization of the purpose can be achieved by virtue of behaviour which is differing from that required by the text. As a result, the judge changes the deontic modality of the norm: instead of being forbidden, the behaviour in question will rather be, for example, permitted. This is a kind of 'evolutionary interpretation.' It results from an enlargement of the elements of choice.

Although such ideas might seem morally attractive, these arguments do not justify the adoption of alternative legislation by the judge. However, the Bulgarian CC is not legally empowered to produce such rules, i.e. to amend the Constitution or the statutory legislation. For this reason, this activity is concealed in the form of 'interpretation.' This can be explained by the fact that interpretation in this sense is not perceived as a cognitive activity of determining the content of a normative text, i.e. 'interpretation is not just discovery. It is also creation. The question is, what 'creation' is best.'[22] The judge, instead of limiting himself to the admissible outcomes according to the wording of the

20 For Aharon Barak the purposive interpretation 'combines subjective elements (subjective purpose; author's intent; subjective teleology) with objective elements (objective intent; the intent of the reasonable author and the legal system's fundamental values; objective teleology) so that they work simultaneously, rather than in different phases of the interpretive process.' Aharon Barak, *Purposive Interpretation in Law* (Princeton University Press 2005) 88. However, when the data on the subjective and objective purpose of a constitution are inconsistent, the purposive interpretation gives weight to objective purpose in constitutional interpretation because 'only then can the constitution fulfill its aim; only then can it guide human behavior over generations of social change; only then can the constitution respond to modern needs; only then can it balance the past, present, and future. The past guides the present, but it does not enslave it'. Ibid., 384–385.

21 Case 7/2015, of 17 September 2015.

22 See Aharon Barak (n 20) 218.

text, decides what the law in his opinion ought to be and combines a different set of legal norms within the same text.[23]

In the field of constitutional review a new technique has emerged because of the problem of legitimacy posed by the possibility of invalidating acts of Parliament passed by democratically elected representative assemblies – the Parliaments. This technique is defined as 'conformity interpretation.' The CC has to find a way to simultaneously guarantee the rights of citizens or the parliamentary opposition without entering into a frontal conflict with the parliamentary majority that has adopted the challenged law. The Bulgarian Constitution admits only two outcomes of this dilemma: to declare the legislative provision to be either unconstitutional or in compliance with the Constitution. The 'conformity interpretation' is not explicitly provided by the Constitution. Instead, it is created by the CC as a third, 'intermediate' solution. This technique has its supporters in the Bulgarian doctrine.[24]

The 'conformity interpretation' consists in proclaiming that a legislative text that contains at least two or more meanings is constitutional according to one or more of the meanings and unconstitutional according to another meaning(s). An example of such practice is the decision of the CC to rule on the compliance with the Constitution of a text of the Regulation for the Organization and Activity of the National Assembly (ROANA).[25] The text stipulates that the NA and the respective parliamentary committee may impose an obligation to state official or citizen to appear in front of it and to deliver answers to the questions posed by the committee. There has been claim that this provision of ROANA is contrary to Art. 8 of the Constitution, which provides for the principle of separation of powers.

The CC accepts that the NA may require from any Bulgarian citizen or state official, regardless of their rank, to appear in front of the Parliament. In this sense, the ROANA's provision, which is claimed to be unconstitutional, is actually not in contradiction with the Constitution. However, the CC stipulates in the motives to the decision that due to the principle of separation of powers here are several office holders that must be granted exception from the obligation to appear in front of the committee and to respond to questions of the MPs. The range of these privileged persons includes the President, the Vice President, the CC judges and all magistrates. The CC acknowledges that the ROANA's provision under consideration is not inconsistent with the Constitution and therefore does not declare it unconstitutional. However, the Court requires explicit definition of the persons to which the obligation to appear in front of the committee and to deliver information does not apply.

The technique of 'conformity interpretation' implies the necessity of interpreting the text, which reveals its different meanings. However, in essence, it consists

23 See Otto Pfersmann (n 16) 49.

24 Zhivko Stalev, 'Legal force of the decisions of the Constitutional Court declaring a statutory legislation as unconstitutional' in Stalev & Nenovski, (n 11) 34–35; Neno Nenovski, 'About the "conditional conformity" of the statutory legislation with the Constitution' (1997) 3–4, *Legal thought*, 25 (*in Bulgarian*).

25 Case 3/95, of 17 May 1995; see also Case 19/1996, of 14 November 1996.

of partial annulment, and sometimes in the creation of new norms by virtue of adding to the text of meaning, which the Court considers to be missing, i.e. substitution by alternative legislative provisions. Thus, this kind of judicial review allows the CC to act as an alternative positive legislator. This way, the Court extends its powers, judging which of the norms expressed in a legislative provision should remain in force, which should be removed, and which should be amended. The exercising of such power requires explicit constitutional empowerment. Such empowerment, however, cannot be found in the Bulgarian Constitution.

The Bulgarian CC often refers to the jurisprudence of the European Court of Human Rights (ECtHR) when it is necessary to determine the content of constitutionally established rights and freedoms. It interprets the constitutional texts in conformity with the ECtHR's case law.[26] The CC holds that 'the interpretation of the relevant provisions of the Constitution in the field of human rights should be as consistent as possible with the interpretation of the European Convention on Human Rights (ECHR) norms.'[27] According to the CC, 'this principle of interpretation in conformity with the ECHR is also consistent with the internationally recognized binding jurisdiction of the ECtHR over the interpretation and application of the ECHR.'[28] The CC defends its position by considering that the 'ECHR norms in the field of human rights have a pan-European and civilizational significance for the legal order of the States which are parties to the ECHR, and thus have the status of norms of the European public order.'[29]

In short, the position of the CC makes it clear that constitutional texts in the field of fundamental rights must have a meaning that is consistent with the ECHR. The ECtHR is competent to interpret the provisions of the Convention in a legally binding manner. Consequently, the CC considers that the constitutional texts should also be consistent with the interpretation provided by the ECtHR. That is why, the CC refers also to ECtHR decisions which do not directly address violations of the ECHR accomplished by the Republic of Bulgaria.

The quasi-legislative activity of the CCs accomplished in the form of interpretation is usually contained in the motives to the Courts' decisions rather than in the dispositive part. The status, role, and function of the motives to the CC's decisions is central for constitutional theory. The thesis for the binding legal force of the motives to the CC's decisions is generally supported in the Bulgarian legal doctrine.[30] The CC did not expressly rule on the issue, accepting that 'the question of the binding force of the motives to the CC's decision requires special discussion and principled resolution, and the Court cannot rule on this issue incidentally.'[31]

26 The CC does not analyze the practice of other CCs as it does with the judgements of the ECtHR.
27 Case 15/97, of 18 February 1998.
28 Ibid.
29 Ibid.
30 Pencho Penev, Normative and practical outlines of the Bulgarian constitutional justice ('Svetulka 44' 2013) 161–162; See Stalev, (n 11) 16–18.
31 Case 26/95, of 6 February 1996.

Motivation of decisions can be seen as a safeguard against arbitrariness of the Court's decision-making because it constitutes an obligation of reasoned justification of the normative production resulting in the dispositive part of the decision. Indeed, the motives are not norms. They differ from the norms in a substantial manner.[32] Justification for the adoption of a legal rule is an element of the rule of law, but the transformation of the motives into norms may actually endanger the rule of law. Blurring of the limits between reasoning and norm creation transforms the CC from a 'guardian of the Constitution'[33] into an alternative positive legislator. Such a way of reasoning may trigger gradual and implicit transformation of the civil law systems into a variant of a mixed system with elements of a common law system.

Now, let's turn to the question of whether the CC's judgements are respected by the courts. The CC's decisions are binding on all government bodies, legal entities, and citizens (Art. 14, para. 6 of the CC Act) It has already been explained that the CC acts upon the initiative of the Supreme Court of Cassation, the Supreme Administrative Court, the Supreme Court of Cassation, and the Supreme Administrative Court shall suspend the proceedings on a pending case and shall refer the matter to the CC if they find a discrepancy between an act of Parliament and the Constitution. The Code of Civil Procedure states that the court suspends the case when the CC allows substantive examination of a claim challenging the constitutionality of the act of Parliament applicable to the case (Art. 229, para. 1, p. 6); a similar text is applicable also in the administrative process (Art. 54, para. 1, point 4 of the Administrative Procedure Code). In practice, when the courts hear the case, they take into account the decisions of the CC.

The Bulgarian doctrine maintains that the courts are legally obliged to invoke the reasons of the CC's decisions since they are legally binding. There is no explicit answer to this question in positive law (including case law). Courts often refer to the CC's motives without indicating whether they regard them as binding normative statements or just as a source of inspiration. For example, the Supreme Administrative Court, referring to the motives of Decision No. 2 of 21 February 2019 on constitutional case No. 2/2018, annuls a decision for state prosecutor dismissal taken by the state prosecutor's panel of the SJC.[34] The Supreme Administrative Court accepts that the Supreme Judicial Council may remove a magistrate from office and instructs the Supreme Judicial Council to give reasons for its decision.

32 See Régis Ponsard, 'Questions de principe sur "l'autorité de la chose interprétée par le Conseil constitutionnel": normativité et pragmatisme', in B. Mathieu & M. Verpeaux (ed.), *L'autorité des décisions du Conseil constitutionnel*, (Dalloz 2010) 29; Otto Pfersmann, 'Le problème des normes paratopiques', in M. Fromont, M-A. Frison-Roche, T. Morais Da Costa, G. Viereira Da Costa Ceraqueira, B. Graeff & T. Marinini Vilarino (ed.), *Droit français et droit brésilien: perspectives nationales et comparées*, (Bruylant 2012) 557.

33 Hans Kelsen. *Qui doit être le gardien de la Constitution?* (Michel Houdiard Editeur 2006).

34 See Case 13600/2018, of 28 June 2019 (Supreme Administrative Court); Interpretative decision of the Supreme Court of Cassation No. 3 of 22 December 2015; Decision No. 24 of 1 February 2016.

There is one more interesting issue, which still has no answer in case law. The amendment of the Code of Civil Procedure adopted in 2017,[35] allows for appeals to the Supreme Court of Cassation to be based on claims for contradiction of the appellate courts' decisions with decisions of the CC of the Republic of Bulgaria (Art. 280, para. 1, point 2 of the Code of Civil Procedure). However, it is not clear whether a decision which contradicts the arguments set out in the motives of the CC's decisions can be considered as a legitimate ground for cassation appeal. More precisely, the question may be raised as to whether a decision of the appellate courts, which is not in compliance with the conformity interpretation of the CC related to a particular provision of an act of Parliament, can be considered as contradictory to the case law of the CC. Here again, the question is whether the motives for the CC's decisions are legally binding.

The Court, especially in its interpretative decisions, implies or changes (broadens or narrows) the meaning of the constitutional texts. The Court does so both in the motives and in the dispositive part of the decisions.

A typical example of a decision extending the meaning of a text is Decision No. 3 of 10 April 2003 on constitutional case No. 22/2002. Here the Court defines the elements of the 'form of government and the form of territorial distribution of power' according to Art. 158 of the Constitution,[36] which establishes the formal soft 'core' of the Bulgarian Constitution. This constitutional core can easily be highlighted as it enjoys enhanced constitutional protection consisting in rigid amendment procedure, which is much more sophisticated than the 'ordinary' amendment procedure.

However, by virtue of this decision, the Bulgarian CC shifts the boundaries between both procedures for amendment of the constitution. The Court assumes that, due to the importance of certain constitutional norms, they must enjoy special protection. This is particularly noticeable in the Court's decisions, in which it accomplishes wider and extensive interpretation[37] of the 'form of government.' In the dispositive part of Decision No. 3 of 10 April 2003 on constitutional case No. 22/2002, the Court provides that the form of government is defined not just by the nature of the state, which may be a parliamentary or presidential republic or monarchy, but includes the system of supreme state institutions such as the National Assembly, the President and Vice President, the Council of Ministers, the CC, and the Judiciary, their existence, position within the relevant power, organization, conditions, constitution, and tenure. According to the Court, the form of state government includes also the functions and competences that the Constitution vests in these institutions in accordance with the main constitutional principles.

According to the decisions of the CC a change *within* the established form of government: a parliamentary republic, may lead to a change *of* the form of government. The CC thus mixes the notions of the form of government and the

35 State Gazette No. 86, of 27 September 2017.

36 Art. 158 states that a Grand National Assembly shall resolve on any changes in the form of State structure or form of government.

37 Case 22/2002, of 10 April 2003.

existence and functioning of government bodies, within the limits imposed by that form. The argumentation is not very solid, but rather based on political expediency.[38] Later, in 2016, the CC invoked the reasons for this decision (of 2003) in order to justify that the reduction in the number of deputies constitutes a change in the form of government that cannot be voted on in a referendum. It reached this conclusion, citing the motives of the 2003 decision. The CC argued (in the motives of its decision) that 'the dispositive part and the motives cannot be separated, because only in their integrity and unity they form the CC's biding interpretative act.'[39]

Another example of a decision by virtue of which the CC extends the meaning of a constitutional text is Decision No. 13 of 25 July 1996 on constitutional case No. 11/1996. The state prosecutor general approached the CC with a demand for a binding interpretation of Art. 129 para. 2 and Art. 102 para. 1 in relation to Art. 98 and Art. 102 paras 2 and 3 of the Constitution. Interpretation was required for the following two questions. First, have all the decrees of the President of the Republic of Bulgaria issued under Art. 129 para. 2 of the Constitution to be countersigned, and in case of a positive answer, by whom? Second, what is the legal effect of countersigning the decree of the President of the Republic and does a refusal to countersign it affect its validity?

The CC in the dispositive part of the decision gave the following interpretation. The presidential decrees listed in Art. 102 para. 3 of the Constitution are an expression of his discretionary powers, therefore, these do not have to be countersigned. The list of the presidential decrees which do not require countersignature is not exhaustive. The presidential decree appointing the chairmen of the Supreme Court of Cassation, the Supreme Administrative Court, and the Chief Prosecutor on proposal of the Supreme Judicial Council shall not be countersigned because it does not concern the executive power but the Judiciary. The decree shall enter into force upon signature by the President and its compliance with the Constitution shall be controlled by the CC. Countersigning of the presidential decree by the Prime Minister or by a minister in accordance with Art. 102 para. 2 of the Constitution results in assuming the political responsibility by the government. The government may be held responsible by the Parliament for the results stemming out of this countersignature. The countersignature is a constitutive element for the validity of the decree.

38 Inconsistent in its argumentation, in 2004, in the context of Bulgaria's accession to the EU, it considered that 'a shared exercise of sovereignty, in which the Member States jointly carry out part of their tasks and exercised their common sovereignty,' from which follows 'the partial transfer of competences by the National Assembly to the legislative activity' of the European bodies does not constitute a change in the form of government since there is no withdrawal of its 'core functions'. Thus, it can be stated that if certain powers of the National Assembly were transferred to another body operating within the established form of government, this could be a change in the form of government, but the transfer of such powers to an international body is not. Case 3/2004, of 5 July 2004.

39 Case 8/2016, of 28 July 2016.

It is clear that in this case the CC adds meaning to the nature and the consequences of the countersignature, which does not immediately stem out of the constitutional text. In particular, the Court broadens the list of Art. 102 with additional decrees, which do not require countersignature.

Decision No. 6 of 12 July 1994 on constitutional case No. 6/94 is an example of a decision by virtue of which the CC narrows the meaning of the text of a constitutional provision. Here the Court interprets the meaning of the text of Art. 84, para. 11 of the Constitution according to which, 'the National Assembly shall approve any deployment and use of Bulgarian armed forces outside the country's borders, and the deployment of foreign troops on the territory of the country or their crossing of that territory.' The text of the Constitution makes the impression that the competence of the NA applies to all foreign troops, without exception. However, the CC narrows the meaning of the text. In the dispositive part of the judgement the Court provides that the term 'foreign troops' refers to the personnel of any organized military unit of any kind of troops of a foreign state or international organization and its military assets and property. According to Art. 84, Subpara. 11, the National Assembly has exclusive competence to permit the presence of foreign troops on the territory of the country or their passage through it, when it is of a military or military-political nature. Permission for the presence of foreign troops on the territory of the country or their passage through it, when it is not of a military or military-political nature, is granted by other state bodies designated by law.

The principle of rule of law requires that the legal system should be systematically structured according to clearly organized procedures for norm production and for checking of norm application. The acts of the CC by virtue of which it performs as legislator do not really contribute for the just-mentioned requirements of rule of law. They are not identifiable by their formal properties (the procedure for norm production) and are dispersed in the legal order. The CC's decisions by virtue of which it acts as legislator make the Constitution and the statutory legislation difficult to identify and rather fuzzy. The legal rules with the force of parliamentary legislation are no longer found only in the acts of Parliament (as produced following the ordinary or specialized legislative procedure as provided by the Constitution), but they can be found in an unlimited number of Court's decisions. In particular, the Court's decisions as alternative legislative acts are frequently to be found not in the dispositive part of the decision but in its motives.

The decisions of the Bulgarian CC, by virtue of which it declares the acts of Parliament as unconstitutional have legal effect only for the future. They do not have retroactive force. The decisions enter into force three days after their publication in the State Gazette. The CC is not competent to postpone the invalidation of the act, which has been declared as unconstitutional. In principle, neither the Constitution nor any other normative act empowers the Court to restore acts of Parliament which have been repealed or amended by another act of Parliament subsequently declared as unconstitutional. However, the Court has empowered itself with such competence. In 1995, the Court had been approached with a demand to adopt an interpretative decision by virtue of which to resolve the issue of what are the legal consequences of the CC's decisions in the case when it declares unconstitutional an act of Parliament, which has been adopted in order to amend or abolish another act of Parliament. In its Decision No. 22 of 31 October 1995 on constitutional case No. 25/95 the CC provides that when an act of Parliament, which has abolished or amended previous act of Parliament, is declared unconstitutional by the CC, the previous act is restored and regains its legal validity by virtue of the Court's decision. Thus, the CC in fact amends the Constitution by acquiring this new competence, which is not provided by the formal constitutional text. In fact, by 'restoring' an abolished act of Parliament the Court actually performs legislative activity.

The CC justifies this 'restorative effect' of its decisions with the risk of emergence of legal gaps. However, this effect of the Court's decisions poses potential risk for violating constitutionally enshrined rights. Moreover, the existing legal order and legal certainty may also be in peril. The unlimited continuation of the validity of the restored act of Parliament is especially problematic. The Constitution does not contain a provision that obliges the NA to adopt the new act of Parliament instead of the unconstitutional one within a specified period. According to the CC, this is intolerable and unconstitutional, 'because it does not conform to the spirit and the provisions of the Constitution.' According to the Preamble and Art. 4, para. 1 of the Constitution, the Republic of Bulgaria is governed by the principle of rule of law. The constitutional framework is based on the principle of intolerance against unconstitutional laws. The existence of a legal gap in the legal order is also inadmissible. Undoubtedly, in this situation, the unconstitutional act of Parliament and the resulting legal gap must be eliminated, which is a requirement of the Constitution itself. According to the CC it is unacceptable that the unconstitutional laws should be abolished while the legal gap that has emerged instead can be tolerated for an unlimited period of time.

The CC stipulates that the act of Parliament, which is declared unconstitutional, loses its validity for the future with the entry of the Court's decision into force. Simultaneously, the abolition of the previous act of Parliament, which has been previously abolished by the unconstitutional act of Parliament, shall be restored as of the same moment. The CC considers that its Decision No. 22 of 31 October 1995 on constitutional case No. 25/95 is not an instance of legislation but only of an abstract normative interpretation in accordance with Art. 149, para. 1, p. 1 of the Constitution. Nevertheless, the CC essentially extends its competence without any explicit constitutional empowerment. The Constitution in its Art. 149, para. 2 requires that no competence should be granted to the CC without an explicit constitutional authorization. Hence, such self-empowerment of the Court by virtue of its own decision seems to be unconstitutional. However, the decision of the CC is supported in the doctrine.[40]

In spite of the legitimate aims pursued by the CC in restoring previously repealed statutory legislation, the opposite results can often be achieved in this way leading to a less favourable situation than the annulled one. An example is Decision No. 2 of

40 See Stalev, Nenovski (n 3).

21 February 2019 on constitutional case No. 2/2018. In this decision, the CC ruled on the constitutionality of Art. 230 of the Judicial Power Act (JPA). According to the act, in the hypothesis of Art. 132 of the Constitution, when a judge, prosecutor or investigator is indicted for a criminal offence, the relevant panel of the Supreme Judicial Council temporarily removes him or her from office until the completion of criminal proceedings. According to Art. 230, para. 2 of the JPA where, except in the cases of para. 1, a judge, prosecutor or investigator is indicted for a criminal offence as a defendant for a crime of a general nature, the relevant panel of the Supreme Judicial Council may remove him or her from office until the completion of the criminal proceedings. The panel may perform hearing of the judge, prosecutor or investigator before making a decision.

The CC declares the provisions of Art. 230, para. 1 of the JPA and Art. 230, para. 2 of the JPA in the part 'outside the cases of para. 1' of the JPA to be unconstitutional.[41] The Supreme Court of Cassation, in its statement to the CC, claims that the challenged provisions are contrary to Art. 4, para. 1 (rule of law), Art. 6, para. 2 (equality before the law and prohibition of discrimination), Art. 31, para. 4 (presumption of innocence), Art. 48, para. 1 and para. 3 (right to work and free choice of profession), in connection with Art. 16 (guarantee and protection of labor by law), and Art. 56 (right to defence) of the Constitution.

As a result of the Decision No. 2 of 21 February 2019 on constitutional case No. 2/2018 of the CC, the old version of Art. 230, para. 1 before the amendment of 10 November 2017 came back into force.[42] The old (new) version of the text of para. 1 (which becomes effective as a result of the Court's decision) states that when a magistrate is recruited as a defendant for an intentional crime of a general nature, the relevant SJC panel temporarily removes him from office until the completion of the criminal proceedings.[43] The repealed text cites as a ground for dismissing a charge of criminal *intentional crime in the performance of official duties*, the new (old) text cites as a ground a charge of *intentional crime of a general nature*. In both cases, the SJC is obliged to remove the magistrate. The Court's motive to declare Art. 230, para. 1 unconstitutional is the SJC's lack of discretion to decide whether to dismiss a magistrate accused of a crime in the course of his official duties. In the new (old) text, such a possibility is again missing. Consequently, the CC restores or even creates a legislative provision which is contrary to the Constitution.

The CC goes even further. It not only empowers itself to restore abolished or amended law, but also controls the restored acts for their constitutionality. The Court accepts requests for control of constitutionality over such restored acts of Parliament and defines them admissible. Moreover, it admits its competence to 'give a ruling on the previous versions of the legislative provisions (…) if a there is a request for control for constitutionality of the subsequent act of Parliament.'[44]

41 Promulgated, *State Gazette* No. 64 of 7 August 2007, last amended, *State Gazette* No. 77/18/2018
42 *State Gazette* No. 90 of 10 November 2017.
43 *State Gazette* No. 65 of 11 August 2017.
44 Case 6/1997, of 26 June 1997; case 12/1998, of 9 April 1998.

This seems confusing and again unfounded (even in the case that we assume the CC is competent to restore abolished acts of Parliament). In fact, the CC controls the compliance with the Constitution of acts of Parliament, which do not exist because they have been abolished.

Another important decision in this regard is Decision No. 12 of 25 September 1997 on constitutional case No. 6/97 for declaration of unconstitutionality of the provision in Art. 50 paras. 1 and 2 of the Pensions Act, and the previous versions of that provision. Art. 50 of the Pensions Act in its new and previous versions, defines the principle of restriction or withdrawal of the entitlement to pension when pensioners work and earn income.[45] In the dispositive part of Decision No. 12 of 25 September 1997 on constitutional case No. 6/97 the Court declares Art. 50, paras. 1 and 2 and the previous versions of this text to be unconstitutional.

4 Conclusion

Considering the significant role of CCs in modern constitutional democracies, it is necessary to reconsider the concept of democracy, as established since the French Revolution, i.e. democracy based on the principle of a simple elected majority. A regime of liberal constitutional democracy is characterized by the adoption of a system of superior legal norms that the ordinary parliamentary majority cannot change by a simple majority. An amendment of these norms requires super-majority agreement achieved in accordance with a specific procedure and constituting a formal constitutional amendment. In that case, there has to be a procedure of review to determine whether the elected simple majority has actually respected these borders.[46] The Bulgarian CC, acting as a negative lawmaker, is a body which is empowered with such competence.

Constitutional control was introduced relatively lately in Bulgaria, last but not least, due to ideological reasons. It is even more difficult to accept that the

45 The CC assumed that the entitlement to pension is conditional upon certain law-established factors. This entitlement is kind of entitlement to social security. As such it is subject to the Constitution-sanctioned protection in Art. 51 para. 1 of the Constitution. It is only the Constitution that can allow restriction of a right that has derived or been acquired, however, the Constitution, neither directly nor indirectly, provides for such restriction in the case in question. The right to social security is a separate Constitution-sanctioned right just like the right to work (Art. 16 and Art. 48, para. 1). The latter is guaranteed and protected by the Constitution on its own. The exercise of each of these rights is not conditional upon the exercise (respectively non-exercise) of the other. Considerations that the pensioning legislation affects the labour market are from the domain of the interplay of social facts and processes but are not characterized by direct Constitution relevance and therefore do not condition a decision on the issue raised concerning compliance with the Constitution other than the decision passed.

46 Pasquale Pasquino, 'Majority Rules in Constitutional Democracies. Some Remarks about Theory and Practice', in S. Novak & J. Elster (ed.), *Majority Decisions: Principles and Practices* (Cambridge University Press 2014) 219. Pasquale Pasquino, 'Le principe de majorité: nature et limites', La Vie des idées (06 November 2019) www.laviedesidees.fr/Le-principe-de-majorite-nature-et.html.

controlling bodies such as the CC should in turn be controlled. This is both a conceptual and a practical issue consisting in the impossibility of multiplying the control bodies without overloading the legal system.[47]

Just as the separation of powers or democracy, the rule of law can often be found in the vocabulary of a number of political actors and lawyers. However, the meaning of these concepts seems very indeterminate and rather elusive.[48] Nevertheless, there are two fundamental requirements, which lie at the core of the notion of rule of law. These are the principle of legal certainty and the requirement of independent judicial review of administrative and legislative acts. Constitutional control contributes a lot to the safeguarding of the second requirement. It is a technique aimed at improving the rule of law because it provides for a legal structure allowing each act for normative concretization adopted by the administrative or the legislative bodies to be examined by an independent organ with regard to its conformity with superior norms that determine the requirements of its production and content.[49] However, the 'alternative legislative acts' adopted by the CC may affect the first criterion: the legal certainty.

The decisions of the CC, having the practical effect of constitutional or legislative law-making, can often be morally acceptable. However, this does not explicitly empower the Court to adopt constitutional or legislative amendments. Thus, the impact of the CCs on rule of law is dubious. Their activity as law-makers offers enhanced protection of human rights. Simultaneously, it may be problematic from the viewpoint of separation of powers and democracy and sometimes may diminish legal predictability as an element of rule of law.

The CC defines the concept of the rule of law to include both the principle of legal certainty (the formal element) and the principle of substantive justice (the substantive element).[50] The Court considers that the 'rule of law' means the exercise of state authority on the basis of a constitution, within the framework of acts of Parliament that are materially and formally in conformity with the constitution, and which are designed to preserve human dignity, to achieve freedom, justice, and legal certainty, and undoubtedly include the requirement for a clear, precise definition of the organs and their functions and

47 See, e.g. Otto Pfersmann, 'Prolégomènes pour une théorie normativiste de 'l'Etat de droit', in Olivier Jouanjan (ed.), *Figures de l'Etat de droit. Le Rechtsstaat dans l'histoire intellectuelle et constitutionnelle de l'Allemagne*. (Presses Universitaires de Strasbourg 2001) 53.

48 About the concept of Rule of Law, see, e.g. European Commission for Democracy through Law (Venice Commission), Rule of Law checklist, CDL-AD(2016)007. Otto Pfersmann, (n. 51); M. Krygier, 'The Rule of Law' in M. Rosenfeld & A. Sajó (ed.), *Oxford Handbook of Comparative Constitutional Law* (Oxford University Press 2012) 233. K. Touori, 'L'État de droit' in M. Troper & D. Chagnollaud (ed.), *Traité international de droit constitutionnel*, Tome 1, (Dalloz 2012), 643. D. Mockle, 'Rule of Law' in M. Troper & D. Chagnollaud (ed.), *Traité international de droit constitutionnel*, Tome 1, (Dalloz 2012), 671.

49 See Favoreu et al. (n 4) 81–82.

50 Cases: 12/1998, of 27 January 2005; 3/2018, of 27 July 2018.

relationships.[51] In other words legal certainty is a requirement for a relatively clear and determined legal framework. In this sense, the legal norms are supposed to be adopted and amended not arbitrarily, but only in a way explicitly mentioned in other legal norms. Unclear and indeterminate legal rules would prevent citizens from foreseeing what the legal consequences of their behaviour would be. The CC sometimes infringes the requirement of legal certainty. The most important examples of such activity are the reviving of abolished acts of Parliament (which are sometimes even unconstitutional) and the discretionary and unlimited broadening or narrowing of meaning of constitutional provisions by virtue of constitutional interpretation.

51 Cases: 8/2004, of 27 January 2005; 12/2000, of 15 December 2010; 3/2013, of 4 February 2014.

6 Law-making activity of the Czech Constitutional Court

Jan Malíř and Jana Ondřejková[1]

1 The constitutional design and legal status of the Czech Constitutional Court

Although the origins of the modern judicial review in the Czech lands can be traced back to the Kremsier Constitutional Assembly of 1848,[2] the Constitutional Court of the Czech Republic (CCC) was only established through the Constitution of the Czech Republic that was adopted on 16 December 1992. The CCC has, however, two predecessors in Czechoslovakian constitutional history. The first is the Constitutional Court created under the Czechoslovak Constitution of 1920, which was not, however, re-established after the Second World War.[3] The second is the Constitutional Court of the Czech and Slovak Federal Republic, whose creation was linked to the federalization of Czechoslovakia in 1968. Nevertheless, due to political reasons, the Constitutional Court of the Czech and Slovak Federal Republic only came into being pursuant to Constitutional Act No. 91/1991 Coll. on the Constitutional Court.

As for the legal status of the CCC, Article 83 of the Constitution of the Czech Republic stipulates that the CCC 'is a judicial body charged with protecting constitutionality.' Although the Constitution assigns the CCC with a special role outside of the traditional separation of powers, the provisions on the CCC are

1 This contribution in part concerning the evolution and the political role of the Constitutional Court of the Czech Republic was made possible thanks to support from the Czech Science Foundation (GAČR), Project No. 17–08176S. All the decisions of the CCC, including those cited in this contribution, can be found at the NALUS database available at https://nalus.usoud.cz/Search/Search.aspx; the English translations of some of the CCC decisions can be found at https://www.usoud.cz/en/decisions/.

2 See e.g. Werner Ogris, 'Germany and Austria in the 19th Centuries' in Alain A. Wijffels, C. H. van Rhee (eds.), *European Supreme Courts. A Portrait Through History* (Third Millennium Publishing 2013), 120, 132–134; for a detailed treatment, see Kurt Heller, *Der Verfassungsgerichtshof: Die Entwicklung der Verfassungsgerichtsbarkeit in Österreich von den Anfängen bis zur Gegenwart* (Verlag Österreich 2010), pp. 85–137.

3 See e.g. Vít A. Schorm, 'La Cour constitutionnelle de la République tchécoslovaque d'entre deux guerres: une première oubliée', (2001) Annuaire international de justice constitutionnelle XVII, pp. 11–28; for a detailed treatment, see e.g. Jana Osterkamp, *Verfassungsgerichtsbarkeit in der Tschechoslowakei (1920–1939)* (Klostermann Verlag 2009).

DOI: 10.4324/9781003022442-7

formally included in Chapter IV of the Constitution entitled 'The Judiciary.' Two other articles of the Constitution must be mentioned as well. Firstly, Article 9(2) of the Constitution, which states that the essential attributes of a democratic rule-of-law State shall not be amendable. In the Melčák Judgement, the CCC invoked this provision in order to scrutinize and annul Constitutional Act No. 195/2009 Coll. on the Prorogation of the Fifth Term of Office of the Chamber of Deputies.[4] The CCC thus accepted that it would review not only the constitutionality of ordinary Acts of Parliament but also Acts of Parliament of a constitutional rank ('constitutional Acts of Parliament'), at least as long as these were adopted by the Parliament as the secondary Constitution-giver. Secondly, Article 89(2) of the Constitution, laying down that enforceable decisions of the CCC shall be binding on all authorities and persons, often serves as justification for extending the effects of the CCC judgements beyond individual cases.

The Constitution contains only basic provisions on the CCC's role, composition and procedures. More detailed rules are laid down in Act No. 182/1993 Coll. on the Constitutional Court (CCA) – technically a 'mere' ordinary Act of Parliament lacking constitutional rank – which means that, in principle, its rules can be flexibly amended.

As for its basic design, the CCC can be characterized as a centralized, Kelsenian-type of constitutional court. It is a judicialized constitutional court and legal qualifications are a prerequisite for appointment to the CCC.[5] Taking a closer look at some features of the CCC could serve as a demonstration of a constitutional 'bricolage.' For example, the process relating to how CCC justices are appointed is directly modelled on the process of the appointment of justices in the US Supreme Court;[6] however, in the Czech Republic, the process is applied in a multi-party parliamentary system.[7] On the other hand, unlike in the USA, the CCC's justices are not appointed for life in the Czech Republic but for a ten-year period that can be renewed.

2 Competences of the Czech Constitutional Court and their use in practice

The powers conferred on the CCC can be divided into three principal groups.

Firstly, the core of the CCC's powers consists in carrying out review of constitutionality *proprio sensu*. Under Article 87(1)(a) and (b) of the Constitution, the

4 Pl.ÚS 27/09, of 10 September 2009, see e. g. Miluše Kindlová, 'Formal and Informal Constitutional Amendment in the Czech Republic' (2018) 8 *The Lawyer Quarterly* 512, 518–520.

5 See, in particular, Art. 84(1) in conjunction with Art. 84(3) of the Constitution under which all of the fifteen justices of the CCC must possess a university degree in law and at least 10 years of experience in a legal profession.

6 Under Art. 84 of the Constitution, the President of the Republic appoints CCC justices with the consent of the Senate, the upper chamber of the Czech Parliament.

7 See Stanislav Balík & Vít Hloušek, 'The Development and Transformation of the Czech Party System after 1989' (2016) 8 *Acta Politologica* 103.

CCC has the power to review the conformity of Acts of Parliament or sub-statutory law with the constitutional order upon a motion from selected constitutional actors. Furthermore, under Article 87(1)(d) of the Constitution, the CCC may review any decision or other act taken by public authorities upon a constitutional complaint lodged by any natural or moral person who claims his or her fundamental rights or freedoms have been breached. In addition, under Article 87(2) of the Constitution, selected constitutional actors may initiate scrutiny into whether a treaty that is to be ratified is compatible with the Czech constitutional order.

Secondly, the CCC has been conferred powers in cases which could be designated as *justice politique*; for example, the CCC has jurisdiction to try the President of the Republic on account of treason and a gross breach of the constitutional order (Article 87(1)(g) of the Constitution) or to decide whether the dissolution of a political party conformed to the Constitution (Article 87(1)(j) of the Constitution).

Thirdly, the Constitution assigns the CCC with a special role with respect to overseeing the horizontal and vertical separation of powers, provided that the jurisdiction to hear disputes over this separation has not been delegated to the Supreme Administrative Court (Article 87(1)(c) in conjunction with Article 87(1)(k) of the Constitution).

The CCC thus, prima facie, appears to be a strong constitutional court. In practice, however, only three types of procedures are frequent; namely, (1) the constitutional complaint procedure, (2) review of conformity of Acts of Parliament/sub-statutory law with the constitutional order, and (3) revisions of previous CCC decisions following a decision by an international tribunal. Constitutional complaints clearly dominate the workload of the CCC. In 2018, constitutional complaints accounted for 99% of the decisions rendered by the CCC (4367 out of 4395 decisions).[8] By contrast, the power to review the compatibility of treaties with the Constitution has only been used twice since 2001 when it was introduced into the Constitution.[9]

As for access to the CCC, it is rather broad. Two aspects must be specifically mentioned in this respect. Under Article 74 of the CCA, a person who has lodged a constitutional complaint may simultaneously apply for the review of the Act of Parliament/sub-statutory law, provided that its application resulted in lodging the constitutional complaint and, in the complainant's opinion, it conflicted with the Constitution. Secondly, review of Acts of Parliament/sub-statutory law before the CCC can also be initiated by any ordinary court, where such a court, when deciding on a particular case, considers the Act of Parliament that court should

8 The corresponding data are available at https://www.usoud.cz/fileadmin/user_upload/ustavni_soud_www/Rocenky/Ustavni_soud_Rocenka_2018.pdf (30 September 2019); in only 166 cases the CCC found (at least partial) infringement of a constitutionally protected fundamental right.

9 The review of the Lisbon Treaty Pl.ÚS 19/08, of 26 November 2008, and Pl. ÚS 29/09, of 3 November 2009; the motion to review the Treaty concerning the accession of the Czech Republic to the EU brought by a group of deputies was rejected as inadmissible as it was brought only upon the ratification of this Treaty by the President of the Republic, see ruling Pl.ÚS 1/04, of 4 March 2004.

apply to conflict with the constitutional order (Article 95(2) of the Constitution in conjunction with Article 64(3) of the CCA).

From the perspective of exploring law-making by the CCC, it should be noted that decisions in which the CCC rules on the merits of the matter of conformity of an Act of Parliament/sub-statutory law with the constitutional order are called judgements (*nálezy*) and are obligatorily published in the *Collection of Laws of the Czech Republic* (*Sbírka zákonů České republiky*), the official digest of laws (Article 57 of the CCA). The CCC can also decide that judgements rendered in constitutional complaint proceedings should be published in the *Collection of Laws,* but this rarely happens.[10] The other decisions rendered by the CCC are published in the printed *Collection of Judgments and Rulings of the Constitutional Court* (*Sbírka nálezů* a *usnesení Ústavního soudu*) and are also available online on the CCC's website.

Furthermore, the CCC considers itself to be bound by the legal reasoning contained in its own previous judgements, including those rendered by three-member panels (where the concurring votes of two justices are sufficient to render the judgement). Such legal reasoning can only be overruled by the full CCC in the form of a so-called opinion (*stanovisko pléna*) that can be adopted where at least nine justices concur (Article 23 in conjunction with Article 13 of the CCA). The legal reasoning contained in a CCC judgement is therefore unlikely to be changed easily.

3 The current level of social trust in the Czech Constitutional Court and the social degree of acceptance for its rulings

Conclusions on the social trust in the CCC can be made on the grounds of available public opinion surveys. When examining the long-term data, public trust in the CCC has remained broadly the same as in the 1990s, even though public trust in the CCC was a bit higher in the 2000s.[11] Another factor to be mentioned is that the current Chief Justice, P. Rychetský, formerly a popular politician, has been one of the most trusted officials of the Czech State in the long term.[12]

Some facts can also be inferred from the way in which the CCC is treated by the parallel branches. A recent study demonstrated that references to the CCC and its case law were frequent in parliamentary debates in the legislation period of 2013 to 2017.[13] The study concluded that Members of Parliament

10 Seven judgments since 1993 according to the NALUS database.

11 The data on the trends from 1994–2019 are available at https://www.stem.cz/duvera-v-nejvyssi-soudni-instituce-se-oproti-lonskemu-roku-mirne-snizila/ (30 September 2019).

12 When P. Rychetský entered his office, the social trust in him (65%) exceeded that of V. Klaus, the President of the Republic (61%) at the time; currently, the public trust in P. Rychetský is lower (43%) but still the same as that for M. Zeman, the present President of the Republic, see https://www.irozhlas.cz/zpravy-domov/duvera-v-politiky-pruzkum-rychetsky_1906101810_jak (30 September 2019).

13 Jan Chmel 'Parlament a judicializace politiky: reflexe rozhodovací činnosti Ústavního soudu České republiky v poslaneckých debatách' (2018) 27 *Jurisprudence* 3, 6–8. On the use of the CCC by the opposition, see e.g. Lubomír Kopecek & Jan Petrov 'From Parliament to Courtroom: Judicial Review of Legislation as a Political Tool in the Czech Republic' (2016) 30 *East European Politics and Societies and Cultures* 120.

generally considered the CCC's case law as binding *erga omnes* and accorded substantial authority to it.[14]

The notable exception in this respect were the responses to the Melčák Judgement, which triggered strong reactions. At the time, the President of the Republic even suggested the launch of a debate on stripping the CCC of its power to review Acts of Parliament of constitutional rank.[15] Generally, however, the criticism of the CCC does not go beyond expressing disagreement over the content of the individual decisions. Contrary to some other countries, there have been no serious attempts to eliminate the effects of the CCC case law through constitutional amendments or *lois de validation*. although there were some misunderstandings over the interpretation of the Constitution between the Constitutional Court and the Parliament in the so-called judicial sagas (see p. 126).

4 Law-making activity of the Czech Constitutional Court

Generally, the CCC emphasizes that it has been established in order to play the role of a negative rather than a positive legislator. The origins of this position date back to the CCC's beginnings. As early as 1997, the CCC (albeit a three-justice panel) ruled that the CCC 'is not empowered to act as a positive legislator.' If the CCC did so, 'it would unacceptably interfere with powers of the Legislative Assembly,' placing it in conflict with its role as a negative legislator. Such a role, in the CCC's view, implies that the CCC has the power to annul 'the provisions of the Acts of Parliament that conflict with the Constitution or treaties under Art. 10 of the Constitution' but not 'to supplant these provisions with its own decisions.'[16] This position has become an integral part of the CCC's settled case law. This can be exemplified by a judgement in which the full CCC was to pronounce on the constitutionality of provisions of the Civil Procedure Code concerning default judgements. The CCC concluded that the contested provisions were not unconstitutional and that their constitutionally conforming interpretation was possible. Even though the CCC admitted that controversies over the pertinence of the provisions in question were legitimate, the CCC resolutely stressed that the power to amend the disputed provisions did not rest with the CCC, but exclusively with the Parliament of the Czech Republic because 'the CCC is not a positive legislator.'[17]

The CCC has also accentuated that it is bound by the imperative of judicial self-restraint, which, in one context, has even been coined to constitute 'the leading principle governing constitutional review in democratic rule-of-law states' by the CCC.[18] Again, references to judicial self-restraint can be traced back to the 1990s. In the last decade, judicial self-restraint has even been viewed as excluding the constitutional review of some decisions taken by political branches in a way that

14 See Chmel (n 13) 14.

15 https://www.tyden.cz/rubriky/domaci/klaus-se-pustil-do-ustavniho-soudu-jde-o-pravomoci_138182.html (30 September 2019).

16 II. ÚS 74/97, of 2 December 1997.

17 Pl.ÚS 49/10, of 28 January 2014, para. 68.

18 Pl.ÚS 11/16, of 24 May 2016, para. 15.

reminds one of the US political question doctrine that has even been, albeit occasionally, expressly mentioned by the CCC.[19] The CCC, for example, declined 'correcting' the original wording of the Constitution when invited to review the constitutionality of a forty-year limit circumventing the eligibility to stand as a candidate for the Senate.[20] Elsewhere, the CCC ruled that 'unless constitutional rules stipulate otherwise, it is up to the Legislature to decide whether it will establish any public office or not', limiting, thus, its own powers of review.[21] More regularly, the CCC employs the avoidance canon and opines that the conforming interpretation shall always precede the annulment of the provisions in question.[22] The CCC also holds that it is obliged to follow the 'maxim of the minimization of its interference' with law that is in force,[23] which, in practice, is not dissimilar to 'narrowness' as pleaded for by the proponents of judicial minimalism.

In theory, to the extent that the CCC views its role as being in line with the Kelsenian model of a negative legislator and considers itself to be bound by the imperative of judicial self-restraint, space for 'judicial legislation' by the CCC should be non-existent or substantially limited. In reality, however, the CCC has had a non-negligible impact on the evolution of the Czech constitutional and legal systems and has often found itself verging on taking on the role of a positive legislator.

The primary channel through which the CCC can make law is the process of annulling legislative provisions as a result of *in abstracto* and *in concreto* review. Even when the CCC does not annul a legislative provision, its law-making capacity can be linked to a creative interpretation of constitutional rules. Although neither the Czech case law nor legal doctrine normally distinguish between *Auslegung* and *Rechtsfortbildung* as in Germany,[24] such a distinction would also be justified in the Czech situation. Frequently, when interpreting constitutional rules, the CCC goes far beyond a literal reading of the rules in question and, in particular, by employing a purposive interpretation, it not only expands the scope of constitutional rules but, in some cases, it also fills in the gaps in the Czech law.

There are, moreover, indirect channels through which the CCC may influence the constitutional and legal systems.

Firstly, the CCC has developed the practice of rendering interpretative judgements (*interpretativní výrok*). In these judgements, the CCC declines ruling that the provision in question is unconstitutional and annulling it. Such a conclusion, however, applies only as long as the provision in question is interpreted in line with the way in which the CCC has 'indicated' this in its judgement so as to best conform to the Constitution.[25] This practice, which was probably not envisaged

19 See e.g. II.ÚS 404/97, of 19 August 1998 or, more recently, Pl.ÚS 2/15, of 3 May 2017.

20 Pl.ÚS 34/16, of 7 March 2017, para. 18.

21 Pl.ÚS 21/15, of 4 September 2018, para. 69.

22 Pl.ÚS 48/95, of 26 March 1996.

23 Pl.ÚS 39/08, of 6 October 2010, para. 60.

24 Martin Brenncke, *Judicial Law-Making in English and German Courts* (Intersentia 2018) 54 et seq.

25 Pl.ÚS 49/10, of 28 January 2014, para. 70.

by the authors of the Constitution[26] but is justified by the duty to minimize the CCC's interference with the powers of the parallel branches[27] amounts to it rendering conditional judgements. In the course of indicating the interpretation that should be taken up, the CCC has a non-negligible space for shaping the way the provisions are applied by the Parliament, the Executive, and ordinary courts. The practice of rendering interpretative judgements thus approaches that of indirect judicial legislation. This conclusion even seems to be confirmed by the CCC itself. When, for example, it reviewed provisions which did not allow for lump sum reimbursements of the costs incurred by a party not represented by a barrister in civil proceedings before an ordinary court, the CCC openly stated that its interpretative judgement would permit the provisions in question to be read in a way that would not conflict with the right to equal representation before a court of justice stemming from a right to a fair trial 'until a new statutory or a sub-statutory regulation is eventually adopted.'[28] This suggests that the CCC considers that by using interpretative judgements, it is empowered to 'shore up' the inconsistencies in the legal system until the Legislator acts, which, in fact, can take years.

Secondly, the CCC has profited from distinguishing between *ratio decidendi* and *obiter dicta* in order to somewhat escape from the separation of powers and to make open pronouncements on the existing law and the necessity for shifts in legal politics. Although, formally, the CCC does not step into the areas reserved for political branches and does not issue advisory opinions *proprio sensu*, its pronouncements – made *obiter dicta,* as is often emphasized verbatim – limit the choices the Parliament or the Executive can make with respect to the form and content of the law. Sometimes, the CCC even indirectly prescribes that the Parliament should adopt a certain approach to a specific problem. Such pronouncements may, in turn, effectively create the limits, which the Parliament or the Executive will find difficult to surmount.

A rather uncontroversial example of such pronouncements can be found in one of the decisions concerning mandatory vaccinations. In 2015, the full CCC rejected a constitutional complaint in which the constitutionality of the provisions of the Public Health Act – setting up the mandatory vaccination schedule – and those of the Administrative Offences Act – providing for the possibility of fining those who have refused to be vaccinated – was challenged. The CCC held that although its review did not result in the annulment of the provisions at stake, 'where the State lays down the sanctions for cases where a person rejects to

26 Occasionally, this leads some of the constitutional justices to express doubts about the justification of this practice, which is sometimes described as a practice that transforms the CCC into a forum that serves the purposes of authoritatively deciding on doctrinal disputes and usurping the powers of the legislative and executive branches, see Pl.ÚS 39/13, of 7 October 2014, Filip, J., dissenting, para. 11, or even that the practice exceeds the powers conferred on the CCC and thus it acts in breach of the separation of powers, see Pl.ÚS 35/11, of 13 May 2014, Sládeček, J., Suchánek, J., dissenting, para. 5.

27 Pl.ÚS 39/13, of 7 October 2014, para. 41.

28 Ibid., para. 44.

undergo vaccination, the State has to reflect upon the situation where it eventually causes a harm to the vaccinated person though law enforcement.'[29] Thus, the CCC called upon the State to seriously analyse the possibility of introducing the statutory scheme providing for compensation for harm suffered as a result of obligatory vaccinations; indeed, such a bill was introduced to the Chamber of Deputies in 2019.

As for more controversial pronouncements concerning the law that should be adopted, in 2010, the CCC concluded that the omission of the Parliament regarding adopting an act on the property settlement with churches and religious societies – to undo injustices resulting from the confiscation of their property in the Communist period – was in breach of the Constitution. The CCC simultaneously dealt with some of the principles that the future relationship between the State and churches should be based on.[30] The Act on Property Settlement with Churches and Religious Societies was then adopted in 2012, but it triggered a serious political dispute that has continued to date and has given rise to repeated challenges before the CCC.[31]

5 Evolution in the case law of the Czech Constitutional Court regarding the approach to its law-making activity

Although, especially at the beginning, the CCC did not hesitate in using 'heroic' language; in the long term, the CCC seems to have built an image of a body that normally interprets the Constitution, rather than of an activist court intervening in the realms of the parallel branches. Only rarely has the CCC openly admitted that its decision-making has amounted to judicial law-making.

Concerning the shifts in the CCC's attitude towards law-making, decisions concerning 'regulatory fees' in the healthcare sector are worth noting. Under Article 31 of the Charter of Fundamental Rights and Freedoms, citizens 'shall have a right to free-of-charge healthcare and medical devices under the conditions laid down in the Act of the Parliament.' This rather generous wording has given rise to diverging interpretations.

In 2007, the right-wing coalition of the day introduced 'regulatory fees,' a kind of lump sum to be paid when using specific types of medical services and fees, in addition to payments from public health insurance. In 2008, following a challenge to the provisions on regulatory fees, the CCC concluded that, when implementing the provisions on social rights such as the right to healthcare, the Legislator had a wide margin of appreciation, limited only by the obligation not to deny the very existence of these rights. Consequently, a judicial review of the choices made by the Legislator in this area had to be substantially limited.[32] As a result, the CCC upheld the constitutionality of the regulatory fees.

29 Pl.ÚS 19/14, of 27 January 2015, para. 87.
30 Pl.ÚS 9/07, of 1 July 2010, para. 103.
31 See: Pl. ÚS 10/13, of 28 May 2013; Pl.ÚS 5/19, of 1 October 2019.
32 Pl.ÚS 1/08. of 20 May 2008, para. 90 et seq.

In 2013, however, the CCC struck down new statutory provisions, which were, inter alia, intended to increase one of the regulatory fees and to strengthen their enforcement.[33] As for the increase in the regulatory fee in question, the CCC basically argued that, due to changes in the regulatory but also in the economic and social environment, a further review of its constitutionality was justified.[34] Although the CCC indicated that it would start from the conclusions contained in its previous case law, without mentioning the wide margin of appreciation of the Legislator, it found that the new provisions increasing one of the regulatory fees did not sufficiently differentiate between specific medical services and, moreover, did not set out any maximum limits.[35] These findings implied the necessity of annulling the statutory provisions in question. The CCC thus partially overruled its previous conclusions concerning the wide margin of appreciation on behalf of the Legislator and the limited scope of the judicial review in terms of the choices made in the area of social rights. Moreover, in 2013, the CCC provided the Legislator with much more detailed guidance on the extent to which payments and fees could be required within the framework of public health insurance.

Unlike the CCC decisions as such, dissenting opinions provide testimony that CCC justices are well aware that their decisions can have a legislative dimension. As for the reasons that are cited in support of law-making on behalf of the CCC, fundamental values on which the constitutional order is based, or the essential attributes of democratic rule-of-law States are frequently invoked. Conversely, when it comes to the CCC disapproving of judicial legislation, the imperatives stemming from the principle of the separation of powers or the exclusive character of the role of a negative legislator are cited.

By way of example, dissenting opinions joined to cases concerning the review of the amnesty decisions taken by the President of the Republic can be mentioned. When, in 2013, the CCC declined to review the decision by which the President of the Republic had granted amnesty, P. Rychetský, Chief J, regretted that his colleagues had not opted for reviewing the amnesty decision, although they would have had to face the risk of being accused of judicial activism, as judicially applicable standards of review are not contained in the Constitution.[36] Conversely, in 2018, when the CCC held that the President of the Republic did not have the power to decide whether the conditions under which the amnesty was granted were breached in individual cases, two justices, in their joint dissenting opinion, were critical, stating that, by ruling so, the CCC had breached the principle of the separation of powers. Far more generally, the two justices argued that for the CCC, 'due to its (the CCC's – the authors added) specific role of a body which has "no superior" on the domestic level, it is of extraordinary importance that it keeps within the limits of its powers and does not set a bad example to the other public bodies that a good intention may even justify a breach of powers.'[37]

33 Pl.ÚS 36/11. of 20 June 2013.
34 Pl.ÚS 36/11. of 20 June 2013, para. 55.
35 Ibid., para. 60.
36 Pl.ÚS 4/13, of 5 March 2013, Rychetský, Chief J., dissenting, para. 2.
37 Pl.ÚS 36/17, of 19 June 2018, Fenyk, J., Fiala, J., dissenting, para. 4.

The dissenting opinions filed in both cases seem to perfectly illustrate that where there are no express provisions on the issue under review contained in the Constitution, the view on whether and how far the CCC should 'legislate' is not often unanimous inside the CCC.

6 Law-making activity of the CCC at the constitutional level

Although the role of a negative Legislator should substantially limit the possibility of a constitutional court to 'legislate,' a fortiori, to modify the Constitution, the CCC has actually developed various constitutional notions and, in some cases, has no doubt filled in the gaps, which had been present in the constitutional design.

At least two cases must be mentioned in this respect.

Firstly, the CCC has a substantial impact on the understanding of what constitutes the Czech Constitution as such. In its Article 112(1), the Constitution introduces the notion of the constitutional order (*ústavní pořádek*) and provides a list of constitutional laws, which this constitutional order shall be constituted of. The *raison d'être* of the notion of the constitutional order was to delimit what the Constitution is.[38] The notion was also meant to define where to seek the reference standards that the CCC should employ when scrutinizing the conformity of Acts of Parliament or acts of public authorities with the Constitution.[39] Moreover, when carrying out constitutional review, in line with Article 88(2) of the Constitution, CCC justices shall be bound to follow the constitutional order, apart from the CCA. The notion of the constitutional order and its components is thus of primary structural importance.

The list of components of the constitutional order contained in Article 112(1) of the Constitution, however, has not retained its exhaustive character, as the CCC has expanded its scope. This judicial rewriting of Article 112(1) of the Constitution followed the so-called Euro-amendment of the Czech Constitution (Constitutional Act No. 395/2001 Coll.), which was a response to the fact that the original wording of the Constitution was extremely laconic when it came to the relationship between the Czech law and international/EU law.[40] Since the entry into force of the amendment, any duly published treaty ratified with the consent of the Parliament and binding on the Czech Republic shall be a part of the Czech legal order and shall be given primacy over any conflicting Act of Parliament. The Euro-amendment thus not only abandoned the previous (and unclear) distinction between treaties on human rights and other treaties, but it was also meant to guarantee the direct applicability to a much wider range of treaties. A new

38 Jan Filip, 'Commentary on Art. 112 Constitution' in Bahýľová, L. et al., *Ústava České republiky. Komentář* (Linde 2010) 1470.

39 Under Art. 87(1) of the Constitution, it is precisely the conflict between an Act of Parliament/a sub-statutory legal act on the one hand and the constitutional order on the other that permits the CCC to strike down a provision of the given Act of Parliament/sub-statutory legal act.

40 Eric Stein, 'International Law in Internal Law: Toward Internationalization of Central-Eastern European Constitutions?' (1994) 88 *AJIL*, 427 et seq.

section was also inserted into Article 1 of the Constitution that stipulates that the Czech Republic shall respect the obligations from international law. Last but not least, the Euro-amendment was meant to permit ordinary courts to directly exclude the application of any national legislation conflicting with treaties under Article 10 of the Constitution without the need to initiate a review before the CCC.

Soon after the Euro-amendment entered into force, the CCC reviewed the constitutionality of some of the provisions that fixed the rules on the reimbursement of the costs of bankruptcy trustees in certain circumstances. The CCC struck down the provisions at stake, holding that they conflicted with the Charter of Fundamental Rights and Freedoms and, beyond the motion from the ordinary court, also with the International Covenant on Civil and Political Rights (ICCPR). In order to justify an unusual reference to the ICCPR, the CCC held that, due to the new Article 1(2) of the Constitution, 'the scope of the notion of constitutional order cannot be read only with regard to Art. 112 (1) of the Constitution but also with regard to Art. 1(2) of the Constitution.'[41] Such an opinion implied that 'ratified and published treaties on human rights and fundamental freedoms must be included' in the scope of the notion of the constitutional order.[42] The CCC thus redefined the notion of the constitutional order and included treaties on human rights – precisely, the category of treaties whose independent existence the Euro-amendment sought to abandon – within its scope. The CCC argued that any amendment of the Constitution should not be construed in a way that was detrimental to the level of procedural protection of fundamental rights that had already been achieved; such a step would amount to a breach of the essential attributes of a democratic rule-of-law State, which, under the terms of Article 9(2) of the Constitution, shall be unamendable. The ruling, however, also signified that ordinary courts would continue to be obliged to stay proceedings before them and refer to the CCC whenever they had doubts about the conformity of Acts of Parliament with treaties on human rights.

Secondly, the CCC has co-defined the content of the notion of the essential attributes (*podstatné náležitosti*) of a democratic rule-of-law State enshrined in Article 9(2) of the Constitution. Due to the divergences during the drafting of the Constitution, a consensus was not reached on which precise elements of the Constitution shall be unamendable;[43] rather, an indefinite notion of the essential attributes of a democratic rule-of-law State was instead employed.[44]

The CCC has never accepted that it should provide a comprehensive definition of the notion of these essential attributes nor that it should even draw up an

41 Pl.ÚS 36/01, of 25 June 2002, section VII.

42 Ibid.

43 The President of the Republic proposed declaring basic provisions contained in the first part of the Constitution to be proclaimed unamendable; however, the proposal was not accepted, see Jindřiška Syllová & Miroslav Sylla, *Ústava České republiky. Dokumenty a ohlasy* (Wolters Kluwer 2018), 132.

44 For a more in-depth treatment, see e. g. Vojtěch Šimíček, 'Commentary on Art. 9' in Bahylova (n 38) 149–177.

exhaustive list of them.[45] On several occasions, however, the CCC has indicated the structure of the notion 'through a partly abstract method and partly on a case-by-case basis.'[46] In particular, the CCC has clarified that the notion of a rule-of-law State refers to the concept of a material rule-of-law State, not only a formal one.[47] From such a perspective, the CCC has ruled that the notion of essential attributes encompasses not only the principle of the sovereignty of the people, the principles of democracy, or the provisions of the Charter of Fundamental Rights and Freedoms inspired by natural law,[48] but also the basic principles of electoral law[49] or the separation of powers.[50] In the Melčák Judgement, it was the lack of normativity, which was considered incompatible with the notion.[51]

The CCC has also expanded the legal effects of the notion. Although Article 9(2) of the Constitution appears as a provision whose principal goal is to establish limits on the domestic process of constitutional amendments, with the prospect of the EU membership, the CCC held that any transfer of sovereignty from the Czech Republic to an international organization or institution shall be compatible with the constitutional order only as long as such a transfer does not affect the essential attributes of a democratic rule-of-law State under Article 9(2) of the Constitution, as powers to carry out such a transfer 'are outside the reach of the Constitution-giver himself.'[52]

Highly controversially, and rather unexpectedly,[53] the CCC has also agreed to scrutinize the respect for Article 9(2) of the Constitution and to annul Acts of Parliament possessing constitutional rank if these Acts conflict with the essential attributes.[54] It is noteworthy that Article 9(2) of the Constitution is silent on who shall control the respect for the essential attributes of a democratic rule-of-law State and whether political or judicial instruments shall be employed.[55] Moreover, as under Article 88(2) of the Constitution, CCC justices shall be bound by the constitutional order, and under Article 112(1) of the Constitution, the notion of the constitutional order shall encompass, constitutional Acts of Parliament designed to amend the Constitution, review of constitutional amendments by the CCC seemed to have been expressly excluded. In the Melčák Judgement, nevertheless, the CCC struck the constitutional amendment down as, in its opinion, it was a 'one-use-only' constitutional Act of Parliament and, therefore, lacked normativity, in stark conflict with the notion of the essential attributes, irrespective of the fact that a comparable constitutional amendment had been adopted

45 Pl.ÚS 19/08, of 26 November 2008, para. 93.
46 Pl.ÚS 27/09, of 10 September 2009, sub IV.
47 Pl.ÚS 19/93, of 21 December 1993.
48 Pl.ÚS 27/09, of 10 September 2009, sub IV.
49 Pl.ÚS 42/00, of 24 January 2001.
50 Pl.ÚS 19/08, of 26 November 2008, para. 93.
51 Pl.ÚS 27/09, of 10 September 2009, sub VI./a.
52 Pl.ÚS 19/08, of 26 November 2008, para. 130.
53 Jan Filip, *Ústavní právo 1*' (Doplněk 2003), 112.
54 Pl.ÚS 27/09, of 10 September 2009.
55 Šimíček (n 44) 160.

in the past.[56] As such, the Melčák Judgement bears all the signs of a 'judicial rewriting' of the constitutional text.

More commonly, the CCC shapes constitutional law in less spectacular ways, in particular, through a creative interpretation of the Constitution.

An instructive example dates back to 1997 and concerns the dispute over the calculation of the deadline in case the President of the Republic uses his or her power of legislative veto.[57] Article 50(1) of the Constitution grants the President the power to veto ordinary bills during a period of 15 days from the day when the bill adopted by the Parliament was delivered to him or her. In this case, the deadline fell on Saturday, while the bill was returned to the Chamber of Deputies by the President only on the following business day, that is, Monday. Subsequently, the Chamber of Deputies failed to recognize the presidential veto as valid because, in their opinion, the 15-day period had lapsed. The President, however, invoked what he designated as a general principle of the Czech law under which, where the deadline fell on a weekend or on a holiday, the *dies ad quem* was actually the following business day. The CCC pointed out that the dispute was 'not a mere dispute over the lapse of time in constitutional law but, principally, a dispute over how to understand law in a democratic society.'[58] Consequently, not only did the CCC analyse the calculation of periods in constitutional law but also the role of constitutional conventions and general principles of law in the constitutional system. Finally, the CCC upheld the President's opinion on the calculation of the deadline and struck down the Act that had been promulgated, irrespective of a valid presidential veto, although it admitted that the Constitution-giver or Legislator might adopt different rules in future.

7 Law-making activity of the Czech Constitutional Court at the sub-constitutional level

The impact of the CCC on sub-constitutional law is extremely varied.[59]

This can be effectively demonstrated by the recent case law on mandatory vaccination schedules. A recent decline in public confidence in vaccinations has resulted in disputes over the conformity of the mandatory vaccination schedule with the Constitution (or, more precisely, constitutional order). The disputes – some of which are close to strategic litigation – have mostly originated from parents who have refused to have their children vaccinated and who have contested the conformity of the statutory provisions laying down the mandatory vaccination schedule and sanctions for their disrespect with the Constitution.

56 In a similar vein, a 'one-use-only' constitutional Act of Parliament, which shortened the mandate of the Chamber of Deputies, was adopted in 1998, but its constitutionality was never challenged and the CCC never criticized this Act.

57 Pl.ÚS 33/9,7 of 17 December 1997.

58 Ibid.

59 See supra sub 4 or Zdeněk Kühn, 'Czech Republic' in Allan R. Brewer-Carías, *Constitutional Courts as Positive Legislators: A Comparative Law Study* (Cambridge University Press 2011), 445.

The CCC has never accepted that the relevant statutory provisions would conflict with the Constitution.[60] On the other hand, by obliging public authorities to read the statutory provisions in question in conformity with the Constitution and by imposing certain conditions on their application, the CCC has contributed to the transformation of their content. As already mentioned, soon after the first confrontations with the mandatory vaccination schedule, the CCC criticized Czech law, as it did not provide for the reimbursement for harm caused by any of the vaccinations under the mandatory vaccination schedule (see p. 117). In addition, the CCC rejected that fines for violations of the mandatory vaccination schedule could be imposed 'automatically,' in particular, where there were some special circumstances capable of justifying declining to enforce 'the mandatory vaccination ... in exceptional cases.'[61] The CCC has also clarified how 'the obligation to undergo a vaccination ... must be accompanied by the checks that are capable of minimizing the cases of its abuse and of excluding the medical intervention where the conditions to carry it out are not met.'[62] More controversially, the CCC has also ruled that a failure to undergo a vaccination under the mandatory schedule might be exceptionally justified by conscientious objections linked to religious beliefs[63] and even the so-called secular freedom of conscience,[64] although the CCC has given assurances that its conclusions cannot be read as a general exoneration from the vaccination obligation. Recently, the CCC has, moreover, pointed out that, where there is a dispute on whether a child shall undergo a vaccination, the opinion of the child shall be heard.[65] Although the CCC has never used its powers of a negative legislator in the area of mandatory vaccinations, it has contributed to transforming the modus operandi of mandatory vaccinations.[66]

8 Occurrence of the law-making elements in the structure of the Czech Constitutional Court judgements

As the CCC is hardly likely to admit that it makes the law, most law-making elements can be identified in the reasoning of its decisions, including the paragraphs that the CCC expressly labels as *obiter dicta*.[67] When, however, the CCC renders interpretative judgements, such interpretations are contained in the operative part

60 See, in particular, Pl.ÚS 19/14, of 27 January 2015, and Pl.ÚS 16/14, of 27 January 2015.

61 III.ÚS 449/06, of 3 February 2011, sub IV./c.

62 Pl.ÚS 19/14, of 27 January 2015, para. 71 and Pl.ÚS 16/14, of 27 January 2015, para. 95.

63 III.ÚS 449/06, of 3 February 2011, sub IV./b.

64 I. ÚS 1253/14, of 22 December 2015, paras 42–43.

65 II.ÚS 725/18, of 8 October 2018.

66 For a critical response, see e.g. 4 As 114/2016–43, of 25 October 2016 (Supreme Administrative Court).

67 For example, this was the case with the extension of the notion of the constitutional order to include treaties on human rights, see supra sub 6; the notion of *obiter dicta* had not been historically employed in the Czech law.

of the judgements.[68] Furthermore, some of these interpretative judgements are expressly qualified as such in the database of the CCC's decisions (57 cases from 1993 to 2018, with most of them being made by the full CCC), even though the doctrine argues that this type of judgement first appeared only in 2004.[69]

Another type of judgement, which formally corresponds with the logic of a negative legislator but simultaneously implies the positive law-making elements in the operative part, is called judgements on the scope of the legal regulation (*rozsahový výrok*). Such judgements are exceptional and serve the CCC in terms of excluding some types of application of a legal regulation without, however, annulling the contested legal regulation. By way of illustration, the operative part of the judgement on Judges' Pay XV can be cited.[70] While the contested provision applied to judges, it did not contain the word 'judges' at all but spoke generally about the calculation of the basic salary for all public officials.

9 Reactions of the courts and public authorities to the law-making activities of the Czech Constitutional Court

Due to the high level of social trust in the CCC, and the political costs involved in potential non-compliance with the CCC's case law, the law-making activity of the CCC is generally respected.

With regard to ordinary courts, it must also be noted that because of the wide access to the CCC via the constitutional complaint procedure(in which decisions of ordinary courts can be challenged), the CCC is rather effective in controlling whether ordinary courts – including the Supreme Court and the Supreme Administrative Court – comply with its decisions. Rare cases of the explicit law-making activity of the CCC expressed in the operative part of the judgement usually concern situations in which the CCC wants to ensure that its legal opinion will be followed, although it may reflect the past *guerres des juges* or the temporary resistance of ordinary courts to the legal opinions of the CCC, as was the case, in the past, in controversies over compulsory military service or the acquirement of an ownership right from non-owners. In these cases, the CCC also heavily relied on references to foreign legal materials.[71]

On the other hand, the CCC, at least rhetorically, invites ordinary courts to enter into a judicial dialogue with the CCC and holds that where ordinary courts have suggested a more adequate constitutional interpretation, the CCC is willing to accept it.

68 In the sentence of the judgment, see e.g. the case of the lump sum reimbursement of the costs incurred by a party which had not been represented by a barrister supra sub 4.
69 See Kühn (n 59) 456–457.
70 Pl.ÚS 28/13, of 10 July 2014.
71 C.f. Jana Ondřejková, Kristina Blažková & Jan Chmel, 'The Use of Foreign Legal Materials by the Constitutional Court of the Czech Republic' in Giuseppe Franco Ferrari (ed.), *The Use of Foreign Case Law and International Law by Supreme or Constitutional Courts* (Brill 2019), 589, 610–611.

Inter-institutional dialogue has also occurred between the CCC and the Parliament. In several cases – where the CCC struck down Acts of Parliament and indicated what requirements should be met so that the Acts of Parliament were upheld – the Parliament did not fully adhere to the CCC's opinions. The CCC then either implicitly accepted the opinion of the Parliament[72] or the disputes evolved into 'judicial sagas,' the best known of which are probably the Judges' Pay saga (16 decisions rendered between 1999 and 2016) and the Slovak pensions saga (27 decisions rendered between 2003 and 2014). In these sagas, the CCC militated against what it considered as disrespect for its decisions by the Parliament. In the former case, it concerned the issue of the potential lowering of judicial salaries in the context of reducing public spending. In the latter case, it was the application of the Agreement between the Czech Republic and the Slovak Republic on Social Security after the dissolution of the Czech and Slovak Federal Republic and its scope.[73]

10 Academia's standpoint

When assessing positions of legal doctrine, one must be aware of the fact that many justices and employees of the CCC are professors of constitutional or administrative law and continue their academic careers once their tenure at the CCC expires, while others actively 'market' their legal opinions through contributing to legal journals and publications. Therefore, it is not difficult to find authors and analyses, which are not only uncritical of the law-making activity of the CCC but that also make a strong plea for the *erga omnes* binding character of the CCC's decisions.[74]

Other scholars more scrupulously distinguish according to different types of decisions and different procedures within which decisions were rendered when it comes to judicial legislation by the CCC.[75] As noted above, the operative part of the judgement where an Act of Parliament or sub-statutory law or sections thereof are annulled is undisputed by most academic circles. The same cannot be said about interpretative judgements or judgements concerning the scope of the legal regulation, the use of which is sometimes criticized by the justices themselves in

72 For example, in the case of the threshold for electoral expense contributions to political parties from the State budget, the CCC advised the amount should equate to 1% of the valid votes cast, yet the Parliament adopted a 1.5% threshold, see Pl.ÚS 30/98, of 13 October 1999.

73 See e.g. Richard Král, 'Questioning the Recent Challenge of the Czech Constitutional Court to the ECJ' (2013) 19 *European Public Law* 271 or Robert Zbíral, 'Czech Constitutional Court, judgment of 31 January 2012, Pl.ÚS 5/12. A Legal revolution or negligible episode? Court of Justice decision proclaimed ultra vires' (2012) 49 *Common Market Law Review* 1475.

74 See e.g. Pavel Rychetský et al., *Ústava České republiky. Ústavní zákon o bezpečnosti České republiky. Komentář* (Wolters Kluwer 2015) 929.

75 See e.g. Vladimír Sládeček et al., *Ústava České republiky. Komentář* (C. H. Beck 2016) 1018–1027; Michal Bobek, Zdeněk Kühn et al. *Judikatura a právní argumentace* (Auditorium 2013).

their academic writings.[76] For the treatment of other legal opinions expressed in the reasoning of the CCC's judgements, the term 'discursive bindingness' has been proposed,[77] which further limits the effects of the CCC's law-making.

11 Conclusions

As is clear from the examples mentioned in the preceding text, the law-making activity of the CCC does exist. While, most frequently, this law-making activity is linked to creatively clarifying the meaning of selected provisions of the Constitution or filling in the gaps existing in the constitutional text, on several occasions the CCC has not even hesitated to redefine the core notions of Czech constitutional law and, thus, to transform, albeit to a limited extent, the Czech Constitution. The truth is, however, that the CCC generally puts the emphasis on the fact that its role is that of a negative legislator, which implies that law-making is reserved for rather exceptional cases, which the CCC considers to be of constitutionally high importance. Moreover, the impact of case law, which has a law-making dimension, is never a priori certain and depends on the capacity of the CCC to persuade other constitutional actors that its decisions should indeed be taken seriously and be as binding as possible, which seems to be more of a practical task rather than a legal exercise.

76 For the criticism of the first interpretative judgment according to the legal doctrine, see e.g. Pavel Rychetský, 'Několik poznámek k roli českého ústavního soudnictví při ochraně ústavně zaručených práv a svobod' in Vojtěch Šimíček (ed.), *Role nejvyšších soudů v evropských ústavních systémech – čas pro změnu?* (Masarykova univerzita, 2007) 105.

77 Jan Wintr, 'Position of the Binding Effect of Case Law in the Interpretative Methodology of Continental Law' in Pavel Šámal, Guido Raimondi & Koen Lenaerts et al., *Binding effect of judicial decisions – national and international perspectives* (Kluwer Law International 2018) 97.

7 The Hungarian Constitutional Court as a law-maker

Various tools and changing roles

Zoltán Pozsár-Szentmiklósy

1 Legal status of the Constitutional Court in Hungary

The establishment of the CC is one of the main achievements of the transition from the state-socialist period to pluralistic democracy in Hungary, in 1989. The peaceful transition was controlled by the National Roundtable, composed of three 'sides': the then governing state-socialist party, the coalition of the opposition movements (the so-called Opposition Roundtable) and some civic movements, which were involved in the negotiations by the state-socialist party.[1] The members of the National Roundtable did not have an intention to formulate a new constitution for the country, rather to implement the essential legal conditions and safeguards for free elections to be organized. According to the consideration of the members of the National Roundtable, the new constitution of the democratic Hungary should be enacted by the new, freely elected parliament. Therefore, the results of the negotiations at the National Roundtable aiming at establishing the basic conditions for free elections were enacted by the one-party Parliament (elected in 1985). However, this process resulted in a comprehensive amendment to the state-socialist constitution, which was in force at that time,[2] the enactment of a dozen of new acts, and the proclamation of the Republic of Hungary.[3] As part of the safeguards of the transition, the establishment of the CC was included in the comprehensive amendment to the Constitution and the Act on the CC[4] (hereinafter CC Act 1989) was enacted.

The CC started to function from 1 January 1990. From the very first period of functioning, it had a significant impact on the building process of the state governed by the rule of law. By answering the most challenging dilemmas related to fundamental rights (e.g. death penalty, 1990),[5] governmental structure (e.g. 1991 and 1992 decisions on the function and competences of the head of the

1 For a detailed analysis of the social background of the political transition see Rudolf Tőkés, 'Political Transition and Social Transformation in Hungary' (1996) 34–35 *Afers Internacionals* 79–101.

2 Act XX of 1949.

3 23 October 1989.

4 Act XXXII of 1989 on the Constitutional Court.

5 Decision 23/1990, of 31 October 1990.

DOI: 10.4324/9781003022442-8

state),[6] revealing the content of constitutional principles (e.g. separation of powers, 1993,[7] proportionality, 1992,[8] people's sovereignty, and the exercise of representative and direct democracy, 1993),[9] it became quickly trusted in Hungarian society, as well as recognized at the international level.[10]

As to the role the CC played in the governmental system of Hungary, two periods can be mentioned. The first period marks the first 20 years of the CC, lasting from its establishment (1 January 1990) till the end of the parliamentary cycle 2006–2010 (13 May 2010). In this period, the legal status and the competences of the CC were prescribed in the 1989 Constitution[11] and the CC Act 1989. According to the regulation, the Court was composed of eleven members. The justices were nominated by a special parliamentary committee, which functioned on a parity basis. The justices were elected by a two-thirds majority of the members of parliament for a nine-year mandate, which was renewable once. The members of the CC elected the president of the Court among themselves.[12]

The most significant competence of the Court was posterior, abstract norm control, which could be initiated by every individual claiming the interest of the public *(actio popularis)*. Individuals could also initiate the procedure of the Court in the case of legislative omissions, which resulted in a state of affairs that contradicted the provisions of the Constitution. The other competences of the Court were: prior norm control of statutes (initiated by the head of the state in a form of a legislative veto); prior norm control of international treaties; concrete norm control initiated by judges while suspending a judicial case in which a questionable piece of legislation had to be applied; constitutional complaints initiated by individuals, claiming the limitation of a fundamental right caused by an unconstitutional piece of legislation applied in the individual judicial case; abstract constitutional interpretation (initiated by qualified state organs); and handling disputes on the conflicting competences between state organs.[13] One can evaluate the position of the CC as a powerful counterbalance of the political powers (the legislative and the executive power).[14]

The enactment of the Fundamental Law of Hungary (hereinafter Fundamental Law), the new constitution of the country, which entered into force on 1 January 2012, and the preceding legislative steps taken by the National Assembly, which

6 Decisions 48/1991, of 26 September 1991, and 36/1992, of 10 June 1992.
7 Decision 38/1993, of 11 June 1993.
8 Decision 30/1992, of 26 May 1992.
9 Decision 2/1993, of 22 January 1993.
10 László Sólyom, 'The Role of CCs in the Transition to Democracy. With Special Reference to Hungary' (2003) 18 *International Sociology* 1 133–161.
11 In legal literature, after the enactment of Act XXXI of 1989, and Act XL of 1990, as comprehensive amendments to it, the former Constitution, Act XX of 1949, is considered a substantially new constitution, often called 'Constitution 1989'. See: István Kukorelli, 'Húsz éve alkotmányozunk' (2009) 2 *Közjogi Szemle* 3, 1–10.
12 CC Act 1989 Chapter II.
13 CC Act 1989 Chapter IV.
14 István Stumpf, 'The Hungarian Constitutional Court's Place in the Constitutional System of Hungary' (2017) 13 *Civic Review* (Special Issue) 239, 242.

started its mandate on the 14 May 2010, as well as the new Act on the CC (hereinafter CC Act 2011),[15] changed the legal status, competences, and profile of the CC profoundly.[16] This period, marked by heated debates on constitutionality,[17] also resulted in significant changes in the status and competences of the CC, as well is its relations with other state organs. The Court is composed of fifteen justices, who are appointed by a special parliamentary committee, which – contrary to the former, parity-based functioning – functions on a majoritarian basis. Identical to the former regulation, the justices are elected by the two-thirds majority of the members of parliament. The mandate of the justices is twelve years and it is not renewable. The president of the Court is elected by the Parliament, among the acting justices.[18]

As to the competences of the Court, abstract posterior norm control is still among the powers of the Court, however, according to the present regulation, this procedure cannot be initiated by individuals, only by qualified state organs.[19] It is deeply controversial that – according to the Fundamental Law – fiscal laws cannot be subject of posterior abstract norm control[20] – as a consequence, the system of protection of constitutional norms is not comprehensive. On the other hand, the CC Act 2011 prescribes that the 'uniformity decisions' of the Curia (the supreme organ of the ordinary judicial system), which have normative force and are compulsory for the ordinary judges, can be subject of posterior norm control.[21] The examination of legislative omissions cannot be initiated – it is up to the Court to reach the conclusion of omission as a result of another procedure.[22] The other competences of the Court (prior norm control of legislative acts, prior norm control of international treaties, concrete norm control initiated by judges while suspending a judicial case, abstract constitutional interpretation) did not change compared to the former regulation.[23] The constitutional complaint can be submitted to the Court on three grounds – claiming in all cases the limitation of fundamental rights: (1) in the case of a judgement based on an unconstitutional piece of legislation (identical to the former regulation), (2) in the case of a judgement based on a legislative interpretation, which is in contradiction with the provisions of the Fundamental Law (the so-called 'German-type' constitutional complaint), and (3) if a piece of legislation causes limitation of fundamental rights

15 Act on the CLI. of 2011 on the CC.
16 See e.g. Fruzsina Gárdos-Orosz, 'The Hungarian CC in Transition – from Actio Popularis to Constitutional Complaint' (2012) 53 *Acta Juridica Hungarica* 4, 302–315.
17 See e.g. European Commission for Democracy through Law (Venice Commission), 'Opinion on the New Constitution of Hungary' (2011) Opinion no. 621/2011; Gábor Attila Tóth (ed.), *Constitution for a Disunited Nation* (CEU Press 2012); Lóránt Csink et al. (eds.), *The Basic Law of Hungary. A First Commentary* (Clarus Press 2012).
18 Fundamental Law Article 24; CC Act 2011, Sections 5–9.
19 Ibid., Article 24 para. (2) point (e).
20 Ibid., Article 37 para. (4).
21 CC Act 2011 Section 37 para (2).
22 Ibid., Section 46.
23 Ibid., Chapter II.

directly, without its application in an individual case ('direct constitutional complaint').[24] As a consequence, one can conclude that according to the new regulation, the CC is not a significant counterbalance of political powers anymore, rather of the ordinary judiciary.[25]

As mentioned above, due to the fact that, by its categorical interpretations, the CC took an active role in the building process of the state governed by the rule of law, so that it became an institution which enjoyed social trust in the early years after the transition.[26] On the other hand, as its decisions necessarily narrowed the room of manoeuvre of political actors, in legal and political discourse, soon after, debates appeared related to the 'activist' role taken by the Court and its 'strong' competences.[27] However, in-depth analyses of the practice of the Court demonstrate that it took a rather constructive approach in its relations with the legislature.[28] When the National Assembly, which enacted the Fundamental Law, started its mandate (2010), the activity of the CC was the subject of strong political critiques from the side of the governing parliamentary majority as context for the enactment of the new regulation relating to the legal status and competences of the Court. In legal science, political constitutionalism[29] and juristocracy[30] can be considered as relatively new concepts, which influence the current debates on constitutional adjudication.

2 Overview of the law-making activity of the Constitutional Court

The CC Act 2011 authorizes the CC to establish its Rules of Procedure.[31] The Rule of Procedure[32] takes the form of a normative decision, which is binding only for the Court itself. This document contains provisions related to the organizational structure of the Court, competences of the president, vice-president and judges, as well as general and special procedural rules. The Rules of Procedure is

24 Ibid., Sections 26–27.

25 Eszter Bodnár, Fruzsina Gárdos-Orosz, Zoltán Pozsár-Szentmiklósy, 'Hungary. The state of liberal democracy' in Richard Albert et al. (eds.), *2017 Global Review of Constitutional Law* (I-CONnect – Clough Center 2018) 129.

26 For a detailed analysis see László Sólyom, 'The Hungarian CC and Social Change' (1994) 19 *Yale Journal of International Law* 1 223–237.

27 See e.g. Gábor Halmai, 'Az aktivizmus vége? A Sólyom-bíróság kilenc éve' (1999) Fundamentum 2 5–27; Béla Pokol, 'Demokrácia, jogállam, konstitucionalizmus: a magyar alkotmányos berendezkedés feszültségei' in Kurtán Sándor, Sándor Péter, Vass László (eds.), *Magyarország politikai évkönyve 1998* (Demokrácia Kutatások Magyar Központja Alapítvány 1998) 409–417.

28 See Kálmán Pócza, Gábor Dobos, Attila Gyulai, 'The Hungarian CC. A constructive partner in constitutional dialogue' in Kálmán Pócza (ed.), *Constitutional Politics and the Judiciary. Decision-making in Central and Eastern Europe* (Routledge 2018) 96–125. The analysis is related to the period 1990–2015.

29 Attila Antal, 'Politikai és jogi alkotmányosság Magyarországon' (2013) XXII *Politikatudományi Szemle* 3, 48–70.

30 Béla Pokol, *A jurisztokratikus állam* (Dialóg Campus 2017).

31 CC Act 2011. Section 50 para. (2) point (c).

32 Decision 1001/2013, of 27 February 2013.

the sole legal norm issued by the CC based on an explicit, formal authorization of a statute, therefore, it can be named as '*explicit law-making*.'

Alongside issuing the Rules of Procedure, the CC plays a significant role in the development of the law, both on the constitutional and sub-constitutional levels.

On the constitutional level, the CC a dozen times has informally amended the constitution by way of constitutional interpretation: ten times based on the 1989 Constitution and twice after the enactment of the Fundamental Law.[33] All these cases were based on the interpretation of those provisions of the constitution which were vague, and therefore needed clarification. By clarifying the content of these provisions, the Court often has identified new constitutional norms, therefore, this activity can be described as '*law-making by constitutional interpretation*'.

On the sub-constitutional level, the most powerful effect of the activity of the CC on the content of the legal system is its classic role of '*negative legislator*' by declaring unconstitutionality of legal norms and annulling these.[34] In this regard, the Hungarian CC exercises the strong form of judicial review as its decision is final, authoritative, and binding.[35] As a result of the decision of the Court, the normative content of a particular legal field changes, in the sense that the examined piece of legislation is not part of the legal system anymore. This creates an interest and duty on the side of the legislature to replace the annulled piece of legislation with a new version, which presumably was not in contradiction with the provisions of the constitution anymore. Accordingly, the Court formulates the substance of legal norms only from the negative side by setting bans related to their content.

Moreover, when exercising its competences, the Hungarian CC can turn to two formal tools, which can formulate the content of the law in a more direct way. The Court can determine '*legislative omission*' in the case that a state organ has missed genuinely accomplishing its regulating task following from the Constitution.[36] This type of ruling creates a direct duty of regulation or re-regulation on the side of the legislature. In other cases, the CC can express '*constitutional requirements*,' i.e. the compulsory interpretation of the challenged piece of legislation, which has to be taken into consideration by every state organ when applying the law in question.[37] Both the legislative omissions and the constitutional requirements are expressed in the ruling part of the decisions, therefore have clear normative (constitutional) basis and direct binding effect. As these cases require the analysis of the relevant provisions of the constitution, as well of the challenged piece of legislation, negative legislation, and in a more direct way, declaring

33 Tímea Drinóczi, Fruzsina Gárdos-Orosz, Zoltán Pozsár-Szentmiklósy, 'Formal and informal constitutional amendment in Hungary' (2019) *MTA Law Working Papers* 18 https://jog.tk.mta.hu/uploads/files/2019_18_Drinoczi_GardosOrosz_PozsarSzentmiklosy.pdf.

34 Fundamental Law Article 24 para. (3).

35 On the forms of judicial review see: Mark V. Tushnet, 'Alternative Forms of Judicial Review' (2003) 101 *Michigan Law Review* 2781, 2784.

36 CC Act 2011. Section 46 para. (1) and (2).

37 Ibid., Section 46 para. (3).

legislative omission and constitutional requirement can be considered as '*law-making by constitutional and legal interpretation.*'

One may add that since the enactment of the Fundamental Law, the CC turns more often to these legal consequences instead of anulling the challenged pieces of legislation, compared to the previous period.[38] A plausible explanation for this tendency could be the Court's intention not to enter into direct conflicts with the political powers. Not surprisingly, this trend seems to be more acceptable to the National Assembly and the Government.

Another aspect can be mentioned related to the decisions of the CC. According to the CC Act 2011, the decisions of the CC are binding[39] – accordingly, every state organ shall respect and follow these. However, it is not clear whether only the ruling part, or even the reasoning part, of the decisions is compulsory. There are strong arguments demonstrating that the ruling part has the strongest normative basis: the norms of the constitution and of the CC Act include clear provisions, which establish the powers of the Court and the possible legal consequences it can impose – all these relate to the ruling part of the decision. Therefore, the 'law-making effect' of the Court's decisions can be precisely identified in the case of decisions, which include '*positive law-making considerations*' in their ruling part: informal constitutional amendments, legislative omissions, and constitutional requirements. In the following pages of this chapter, I will analyze the Court's practice related to these legal institutions.

Some considerations related to legal interpretation are also relevant. Irrespective of the outcome of a particular decision, the Court has to express its position on the precise meaning of the examined piece of legislation in order to answer the question of its compliance with the norms of the constitution. This kind of legal interpretation is inevitable and required to be in accordance with the professional standards followed by other stakeholders active in the particular legal field (law-enforcement agencies, state authorities, judges, attorneys, academia, etc.). However, it can happen that the legal interpretation of the Court is '*creative*' in the sense that it does not harmonize with these standards, and creates a new perspective or even a possible new normative content related to the challenged piece of legislation. In the unlikely situation that this new interpretation is accepted by stakeholders active in the particular legal field, it can also be assessed as '*law-making by legal interpretation.*' However, as in such cases the interpretation of the challenged piece of legislation is not directly linked to the provisions of the constitution and is included in the reasoning part of the decision (not in the ruling part of it), the legislation has a much weaker effect on the activity of other stakeholders.

Nevertheless, in one aspect the CC can turn 'creative interpretation' into a more precise examination of constitutionality of the challenged piece of legislation. In the early years of its functioning, the Court started to refer to the '*living law doctrine.*'[40] In the Hungarian context, this doctrine calls for the examination of

38 See Eszter Bodnár, Fruzsina Gárdos-Orosz, Zoltán Pozsár-Szentmiklósy (n 25) 129.
39 CC Act 2011. Section 39 para. (1).
40 Decision 57/1991, of 8 November 1991.

the application, enforcement of the law (piece of legislation), which is the subject of the procedure before the CC. Accordingly, the meaning of the challenged piece of the legislation is not identified solely based on the text and certain methods of legal interpretation, but rather by taking also into consideration the practice related to it. As a consequence, the examination of constitutionality can be more precise in the sense that the Court can take into consideration the effects of the application of the law on constitutional principles or individual rights. In other words, in cases when the content of the regulation itself is not problematic, but the practice related to it could be in conflict with constitutional standards, this doctrine allows the Court to examine the context of the law. As explained under the following heading, the living law doctrine is particularly relevant in the case of constitutional requirements.

3 Analysis of the law-making practice of the Constitutional Court

3.1 Explicit law-making activity (Rules of Procedure)

As mentioned above, the Rules of Procedure is the sole legal norm issued by the CC based on an explicit, formal authorization of law. According to the previous regulation, marked by the 1989 Constitution and CC Act 1989, the National Assembly was responsible for the enactment of the Rules of Procedure of the CC, on the proposal of the Court itself.[41] Even this provision seems to be problematic from the point of view of the principle of separation of powers; the CC declared that this procedure does not necessarily lead to the restriction of the independence of the Court as the regulation requires a cooperation between the different branches of government.[42] However, the National Assembly did not enact the Rules of Procedure of the CC while the CC Act 1989 was in force. As a reaction to this situation, the Court declared that this cannot be assessed as legislative omission taking into consideration that the legislative duty of the National Assembly does not directly follow from the provisions of the Constitution.[43] As a result, the Court issued its Temporary Rules of Procedure, taking the form of a normative decision.[44] The Temporary Rules of Procedure were in force until the issuance on the Rules of Procedure, based on the authorization of the CC Act 2011.

The CC Act 2011 expressly authorizes the CC to issue its own Rules of Procedure[45] – therefore, the National Assembly has no formal role in the process. The Court issued its first Rules of Procedure based on an explicit legal authorization in 2012,[46] which took the form of a normative decision voted by the plenary session of the Court. One year later, this document was replaced by new Rules of

41 Section 29. CC Act 1989.
42 Decision 2/2002, of 25 January 2002.
43 Ibid.
44 Decision 3/2001, of 3 December 2001.
45 CC Act 2011. Section 70 para. (1).
46 Decision 1/2012, of 3 January 2012 on the Rules of Procedure of the CC.

Procedure[47] – a normative decision, which is actually in force. Until the present, the Rules of Procedure have been amended six times.[48]

As to the particularities of the Rules of Procedure, it may be said to have highlighted the basic components of the Hungarian legal system. According to the Fundamental Law, generally binding rules of conduct can be included only in laws, issued by organs having legislative competence and specified in the Fundamental Law.[49] Alongside the laws, the Hungarian legal system also knows the 'public regulatory instruments,' namely, normative decisions and normative instructions.[50] These legal instruments can regulate the organization, operation, activities, and action plans of the issuing organ – accordingly, these may not include any provisions which regulate the activities of others. According to the Act on law-making, the CC is expressly authorized to regulate these questions in its case in a normative decision[51] – this is the legal form of the Rules of Procedure.

The Rules of Procedure contains detailed provisions related to the organizational structure of the Court, including the competences of the president, the justices, and the secretary general, the composition of the committees, as well of the procedures before the Court, including the preparation process, the interim measures, the adoption and publishing of the decisions, etc. All these elements can be considered as topics related to the internal regulation of the activities of the Court. Some of the rules are repeated provisions of existing laws, e.g. the forms of legal representation, and the requirements related to applications for extension (included in several procedural acts), while the majority of these are about the specification of the procedures of the Court related to its competences prescribed in law. However, in some cases the Procedural Rules contain provisions which affect the rights of others (those persons and entities who turn to the Court) in a way which is neither repetition nor specification of existing laws, rather the prescription of new norms. Some examples of related – questionable – norms: determining (in an exemplificative manner) cases which can lead to the exclusion of a member of the Court due to personal and direct connectedness to the subject of the case,[52] regulating the publicity of the memoranda and voice recordings on the sittings of the Court,[53] prescribing deadlines for open for the submission of the answer of organs to which the Court turns for consultation in individual cases.[54]

47 Decision 1001/2013, of 27 February 2013 on the Rules of Procedure of the CC.

48 Decisions: 1003/2013, of 21 December 2013, 1001/2014, of 20 March 2014, 1003/2015, of 21 July 2015, 1004/2015, of 16 December 2015, 1002/2016, of 21 April 2016, 1005/2016, of 22 June 2016, 1001/2018, of 8 March 2018.

49 Fundamental Law Article (T) para. (1). According to the Fundamental Law (not taking into consideration the state of emergency) these laws shall be acts, government decrees, decrees of the members of the Government, decrees of the Governor of the Hungarian National Bank, decrees of the heads of independent regulatory organs and local government decrees. See Article (T) para. (2).

50 Act CXXX. of 2010. on Law-making Section 1 para. (1), point (b).

51 Ibid., Section 22 para. (1), point (d).

52 Procedural Rules, Section 50.

53 Procedural Rules, Sections 13–14.

54 Ibid., Section 36 para. (3).

Despite the controversial provisions, the Rules of Procedure is a necessary tool to regulate the internal organizational structure and procedures of the Court. Taking into account professional standards, requirements related to the independence of the Court, and the formal separation of powers, one can conclude that it is a better solution to authorize the Court to regulate this field, and not to involve the National Assembly in the process.

3.2 Law-making by constitutional interpretation (informal constitutional amendments)[55]

As highlighted earlier, the CC has amended the constitution informally twelve times, by way of constitutional interpretation. As a result, the normative content of the constitution was changed – a fact which caused three types of reactions on the side of the National Assembly, the state organ competent to amend the constitution in a formal way. In some cases the National Assembly has accepted the interpretation of the Court and did not react to that by way of legislation or formal amendment to the constitution. In other cases the National Assembly included formally in the text of the constitution the normative content of the interpretation of the Court, by way of formal amendment. There are also examples of 'over-constitutionalization,' including provisions to the text of the constitution by way of formal amendment with a content which contradicts the interpretation of the Court.

As examples to the second case (acceptance of the Court's interpretation and including formally the normative content of it into the text of the constitution by way of formal constitutional amendment), there can be mentioned the decisions related to the function and competences of the President of the Republic, the head of the state. In a decision of 1991,[56] the Court held that the President could refuse the appointment of state officials if the conditions required by law are not met or if he or she has well-grounded reasons to conclude that the appointment would lead to a serious disorder in the democratic functioning of the state. The Court made a sound statement on this competence, although the 1989 Constitution did not contain any similar provision, only the duty of the President to appoint state officials based on the proposals of the nominating organs (in most of the cases, Government).[57] The basis of this power, according to the Court, is the function of the President as the guardian of the democratic operation of the state organization.[58] Accordingly, the intervention of refusal is seen as an extraordinary measure to maintain the democratic operation of the state. One year later, the Court further explained the criteria which opened up the possibility for the President to refuse an appointment.[59] Later, in 2007, the Court held that the

55 The basis of this part is an analysis written together with Tímea Drinóczi and Fruzsina Gárdos-Orosz. See Tímea Drinóczi, Fruzsina Gárdos-Orosz, Zoltán Pozsár-Szentmiklósy (n 33) 19–20, 24–25.

56 Decision 48/1991, of 26 September 1991.

57 1989 Constitution Articles 30/A para. (1) points (c) and (i), 33 para. (4).

58 Ibid., Article 29 para. (1).

59 Decisions 8/1992, of 30 January 1992 and 36/1992, of 10 June 1992.

President has a substantial discretionary right to refuse to award prizes in the name of the state (proposed by the Government) if it would violate the values enshrined in the constitutional order of Hungary. One can note that – similarly to the regulation on the appointments – the 1989 Constitution contained only the duty of the President to award prizes based on the proposals of nominating bodies.[60] The Court held that any recommendation for an award or the conferring of an award that violates the constitutional values of the Republic of Hungary or that reflects a different scale of values is unconstitutional as it contravenes constitutional values.[61]

In these cases, the Court had to decide on the modality of resolving the constitutional gap. The Court had chosen constitutional interpretation, even though dissenting opinions were attached to each of these decisions claiming that this choice had been unconstitutional. Judges criticizing the decisions on the refusal of an appointment, were of the opinion that determining criteria for refusal of an appointment fall within the powers of the constitution-making power.[62] Moreover, according to the dissenting judges, the refusal to award a prize based on the constitutional value order would create a non-textual constitutional basis for the President to make political decisions without due constitutional restraints – a state of affairs which is in contradiction with the principle of separation of powers.[63]

After the publication of the decisions of the CC, the relevant state organs (the President, the National Assembly, and the Government) accepted these considerations and performed their activities related to appointments and awards in line with the interpretation of the Court.[64] There were no attempts at over-constitutionalization, formal constitutional amendment, or ordinary legislation in these questions. However, during the drafting process of the Fundamental Law, these considerations were taken into account by the constituent power, and the power of the President to refuse appointments or awards was formally included in the text of the Fundamental Law, among the competences of the head of the state.[65]

Another illustrative example on the law-making activity of the CC at the constitutional level is the case related to constitutional identity. The Court declared in 2016 that by exercising its competences, it can examine whether the joint exercise of competences with EU member states and institutions under 'EU clause'[66] of the Fundamental Law infringes human dignity, other fundamental rights, the sovereignty, or the constitutional identity of Hungary. According to the Court, the constitutional identity of Hungary is rooted in its historical constitution and

60 1989 Constitution Article 30/A para. (1) point (j).

61 Decision 47/2007, of 3 July 2007.

62 See dissenting opinions of Géza Kilényi, Péter Shmidt and Imre Vörös (Decisions 1991, 1992).

63 See dissenting opinions of László Kiss and István Kukorelli (Decision 2007).

64 One can note that presidential refusals of appointments and awards were rare exceptions due to the fact that usually there is cooperation between the state organs in these questions.

65 Fundamental Law Article 9. paras. (6)–(7).

66 Ibid., Article (E) para. (2).

has not been created but only recognized by the Fundamental Law.[67] Even though the Court holds that the constitutional identity of Hungary cannot be featured by an exhaustive listing of values, it nevertheless mentions some of them, such as freedoms, the separation of powers, the republican form of state, and freedom of religion.[68] The decision was issued based on the request of the ombudsperson for abstract constitutional interpretation related to the implementation of the 2015 EU 'refugee quota decision'[69] – against which the Government expressed a definite opposing position. One can note that based on the initiative of the Government in 2016, even a national referendum was organized related to the 'refugee quotas' and the compulsory settlement of non-Hungarian citizens in Hungary. The constitutional ground of the referendum was questionable,[70] however, its result was not valid, due to the fact that the voters did not cast valid votes in the required proportion. Nevertheless, the Government initiated a formal amendment to the Fundamental Law in order to implement provisions to its text on the protection of constitutional identity and bans on the settlement of 'foreign population' in the country. In 2016, the amendment did not pass in the National Assembly, however, the decision of the CC published at the end of the year seemed to react to these notions. In 2016, the explanation on constitutional identity based on constitutional interpretation was inevitably an informal amendment to the constitution, as the Fundamental Law at that time did not contain any provision related to identity or the special protection of the values included in that concept. As a result, the Court created an ambiguous implicit eternity clause.

Later, in 2018, the decision of the CC was the textual basis for the Seventh amendment to the Fundamental Law, which successfully passed. According to the amendment, the exercise of competences of the country as a member of the European Union shall not limit the inalienable right of Hungary to determine its territorial unity, population, form of government, and state structure.[71] Moreover, the protection of the constitutional identity and Christian culture of Hungary shall be an obligation of every organ of the State.[72] As a result, the informal amendment to the constitution expressed in the constitutional interpretation of the CC was not only confirmed by the constitution amending power, rather followed by wording. However, the most controversial element of this process is that in its reasoning the Court followed the former, unsuccessful proposal (2016) for the

67 Decision 22/2016, of 5 December 2016.

68 For a detailed analysis see Zoltán Pozsár-Szentmiklósy – Veronika Kéri, 'The decision of the Hungaria CC on constitutional identity' [Decision 22/2016. (XII. 5.) CC] (2018) 9 *Romanian Journal of Comparative Law* 2 299–327.

69 Council Decision 2015/1601, of 22 September 2015.

70 See Zoltán Szente, 'Analysis: The Controversial Anti-Migrant Referendum in Hungary is Invalid' IACL-AIDC Blog (19 October 2016) https://iacl-aidc-blog.org/2016/10/18/the-controversial-anti-migrant-referendum-in-hungary-is-invalid/; Zoltán Pozsár-Szentmiklósy, 'A Kúria végzése a betelepítési kvótáról szóló népszavazási kérdésről. Országgyűlési hatáskör az európai jog homályában' (2016) VII. Jogesetek Magyarázata 1–2.

71 Fundamental Law Article (E) para. (2).

72 Ibid., Article (R) para. (4).

amendment to the Fundamental Law. Therefore, in this case the informal amendment was influenced even by the intention of the constitution-amending power – an element, which is manifestly problematic from the point of view of the separation of powers.

3.3 Law-making by constitutional and legal interpretation (positive law-making considerations)

As to the law-making at the subconstitutional level, it is worth examining the practice related to those legal instruments which formulate the content of the law in a direct way: the legislative omission and the use of constitutional requirements.

3.3.1 Legislative omissions

After the enactment of the Fundamental Law and CC Act 2011, examining legislative omissions is not a distinct competence of the Court, rather a legal consequence, which can be declared related to other procedures. The Court turns to this consequence relatively frequently; in the period 2013–2018, it has declared the legislative omission 29 times.[73]

From the preceding period, it is worth analysing the decisions related to the formulation of single member constituencies on parliamentary elections, as these are illustrative examples on the functioning of the legislative omission. In 2005, the CC has declared[74] legislative omission regarding the implementation in the law of the requirements related to the principle of equal right to vote, which was explicitly declared in the 1989 Constitution.[75] According to Act XXXIV of 1989 on the election of the members of the National Assembly (hereinafter Election Act 1989), the Government was authorized to prescribe in a decree the boundaries of single member constituencies. The law applied a mixed system for the election of the 386 members of the National Assembly: 176 MPs were elected in single member constituencies on a majority basis, while the other MPs could win their mandates on a proportional basis by taking into consideration the votes of the citizens on the 'territorial lists' of the political parties and the surplus votes of the 'national list'. According to the petitioner's arguments, it was problematic that the law did not prescribe any re-examination of the boundaries of single member constituencies, although demographic changes could cause extreme differences in the number of the population of the different constituencies during the previous years. Therefore, the functioning of the equal right to vote was challenged.

73 Public data on the practice of the Court based on the new regulation is available only related to this period. More specifically: the Court declared legislative omissions twice in 2013, once in 2014, six times in 2015, three times in 2016, seven times in 2017, and ten times in 2018. See https://alkotmanybirosag.hu/ugyforgalmi-es-statisztikai-adatok?ev=2011.

74 Decision 22/2005, of 17 June 2005.

75 Constitution 1989 Article 71 para (1).

When interpreting the equal right to vote, the CC referred to the double nature of this principle: equality in the number of votes and equality in the weight of the votes. By explaining the content of the latter requirement, the Court also took into consideration the Code of good practice in electoral matters of the Venice Commission.[76] According to this, only a 10% difference in the size of the population of the electoral district (constituencies) is acceptable, while this difference may not exceed 15% at any case. The boundaries of the constituencies shall be re-examined in every 10 year by taking into consideration the administrative structure, ethnical and cultural peculiarities of the country and the region, as well as the opinion of independent experts. Based on these professional standards, the Court reached the conclusion that the equal right to vote requires explicit safeguards in the Election Act 1989 for the regular re-examination of the boundaries of the constituencies. In this regard, the Court declared a legislative omission and set a two-year deadline for the National Assembly to include the related norms into the regulation. Moreover, the Court expressed constitutional requirements directly affecting the future regulation. According the Court, it is required to have the least possible difference in the number of voters belonging to different constituencies. It is worth mentioning that in the reasoning part of the decision the Court has expressed its opinion from the point of view of functioning of the professional standards and excluding manipulation, and did not focus on the form of the regulation, i.e. on the fact that the Government is authorized to determine the boundaries of the constituencies.

The National Assembly did fulfil its legislative duty prescribed by the CC, and two consecutive parliamentary elections (2006, 2010) were held based on the identical – problematic – regulation. Based on new petitions, in 2010, the CC examined again the questions related to the equal right to vote and the boundaries of the single member constituencies.[77] As a result, the Court annulled the authorization of the Government to regulate the boundaries of the constituencies included in the Election Act and the related governmental decree.[78] (The annulment was declared on a *pro futuro* basis, with the 31 December 2011.)

Based on the petitions, in this case the Court focused on the level of regulation and the hierarchy of norms. According to the Constitution 1989, the rules related to the exercise fundamental rights shall be included in laws.[79] The Court also took into consideration the existence of so-called 'two-thirds laws': laws on legislative topics, which – according to the Constitution – require two-thirds vote of the

76 European Commission for Democracy through Law (Venice Commission), 'Code of good practice in electoral matters. Guidelines and explanatory report' (2002) Opinion no. 190/2002.

77 Decision 193/2010, of 8 December 2010.

78 2/1990. (I. 11.) Decree of the Council of Ministers.

79 Constitution 1989. Article 8 para. (2).

MPs present at the sitting of the Parliament.[80] As the Constitution declared that the election of MPs is a 'two-thirds legislative topic,' the Court structured specified this requirement. According to the Court, the safeguards of the right to vote and the basic elements of the electoral system – including safeguards and standards for the re-examination of constituencies – shall be included in a law enacted by the two-thirds majority. Other provisions – such as the boundaries of the constituencies – can be included in an ordinary law, while only technical rules can be set at the level of a governmental decree.

At this point two comments can be made. First, even in the 2010 case, the Court did not declare a legislative omission and also did not refer to constitutional requirements, and in its reasoning made more precise considerations for the legislature to take into account. As a consequence, the National Assembly was forced to enact a new regulation in this field – which finally took place in the form of the enactment of the new act on parliamentary elections.[81] One can note that, based on the provisions of the Fundamental Law, the National Assembly would enact the new regulation in the absence of the decision of the Court as well. This act reacted to some extent to the requirements prescribed by the CC – however, only partly. Even the boundaries of the constituencies are set in the law, and there are no safeguards for a regular re-examination of these based on professional standards. Moreover, as the boundaries of constituencies are included in a cardinal law – so it may happen in the future that this norm would not be flexible enough to react on the necessary changes based on the time passed.[82]

Second, in these cases the Court made clear its source of inspiration: the Code of good practice in electoral matters. It is worth mentioning that in other cases the Court refers to the practice of international entities and foreign courts rather including additional arguments in its reasoning. Accordingly, in this case the international standards influenced the Hungarian formal legislation by the transmission of the law-making activity of the CC.

3.3.2 Constitutional requirements

In the case of constitutional requirements, the trend is opposite compared with legislative omissions. The CC Act 1989 did not explicitly contain the possibility of the Court to issue constitutional requirements – therefore, the use of this legal consequence itself can be assessed as an example to law-making activity of the Court on the sub-constitutional level. The CC Act 2011 explicitly declared the possibility of the Court to issue constitutional requirements – accordingly, in this

80 At present, according to the Fundamental Law, these laws are called cardinals laws. It is important to note that these laws are at the same level as ordinary laws in the hierarchy of norms. See Zoltán Pozsár-Szentmiklósy, 'Supermajority in parliamentary systems – A concept of substantive legislative supermajority: Lessons from Hungary' (2017) 58 Acta Juridica Hungarica. *Hungarian Journal of Legal Studies* 3 281–290.

81 Act CCIII. of 2011. On the election of the members of the National Assembly (Election Act 2011).

82 See Election Act 2011. Section 4.

regard, the legislator has formally accepted the result of the law-making activity of the Court. The CC turns to this legal consequence even more frequently than to legislative omissions: in the period 2013–2018, the CC has declared constitutional requirements 39 times.[83]

An illustrative example from the recent practice of the Court related to constitutional requirements is its approach expressed in the decision examining the 'criminalization of homelessness.' The basis of the legal question is the new provision of the Fundamental Law, which was incorporated into the text by the Seventh Amendment (2018). According to this new provision, 'using a public space as a habitual dwelling shall be prohibited.'[84] As a consequence, the National Assembly inserted a new section in the Act on Misdemeanours,[85] which declares habitual dwelling a petty offence. According to these rules, habitual dwelling does not lead to sanction, in the case the concerned person stops this activity due to the warning of the police or accepts the social services provided for homeless people. However, in the case the police warns a person for the third time within a 90-day period, the misdemeanour proceeding must be started. In such a case, the person has to be detained and a court hearing has to take place within three days. The court can use warning, community service or confinement as a sanction. Shortly after entering into force of the new regulation, several misdemeanour proceedings started against homeless people. However, some judges suspended the court hearings and initiated norm control in the concrete cases[86] claiming that the new regulation was unconstitutional; later a constitutional complaint was also filed. The petitioners claimed the violation of human dignity, the requirement of equal treatment and the principle of rule of law. Amicus curiae letters were also filed by NGOs and former justices of the CC.

The CC published its decision in this case in June 2019,[87] which was the subject of intensive criticism.[88] The Court did not find the challenged piece of legislation unconstitutional, rather expressed constitutional requirements related to the application of the law in the ruling part of the decision. According to this statement, in the case of habitual dwelling, sanctions can be imposed only if the homeless person had a verifiable possibility to access the social services provided for homeless people. Moreover, imposing the sanction has to be in accordance with the purpose of the regulation, namely, the involvement of homeless people into the system of supportive (social) services.

83 Public data on the practice of the Court based on the new regulation is available related only to this period. More specifically: 13 times in 2013, 7 times in 2014, 5 times in 2015, 2 times in 2016, 8 times in 2017, 4 times in 2018. See https://alkotmanybirosag.hu/ugyforgalmi-es-statisztikai-adatok?ev=2011.

84 Fundamental Law Article XXII para. (3).

85 Act II of 2012 on Misdemeanours, misdemeanour proceedings and the registration of misdemeanours Article 178/B.

86 CC Act 2011. Section 25.

87 Decision 19/2019, of 18 June 2019.

88 See Viktor Z Kazai, 'No one has the right to be homeless …' Verfassungsblog (13 June 2019) https://verfassungsblog.de/no-one-has-the-right-to-be-homeless/.

When interpreting the related provision of the Fundamental Law, the Court stated that its purpose is the protection of proper use of public spaces as a public interest, that is why the constitution contains a ban related to activities (like habitual dwelling), which counter the functioning of this public interest. On human dignity and freedom of autonomy considerations, the Court emphasized that the individual can exercise his or her rights as a member of the community. As such, when exercising rights, the individual has to cooperate with other members of the community and the state, which is responsible for providing all institutional conditions that support the exercise of fundamental rights and the functioning of public interest. According to the Court, the new sanctions included in the Act on misdemeanours do not sanction people based on their special living conditions, rather the absence of their willingness to cooperate. In the Court's consideration, the new regulation is applicable in the case of all individuals who do not cooperate with the state organs; therefore, it is not discriminatory. The Court also did not find the content of the challenged piece of legislation to be in contradiction with the requirement of clarity of norms.

The case illustrates precisely the present, general attitude of the CC to politically sensitive cases: instead of examining in detail the challenged piece of legislation based on constitutional standards and declaring unconstitutionality, it rather prescribes aspects to take into consideration for law-enforcement agencies and courts, even in unambiguous cases.

As for the application of constitutional requirements, one can point to other considerations as well. As mentioned on p. 133, in the early years of its functioning, the CC often referred to 'living law.'[89] According to this doctrine, in Hungarian jurisprudence, not only the text of examined piece of legislation shall be taken into consideration during norm control, rather the practice of law-enforcement agencies and court related to it. In cases when a certain piece of legislation was not problematic in its own, but its interpretation was in contradiction with the constitution, the Court often used constitutional requirements not to annul the challenged piece of law, but to react on the problematic application of it. One can note that in the 2019 case on the 'homeless regulation' there was no considerable judicial practice, therefore, no 'living law' to be examined. Instead of focusing on the constitutionality of the law, the CC focused on the prevention of possible future violations of the constitution by law-enforcement agencies and ordinary courts.

Another consideration relates the independence of the judiciary and the competence of the Curia (the Supreme Court). According to the Fundamental Law, the Curia has the right to issue uniformity decisions, which are binding on

89 One can note that the Hungarian 'living law' concept is close to the 'living tree' doctrine elaborated by the Supreme Court of Canada, which is the basis of the evolutive constitutional interpretation. However, the Hungarian concept is different, taking into consideration that it focuses on social context of the law, not of the constitution. For a detailed explanation of the living tree doctrine, see W. J. Waluchow, 'The Living Tree' in Peter Oliver, Patrick Macklem, Nathalie Des Rosiers (eds.), *The Oxford Handbook of the Canadian Constitution* (Oxford University Press 2015).

ordinary courts.[90] The Curia issues uniformity decisions if there is a trend that in a certain legal question the interpretation and practice of judges is different, even based on an almost identical factual background. In such cases the Curia prescribes the uniform interpretation of the piece of law in question within a certain context, which has to be followed by ordinary courts. Similarly, if the Curia intends to reformulate a former uniformity decision, it can issue a new one. Due their normative force, uniformity decisions are the subject of norm control before the CC.[91] Constitutional requirements issued by the CC are not much different from the uniformity decisions of the Curia by taking into consideration their effect: both tools are binding on courts, therefore, to some extent both limit the independence of the individual judge. Strong arguments demonstrate that the CC shall issue constitutional requirements only in cases of manifest unconstitutional practice ('living law'). Other types of problematic legal practice can be handled by the Curia with uniformity decisions. More importantly, in cases of manifest unconstitutionality of the challenged piece of legislation, the Court shall exercise its power of annulment.

4 General considerations related to the law-making activity of the Constitutional Court

As a general assessment, one can note that compared to the first two decades of its functioning, at present, based on the Fundamental Law and CC Act 2011, the competences of the Hungarian CC changed in the direction of strengthening the control of the judiciary and weakening the scrutiny related to the activity of central political powers. Moreover, based on the attitude of the Court, this difference is even more sharp: the Court is often reluctant to annul pieces of legislation which relate to sensitive political questions.

Law-making was always present in the activity of the Court, since its establishment (1990). The *explicit law-making* activity relates to the Rules of Procedure – the 2011 regulation operates with an explicit authorization, which strengthens the Court's position in this regard compared to the former regulation. *Law-making by constitutional interpretation* has a significant practice by way of informal constitutional amendments. Even though the constitution-amending power often accepted these interpretations, in the present practice the cooperation between the Court and the National Assembly seems to be more intense in these questions. Law-making by constitutional and legal interpretation is manifest and direct by declaring *legislative omissions* or *constitutional requirements.* At present, none of these can be initiated by petitioners or qualified state organs, but both of these can be expressed in every case before the Court. There is a trend to operate more frequently with these instruments instead of annulling the challenged pieces of legislation. This trend strengthens the cooperation with the legislature, but leaves the question open, whether the system of protection of the constitutional norms is effective?

90 Fundamental Law Article 25 para. (2).
91 CC Act 2011. Section 37 para. (2).

8 The Constitutional Court of the Republic of Latvia as a law-maker

Current practice

Anita Rodiņa and Alla Spale

In Latvia, the exclusive function of safeguarding the Constitution[1] or ensuring the existence of a legal system that complies with the Constitution of the Republic of Latvia – the *Satversme*[2] – is in the hands of the Constitutional Court of the Republic of Latvia (hereinafter, the CC).

Nowadays, the role of the CC as a simple body for dispute resolution has changed. In Latvia, as in other democratic countries governed by the rule of law, politics and law-making are very much 'judicialized.'[3] Besides striking down legal norms, the CC can influence politics and the content of new legal norms and, if necessary, it can also create and establish the legal order. As mentioned in the doctrine, this mix of 'court-like' and quasi-legislative features and functions 'is neither surprising nor inherently problematic.'[4] It is true that in Latvia the public power has accepted the role of the CC in the State. The same conclusion can be drawn with respect to society. Therefore, by fulfilling the so-called negative legislator function, the CC plays a significant role in the State, and if required to do so, it also determines the legal order within its competence and legal status.

1 The legal status of the Constitutional Court of the Republic of Latvia

After the collapse of the Union of Soviet Socialist Republics (USSR), in many new democracies or new countries in Eastern and Central Europe, CCs were established as the guardians of the Constitution.[5] The first legal act at the constitutional

1 Case No. 2009-11-01, of 18 January 2010, Para. 5.
2 The Constitution of 15 February 1922, http://saeima.lv/en/legislation/constitution/.
3 Alec Stone Sweet, *Governing with Judges. Constitutional Politics in Europe* (Oxford University Press 2000) 1.
4 Tom Ginsburg & Zachary Elkins, 'Ancillary Powers of Constitutional Courts' (2008–2009) 87 *Tex. L. Rev.* 1431, 1461.
5 Radoslav Prochazka *Mission Accomplished. On Founding Constitutional Adjudication in Central Europe* (Central European University Press 2002) 33–73; Herman Schwartz *The Struggle for Constitutional Justice in Post-Communist Europe* (The University of Chicago Press 2000) 5–21.

DOI: 10.4324/9781003022442-9

level, envisaging the establishment of a CC in Latvia, was the declaration adopted by the Supreme Council of the Latvian Soviet Socialist Republic (LSSR) on 4 May 1990, 'On the Restoration of the Independence of the Republic of Latvia.' The second sentence in para. 6 provided that '[d]isputes over the issues regarding the application of a legal act shall be resolved by the CC of the Republic of Latvia.'[6] Later, the law of 15 December 1992 'On Judicial Power' envisaged entrusting the Supreme Court with the function of constitutional supervision.[7] Quite soon afterwards, political and legal thought shifted, moving away from the idea of entrusting the right to constitutional supervision to the Supreme Court, and developing the concept of a special court – the CC. On 5 June 1996, the law, 'Amendments to the *Satversme* of the Republic of Latvia,' and also the CC Law, were passed.[8] The CC, as the youngest constitutional institution in Latvia, commenced its activities on 9 December 1996 and passed its first judgement on 7 May 1997.[9]

The constitutional status and regulation of the CC are included in one Article of the *Satversme* – Article 85.[10] The constitutional regulation of the CC does not go into much detail, because it was necessary to retain the very laconic style of the *Satversme*.[11] Therefore, the *Satversme* simply indicates the competence of the CC by giving the authorization to specify it in law; it regulates the legal status of Justices, and the right of the CC to declare laws or other enactments, or parts thereof, as invalid. The CC Law further defines the persons who can stand before the CC, and regulates the procedure of submitting an application and the rules for adjudicating cases.

In accordance with the doctrine of the separation of powers, the CC belongs to the judicial power and performs its functions by administering justice, ensuring control over the two other branches of power.[12] As the aim of the CC is to fulfil

6 Declaration of the Supreme Soviet of the Latvian SSR 'On the Renewal of the Independence of the Republic of Latvia' on 4 May 1990, https://www.uta.edu/cpsees/latind.htm.

7 Law 'On Judicial Power' of 15 December 1992, http://unpan1.un.org/intradoc/groups/public/documents/UNTC/UNPAN018383.pdf.

8 Grozījums Latvijas Republikas Satversmē: LR likums, *Latvijas Vēstnesis*, No. 100/101 (585/586), 12.06.1996.

9 Case No. 1997-04-01, of 7 May 1997.

10 Article 85 of the *Satversme* provides: '[I]n Latvia, there shall be a Constitutional Court, which, within its jurisdiction as provided for by law, shall review Cases concerning the compliance of laws with the Constitution, as well as other matters regarding which jurisdiction is conferred upon it by law. The Constitutional Court shall have the right to declare laws or other enactments or parts thereof invalid. The *Saeima* shall confirm the appointment of judges to the Constitutional Court for the term provided for by law, by secret ballot with a majority of the votes of not less than fifty-one members of the *Saeima*.'

11 The fundamental principles of the constitutional order of the Latvian State are determined by the *Satversme*, adopted on 15 February 1922, which can be recognized as one from among the oldest constitutions in Europe. Following the restoration of independence, the Republic of Latvia did not draft a new constitution but reinstated the constitution that had been adopted prior to occupation.

12 Case No. 2001-06-03, of 22 February 2002, Para. 1.2.

an exclusive function – to safeguard the Constitution – and, differently to other courts belonging to the general court system, the CC solves disputes regarding the compatibility of legal provisions with the provisions of higher legal force.[13] The competence of the CC is included in the *Satversme* (Article 85), and the CC Law (Section 16).[14] The CC reviews: (1) the conformity of laws with the *Satversme*; (2) the conformity of international agreements signed or entered into by Latvia (also until the confirmation of the relevant agreements in the *Saeima*) with the *Satversme*; (3) the conformity of other laws and regulations or parts thereof with the norms (acts) of higher legal force; (4) the conformity of other acts of the *Saeima*, the cabinet, the president, the speaker of the *Saeima* and the prime minister, except for administrative acts, with the law; (5) the conformity with the law of such an order with which a minister authorized by the cabinet has suspended a decision taken by a local government council; and (6) the conformity of the Latvian national legal norms with those international agreements entered into by Latvia that are not in conflict with the *Satversme*.

The establishment of the CC is to be considered as a significant addition to the parliamentary order of Latvia. The importance of the CC has been aptly described by the President of the CC, Professor I. Ziemele, who noted that the CC had played an important role in strengthening Latvian statehood by assessing issues of constitutional importance and developing the interpretation of the Constitution in accordance with a democratic rule-of-law state and the ideas and principles of constitutionalism.[15] It is true that with the help of the CC, the Latvian legal system was transformed from the Soviet system of old.[16] The CC of today is still creating and consolidating the Latvian legal system. Moreover, it has also formulated the values upon which the constitutional identity of the State is founded, and those consist of basic rights and fundamental freedoms, democracy, the sovereignty of the State and people, the separation of powers, and the rule of law.[17] Undeniably, the CC rulings are of principal importance in the functioning of the legal system, as well as in the protection of the constitutional order.[18] In other words, Latvia is one of those states where the emergence of the CC in general is characterized as one of the most successful improvements in the traditional European concepts of democracy and the rule of law.[19]

13 Case No. 2011-11-01, of 3 February 2012, Para. 11.1.
14 Constitutional Court Law. http://www.satv.tiesa.gov.lv/?lang=2&mid=9.
15 Ineta Ziemele *Introduction*, http://www.satv.tiesa.gov.lv/en/.
16 Ineta Ziemele, 'Role of the Constitutional Courts in Upholding and Applying the Constitutional Principles: The Case of Latvia' (conference paper), http://www.satv.tiesa.gov.lv/en/articles/role-of-the-constitutional-courts-in-upholding-and-applying-the-constitutional-principles-the-case-of-latvia/.
17 Case 2008-35-01, of 7 April 2009, Para. 17.
18 Janis Pleps & Dita Plepa 'Satversmes tiesas ietekme uz Latvijas tiesiskās sistēmas attīstību' (2016) 49 (952) Jurista Vārds, https://juristavards.lv/doc/269772-satversmes-tiesas-ietekme-uz-latvijas-tiesiskas-sistemas-attistibu/.
19 Lech Garlicki, 'Constitutional courts versus supreme courts' (2007) 5 *International Journal of Constitutional Law* 44, 44.

The authority that the CC has to veto legislation as unconstitutional is only one dimension of its powers. Another dimension, characterized as 'prospective, indirect, and creative,'[20] should also be evaluated. In the contemporary Latvian legal space, there is no doubt that laws (legal norms) should be interpreted in the light of the interpretation provided in the CC judgements. This requirement is fulfilled because of two main reasons. First, normative regulation establishes the binding legal force of the CC judgements, as the judgements have *erga omnes* effects. Second, the CC enjoys a high level of authority among public institutions. Practice shows that references to the CC judgements are included not only in court rulings but also in legislation and policy documents. Most importantly, the parliament and the government draft laws to comply with the relevant case law or to anticipate the direction of future disputes. Unfortunately, there are no official polls about the Court's authority. Its influence and authority, however, can be seen and evaluated by taking into consideration other aspects, for instance, the legislator's response (in the broader meaning) to the Court's judgements. Until now, there have been just a few cases when the legislator has not enforced the judgements of the CC in full. There have also been some delays in passing normative regulations. However, in general, the CC judgements are enforced.

2 The CC as a law-maker

In accordance with the theory of constitutional review, the CC adjudicates cases and provides a binding interpretation of legal norms in its judgements.[21] After a case is decided in the CC, and even prior to that, political outcomes can be influenced by the CC's judgements. This is the reason why the term the 'judicialization of politics' is quite well-known in Europe and it is obvious in the Latvian political agenda.

The role and importance of the Latvian CC in law-making can be examined from various perspectives. The peculiarity of the CC's law-making manifests itself in the fact that it does not regulate legal relationships directly but, by specifying the content of the *Satversme* provisions and the general legal principles, it ensures that the legal regulations comply with the *Satversme,* so that in the future, they can be applied correctly in the specific legal relationship. However, sometimes the CC also uses the possibility of being able to directly regulate a specific legal relationship; however, only for the period until the legislator adopts a legal norm that is compatible with the *Satversme*. Law-making in the practice of the CC can be reflected in different forms: (1) the CC can establish legal norms based on the direct authorization of the legislator; (2) the CC can develop the law at the constitutional level and also at the sub-constitutional level; (3) the CC has also decided on the so-called legal

20 Sweet (n 3) 73.

21 M. De Visser, *Constitutional Review in Europe. A Comparative Analysis* (Hart Publishing 2014) 291.

lacuna cases and others, thus establishing the content of a norm in accordance with today's reality; and (4) the CC has provided legal regulation until new norms (after the judgement of the CC becomes effective) are passed.

2.1 Legal norms established by the CC based on the direct authorization of the legislator

The CC adjudicates all cases according to a specific procedure. Procedures laid down by law for adjudicating cases are determined by the CC Law and the Rules of Procedure of the CC.[22] Section 14 of the CC Law provides that the structure and the organization of the CC's work is determined by the CC's Rules of Procedure that are adopted by the Court itself.

Initially, the CC Law was adopted with Transitional Provisions, envisaging that until the CC Procedure Law entered into force, the procedure for hearing cases would be regulated by the CC Law and the Rules of Procedure of the CC. This legislator's intention was not implemented; instead, the existing CC Law was supplemented by a provision on the CC's competence to decide on issues that were not regulated in the law (Section 26). This means that other procedural issues that are not regulated by the CC Law, by the Rules of Procedure of the CC, nor by other legal acts are decided by the CC itself in accordance with Section 26 (1) of the CC Law, which authorizes the Court to decide on 'other procedural issues.'

The CC has been exercising its right to create regulatory enactments by establishing procedural legal norms related to case hearings since the very first day when the CC Law entered into force. However, the legislator has entrusted the CC with deciding on which issues are, in fact, unregulated procedural issues, while still bearing in mind that a 'procedural issue' cannot be understood as merely 'any' issue. An unregulated procedural issue is an issue that pertains to the legal proceedings of the CC, comprising both the examination of cases based on their merits and other issues linked to the examination of cases that have not been legally regulated (in the CC Law and in the Rules of Procedure).[23] For example, a classical unregulated procedural issue could be returning to the previous state of the CC's legal proceedings[24] or a decision to change the date of a court hearing.[25] In 2017, during its assignment sitting, the CC dealt with an unregulated procedural issue relating to the procedure for referring a question for a preliminary ruling to the Court of Justice of the European Union (CJEU),[26] as well as deciding on a request to restrict access

22 CC Rules of Procedure of 5 February 2014.

23 Anita Rodiņa, Dita Amoliņa 'Lietas ierosināšana Satversmes tiesā' (2013) 1 *Central and Eastern European Legal Studies* 49, 43–97.

24 Case 2013-04-01, of 10 December 2013.

25 Case 2014-03-01, of 3 December 2014.

26 Decision of 28 February 2017 on the order in which the decision to refer the matter to the CJEU for a preliminary ruling is taken. *Latvijas Vēstnesis*, No. 46 (5873), 02.03.2017.

to information included in the application.[27] An unregulated procedural issue may not be linked, for example, to the jurisdiction (competence) of the CC. Thus, not each and every request made by an applicant can be considered as being an unregulated procedural issue. However, the procedural issues, which are not included in the normative acts mentioned above, are determined by the CC, thus creating the legal order and legal norms binding upon all persons involved in the CC procedure.

2.2 The development of the law

Section 29 (2^1)[28] and Section 32 (2) of the CC Law, referred to on p. 148, establish the mandatory nature of the interpretation of a respective norm provided by the CC. This means that the CC has been granted an exclusive competence to interpret legal norms; that is, only the interpretation of legal norms performed by the CC has a general effect and is binding upon all parties. The CC interprets norms only within the framework of a constitutional review; that is, by adjudicating cases within its competence.

In establishing the CC, the model of the German Federal CC was studied. Undoubtedly, the case law of the German Federal CC has served as the basis for creating the methodology for assessing restrictions placed on fundamental human rights.[29] The German Federal CC has played a significant role in the development of legal proceedings before the CC. The influence of other CCs can be discerned in developing the rights of the CC to determine legal regulations and to renew previously existing legal norms (see the further analyses on p. 160–162). The CC has also carefully studied the experience of the CC of Austria, and, based on the experience of those (Austrian and German) courts, ruled that if it is possible and necessary, the CC in the substantive part of the judgement may declare that the legal norms, which have been amended by the challenged act, and which the CC has recognized as incompatible with the legal norms of higher legal force, regain their legal force.[30]

2.2.1 The development of the law at the constitutional level

In a democratic state governed by the rule of law, the interpretation of the Constitution is of essential importance. The objective of the interpretation is to arrive

27 Decision of 22 November 2016 on the procedure by which the request to limit access to the information contained in the application is decided at the stage of reviewing the application. *Latvijas Vēstnesis*, No. 229 (5801), 24.11.2016 and Decision of the Assignment Meeting of 4 October 2016 in Cases: 2016-14-01, 2016-15-01, 2016-16-01, 2016-17-01, 2016-18-01, and 2016-19-01, *Latvijas Vēstnesis*, 194 (5766), 06.10.2016.

28 Section 29, (2^1) of the CC Law says: 'Interpretation of the legal norm provided in the CC decision to terminate the judicial proceedings shall be obligatory for all State and local government authorities (also courts) and officials, as well as natural and legal persons.'

29 Case 2001-05-03, of December 19, 2001, Para. 6.

30 Case 2005-12-0103, of 16 December 2005, Para. 25.

at a constitutionally correct conclusion on the scope of the constitutional norm and to substantiate it, thus creating legal certainty and clarity regarding the constitutional regulation.[31]

The CC, in characterizing the Latvian Constitution, the *Satversme*, has underscored, in particular, that 'the *Satversme*, essentially, is a concise, yet, nevertheless, a complex document.'[32] It is the concise style of expression that allows for interpreting the norms of the *Satversme* in accordance with the spirit and the requirements of the time, focusing on the legal findings of a contemporary democratic legal system. Therefore, each judgement of the CC in each particular case fills a specific norm of the *Satversme* with content.

In the transitional period, the transformation of the Latvian legal system was (from the Soviet system to the Romano-Germanic legal system) facilitated by revealing the content of Article 1 of the *Satversme*, which states that 'Latvia is an independent democratic republic' in the CC rulings. In the course of transforming the Latvian legal system, the legal principles had to be learned and understood anew as well as effectively embodied. At present, Latvian legal science and practice are characterized by the dominance of the concept of natural law, as well as by the extensive recognition and application of the general principles of law and actual legal norms related to it. The contribution by the CC to the application and explanation of the general principles of law is invaluable. In revealing the content of Article 1 of the *Satversme*, the CC has noted that the general principles of law that are derived from the basic norm of a democratic state governed by the rule of law fall within the scope of Article 1 of the *Satversme*.[33] The CC, in its case law, has gradually integrated the content of the general legal principles in the norms of the *Satversme*, thus ensuring harmonization of the general legal principles and the written norms of the *Satversme*.[34] The objective of the principles derived from Article 1 of the *Satversme* is to ensure that other legal norms, also those included in the *Satversme*, are applied correctly and that the application thereof, as well as the outcome of such an application, would meet the requirements of a state governed by the rule of law in full.[35] By enshrining in its case law the finding that Article 1 of the *Satversme* also comprises the principle of a state governed by the rule of law, the CC opened up extensive interpretive possibilities in terms of reviewing any regulation in the light of a rule-of-law state, since the 'principle of rule of law provides that legal acts and laws are binding upon all institutions of state power, also the legislator itself.'[36] With the development of the case law, the CC has specified the content of a number of principles: the principle of the continuity of the Latvian State; the principle of the separation of powers; the principle

31 Janis Pleps, *Satversmes iztulkošana* (Latvijas Vēstnesis 2012) 135.
32 Case 2005-12-0103, of 12 December 2005, Para. 17.
33 Case 2016-07-01, of 8 March 2017, Para. 16.3.
34 Ineta Ziemele 'Satversmes tiesas loma konstitucionālo principu aizsardzībā un piemērošanā' (2017) 48 (1002) *Jurista Vārds*, 20–24.
35 Case 2005-12-0103, of 16 December 2005, Para. 24.
36 Case 2011-11-01, of 3 February 2012, Para. 16.

of legitimate expectations and legal security, of justice and proportionality; and the principle of good legislation.

A significant part of the CC's case law is constituted by revealing the content of the fundamental rights included in the *Satversme*. Chapter VIII of the *Satversme* – 'Fundamental Human Rights' – has been drafted in the same laconic style as the other norms of the *Satversme* that were adopted at the beginning of the twentieth century. Therefore, the case law of the CC, in specifying the content of the fundamental rights, constitutes a major part of the interpretation provided by the CC. Already in 2000, in the so-called KGB case,[37] the CC defined the finding on the interpretation of the *Satversme* in interconnection with the international norms of human rights and by applying the findings approved in the case law of the European Court of Human Rights (ECtHR). By referring to Article 89 of the *Satversme*,[38] the CC explained that in 'interpreting the *Satversme* and international liabilities of Latvia, it is necessary to find such a solution that would ensure harmony of norms. Consequently, international law and practice of the application thereof may serve as an instrument for investigating the content of the legal norms and principles established in the *Satversme*.'[39] This means that the content of the human rights included in the *Satversme* should be determined and they should be interpreted, to the greatest extent possible, in compliance with the interpretation that is used in the practice of applying the international norms of human rights. This obligation of the parties applying the law follows from Article 89 of the *Satversme* as well as from the principle of the *Satversme's* openness.[40] Latvia is characterized by the maximum openness of its constitutional law vis-à-vis the international law, integrating the progressive development of international law, through interpretation, into its constitutional regulations.[41]

On the basis of the interpretation of the European Convention on Human Rights (ECHR) norms by the ECtHR, the CC has specified the norms of the *Satversme* that guarantee certain fundamental rights. For example, Article 92 of the *Satversme*, which guarantees the right to a fair trial, is rather laconic: 'Everyone has the right to defend his or her rights and lawful interests in a fair court.' However, the CC, in revealing its content, has indicated that the concept of 'a fair court' referred to in this Article comprises two aspects; that is, 'a fair court' as an independent institution of the judicial power that hears the case, and 'a fair trial' as a due procedure, compatible with a state governed by the rule of law in which the case is heard.[42] In interpreting Article 92 of the *Satversme*, the CC has noted that:

37 Case 2000-03-01, of 30 August 2000.

38 Article 89 states: 'The State shall recognize and protect fundamental human rights in accordance with this Constitution, laws and international agreements binding upon Latvia.'

39 Case 2008-35-01, of 7 April 2009, Para. 13.

40 Anita Kovaļevska, 'Satversmes 89. pants: vai deklaratīva norma Satversmē', (2008) 26 *Jurista Vārds*, 8.

41 Egils Levits,'Piezīmes par Satversmes 8. nodaļu – Cilvēka pamattiesības' (1999) 9–12 *Cilvēktiesību Žurnāls* 22–25.

42 Case 2001-10-01, of 5 March 2002, Para. 2

> a fair trial as due legal proceedings compatible with the state governed by the rule of law, comprised a number of interconnected elements, for example, the right to access to court, the principle of the equality of parties and adversary proceedings, the right to be heard, the right to a reasoned ruling by a court, as well as the right to appeal. Only such legal proceedings that ensure that the elements referred to above are implemented, guarantee to a person effective protection of his rights.[43]

Similarly, the res judicata principle has been derived from the content of the right to a fair trial established in Article 92 of the *Satversme*.[44]

The case law of the CC, in revealing the content of the *Satversme's* provisions, is very extensive, which can be explained by the particular form of the Latvian Constitution, as the *Satversme* presents its content in a very concise style, thus giving the CC broad discretion to explain its content in accordance with the social need and, at the same time, imposing a huge burden of responsibility to determine the content of legal norms with the highest legal force. At the same time, the CC has noted that it has the obligation to abide by the findings expressed in its own rulings due to the requirements for the stability and continuity of the legal system as well as fairness and equality. However, in those instances where the contested norm is incompatible with the actual social reality or is contrary to the legal relationship that, in the course of social development, has become dominant, the constitutionality of this norm may be reviewed.[45] No judgement by the CC provides the final interpretation of a *Satversme* norm, as with the appearance of new cases, the case law of the CC in interpreting a particular norm of the *Satversme* expands and ramifies, and at the same time, never reaches full completion.[46] The CC's findings are developed and perfected by interpreting a particular norm of the *Satversme*, while at the same time not revealing the full content of the norm of the *Satversme*, including the content of the general legal principles, which are in constant and continuous change following the dynamics in the development of legal relationships.[47]

2.2.2 The development of the law at the sub-constitutional level

One can agree with the opinion that judges make law when choosing from among a number of potential rules or interpretations.[48] It is the task of the CC to understand and to reveal the content of a legal norm by applying the methods for

43 Case 2017-23-01, of 14 June 2018, Para. 12.
44 Case 2013-08-01, of 9 January 2014, Para. 7, Para. 11.
45 Case 2011-01-01, of 25 October 2011, Para. 4.3.1.
46 Janis Pleps & Edgars Pastars, 'Satversmes lasīšana Satversmes tiesā' (2007) 42 *Jurista Vārds.*
47 Daiga Rezevska, 'Vasilijs Sinaiskis un juridiskā metode: vērtības, taisnīgums un interpretācija' in *Latvijas Republikas Satversmei – 95. Latvijas Universitātes 75. zinātniskās konferences rakstu krājums* (LU Akadēmiskais apgāds 2017) 160.
48 Mary L. Volcansek, *Constitutional Politics in Italy* (Palgrave Macmillan 1999) 4.

construing or interpreting it, to carry out an assessment of its intertemporal and hierarchic applicability, the use of case law and the legal doctrine, as well as the development of the law.[49]

At the sub-constitutional level, the CC directly influences legal regulation, as it is authorized to decide on the existence of the legal norm in the Latvian legal system. In other words, the CC can declare a law and other enactments or parts thereof invalid. This means that the Court will decide on the 'destiny' of a norm that is challenged at the CC. In accordance with Section 32 (3) of the CC Law, a legal provision, which has been declared by the CC as non-compliant with a norm of a higher legal force, must be regarded as being not in effect from the day of publication of the CC's Judgement (*ex nunc*). However, the CC Law has granted to the Court broad discretion to decide on the date as of which a legal norm, which is incompatible with the *Satversme*, becomes invalid. The CC, by substantiating its opinion, can rule that the unconstitutional legal norm will become invalid from the day it was adopted (*ex tunc*) or on another day (*ex tunc*), or the date may be set in the future (*pro futuro*).[50] To decide on the moment when the legal norm loses its legal force, the CC takes into account several principles: the principle of justice, the principle of legality, the principle of the separation of powers, legitimate expectations, and legal certainty.[51]

Although the CC cannot directly act as a legislator, it has directly influenced, firstly, the adoption of specific legal norms and, secondly, the contents of norms; that is, the legislator usually transfers the ideas and interpretation of a legal norm provided in judgements to the actual text of a law. For example, in 2010, the CC recognized norms of the Civil Law, which provided that a person had to be acknowledged as lacking the capacity to act if he or she was mentally ill or lacked all or a large part of their mental capacity, as non-compliant with Article 96 of the *Satversme*. In other words, the norms in force at that time provided recognition of a full lack of capacity to act and therefore a person was denied the possibility of making substantial decisions independently.[52] The CC held that such a restriction, which envisaged only full incapacitation, was disproportional and therefore unconstitutional. The Court mentioned in the judgement that it was possible to regulate and restrict legal capacity differently, and provided a possible solution to that situation based on the experience of other countries.[53] After the judgement of the CC became effective, amendments to the Civil Law were made.[54] However, two aspects should be mentioned within this specific case with respect to relations between constitutional bodies; namely, the CC and the parliament. Firstly, the annotation to the draft law proves that the legislator considered the CC's judgement very carefully while preparing the draft law (amendments to the Civil

49 Case 2014-16-01, of 2 March 2015, Para. 13.

50 Cases: 1997-04-05, of 11 March 1998, Para. 5; No. 2016-12-01, of 18 May 2017, Para. 15.

51 Ibid.

52 Case 2010-38-01, of 27 December 2010.

53 Ibid., Para. 13.

54 Grozījumi Civillikumā, *Latvijas Vēstnesis*, No. 200 (4803), 20.12.2012.

Law).[55] Secondly, the CC noted in the judgement that the adoption of the new regulation required a reasonable time period and therefore the Court decided that challenged norms would become null and void as of 1 January 2012. Since the judgement became effective at the end of 2010, the CC gave a year for preparing the necessary norms. However, until the set term had been reached – on 1 January 2012 – no new legal regulation in the field of incapacity was developed and, thus, for some time, Latvia had no legal regulation at all on restricting a person's capacity to act. Therefore, on 2 February 2012, the *Saeima* adopted, in an urgent procedure, a law that introduced a transitional legal regulation on establishing temporary custody for a mentally ill person and on declaring a person incapable. Finally, on 29 November 2012, the legislator adopted the law 'Amendments to the Civil Law,' by which it enforced the ruling by the CC in this case.

The so-called interpretative judgements are found in the case law of the CC, which are used when the disputed norm has different meanings that are used in different ways, in the practice of which some are constitutionally admissible and some not.[56] The so-called interpretative judgements very clearly demonstrate how the CC exercises its interpretative powers, as it rules that only one interpretation of a norm declared by the Court 'saves that text from being judged unconstitutional.'[57] For example, the State Human Rights Bureau challenged Section 74 of the Latvian Penalty Execution Code, which regulated the regime of punishment and disciplinary solitary confinement and provided that convicted persons placed in penalty or disciplinary solitary confinement cells could not exercise the right to mail letters.[58] By interpreting legal norms systematically (in interconnection with other norms), the Court determined that the norm did not forbid the writing of submissions, letters, and complaints to State institutions. Therefore, the restriction had to be applied only to sending letters to private persons. In the judgement, the Court decided that this restriction with respect to sending letters to private persons complied with the *Satversme*, and also explained that the term 'letters,' included in the first part of Section 74 of the Latvian Penalty Execution Code, had to be interpreted in a narrow sense as 'letters to private persons.'[59] This is a very obvious example of how, by interpreting legal norms and giving a binding interpretation of a norm, the CC establishes a legal order.

In a state governed by the rule of law, courts play an important role in safeguarding national values – both the CC and the courts of the court system (other courts). Direct relations between the CC and a court of the court system, with respect to enforcing the CC's judgements, can be analysed through two aspects.

55 Likumprojekta 'Grozījumi Civillikumā' sākotnējās ietekmes novērtējuma ziņojums (anotācija), http://titania.saeima.lv/LIVS11/SaeimaLIVS11.nsf/0/F81AEAE4B081B277C225794A00253F71?OpenDocument.

56 Nejc Brezovar, 'Judicial Activism Contributing to the Understanding of Social State Principle(S) – Constitutional Court of Slovenia at the Crossroads' (2017) 8 DANUBE: *Law, Economics and Social Issues Review* 19, 25.

57 Sweet (n 3) 72.

58 Case No. 2005-17-01, of 6 February 2006.

59 Ibid.

Firstly, in CCs, which are based upon the European model, the judicial review can be realized in the form of concrete control, which also exists in Latvia.[60] After a judgement of the CC comes into legal force, the court will resolve the initial dispute through abiding by the CC's judgement. The interpretation of a legal norm that raised doubt in a court, which then turned to the CC, is usually applied in the court's decision or, in other words, the court provides the final resolution of a case. Secondly, the courts of the general court system take into consideration the interpretation of a given norm provided by the CC in interpreting legal norms. In practice, it means that courts do abide by the judgements of the CC. Moreover, in view of the authority of the CC's judgement, its judgement may be the grounds for amending the jurisprudence of the courts of general competence. Thus, for example, until 2018, administrative courts in Latvia, including the Supreme Court, held that cases concerning requests for information from a municipal council member were not to be considered in the administrative procedure because they pertained to relations within the State administration. By deciding a case at the CC, the CC explained that the examination of the violation of a local government council's deputy's subjective public rights, on the basis of an application by the deputy, should be performed by an administrative court.[61] Based on this interpretation of the subjective rights of a deputy, the Department of Administrative Cases of the Supreme Court changed case law, stating that it departed from the previous point of view that cases regarding requests for information from a local government council were not to be considered in administrative procedures, and therefore in accordance with the principle of a democratic state under the rule of law and Article 2 of the Administrative Procedure Law, such a dispute was subject to control by an administrative court.[62]

Besides *ratio decidendi*, in some judgements the CC has included *obiter dicta*, pointing out its view on the further development of the law. Also, in Latvia, *obiter dicta* can be evaluated as an incidental element in the decision that does not affect the essential content of the decision.[63] Usually, *obiter dicta* are rules or the grounds to be considered. The importance of *obiter dicta* in establishing a law can be demonstrated by the following example. In a case where a person challenged Limbaži City Council's binding Regulation No. 4 on the 'Graphical Part of the Spatial Plan of Limbaži City and Regulations of Utilization and Construction of the Territory,' which restricted the person's property rights, the question about

60 Since amendments to the CC Law were adopted, pursuant to Section 19^1 of the CC Law, an application to the CC can be submitted by a court that is adjudicating a civil matter or criminal matter and a court that is adjudicating an administrative matter, if the court considers that the norm that should be applied in this matter does not comply with the norm (act) of a higher legal force. Simultaneously with a decision to turn to the CC, the court also decides on suspending legal proceedings. Grozījumi Satversmes tiesas likumā, Latvijas Vēstnesis, 460/464 (2371/2375), (20.12.2000).

61 Case 2017-12-01, of 11 April 2018, Para. 25.2.

62 Case 670019217, SKA-888/2018, of 27 November 2018, Para. 8 (Supreme Court).

63 Maria José Falcón y Tella et al., *Case Law in Roman, Anglosaxon and Continental Law* (Brill Academic Publishers 2011) 34.

the time limit to submit a constitutional complaint arose. At that time, there was no requirement regarding the term for submitting a complaint and challenging the regulations of a local government on urban planning. The Court established that neither the CC Law nor other normative acts regulating spatial planning provided for the term during which a person could appeal against the spatial plan of the local government to the CC. The Court took a clear stand that the lack of such a term could be in conflict with the principle of legal stability, especially in cases where the spatial plan of a local government was appealed against a considerable time after confirmation thereof, while other persons had relied on the permanence of the spatial plan and had planned their actions accordingly.[64] The Court, of course, in such a situation could not establish any regulation on the term, thus respecting the functions of the legislator. Therefore, the CC could make notes *obiter dicta*. However, the legislator did not respond to the Court's *obiter dicta*. Later, in another case, the CC again faced the problem when it had to decide on a case regarding detailed planning, which had been in force for more than three years. The Court repeatedly emphasized the need for establishing a term to challenge such a regulation at the CC and gave a clear signal to the legislator that it was within the competence of the legislator to set such a time limit, and that the absence of such a time limit could run counter to the principle of legal stability.[65] This was a strong signal to the legislator and finally the CC Law was amended and new norms establishing a term for challenging specific laws were introduced. Currently, Section 19^3 provides that an application regarding the initiation of a matter in relation to the spatial planning or local planning of a local government may be submitted to the CC within six months after the day of the relevant binding regulation coming into force. However, everybody who followed the developments in the CC knew that the term was established because of the CC's involvement. On the one hand, it is clear that *obiter dicta* are just a signal to the legislator. However, at the same time, they are not 'just' a signal. A rational legislator always pays attention to the *obiter dicta* of the CC.

2.3 Legal lacuna cases and a creative interpretation

As mentioned in the legal literature, the powers of the CC to assess the constitutionality of legal gaps are derived from the very essence of the implementation of constitutional justice.[66] Also, the CC sometimes initiates and reviews cases where the narrow scope of a legal norm is examined. This means that a legal norm has begun to regulate a matter, but the task has not yet been completed. It must be underscored that the CC distances itself from its right to decide on matters that have not been regulated at all. On the one hand, in such instances, the CC

64 Case 2006-38-01, of 11 April 2007, Para. 9.2.

65 Case 2008-23-03, of 13 February 2009, Para. 10.

66 Gediminas Mesonis, 'Judicial Activism in the Context of the Jurisprudence of the Constitutional Court' in *Judicial Activism of a constitutional court in a democratic State* (CC of the Republic of Latvia 2016) 342, 352.

formally rules on the absence of a legal regulation, the establishment of which, as well as deciding on the need for such a regulation, falls within the legislator's competence. However, if the law is silent or it fails to regulate a certain legal situation and this situation may lead to a breach of the *Satversme*, it is in the hands of the CC to decide on such a situation. In general, during the 23 years of the CC's existence there have not been many cases like this. However, when the absence of legal regulations causes incompatibility with the *Satversme*, it is obvious that the CC must become involved in the resolution of the particular matter. For example, in one case a person challenged a norm of Cabinet Regulation No. 423 'Regulations of Internal Procedure in Establishments for Deprivation of Liberty' (the Annex to the Regulation) at the CC, insofar as this norm failed to allow for the keeping of religious objects. In other words, the legal regulation provided a list of objects that could be kept by prisoners, but the norm did not provide for the right to keep religious objects, for instance, icons, crosses or rosaries.[67] By interpreting Article 99 of the *Satversme,* which provides the right to the freedom of thought, conscience, and religion, together with international documents on human rights as well as the practice of their application thereof, the Court found that this restriction was not proportional and therefore it failed to comply with Article 99 of the *Satversme*. The Court also noted that normative regulatory frameworks should allow an imprisonment institution to decide either to allow or to prohibit prisoners from keeping religious objects by taking into account the circumstances of each individual case, and it should also be ensured that such a practice was based on common principles.[68] In other words, the CC, first of all, evaluated the so-called legal lacuna and, secondly, decided that such a regulation was necessary. After the judgement came into effect, the legislator (executive branch) prepared amendments to the regulation, establishing the right of a prisoner, upon receiving the permission of the head of the custodial institution, to keep religious objects in a cell or in a living room.[69] The judgement of the CC came into effect on 22 March 2011, and the new regulation was passed on 1 November 2011. It was noted in the annotation that amendments to the normative regulation had been drafted to ensure enforcement of the CC's judgement.[70] So, it took almost eight months to pass such a legal regulation. However, nobody questioned the right of the CC to rule in such cases.

As noted in the legal theory, the theory of the mixed purpose of interpretation prevails in the legal system of a contemporary state governed by the rule of law.[71] This means that the party applying the legal norms, in examining the outcome of

67 Case 2010-50-03, of 18 March 2011.

68 Ibid, Para. 15.

69 Regulations of the Cabinet of Ministers No 847 of November 1, 2011. Amendments to the Cabinet of Ministers Regulations No.423 of 30 May 2006 'Internal Rules of the Imprisonment Institution.' *Latvijas Vēstnesis*, Vol.176 (4574), 08.11.2011.

70 Ministru kabineta noteikumu projekta 'Grozījumi Ministru kabineta 2006.gada 30. maija noteikumos Nr.423 "Brīvības atņemšanas iestādes iekšējās kārtības noteikumi"' sākotnējās ietekmes novērtējuma ziņojums (anotācija).

71 Rezevska (n47) 161–162.

the interpretation on the basis of the legislator's historical will, must identify the meaning of the law today in its reasonable understanding. Legal norms should be interpreted by taking into consideration the contemporary reality. This privilege of the CC was very clearly demonstrated in one of the most recent and sensitive cases in Latvia. Thus, a person – Ms Ždanoka – challenged the legal norms, which restricted her right to be elected in the parliament. These challenged legal norms – the *Saeima* Election Law, Article 5 (6) – were worded as follows: 'Persons who after 13 January 1991 had been active in the Communist Party of the Soviet Union (the Communist Party of Latvia), [.] are not to be included in the lists of candidates for elections of the *Saeima* and are not eligible to be elected to the *Saeima*.'[72] The court of general jurisdiction had established the fact that a person who had applied to the CC had been active in the Communist Party after 13 January 1991. Therefore, this person could not apply to become a candidate for *Saeima* elections.

This restriction on passive election rights was already evaluated at the CC twice: in 2000 and in 2006. In both cases, the CC recognized this restriction as being necessary in a democratic society. However, already in Case No. 2000-03-01 in 2000, the Court mentioned 'the legislator, periodically evaluating the political situation in the state as well as the necessity and validity of the restrictions should decide on determining the term of the restrictions in the disputable norms, as such restrictions to the passive election rights may last only for a certain period of time.'[73] The requirement to 'keep the statutory restriction under constant review' was mentioned in the ECtHR in the *Ždanoka v. Latvia* case.[74] However, what was most important with respect to the interpretation of the norm was the CC's decision (in 2018) to establish the content and aim of this restriction (norm) in the light of today's reality. Firstly, the CC made it clear that in adopting the norm, the legislator's intention was to deprive persons of the right to be candidates in elections and to be elected to the *Saeima* not only because the respective persons had been active in the mentioned organizations, but also because the respective persons, by being active in those organizations, had imperilled the restored independence and democratic order of the State of Latvia.[75] Secondly, the Court decided to establish the content of this restriction by analysing the way in which the conditions that should be taken into account in interpreting this legal norm had changed over time and what the content was of the norm in 2018. The Court made references to the legal science proving that every legal norm was not frozen, since every society continued to develop, and its legal system also evolved accordingly. The Court very carefully evaluated the consequences of the occupation, the concept of a militant democracy, and the objective meaning of the norm and concluded that the norm should be interpreted to mean that it prohibited

72 The Saeima Election Law, http://www.saeima.lv/en/about-saeima/saeimas-velesanas-1/saeimas-velesanu-likums-1.

73 Case 2000-03-01, of 30 August 2000, Para. 7.

74 *Zdanoka v. Latvia*, ECHR (2006).

75 Case 2017-25-01, of 29 June 2018, Para. 13.2.

those who had been active in the mentioned organizations from standing for the *Saeima* elections and that, by her actions, Ms Ždanoka had imperilled and still continued to imperil the independence of the State of Latvia and the principles of a democratic state governed by the rule of law.[76]

After the above-mentioned judgement, Ms Ždanoka decided to stand for election and was included on the list of the political party called 'Latvia's Russian Union.' The Central Election Commission deleted her from the candidates' list and Ms Ždanoka appealed to the Regional Court, asking it to annul the decision of the Central Election Commission. The Administrative Regional Court, by interpreting the applicable norm that was interpreted by the CC, also used the same interpretation as the one included in the CC's judgement. As the Administrative Regional Court found that Ms Ždanoka's activities posed a threat to the democratic State system and to national security, she was not allowed to stand for the *Saeima* election.[77]

2.4 Legal regulation until new norms are passed

Enforcement of the judgement is one of the stages in constitutional legal proceedings; however, the CC Law does not provide for it *expressis verbis.* Currently, the CC Law does not define who decides on the issues that arise in the course of enforcing a judgement. Inter alia, there are no provisions on who should interpret a CC judgement in case of a dispute. The absence of this regulation, on the one hand, causes certain problems, but, on the other hand, it allows the CC itself to determine in the judgement the mechanism for enforcing it in the particular case upon examining the facts of the case.

If a legal norm is recognized as being void and is excluded from the legal system, various consequences may arise. This can improve the legal regulation but might also lead to a situation that is even worse than the previous regulation (the contested norm) since there would be no regulation at all. Therefore, the CC, in its judgements, meticulously examines the consequences that might arise if the norm is declared void. In its case law, the Court has applied various mechanisms to resolve such situations. Upon declaring a legal norm void, the CC may indicate the regulation that should be applied in legal relationships. For example, until amendments are introduced, legal relationships should be regulated by: (1) applying a legal norm of higher legal force directly; (2) applying the anti-constitutional norm until amendments are introduced, but abiding by the findings expressed in the Court's judgement; or (3) applying the previous regulation.

Usually, a legal norm is recognized as being incompatible with the *Satversme*, providing, at the same time, that the norm becomes void as of a postponed date

76 The Court also mentioned actions that, *inter alia*, deny Latvia as an independent State, support international crimes and can be assessed as actions directed against the independence of the State of Latvia and the principles of a democratic state governed by the rule of law. See Case 2017-25-01, of 29 June 2018, Para. 13.4.

77 Case A43008018, A 43-0080-18/8, of September 3, 2018 (Administrative Regional Court).

(pro futuro) in those cases that require amendments to the legal regulation. That is, the Court gives the legislator time to align the legal regulation and rectify the errors. Different periods of time are granted for improving the regulation – from three months up to a year; however, this matter is not regulated by law. In each particular case, the Court takes into account the scope of the required amendments and whether the legislator would be able to adopt the legal regulation within the respective period (there have been cases when the recess of the *Saeima* or an election falls within this period). Usually, the Court sets a term of six months, which is optimal.

The simplest way to regulate the legal relationship in this case, until the new regulation is adopted, is to determine that a norm of the *Satversme* and the interpretation thereof provided in the judgement must be applied. That is, in the absence of a new regulation, while the previous one has become void, the norm of the *Satversme* and the interpretation provided by the Court must be applied directly. There are judgements in which the CC has noted that until the moment when the legislator improves the legal regulation, institutions and courts must apply the legal norms that have been recognized as being unlawful in accordance with the *Satversme* and international legal norms that are binding upon Latvia,[78] and in compliance with the findings made in the judgement by the CC.[79] For example, in its judgement in Case No. 2017-23-01, the Court included the following wording: 'Until the moment when the legislator has improved the legal regulation with respect to acceptance of a cassation complaint, the right of persons to a fair trial must be ensured by direct application of Article 92 of the *Satversme* and the findings of this judgement.'[80] In this case, the contested norms provided that in assessing the criteria regarding the eligibility of a cassation complaint, a single judge adopts the decision and does not provide the reasoning for this decision. The CC noted that such decisions should be adopted in a collegial manner, providing at least minimal reasoning. Later, an appropriate regulation was added to the Criminal Procedure Law.[81] Thus, in some cases, the CC needs to be involved in filling in the legal lacuna.

In very rare cases, the CC allows the application of an anti-constitutional norm until the legislator adopts a regulation that complies with the *Satversme*. However, in a case like this, the CC weighs up the interests of society in general since the absence of any regulation could be even more detrimental to a person's interests than the revoked regulation.[82] For example, in the case regarding a so-called compulsory lease, the CC noted:

> It is the legislator who, abiding by the judicature of the CC in the matters of compulsory lease, must find the solution to the particular situation, in the

78 Case 2006-03-0106, of 23 November 2006.
79 Case 2006-28-01, of 11 April 2007, Para. 7.
80 Case 2017-23-01, of 14 June 2018, Para. 15.
81 Law 'Amendments in the Criminal Procedure Law' of 27 September 2018, *Latvijas Vēstnesis*, No.201 (6287), 11.10.2018.
82 Case 2006-28-01, of 11 April 2007, Para. 22.

> drafting of which the possible restriction on persons' fundamental rights would be duly examined and that would provide a fair balance between the interests of the landowners and the owners of multi-apartment buildings. A reasonable period of time is required for developing the aforementioned resolution. Therefore it is admissible that the norms that are incompatible with the *Satversme* remain in force until the legislator establishes a new legal regulation on the payment of compulsory land lease.[83]

It is worth noting that the period of time granted to the legislator (1 May 2019) has expired but it did not succeed in regulating the respective matter, therefore, to regulate legal relationships when concluding lease agreements, the Civil Law, and the free market rules had to be applied.

Another way to regulate legal relationships until a new legal regulation is adopted is to provide that the previous legal regulation is in force in this period; that is, in some cases, where it is necessary and possible, it can be recognized in the substantive part of the CC's judgement that the legal norms, which had been amended by such a contested norm (act), which the CC has recognized as being incompatible with the legal norms of higher legal force, regain their legal force.[84] As noted above, this solution was applied in the case law of the CC on the basis of the case law of the German and Austrian CCs. The CC provided reasoning for such a decision saying that it must, to the greatest extent possible, ensure that the situation, which might develop after the moment when the contested norms are recognized as being invalid, and until the moment when the legislator has adopted new norms, would not cause infringements upon persons' fundamental rights guaranteed by the *Satversme* and would not cause significant harm to the interests of the State and society.[85]

3 The CC and the legislator: the present and the future

The role of the CC in interpreting the *Satversme* at the constitutional level is determined by its ability to define, by using methods and means at its disposal, the content of the *Satversme* in accordance with the changing contemporary circumstances and the particular needs of society. Hence, it is possible to arrive at the most appropriate resolution of a real-life situation by a binding interpretation of the *Satversme* rather than by amendments to it. Certainly, the CC's rulings have a methodological and causal impact on aligning the legal system in accordance with the standards of a state governed by the rule of law. Legal scholars hold that the CC facilitates awareness of using auxiliary sources of law and their interconnection in providing reasoning for a ruling.[86] Hence, the quality of applying legal norms improves, inter alia, the general quality of court rulings, which has allowed for the

83 Case 2017-17-01, of 12 April 2017, Para. 24.
84 Cases: 2005-12-0103, of 16 December 2005; 2006-13-0103, of 4 January 2007.
85 Case 2012-15-01, of 28 March 2013, Para. 19.
86 Pleps (n 18) 279–286.

approximation of the Latvian legal system with the circle of Continental law, a legal system that is appropriate for the standards of a democratic state, and has facilitated the successful harmonization of the Latvian legal system with the legal system of the European Union.

When analysing relations between the CC and the parliament, the principle that the Court cannot substitute the legislator, or that the CC cannot act on behalf of a democratically legitimized legislator and assume its legislative competence, is always observed.[87] This premise has also been established in the case law. In deciding on several issues, the Court has noted that it cannot take the legislator's place and decide on issues like a legislator does.[88] Therefore, relations between the CC and the parliament in Latvia can be characterized as respectful and dignified. Only the legislator determines whether and what legal relations require normative regulation, as well as defining the content of such normative regulation. In some cases, the requirement for a need for a legal regulation or even specific content thereof derives from regulatory enactments of a higher legal effect and is not restricted solely by the legislator's will. In such cases, the CC, in its judgement, can impose an obligation on the legislator to adopt a legal provision.

However, the legislator is very closely linked to the CC as it has to abide by the CC's judgements when introducing amendments to the normative regulation or when supplementing it; that is, the rulings previously made by the CC restrict the legislators' rights in the process of creating the law. The parliament, in exercising legislation, enjoys discretion, insofar as the general legal principles and the norms of the *Satversme* are not violated.[89] It has been recognized that the compliance of legal regulations with the *Satversme* can be ensured if the *Saeima*, in exercising its power, has complied with the findings expressed in the CC's judgements.[90] Inter alia, the failure to comply with the CC's findings has led to a situation where a legal norm is recognized as being incompatible with the *Satversme*.[91] To a certain extent, one can agree with the statement of Alec Stone, who has described the legislation process under the impact of the CCs as a 'juridicized legislative process.'[92]

During the 23 years of the CC's existence, the CC's rulings have only not been enforced in some very rare cases. The so-called incapacity case is just such an exception. However, sometimes the legislator had to decide on the matter in an urgent procedure to ensure that the CC's judgement was enforced. For example, in order to enforce the judgement by the CC in Case No. 2016-31-01 by 1 January 2019,[93] which recognized the Latvian system of judges' remuneration as

87 Case 2010-51-01, of 14 March 2011, Para. 10.2.
88 Case 2009-43-01, of 21 December 2009, Para 29.2.
89 Case 2016-14-01, of 19 October 2017, Para. 25.2.
90 Case 2017-17-01, of 12 April 2018, Para. 21.
91 Ibid.
92 Alec Stone, *The Birth of Judicial Politics in France: The Constitutional Council in Comparative Perspective* (Oxford University Press 1992) 119.
93 The Court established that the legislator needs time to create a system of judges' remuneration that would comply with the requirements of Article 83 of the

being incompatible with the *Satversme*, the legislator had to adopt in an urgent procedure – in two readings – amendments to the 'Law on Remuneration of Officials and Employees of State and Local Government Authorities' to enforce the CC's ruling in the case in question.

The CC is involved in strategic interactions with other actors and not only with the legislator. The impact of judicial politics depends not only on links between the Court and political officials, but also society.[94] In general, CC judgements are positively evaluated by legal scholars and society. Public support is crucial for every CC as support shields the Court's authority (strengthening the enforcement of the decision) and its institutional integrity.[95] The real aim of the CC can be achieved if there is recognition from both the public power and society. This premise is also supported by the CC, which has noted that 'the judicial power must enjoy public trust in order to perform its duties successfully.'[96] In Latvia, the CC enjoys the people's trust. Sometimes the CC is treated as the 'last chance saloon' against the other forms of power.

The practice of the CC allows for the conclusion that the Court, by performing its functions meticulously, realizes its role. In some cases, it is even necessary for it to be active as otherwise it would be impossible to fulfil the Court's functions. The Court's activism cannot be excluded, as it could be necessary to perform the Court's functions properly. As Ed McWhinney has noted, the question is not whether judges make law, but on what bases they do it and according to what values.[97]

Satversme – to assess the actual value of remuneration to be ensured to every judge and to review the possibilities of the State budget. Therefore, the Court gave a sufficient term, thus allowing the legislator to draft the necessary legal acts. Consequently, it was decided that the contested norms were to be recognized as being invalid as of 1 January 2019. See Case 2016-31-01, of 26 October, 2017, Para. 23.

94 Henry Robert Glick, *Courts, Politics and Justice* (McGraw-Hill Book Company 1988) 326.

95 Jarosław Kantorowicz, 'Judges as Fiscal Activists: Can Constitutional Review Shape Public Finance?' (2014) 5 DANUBE: Law, Economics and Social Issues Review 79, 90.

96 Case 2015-06-01, of 12 November 2015, Para. 16.2.

97 Edward McWhinney, *Supreme Courts and Judicial Law-Making: Constitutional Tribunals and Constitutional Review* (Springer 1986) 270.

9 Law-making activity of the Polish Constitutional Tribunal

Piotr Czarny and Bogumił Naleziński

The Polish Constitutional Tribunal (CT) is the oldest judicial review body for the constitutionality of laws in the post-communist countries of Central and Eastern Europe. It was established in 1986, even before the political transformations of 1989 to 1990. It was founded with the intention of it being the fundamental guarantor of the superiority of the Constitution in the system of sources of law. The legal solutions that define its organization and powers are based on the model of a concentrated review of the constitutionality of laws, whose foundations were laid down by H. Kelsen. The constitutional provisions currently in force in Poland can be treated as a partial adoption of the Austrian and German regulations, supplemented with some important additional elements.

The implementation of the most important function of any constitutional court – namely, guaranteeing that legislative bodies adhere to the Constitution – means that such courts have a significant impact on the existing legal order. The CT's activity shows that this influence has at least some features that go beyond applying the law, and resemble – although to a limited extent – law-making.

The issue is highly complex.[1] The research assumption that led to the reflections that follow in this chapter was the hypothesis that, in its activity, the CT creates norms, which in practice are treated as if they were part of the applicable law. This process is different at the level of constitutional norms and at the level of statutory (or lower ranking) norms.

1 Establishment of the Constitutional Tribunal in Poland

The establishment of the CT is linked to the amendments to the then-applicable Constitution, introduced by the Act of 26 March 1982 on Amendments to the 1952 Constitution.[2] For the CT to actually be set up, an ordinary statute had to be drafted and then adopted. In view of the highly general formulation of constitutional norms, this was a necessary prerequisite for its

1 Marcin Dąbrowski, *Funkcje Trybunału Konstytucyjnego związane z hierarchiczną kontrolą konstytucyjności prawa* (Wydawnictwo Uniwersytetu Warmińsko-Mazurskiego 2015) 102–103.

2 Polish official journal *Dziennik Ustaw* (DzU) no 11, item 83.

DOI: 10.4324/9781003022442-10

establishment.[3] The Act was passed much later, in April 1985, and it entered into force on 1 January 1986; thus, this later date is viewed as the start of the Polish CT, which issued its first ruling on 28 May 1986.

In accordance with Article 33a inserted into the 1952 Constitution, the CT was established as an authority for the concentrated review of laws, but its decisions had a rather limited impact. This was a consequence of the solution that required CT decisions concerning the unconstitutionality of statutes to be approved by the *Sejm* to take full effect. Thus, this solution formally gave the parliament the final say, and in the broader political context, it enabled reconciliation of the review powers of the CT with the constitutionally guaranteed superior position of the *Sejm* over all other State authorities. From the organizational point of view, the 1952 Constitution also provided for the election of CT judges by the *Sejm*, and for their special status resulting from the principle of independence and subordination only to the Constitution.

Taking into account the timeline of the above events, it is apparent that the CT was created in the political reality of the so-called socialist democracy, in a system governed by the principles of the unity of State power (in terms of the legal aspect) and the hegemonic role of the ruling political party (in terms of the political aspect). This specific normative environment of the CT gradually evolved as the law was amended in the 1990s.[4] Its final stage was the adoption and entry into force of the current Constitution of the Republic of Poland of 2 April 1997.

2 Legal basis, systemic position, and powers of the Constitutional Tribunal

The currently functioning CT has its constitutional anchor in numerous and more detailed provisions of the 1997 Constitution.[5] These include, first of all, Article 10 (2) of the Constitution, according to which the CT belongs – together with the Tribunal of the State (TS) – to a separate segment of the judicial power, and with a separate part of Chapter VIII of the Constitution (Articles 188–197) being devoted specifically to the CT. Two general provisions in this chapter that relate equivalently to all judicial authorities (Articles 173–174) also apply to the CT. The constitutional regulations concerning the CT's functioning also include provisions contained in other parts of the 1997 Constitution. Outside Chapter VIII, one can find regulations on the constitutional complaint procedures, as well as on the powers of the President of the Republic and the National Council of the Judiciary, to submit such applications to the CT.

3 Act of 29 April 1985 on the Constitutional Tribunal (DzU no 22, item 98, as amended).

4 These changes resulted, among other things, in an extension of the original scope of powers of the CT to include the universally applicable interpretation of statutes and the review of the constitutionality of the objectives and activities of political parties.

5 Constitution of the Republic of Poland of 2 April 1997 (DzU no 78, item 483, as amended).

The delegation in Article 197 of the Constitution for the legislator to regulate the issue of the organization of the CT and procedures before the CT was initially implemented by the adoption of the Act of 1 August 1997 on the Constitutional Tribunal.[6] This legal act remained in force for almost eighteen years with hardly any amendments. One of the effects of the constitutional crisis that occurred after the presidential and parliamentary elections in 2015 was major amendments to the statutory regulation of the CT.[7] Nowadays the delegation contained in Article 197 of the Constitution is implemented by two statutes concerning, respectively, the organization of the CT and the procedure it follows,[8] and the status of CT judges.[9]

Determining the CT's position in the system of government established by the 1997 Constitution seems to be much easier than under the regulations in force in the 1980s when the CT was created. This results first of all from the unambiguous wording of Article 10(1) and (2) of the Constitution, which expressly classify the CT as an authority of the judicial power, while making it (together with the TS) part of a separate segment of that power (in relation to courts). This systemic classification is, to a large extent, consistently taken into account in the further systematics of the constitutional provisions. Consequently, matters relating to the CT are regulated (as a rule) in Chapter VIII of the Constitution, entitled 'Courts and Tribunals,' firstly under the heading, 'the Constitutional Tribunal'.

The fact that the Constitution-maker gave the CT the status of a 'third power' authority has significant consequences, due to the requirement to respect the CT's separate nature and independence from other branches of power (Article 173), while including it fully in the structure of a democratic rule-of-law state (Article 2) on whose behalf the CT is to issue its judgements (Article 174).

The actual normative formulation of the principles indicated in Article 173 of the Constitution is directly affected by the content of other provisions of the Constitution relating to the CT. On the one hand, they deprive the principles of 'separateness' and 'independence' of their absolute nature and, on the other hand, they are intended to serve as directives restricting the freedom of interpretation of those provisions in a direction that is incompatible with the requirement of guaranteeing the CT the status enjoyed by judicial authorities. Regardless of this, the principles expressed in Article 173 must be fully implemented by the statutory provisions where the constitutional delegation is clarified to determine the details of the CT's organization and the procedures that it follows.

6 DzU no 102, item 643, as amended.

7 They resulted in the adoption of subsequent Acts on the Constitutional Tribunal, as well as numerous amendments to these statutes, see Piotr Radziewicz & Piotr Tuleja (eds.), *Konstytucyjny spór o granice zmian organizacji i zasad działania Trybunału Konstytucyjnego; czerwiec 2015 – marzec 2016* (Wolters Kluwer 2017).

8 Act of 30 November 2016 on the Organization of the Constitutional Tribunal and the Mode of Proceedings Before the Constitutional Tribunal (DzU, item 2072), further, as the Act on the CT's Organization.

9 Act of 30 November 2016 on the Status of the Judges of the Constitutional Tribunal (DzU 2018, item 1422).

Undoubtedly, the very mechanism of appointing the fifteen CT judges (who are elected individually by the *Sejm* for a nine-year term) is the exemption from the principle of the separateness and independence of the CT from the other branches of power.[10] Additionally, the aforementioned authorization for the parliament to regulate the matters referred to in Article 197 of the Constitution must be seen as a restriction upon the full – organizational and functional – independence of the CT. The political link between the CT and the executive power is a consequence of the fact that the President of the Republic of Poland is granted the power to appoint the CT president and vice-president from among the candidates presented by the General Assembly of CT judges.[11] However, the CT's separateness and independence also concerns its relations with other judicial authorities, including the courts – the Supreme Court (SC) and Supreme Administrative Court (SAC) – and the TS.

The current constitutional regulations also include solutions that undoubtedly strengthen – also in comparison to other judicial authorities – the principles enshrined in Article 173. These include, in particular, guaranteeing CT judges a special legal status resulting from the principle of their subordination only to the Constitution, as well as making the CT's judgements final and universally binding – Article 190(1).

Not only does the CT's separation from the 'court' segment of the third power have significant consequences in terms of a lack of any 'judicial' subordination of the CT to the highest courts (i.e. the SC and SAC), but it also excludes the CT from the scope of application of general systemic solutions (organizational and functional) relating to courts adjudicating in the Republic of Poland. These include, among others, the principle of at least two instances of court proceedings, the presumption that the court has jurisdiction, and the principle of the participation of citizens in the administration of justice. However, there is no doubt that the principle of independence and the accompanying constitutional guarantees (judges being apolitical, their immunity, and freedom from detention) are common to all the bodies of the judicature, in particular, to the judges adjudicating in these bodies. In contrast to the very general and laconic constitutional basis of the CT's activity in the period before 1997, the provisions of the current Constitution set out a detailed and exhaustive list of CT functions, as well as the most important powers vested in the CT for it to perform those functions.

Apart from the organizational sphere, the distinctness and independence of the CT as a judicial authority can be seen in the functions performed by that authority. It should be emphasized that in light of the current Constitution, the following functions may be assigned to the CT: reviewing the constitutionality and legality of laws (Article 188(1) to (3)); adjudicating in matters of constitutional

10 It is a type of continuation of the solution resulting from Article 33a of the 1952 Constitution that the authors of the current Constitution limited themselves to indicating in it only one necessary condition: that candidates for judges of the Tribunal be 'persons distinguished by their knowledge of the law'.

11 Pursuant to Article 144(3)(21) of the 1997 Constitution, the official act of appointment does not require the Prime Minister's signature for its validity.

complaints (Article 79 and Article 188(5)); resolving competence disputes (Article 189); reviewing the constitutionality of aims or activities of political parties (Article 188(4)); and deciding whether the President of the Republic is unable to (temporarily) hold office (Article 131(1)). The first two of the aforementioned functions are of a similar quality, because, due to the constitutional complaint model adopted by the Polish Constitution-maker, the CT's examination of this legal remedy actually also means that the CT reviews the constitutionality of laws. Compared to the laws in force before 1997, the list of CT functions was thus extended, on the one hand, but on the other hand, it was significantly limited – especially in terms of the issues discussed in this book – when the CT was deprived of its power to determine the universally binding interpretation of statutes.[12]

However, the actual role that a public authority plays in a state's system of government is determined not only by the content of the legal norms that form the basis of its organization and functioning, but also by how the norms are applied by the addressees. Even though the Constitution-maker intended the CT to be an element of an independent judiciary, it is exposed to particular threats, which may undermine its (assumed) apolitical status in both its personal and functional aspects. This adverse phenomenon, resulting from the way in which some of the CT's judges were elected, from the procedure it follows, and from the content of its decisions, has been observed in Poland since the 2015 parliamentary election. Its consequences have included denying the constitutional mechanisms of checks and balances, as well as undermining confidence in the CT both among legal scholars and numerous civil society groups.

3 The degree of public confidence in the Constitutional Tribunal and the degree of public acceptance of its judgements

The position of the CT is affected not only by its formal position, but also by the social context in which it operates. When it comes to public trust in the CT, it must be noted that generally, Poles display an overall low level of trust. According to a poll conducted in 2018 by the CBOS,[13] only about 20% of Poles believe that most people can be trusted.[14] From among all the public institutions, local self-government authorities enjoy the highest levels of trust: almost two-thirds of adult Poles declared they trusted them.[15] According to the aforementioned poll, half of the respondents did not trust the CT, with just 25% declaring their trust. The

12 Moreover, as per Article 239(3) of the Constitution, such interpretive resolutions adopted by the Tribunal before the Constitution entered into force lost their universally binding force.

13 The Centrum Badania Opinii Społecznej (Public Opinion Research Centre) is a state foundation whose task is, among others, to collect, process and share data from social opinion polls; it is supervised by the Prime Minister, who appoints the majority of members of the CBOS Board; hence, its full objectivity is sometimes questioned.

14 CBOS, O nieufności i zaufaniu, CBOS poll report no 35/2018, 1 (11 July 2019) www.cbos.pl/SPISKOM.POL/2018/K_035_18.PDF.

15 Ibid., 7.

results for courts were similar in terms of the level of mistrust, but the level of trust was higher (33%). Additionally, it should be noted that slightly more than half of the respondents had no trust in the legislative power; that is, the parliament (53%, with 34% expressing trust).[16]

In an earlier CBOS poll in 2016, 37% of respondents trusted the CT, while 36% did not.[17] It is plain to see that a change in public attitude to the CT took place. The credibility of the CT in the eyes of the public declined most sharply compared to other public authorities: trust in it fell by as much as thirteen percentage points, while distrust rose by fourteen points.

As for the attitude towards the activity of the CT, from 2002 to 2015, the share of negative assessments was slightly above 10%, while positive assessments ranged from 40% to 60%. Since the autumn of 2015, there has been a strong upwards trend in negative assessments (to approximately 45% in the spring of 2017) and, understandably, a downwards trend in positive assessments (to an all-time low of 20% in March 2017).[18] The data from March 2019 shows a gradual improvement in opinions about the CT's activity, although there is still more criticism (34%) than approval (30%).

In general, it can be concluded that in comparison to other constitutional courts, both the level of public trust in the CT and the public assessment of its activities are rather low. This level further decreased significantly from 2015 to 2017, which was undoubtedly one of the effects of the constitutional crisis in Poland.

4 Manifestations of law-making in the Constitutional Tribunal's activity

The current provisions of the aforementioned statutes, which regulate the CT's activity, authorize it to issue normative acts; that is, to make laws. This includes the adoption of the Tribunal's Rules of Procedure, the Statutes of the Tribunal's Chancellery, and the Statutes of the Legal Service Office, as well as the Code of Ethics of Judges of the Constitutional Tribunal.[19] The subject matter of the Tribunal's Rules of Procedure is defined in a fairly detailed way. It mainly determines the rules of the internal organization of the work of the General Assembly and the CT's president. The power to lay down the rules of procedure does not imply that the CT has been granted procedural autonomy, since, in matters not regulated by that statute, the provisions of the Code of Civil Procedure apply *mutatis mutandis* to proceedings before the CT.[20]

16 Ibid.

17 CBOS, Zaufanie społeczne, CBOS poll report no 18/2016, 13–14 (9 July 2019), www.cbos.pl/SPISKOM.POL/2016/K_018_16.PDF.

18 CBOS, Oceny działalności instytucji publicznych, poll report no 44/2019, 5 (12 July 2019), www.cbos.pl/SPISKOM.POL/2019/K_044_19.PDF.

19 In administrative matters, the statute and the Rules of Procedure of the Constitutional Tribunal also confer some limited law-making powers on the president of the CT.

20 Article 36 of the Act on the CT's Organization.

The Code of Ethics of Judges of the Constitutional Tribunal, which should define the standards of behaviour of judges, has a special nature. The Code does not consist of legal norms in the strict sense of the word, but their violation constitutes grounds for disciplinary action.

All the aforementioned legal regulations are adopted by the General Assembly of CT Judges. They may be regarded as sources of internal law and therefore their practical significance is limited. They must be compatible not only with the Constitution, but also with other universally binding legal acts (especially statutes).

In general, it can be said that the aforementioned power to make laws is incidental and marginal in the context of the CT's exercise of its constitutional powers.

The CT's activity that displays major features of law-making and that has a significant impact on the legal order takes place in its case law (decisions on specific cases). This statement is mainly justified through an analysis of the CT's practice, because the Constitution itself does not directly empower the CT to make laws, as it includes this in the judicial authorities whose task is to apply laws. Moreover, the Constitution follows a normative (positivist) concept of the sources of law, expressed primarily in Chapter III. CT judgements are not listed among the sources of law, therefore some Polish scholars even conclude that the Constitution prohibits judicial law-making.[21] In addition, the CT itself stresses that the principle of the separation of powers excludes its participation in the exercise of the legislative power.[22] However, CT judgements have one important feature in common with the sources of law in the formal sense of the word: their universally binding force.[23]

However, the issue is much more complicated than that. In Poland, since the 1960s, opinions have been expressed that general norms (legal principles) may emerge from case law and, even though they do not result directly from the provisions of laws, they may, in practice, function as if they were statutory norms.[24] And as for the closed nature of the system of the sources of law in the 1997 Constitution, it has been pointed out that it is not absolute. This closed nature should mainly concern enactments, so one cannot exclude customary law or court precedents perhaps being treated as sources of law of a specific nature.[25] Although the CT is not a court within the meaning of the constitutional provisions, its judicial law-making activity cannot be regarded as completely unacceptable.

The CT activity that can be treated as actual law-making can be seen, first and foremost, at the constitutional level. The CT is obliged to prepare, *ex officio*, a written statement of reasons for its judgement.[26] In order for the statement of

21 See Dąbrowski (n 1), 262.

22 K 11/06, of 19 July 2007.

23 See Articles 87 and 190(1) of the Constitution.

24 Andrzej Stelmachowski, 'Prawotwórcza rola sądów (w świetle orzecznictwa cywilnego)' (1967) 4–5 Państwo i Prawo 611, 612.

25 Roman Hauser & Janusz Trzciński, *Prawotwórcze znaczenie orzeczeń Trybunału Konstytucyjnego w orzecznictwie Naczelnego Sądu Administracyjnego* (LexisNexis 2008) 10–11.

26 Article 108(3) of the Act on the CT's Organization.

reasons to be correct from the point of view of the legal methodology, and in terms of a convincing correct decision, the CT must compare (juxtapose) the contents of the reviewed legal norm and the constitutional norm that constitutes an adequate basis for a review.

The statement of reasons is important from the point of view of so-called substantive legitimacy. It assumes that 'the very process of making legal decisions, thanks to its rationality and fairness, becomes a substantive source of these decisions' legitimacy.'[27] An important feature of such a process is revealing the reasons for the decision in a clear manner, which matters from the point of view of avoiding arbitrariness.

The substance of constitutional norms should be determined through their interpretation by means of commonly accepted interpretation methods. Due to the highly abstract way some provisions of the Constitution are formulated, the process of establishing their meaning is, by definition, creative, very often involving their concretization; that is, the formulation of more detailed rules (norms).[28] This phenomenon may, in a way, be illustrated with the issue of the substance of the principle of the separation of powers.[29] One of the conclusions derived by the CT from this principle is that each of the three branches should have substantive powers corresponding to its essence and that each of them should retain certain minimum powers required to preserve this essence.[30] Consequently, when examining an alleged violation of Article 10 of the Constitution, in which this principle of the separation of powers is expressed, the CT begins by checking whether the legislator, when determining the powers of particular State authorities, has not limited the power of authority of another branch of power below the minimum level.

In addition, it should be noted that the CT considers itself to be an authority empowered to make binding interpretations of the Constitution. In its opinion, for reasons of legal certainty, it is justified that the Constitution should be interpreted by the CT and not by any court or another authority deciding on a specific case.[31] As we can see, the CT ascribes (tries to ascribe) its legal views to an important feature of legislative instruments: their binding character for other State authorities.

In this context, a partial law-making quality may be attributed to those statements where the CT decides on the choice of one of the various prima facie acceptable results of interpretation. One example of this relates to the understanding of the principle of the secrecy of voting in general elections and the decision as to whether it applies to the organization of the elections and the

27 Grzegorz Wierczyński, 'Uzasadnienie aktu stanowienia prawa jako źródło legitymizacji norm w nim ustanowionych' in Małgorzata Masternak-Kubiak et al. (eds.), *Prawowitość władzy państwowej*, (Beta-Druk 2014) 165,171.

28 Krzysztof Wojtyczek, *Sądownictwo konstytucyjne w Polsce. Wybrane zagadnienia* (Biuro Trybunału Konstytucyjnego 2013) 244.

29 This is particularly evident in the understanding of the rule of law.

30 K 6/94, of 21 November 1994.

31 P 25/12, of 13 November 2013.

authorities holding them or to the voters as well. The constitutional regulation is limited to stating that elections must be held by secret ballot. In one of its judgements, the CT held that 'for a voter, secrecy of the ballot is a privilege that s/he can take advantage of, though without an obligation to do so.'[32] Regardless of our assessment of this standpoint, the creative element is clear here; it is not only a result of an interpretation made by means of the usual methods.

As far as the sub-constitutional level is concerned, it follows from Article 190(3) of the Constitution that the basic effect of the CT's finding that a normative act (or part of it) is incompatible with the Constitution (or another act of a higher rank in the legal system) is that legal act (part) losing its binding force. This is an obvious reference to the concept of the CT as a negative legislator.

However, an observation of the practice leads to the conclusion that the 'deletion' of norms by the CT may also produce other law-making results; namely, changing the content of other binding legal norms. Such a situation occurs in particular when the CT issues a partial judgement, which causes the scope of the application of other provisions to broaden or narrow. For example, in one of its judgements, the CT pronounced the ban on ritual slaughter unconstitutional.[33] The statutory provision contested in that case stated that 'a vertebrate animal may be killed in a slaughterhouse only after it has been made unconscious by persons with appropriate qualifications.' The CT considered it unconstitutional, but only 'insofar as it does not allow animals to be slaughtered in slaughterhouses in accordance with specific methods required by religious rites.' Once this judgement entered into force, the law changed in such a way that the ritual slaughter of animals became lawful and the provision started to apply in a significantly modified form without any direct change in its wording.

The law-making influence of the CT's judgements on the sub-constitutional level results mainly from the so-called complex techniques of formulating the operative part of a judgement on unconstitutionality. In the Polish practice, not only partial judgements, but also interpretive and applicative judgements can be identified.[34] Without delving into details, we should note that there is no legal basis – either in the Constitution or in statutory law – for issuing such judgements. The CT issues them, attempting in general to directly restore the state of compliance of the legal system with the Constitution; that is, without the need for the legislature to take action. The mere acceptance of their admissibility can be seen as an element of judicial law-making.

The law-making aspect of the Polish CT's judgements is also visible when it sets a different date for the loss of the binding force of unconstitutional normative acts than the date when the judgement was promulgated. The CT may postpone the 'entry into force of its judgement' by eighteen months with respect to statutes, and by twelve months with respect to other normative acts.[35] The Constitution

32 K 9/11, of 20 July 2011.

33 K 52/13, of 10 December 2014.

34 For more on the typology of CT judgments, see Monika Florczak-Wątor, *Orzeczenia Trybunału Konstytucyjnego i ich skutki prawne* (Ars Boni et Aequi 2006) 89 et seq.

35 Article 190(3) of the Constitution.

does not specify the situations when the CT should exercise this power.[36] Similarly, it does not provide any guidance on how the length of the 'deferral' period should be determined. This means that the CT enjoys relative freedom in this regard.

We should add that certain 'indirect' powers of the Polish CT to influence the binding law result from the legislation. The CT notifies the *Sejm* and the Senate (both chambers of the Polish parliament), as well as other authorities with legislative power, of the existence of infringements and gaps in the law.[37] This does not give the CT the right to legislative initiative; however, it may indicate the content of future legal provisions to the parliament.

5 Evolution of the Constitutional Tribunal's case law in the area of law-making

For more than the 30 years of the existence of the Polish CT, there have been far-reaching changes in its judicial activism, which has also influenced the scope of its 'positive' influence on the existing legal order. In general, we can distinguish four periods. The first one covers the years from 1986 to 1989, when the adjudicating practice was taking shape. At that time, the CT focused on the issue of the relationship between statutes and government legislation.[38] The second period lasted from 1990 to 1997, when, as a result of a political transformation, the CT was forced to concretize 'new' constitutional principles, which was reflected primarily in a very creative (extensive) interpretation (concretization) of the rule of law. One of the judgements summarizes the entire line of CT case law in this respect as follows:

> One of the most important findings has been the assumption that the democratic rule-of-law clause is a kind of collective expression of a series of rules and principles that, although not explicitly mentioned in the written text of the constitution, result immanently from the axiology and essence of the democratic rule of law. [...] They concerned both substantive law (the existence of certain rights of an individual, such as the right to life, to privacy and, above all, to a fair trial, was considered a necessary element of the democratic rule of law) and the so-called principles of decent legislation (e.g. the prohibition of retroactivity of laws, the obligation to maintain 'appropriate' *vacatio legis*, the obligation to respect justly acquired rights). The general foundation was the recognition that the democratic rule of law requires respect for the principle of citizens' trust in the state and the laws it enacts. The latter requirement (referring to the construction of administrative law, and in

36 The Constitution only indicates that one of the cases is judgments that involve financial outlays not provided for in the Budget Act.

37 Article 35(1) of the Act on the CT's Organization.

38 Leszek. Garlicki et al., 'From scientific editors' in Leszek Garlicki et al. (eds.), N*a straży państwa prawa. Trzydzieści lat orzecznictwa Trybunału Konstytucyjnego* (Wolters Kluwers 2016) 17, 18.

> particular to the German concept of *Vertrauensschutz*), combined with the principle of proportionality (prohibition of excessive interference), laid the general foundations for determining the shape and effects of the clause of the democratic rule of law.[39]

This quote does not indicate all the 'rules and principles,' which the CT formulated during that period on the basis of the democratic rule-of-law principle.

The subsequent period, which covers the years from 1997 to 2015, was characterized by a lesser degree of judicial activism. In this period, the CT supplemented its interpretations of some of the principles mentioned above by formulating general conditions that allowed for departures from them. In its case law, the CT formulated, for example, a test to verify the admissibility of departing from the principle of the protection of acquired rights in a specific situation. The test requires answering the following four questions: '(1) Are the introduced limitations based on other constitutional norms, principles or values? (2) Is it impossible to implement a given constitutional norm, principle or value without infringing on acquired rights? (3) Can the constitutional values, for the implementation of which the legislator limits the acquired rights, in a given specific situation, be given priority over the values underlying the principle of the protection of acquired rights? (4) Has the legislator undertaken the necessary steps aimed at ensuring conditions for the individual to adapt to the new regulation?'[40] This example shows an element that is typical of the process of creating judicial law; namely, the reliance on previous judgements in formulating assessments while introducing certain additions (further concretization).

At the level of statutes, the CT faced the problem of clarifying the effects of its judgements, with particular emphasis on the consequences of different types of judgements with 'complex operative parts.'

The last stage of the CT's activity started at the beginning of the constitutional crisis in the autumn of 2015. Initially, it was necessary to resolve the question of the scope of the legislator's freedom to regulate the position of the CT itself. Then, from December 2016, as a result of significant changes in the composition of the CT, its activism acquired a different character.

6 Selected examples of the Constitutional Tribunal's law-making activity

To illustrate the manifestations of the norm-forming activism of the Polish CT, it is worth presenting examples of specific judgements that not only resulted in a derogation of the binding regulations, but had a creative (positive) influence on the binding laws. Such an influence varies depending on the subject matter and on the basis of the review carried out by the CT, as well as the type of decision taken by

39 K 26/97, of 25 November 1997.
40 K 43/12, of 7 May 2014.

the CT. Undoubtedly, the most frequent form of the 'creative' reading of norms expressed by the legislator is the CT's operative interpretation of general constitutional principles, especially those relating to the legal status of an individual.

At this point, it is worth mentioning the judgements, which, in the contents of this formula and especially in the component principle of the citizen's trust in the state and the law, 'found' further rights that were not expressed in the text of the Constitution. The first is an individual's right to fair proceedings before public authorities. According to the CT, the rule of law enshrined in Article 2 of the Constitution implies 'a general requirement that all proceedings before public authorities conducted to resolve individual cases must comply with the standards of procedural justice.'[41] Another right decoded by the CT from the substance of general principles expressed in Article 2 of the Constitution is the right to good administration. In this case, the CT's argumentation was additionally based on an EU-compliant and international law-friendly interpretation of provisions of the Polish Constitution.[42] In the opinion of the CT, the consequence of Article 2 of the Constitution is in 'granting to an individual (to everyone) the constitutional "right to good administration," understood as a bundle of procedural rights making administrative proceedings similar to court proceedings in which the parties enjoy considerable guarantees.'[43] This group of examples undoubtedly includes the interpretation of the Constitution's provisions adopted by the Polish CT, which allows for 'finding' in them the legal basis for Poland's functioning in the EU and for resolving conflicts between national law and EU law, despite the fact that at the time of the adoption of the Constitution, Poland was outside the structures of this international organization.[44]

This form of activism, which is manifested in the case of constitutional regulations, is of course also possible in relation to regulations contained in lower-ranking legal acts. As already mentioned, the possibility of the CT using so-called interpretive and partial judgements is also important in this context.

It should be emphasized that the effect of a dynamic interpretation of constitutional provisions may also be the 'radiation' of the Constitution to matters where, formally, the basis for a review and/or the subject of a review are the norms laid down in lower ranking legal acts. The consequence of the directive of the interpretation of these legal acts in accordance with the Constitution should be respect for the adopted and consolidated interpretation of its provisions. Such value can be attributed, for example, to the CT's findings concerning the constitutional conditions for enacting sub-statutory legal acts (regulations), in particular, the requirement of formulating correct guidelines that are consistent with the constitutional directive in the authorization contained in the statute.[45] Taking account of this kind of influence, which refers

41 SK 3/11, of 6 December 2011.
42 K 24/02, of 18 February 2003.
43 SK 54/05, of 18 December 2007.
44 K 18/04, of 11 May 2005; P 1/05, of 24 April 2005.
45 K 12/99, of 26 October 1999.

to the axiology and philosophy of constitutional norms, is particularly important in matters within the sphere of the freedoms and rights of the individual. Therefore, examples of the latest judgements of the current Polish CT, in which this aspect of interpretation and then an assessment of the reviewed norms is clearly neglected, must be a cause for concern.[46]

7 How the Constitutional Tribunal formulates decisions of a law-making nature

From the point of view of the structure of the CT's judgements, we can say that elements of law-making at the constitutional level are usually visible in the statements of reasons. Only exceptionally does the CT formulate the infringed constitutional norm in the operative part of a judgement. The CT expresses it in a complex way by indicating that a specific legal regulation is inconsistent with the Constitution (e.g. with Article 2), because it violates a certain 'directive' that the CT considers to be an element of the rule of law. For instance, in one of its judgements, the CT stated that a statutory provision was inconsistent with Article 2 of the Constitution because it violated 'the requirement of definiteness of legal provisions resulting from that provision.'[47] It is clear from the above that the principle set out in the operative part of the judgement must be regarded as an element of the rule of law.

Under statutory law, the statement of reasons is not an integral part of a judgement.[48] As far as its 'normative value' is concerned, there is a widespread view in Poland that the statement of reasons expresses the grounds and arguments, which led the adjudicating panel to reach a specific decision. Therefore, it does not have the same binding force as the operative part.[49] Only statements of reasons issued by the full bench have special status. Where the panel that decides on a particular case intends to depart from a legal opinion expressed in a judgement issued by the full bench, that case must also be referred to the full bench for examination.[50] It is clear that the legal view of the full bench of the CT is binding on all 'smaller' adjudicating panels. Therefore, judgements of the full bench may be attributed a law-making quality, while the legal views expressed in them should also constitute a certain 'pattern' for subsequent CT decisions.

As for the actual impact of the interpretive findings of the CT, a significant problem results from the fact that in Poland, in the official versions of its

46 Kp 1/17, of 17 March 2017.
47 K 24/00, of 21 March 2001.
48 The necessary structural elements of the judgment are listed in Article 105(1) of the Act on the CT's Organization.
49 Zdzisław Czeszejko-Sochacki et al., *Komentarz do ustawy o Trybunale Konstytucyjnym,* (Wydawnictwo Sejmowe 1999) 211.
50 Where the panel which decides on a particular case intends to depart from a legal opinion expressed in a judgement issued by the full bench, that case must also be referred to the full bench for examination (Article 35(1)(1)(e) of the Act).

judgements (published in electronic form in the collection *Orzecznictwo Trybunału Konstytucyjnego*), the judicial theses are not distinguished. This sets the CT apart from other supreme judicial authorities (the SC and SAC), which do apply this practice. The judicial theses, which are one- or multi-sentence quotes from the statements of reasons, usually concern the abstract resolution of interpretive problems that are relevant for other cases as well. As in many other countries, citing the case law of the SC (or the SAC) by quoting the judicial thesis is an important element of pleadings, statements of reasons for court decisions, and views presented in legal journals or monographs.[51] Thus, these judicial theses sometimes become more important than the wordings of the relevant provisions themselves.

In this context, the different practice followed by the CT may come as a surprise. This is all the more so given that the statements of reasons for its decisions are relatively long and it is often difficult to determine which views are important and relevant beyond the given case. On the other hand, it can also be argued that it is an expression of the desire to avoid the petrification of the Constitution's interpretation by treating, in practice, the judicial thesis in a dogmatic (mechanical) manner without taking into account the particularities of other situations. It should be noted, however, that many scholars have attempted to fill this gap.[52] However, the emphasis on certain passages from the statements of reasons for CT judgements in the literature does not have such a practical impact as the judicial thesis 'authorized' by the CT itself would have.

8 Legal scholarship on the Constitutional Tribunal's law-making activity

Since its establishment, the activity of the CT has caused various disputes among legal scholars, not only in the context of the issues discussed here.[53] Apart from the fundamental dilemmas concerning the democratic legitimacy of the CT and its judges to perform the very function of reviewing the constitutionality of statutes, these disputes are also connected to the problem of this authority's activism in the broad sense, including the issue of the normative influence of its case law. The arguments formulated by critics of this activity by the CT are rooted primarily in the concept of the CT as an exclusively 'negative law-maker,' whose powers should be limited to derogating defective provisions from the system of binding laws. In the positive law context, it has also been pointed out that there is no express constitutional normative basis for making the CT a 'creator' or even just a 'modifier' of binding

51 Grzegorz Orłowski, 'Kilka uwag o tezowaniu orzeczeń' (2016) 1 Monitor Prawa Pracy (10 August 2019), https://czasopisma.beck.pl/monitor-prawa-pracy/aktualnosc/kilka-uwag-o-tezowaniu-orzeczen/.

52 See Marek Zubik (ed.), *Konstytucja III RP w tezach orzeczniczych Trybunału Konstytucyjnego i innych sądów* (CH Beck. 2008).

53 See Wojtyczek (n 28), 265 et seq.

legal norms. Additional confirmation of this is sometimes perceived in the fact that, in 1997, the Constitution-maker deprived the CT of the function of determining the universally binding interpretation of statutes.

On the other hand, those who approve of the CT's creative role in the norm-forming sphere emphasize the derivative and purely applicative nature of the CT's influence in the field of law-making. This influence is, after all, a consequence of the decisions taken by the CT – decisions that always concern the problem of the (in)compatibility of the reviewed legal norms. Consequently, it is stressed that the effects of CT judgements escape the simple classification of those operating *ex tunc* or *ex nunc.* As has already been explained above, the problem of the Polish CT's activity in the norm-forming sphere requires different approaches depending on the hierarchical level of the sources of law that this activity may concern. The CT's activism in relation to constitutional norms, which only constitute the basis for the review it conducts, is qualitatively different from the forms it assumes in relation to hierarchically lower legal acts, which are both the subject of and the basis for the review of laws. In the first situation, the 'creative' role of the CT is justified by the need for an operative determination of the meaning of many general terms used in the Constitution. In the latter case, the activity of the CT is significantly enriched by the fact that the CT makes decisions of a quasi-validative nature. Such a qualification can be attributed to those CT judgements, which result not only in derogating the provisions of law, but also (or only) in modifying the scope of application of the legal norms decoded from provisions reviewed in terms of their constitutionality and legality. Disputes among legal scholars, subsequently reflected in judicial decisions, result from the very fact that the CT uses such a tool. The doubts that accompany interpretive judgements or partial judgements are thus transferred to the question of the effects that they may produce in the system of binding laws.

9 Courts' reactions to manifestations of the law-making activity of the Constitutional Tribunal: Selected problems

In general, it can be said that the courts did not question the quasi-legislative activity of the CT at the level of constitutional norms. In principle, acceptance was expressed in an indirect form, by means of quoting legal views contained in the statements of reasons of CT judgements that were related to the understanding of some provisions of the Constitution. Since court decisions are usually based on the provisions of statutes, references to the case law of the CT were infrequent and mainly concerned issues affecting the resolution of doubts about the interpretation of statutory provisions.

There was an exception: the question of the courts' competence to review the constitutionality of statutes. It is not explicitly regulated for in the Constitution. The CT has consistently expressed the position that: '[D]irect application of the Constitution cannot be understood as authorizing courts to refuse to apply statutory provisions in force, instead of referring an appropriate question of law to the

CT.'[54] The SC (in some judgements) presented a different position.[55] Without discussing the substance of the dispute from the point of view of the legitimacy of one view or another, it should be noted that the SC (and in some instances, other courts) mainly questioned the fact that the CT tried to limit their powers, but a subsidiary role was also played by the fact that the position of the CT was alleged to have an essentially law-making quality.

At the statutory level, the evaluation is slightly more complicated. From 1990 to 1997, the CT was authorized to make a generally binding interpretation of statutes. CT resolutions issued on this basis often had a law-making quality in the sense that the interpretation adopted by the CT clearly went beyond a linguistic interpretation and was aimed at achieving a state of law that would correspond (to the greatest extent possible) to constitutional standards. The SC questioned the binding force of such resolutions, chiefly by invoking the principle of judges only being subject to statutes. For obvious reasons, after the Constitution of 1997 abolished the universally applicable interpretation of laws, the controversy came to an end.

Since the 1997 Constitution entered into force, the most important example of a dispute between courts and the CT has been the conflict over the admissibility and legal effects of interpretive judgements. The CT stated in these judgements that a statutory regulation was consistent with the Constitution provided that a certain interpretation was adopted or that it indicated that a certain understanding (interpretation) of a statute was inconsistent with the Constitution. The essence of the objections the courts had about interpretive judgements can be reduced to the statement that the CT had granted itself the power to make such decisions, and thus had itself established a competence norm, acting in excess of its powers. However, the 'axis' of the dispute was actually of a different nature. The point was that the SC was of the opinion that interpretive judgements constituted an unauthorized interference with the interpretive independence of courts to the extent of interpreting statutes (and other sub-constitutional legal acts), while the Constitution did not provide for the CT's power to review judicial decisions, including with regard to how the provisions of law were interpreted in them.

However, what seems of most interest are two other issues, which clearly show that courts do treat CT judgements as a kind of source of law, capable of being the basis for resolving a specific case. The first issue is that of the consequences of the judgements in which the CT finds a certain statutory regulation unconstitutional, but only to the extent that it omits certain groups of similar facts. This particular judicial technique of the Polish CT is based on a distinction between a so-called proper (absolute) legislative omission and a so-called relative (partial) legislative omission. The former involves the lack of regulation of a specific area of social relations, and the CT has no jurisdiction to examine such cases. In the second case, the existing regulation omits specific groups of facts, although in the

54 K 36/01, of 28 November 2001.

55 Leszek Garlicki, 'Sąd Najwyższy' in Wiesław Skrzydło (ed.), *Sądy i Trybunały w Konstytucji i w praktyce* (Wydawnictwo Sejmowe 2005) 15, 22.

light of constitutional principles (in particular, the principle of equality before the law), they should be covered by it. In cases where a relative omission is found, the CT makes a decision on the merits and issues of a specific partial judgement. In the judgement, it states unconstitutionality, but only to the extent of the omission, which does not result in the derogation of the challenged provision.

From the point of view of the subject matter of this study, it is important to state that courts treat these kinds of judgements concerning relative omissions as the basis for determining changes in the state of law and for decisions where the opinion is expressed that a CT judgement is an independent basis for extending the application of a given regulation to also cover the 'omitted' situations without changing the wording of the applicable provisions.[56]

10 Effects of the Constitutional Tribunal's law-making activity and prospects for the future: a summary

In light of the considerations presented in this chapter, the basic hypothesis seems fairly obvious that the CT's activity in the field of the 'creation' of constitutional norms mainly resulted in determining the substance of some constitutional principles with greater precision, thus facilitating the assessment of the constitutionality of statutes, but also affecting the interpretation and application of sub-constitutional legal acts. The consequence of this is a significant reduction in uncertainty as to the substance of these principles.

The principles that the CT formulated in its case law as concretizations of constitutional regulations did not also provoke any major objections because, to a considerable degree, they were an adoption of the case law of other constitutional courts (especially the German Federal Constitutional Court). Whenever the Polish CT's activism in the area of formulating constitutional principles and norms not expressed in the text of the Constitution was criticized, it was for methodological reasons (arbitrariness manifested in the lack of appropriate justification and acting in excess of the powers granted to it by the Constitution).[57]

Practical problems were much more frequent in situations where the CT created (concretized) norms at the statutory level. Particularly in cases involving interpretive judgements, this was met with a certain amount of 'resistance' from courts, especially the SC.

Shaped mainly in the period from 1990 to 1997, the practice, which actually permits the law-making activity of the CT, to a relatively broad extent, will probably continue in the future. However, in connection to the constitutional crisis and the far-reaching changes in the CT's composition, there is a justified concern that it will be used for different purposes and in a different way than before. Currently, out of the members of the Polish constitutional court, as many as two-

56 Monika Florczak-Wątor & Piotr Czarny (eds.), *Oddziaływanie sądu konstytucyjnego na porządek prawny Austrii, Niemiec i Polski* (Księgarnia Akademicka 2019).

57 B Banaszak, *Prawo konstytucyjne*, (C.H. Beck 2012), 87.

thirds of them have been elected by the *Sejm* from among candidates put forwards by one political party.[58]

Without delving into details, it can only be pointed out that some CT judgements and the interpretations or concretizations of constitutional norms they contain may be treated as legitimizing legislative solutions. Such legitimacy is highly doubtful from the point of view of the constitutional axiology. The way the technique of partial judgements is used began to show symptoms of a preventive influence on the direction of case law.[59] In this context, there is a concern that the case law of the CT resulting from its previous practice will serve as an additional argument for the parliamentary majority to justify the 'validity' of the adopted statutes and limit the possibility of judicial reviews of the activities of the executive power. There may also be a specific 'reinterpretation' of the Constitution.

58 Not insignificantly, there are also reservations regarding the correctness of the election of CT judges in November 2015.

59 Helsinki Foundation for Human Rights, '"Pracuje tak, jak powinien?" TK w 2017 r.' (9 August 2019), https://www.hfhr.pl/wp-content/uploads/2018/03/HFPC-Pracuje-tak-jak-powinien-raport-TK-2017.pdf.

10 The Constitutional Court of the Slovak Republic

The many faces of law-making by a constitutional court with extensive review powers

Ján Štiavnický and Max Steuer[1]

1 Introduction

The Slovak Constitutional Court (SCC) has been in the shadows of scholarly attention compared to its regional counterparts. This chapter contributes to dispersing that shadow, a process that has already begun due to several internationally observed developments related to this institution. These include the difficulties in appointing new judges and the unique transitional justice decision to invalidate the amnesties issued by the Prime Minister Mečiar executing presidential powers in 1998 to obstruct possible investigations against several alleged crimes of the state secret service with his own involvement (PL. ÚS 7/2017). After an introduction to the SCC's creation and legal basis, we divide the chapter into two relatively independent parts. The author of heading 3 is an insider familiar with the internal discussion and development of hard cases at the SCC who focuses more on legal features of its law-making activity. Heading 4 represents a view from outside the SCC focusing on its reflections by selected segments of the society. Although written separately, both parts together illustrate the contrasting faces of the SCC. The SCC itself is contrasting, but from a transitive point of view it has engaged in an epic struggle for democracy and the rule of law.

2 Creation and legal basis of the SCC

It is elegant that Czech and Slovak constitutionalists make frequent reference to the pre-war 1920 Czechoslovakian Constitutional Court as co-founder, together with its Austrian counterpart, of European constitutional review. But the real inspiration for the second Czechoslovak Constitutional Court (1968 – only in books, 1991 – in action) and the current SCC was the Constitutional Court of Yugoslavia from

1 Max Steuer's analysis of the societal reflections of selected facets of the Slovak Constitutional Court's decision making has been supported by the Comenius University Grant No. 346/2019 on 'Conceptualization and Measurement of Democratic Performance of Political Institutions: The Case of the Constitutional Judiciary'.

DOI: 10.4324/9781003022442-11

1963.[2] The Yugoslavs implemented a unique merging of judicial review of laws with the unity-of-power concept.[3]

Similarly, today's SCC has centralized and robust powers.[4] The Court is tasked with 'guarding the constitutionality' of the Slovak Republic in Article 124 of the Constitution. The constitutional amendment in 2001 (Act 90/2001 Coll.) brought about a modification in the number of judges and their term limits as well.[5] The increase of the number of judges to 13, accompanied with the extension of the term limit to 12 years, and the prohibition of re-election, may provide more room for law-making activity. In addition, the Court was further strengthened by introducing its competence to temporarily suspend the legal force of legal provisions. In the subsequent years, several other legal changes took place. The Court's competence was further extended by the possibility of reviewing the National Council's decisions on amnesties,[6] and altered by enabling the renewal of the judicial process in case of a reversal decision of international courts – in particular the European Court of Human Rights (ECtHR) – against the decision of the SCC.[7] In 2018, a new Constitutional Court Act (314/2018 Coll.) was adopted and a failed attempt to amend the constitutional mechanism of the appointment process of constitutional judges took place.[8] These developments confirmed the SCC's position as one of the formally most powerful centralized constitutional courts.

3 The SCC's law-making activity: view from 'the inside'

Constitutional courts' decision-making often leads to outcomes which observers would rather expect as value or expert results of political procedure. These outcomes may be understood as positive legislation. This heading reviews situations which generate such outcomes, and explains why they occur. It starts from more

2 Dimitrije Kulic, 'The Constitutional Court of Yugoslavia in the Protection of Basic Human Rights' (1973) 11 *Osgoode Hall Law Journal* 275.

3 Article 245 of the Constitution of Yugoslavia (1963). Compare to Article 125.3 of the Slovak Constitution (1992). Arguably, its structure implied that the Left believed in centralized and scientific solutions for socio-legal problems and the Left's scepticism regarding the ability of civic society to develop pressure towards power to respect freedom.

4 Kálmán Pócza, Gábor Dobos & Attila Gyulai, 'How to Measure the Strength of Judicial Decisions: A Methodological Framework' (2017) 18 *German Law Journal* 1557.

5 Lucia Berdisová, Constitutional Law (Trnavská univerzita 2013) 78–81, full access http://iuridica.truni.sk/sites/default/files/dokumenty/zahranicne-vztahy/en/publications/pdf/02Constitutional%20Law.pdf.

6 Ján Mazák & Ladislav Orosz, 'Quashing the Decisions on Amnesty in the Constitutional System of the Slovak Republic: Opening or Closing Pandora's Box?' (2018) 8 *The Lawyer Quarterly* 1.

7 Ján Mazák, 'Obnova konania pred Ústavným súdom SR: Prvé skúsenosti, pochybnosti a jeden námet' (2017) 23 Bulletin slovenskej advokácie 24.

8 Max Steuer, 'On the Brink of Joining Poland and Hungary: The Night of Surprises in the Slovak Parliament' Verfassungsblog (October 25, 2018), https://verfassungsblog.de/on-the-brink-of-joining-poland-and-hungary-the-night-of-surprises-in-the-slovak-parliament/.

abstract forms of positive legislation, forms which are more related to society and democracy and the political profile of a country. Then it proceeds to more technical, but no less exciting kinds of positive legislation. The heading is divided into the following sub-headings, the SCC as: (3.1) Positive democracy-giver; (3.2) Positive/negative constitution-giver; (3.3) Positive law- and policy-maker; (3.4) Positive constitutional interpretation: disputes between constitutional authorities (organstreit); (3.5) Positive legislator: 'resuscitator' (1); (3.6) Positive legislator: 'resuscitator' (2); and (3.7) Positive legislator – lacunae and 'super-lacunae.'[9]

Let's start with one more note on Kelsen. I would differentiate between his two roles: that of the legal philosopher, and that of the drafter of the 1920 Austrian Constitution and the first president of the Court. Kelsen uses the term *negative act of legislation* in a way taken from (1) theory of norms, and (2) in a technical way. He does not use it in a political way, suggesting that there is no fear about abstract review because constitutional courts are just 'negative legislators.'[10] He was well aware of the legislative and even democratic function of constitutional courts. From this point of view, the distinction between positive and negative legislation is blurred.

Written law: the style of thinking of constitutional courts in central European countries is heavily based on the concept of written law and its 'erasing,' if constitutional courts decide that certain provisions are unconstitutional. Written law as a feature, rather than a mere method of interpretation, is constantly overlooked by constitutional comparatists.[11] Unlike common law systems, after 'erasing' a carved provision from the legal order by the Constitutional Court, the sub-constitutional rules will be different. Explaining why a rule is unconstitutional often implies what kind of different rule would be constitutional; this is a fact which is valid irrespective of formalism in the reasoning of the Court. Consequently, the narrative about negative legislator is more of a symbolic cliché than a practical tool, and the Court is often inevitably in the position of a positive legislator. The fact that a centralized Court can change written law directly has two implications related to the limits of positive legislation: firstly, it has to consider which rule will be valid after the decision, and occasionally what to suggest in its

9 Cf. Ján Svák & Lucia Berdisová, 'Constitutional Court of the Slovak Republic as Positive Legislator via Application and Interpretation of the Constitution' in Allan R. Brewer-Carías (ed.) *Constitutional Courts as Positive Legislators: A Comparative Law Study* (Cambridge University Press 2013) 767.

10 'The decision of the Constitutional Court by which a statute was annulled had the same character as a statute which abrogated another statute. It was a negative act of legislation. Since the Constitution conferred upon the Constitutional Court a legislative function, i.e. a function which, in principle, was reserved to the Parliament, the Austrian Constitution of 1920, provided that the members of the Constitutional Court had to be elected by the Parliament, unlike the other judges, who were appointed by the administration.' In Hans Kelsen, 'Judicial Review of Legislation: A Comparative Study of the Austrian and the American Constitution' (1942) 4 *The Journal of Politics* 183, 187.

11 See, for example, an otherwise perfect standard reference: Alec Stone Sweet, 'Constitutional Courts' in Michel Rosenfeld & András Sajó (eds.) *The Oxford Handbook of Comparative Constitutional Law* (Oxford University Press 2013) 815.

reasoning to Parliament; and secondly, it may unconsciously give an impression of its ability to change a law as being equal to that of the legislator.

3.1 Positive democracy-giver

In the 1990s, Slovakia had a rather complicated trajectory to democracy.[12] In those days our Court often had a tough job with laws regarding privatization and economic transformation, and an even tougher job resolving disputes between government and the President. As far as privatization was concerned, the government usually adopted some new provisions ('plus norm'), opposition MPs challenged them, and the Court frequently agreed with the latter.

In the Czechoslovak Socialist Republic, economic entities were solely in state hands. During federal Czechoslovakia, inventive but controversial privatization was launched in 1991. Practically all citizens could, on demand, become shareholders in former socialistic economic entities or shareholders in newly established investment funds. All this was a strange game, which symbolized the unlimited freedom and extravagance of this era. Some shares became very valuable, but others did not. In 1995, Vladimír Mečiar's government changed this method of privatization from shareholder-like to bond-like. From the economic equality point of view, the new method was fairer, because every citizen got a right to the same amount of money in ten years. Moreover, the law obliged municipalities and housing cooperatives to accept those non-mature state bonds as a form of payment for selling flats.[13]

Part of civic society did not believe that the government would be able to repay the bonds in ten years. Opposition MPs challenged this *changing rules in mid-game*. No one had a clear view as to whether Parliament could do that, but people had a feeling of unfairness.

The Court decided (PL. ÚS 33/95) that it was not possible to determine objectively which method of privatization was the most effective. (The Court is not a policy-maker.) It also stated that there was no basic right to get any property from the State.[14] According to the Court, therefore, Parliament could change the privatization method without violating the property rights of citizens. But it also decided that municipalities and housing cooperatives (HCs) were not obliged to accept bonds as a form of payment. The Court opined that this obligation was an

12 Fareed Zakaria, 'The Rise of Illiberal Democracy' (1997) 11–12 *Foreign Affairs*; Timothy Garton Ash, *History of the Present: Essays, Sketches, and Dispatches from Europe in the 1990s* (Allen Lane 1999) 331; David Kosař, Jiří Baroš, & Pavel Dufek, 'The Twin Challenges to Separation of Powers in Central Europe: Technocratic Governance and Populism' (2019) 15 European Constitutional Law Review 428, 429.

13 During the pre-1989 Socialist era flats were owned either by the State or by giant cooperatives. As part of the economic transition the State 'forwarded' free flats to municipalities. What is important is the fact that municipalities and cooperatives then had the duty to sell flats to the tenants on demand for a low price. One reason was to make people responsible for their housing.

14 Herman Schwartz, *The Struggle for Constitutional Justice in Post-Communist Europe* (The University of Chicago Press 2000) 220.

unequal burden on their property stock. In other words, the Court argued that other entities did not have the same burden as municipalities and HCs. This was the era of rediscovered *laissez-faire*.

Based on the current knowledge of constitutional standards, this norm would be completely acceptable. Applying the principle of proportionality, unequal interference in the property stock of municipalities and HCs would be outbalanced by public interest, producing a historically unique situation in privatization.

So, the decision was strictly speaking legally incorrect (Radoslav Procházka offers a completely opposite view).[15] Besides, it was not friendly to thousands of citizens who might have paid for their flats with their privatization bonds. On the other hand, the decision was very friendly to millions of citizens, because, together with other decisions by the Court, it symbolized that there was (together with the President) one last resort, which stood against Mečiar's expansive government. This decision is an example of poor *positive legislating* because the Court interfered with the economic concepts set out by the government, but otherwise the same decision is a very good decision issued by the Court as *positive democracy-giver*.

There are a few more similar decisions in this scheme of a very strict review of derogation as helping democracy. Two facts are striking: one, our Court did not deal too much with classical human rights, apart from the right to peaceful enjoyment of property. (We should also think about the fact that for undemocratic actions the government does not need any changes in the law.) Two, not a single judge had a dissident background with regard to the Communist regime. Nevertheless, the judges needed a kind of civil courage for that decision-making.

One more actor was courageous: the President of the Republic. Decisions concerning his constitutional position were also part of *positive democracy-giving*. A case related to the appointment of a minister by the President is explained below in the sub-heading on a generally binding interpretation of the Constitution – see page 192.

3.2 *Positive/negative constitution-giver*

The Court as *positive democracy-giver* has been mentioned. In real contrast to this is the Court in the form of not just *negative legislator*, but *negative constitutional legislator*.

The Slovak Constitution is strongly based on the former Czechoslovak federal constitution (originally from 1960, with significant amendments in 1968 and 1991). It has to be said, that during the *un-freedom era* (1948–1989) the Communist Party did not need a constitution as an instrument of permanence (eternity) of their power. Although that Constitution contained an article on the leading role of the Communist Party, the Constitution itself did not contain any other eternity clause. It was built on the concept of popular, not representative,

15 Radoslav Procházka, *Mission Accomplished: On Founding Constitutional Adjudication in Central Europe* (CEU Press 2002) 183.

democracy and the concept of unity of power. Popular democracy was embodied in the Federal Assembly, which was therefore the dominant body in the constitutional system. The Federal Assembly had explicitly not only the power to change the Constitution, but also the power to adopt a completely new Constitution. The current Slovak Constitution contains the same provision (Article 86.a: 'The powers of the National Council of the Slovak Republic shall be *to adopt the Constitution*, constitutional laws and other laws'), and it does not contain any eternity clause.

Reforms of the judiciary and the fight against corruption are constant themes in Slovak public discussion. They led to an ambitious constitutional amendment in 2014 (also a reaction to the SCC's decision on Special Court, which will be discussed later in this chapter).

This amendment introduced one-time screening or lustration of all active judges to check whether they fulfil the criteria for judicial capacity, which provide a guarantee that they will properly perform the office of judge. Undoubtedly, it was a fairly intensive means of securing the integrity of the judiciary. (Both the judiciary and the civil society needed to be reassured that all judges have integrity.) However, there were some built-in mechanisms to avoid misuse: the screening procedure was within the competence of the Judicial Council, and if a judge failed to meet the criteria before the Judicial Council, the judge could ask the SCC to review their screening through a particular procedure, rather than through a constitutional complaint. From the democratic point of view, all this was an effort to demonstrate willingness to reform, to re-legitimize the judiciary. Judges also got something: improved standing. The Judicial Council, through its president, got standing to ask the SCC to review laws relating to the judiciary.

The very first request by the president of Judicial Council to review the law was in fact a request to review not just *any law*, but a request to review a *constitutional amendment* on one-time screening of active judges. In January 2019, the Court derogated these provisions,[16] stating that they were contradictory to its new reference norm: the material core of the Constitution. According to the Court, the material core of the Constitution contains all principles of the rule of law including the principle of independence of the judiciary.[17] In my opinion, thinking about the above-mentioned Article 86.a of the Constitution, and the absence of eternity clauses, foreign inspiration was more influential than our national constitutional text. Comparative constitutional conclusions have almost legal force these days. To sum up:

(1) The Court acted here as *positive supra-constitutional legislator*, because it developed a new reference norm and subsequently its own competence to derogate constitutional provisions if they are contradictory to the implicit material core; (2) The Court acted here as *negative constitutional legislator*,

16 Marek Domin, 'A Part of the Constitution is Unconstitutional, the Slovak Constitutional Court has Ruled' Verfassungsblog (February 8, 2019), https://verfassungsblog.de/a-part-of-the-constitution-is-unconstitutional-the-slovak-constitutional-court-has-ruled/.

17 Cf. Yaniv Roznai and Tamar Hostovsky Brandes, 'Democratic Erosion, Populist Constitutionalism and the Unconstitutional Constitutional Amendment Doctrine' (May 26, 2019) https://ssrn.com/abstract=3394412.

because it derogated part of the Constitution. It should be noted that the amendment was not something like *ad hoc* legislation to neutralize constitutional text, but it was an amendment for complex reform. (3) The Court acted here also as *positive law- and policy-maker* in the sense that rejecting this policy towards the judiciary implied that reforms have to be more prudent or conservative.

3.3 Positive law- and policy-maker

It is not expected from constitutional courts that they will be policy-makers in areas where democracy allows different, equally possible solutions. It is not the role of constitutional courts to set value determinations or substantive policy results. In any case, if a court rejects some policy, it becomes a policy-maker, at least indirectly, because democratic choice is then restricted to the rest of the possible solutions. We may consider it as a kind of *positive legislating*, because the court shows indirectly what is not only constitutional, but also the 'right' approach.

The SCC has repeatedly dealt with laws focusing on the reform of the judiciary. In reaction to the high criminality and corruption in the 1990s, in 2003 Parliament passed Act No 458/2003 Coll. introducing into the judicial system a completely (brave) new Special Court. This was a criminal court with the competence to decide on organized criminality and on corruption of public officials. The Supreme Court was to decide on appeals against decisions by the Special Court. Its judges had to get security screening carried out by the National Security Office, they got higher salaries, and almost personal bodyguarding in order to feel safe. Many judges from the rest of the judiciary did not accept that there was a "privileged" group among them. MPs of the political party which led Slovakia off the rule of law track in the 1990s challenged at the Constitutional Court the constitutionality of the very existence of the Special Court. The Court accepted (PL. ÚS 17/08)[18] the application of the MPs by a tight majority of one vote. One of the main arguments was that the Special Court was partially, in fact, an extraordinary court: its jurisdiction on corruption was restricted personally to constitutional authorities, and security screening might be reviewed by the National Security Office at any time.[19] Such a strict law was not necessary for Slovak society, according to the Constitutional Court.

In Slovak and Czech legal thinking, from the 2000s the contrast between the so-called material rule of law and formal rule of law became the main narrative.[20] According to this contrast, formal rule of law meant mechanical, blind application of legal provisions. Material rule of law meant that judges should look for the

18 The ECtHR dealt with the derogation of the Special Court in *Fruni v. Slovakia*, Application no. 8014/07 (judgement, June 21, 2011).

19 Michal Bobek, *Comparative Reasoning in European Supreme Courts* (Oxford University Press 2013) 176.

20 Pavel Holländer, 'The Role of the Constitutional Court for the Application of the Constitution in Case Decisions of Ordinary Courts' (2000) 4 *Archiv für Rechts- und Sozialphilosophie* 537.

purpose of a written legal norm. Nevertheless, the borderline between material rule of law and arbitrariness may in fact be blurred.

In my opinion, the Court, inspired by the ban on extraordinary courts in foreign constitutions, argued that 'materially' the Special Court was extraordinary, although formally the Special Court would be acceptable. The main argument was in fact formal and of symbolic nature: it turned on the title 'Special Court.' The Court followed the sentiments of judges at the general courts. Public sentiment was different, however, so Parliament again approved a new, slightly modified Court with the title 'Specialized Court.' There is an important link to a decision on derogation of part of the Constitution discussed above (PL. ÚS 21/2014). The Court considered that screening of possible judges for the Special Court was contrary to the principle of independence of judges (although it was up to judges whether they wanted to work at the Special Court). Nine years later, screening was elevated to the constitutional level and widened to include all active judges, but also upgraded with procedural guarantees overseen by the Judicial Council and the SCC.

It can therefore be concluded that the SCC played its part in shaping the scheme of the general judiciary towards its more conventional structure.

The Act on the Constitutional Court allows for convicted persons to ask for reopening of their case, if their conviction was based on an unconstitutional norm. However, in the decision on unconstitutionality of the Special Court, in its operative part, the Court expressed that this decision had no impact on the position of convicted persons.[21] It was, in fact, a little legal amendment by a *positive legislator*, which neutralized hope for convicted persons and the competence of criminal courts to decide on the reopening of their cases. This fact reveals that the Special Court issue was not a question of individual rights, but of institutional design of the Slovak judiciary.

In the Austrian-Czecho-Slovak concept of the judiciary, the Minister of Justice appoints presidents of local and regional courts. In the 2000s, when discussion on the content of judicial independence started, some sort of scepticism towards presidents of local and regional courts developed because they were both judges and part of executive power. Later a complicated search started to establish whether the judiciary should be 'self-created' or created also from the outside.

Our Court decided in case PL. ÚS 102/2011[22] that it is contrary to judicial independence if a minister may freely, on his/her discretion, recall presidents of local courts. The Court stated that such a decision must be reasoned and also reviewable by an administrative court. The Court, further, decided that commissions for selection of candidates for judges' positions could not be composed predominantly by non-judicial (political) representatives, because that is at odds with

21 See § 81, *Fruni v. Slovakia*, Application no. 8014/07, (judgement, June 21, 2011).

22 Samuel Spáč, Katarína Šipulová & Marína Urbániková, 'Capturing the Judiciary from Inside: The Story of Judicial Self-Governance in Slovakia' (2018) 19 *German Law Journal* 1741; James E. Moliterno, Lucia Berdisová, Peter Čuroš & Ján Mazúr, 'Independence Without Accountability: The Harmful Consequences of EU Policy Toward Central and Eastern European Entrants' (2018) 42 *Fordham International Law Journal* 481.

the separation of powers principle. One of the dissenters argued that it is necessary to protect only independence related to the application of laws, and this independence is not affected by the nomination process for local court presidents.

The SCC is balancing on the edge between the reviewing of constitutionality and suggesting a specific design of matters, particularly when deciding on the judiciary. Why is this so? In pre-war Czechoslovakia, judges were more focused on the application of law than the protection of individuals from state power (which is definitely not to suggest that their decisions were not legally correct). During the 'un-freedom era' (1948–1989) the role of judges was definitively bureaucratic. Constitutional judges are in the best position to know that all judges should protect individuals from misuse of power, which is why they need to be independent, and this is why their independence must be protected. This is why constitutional judges are strictly suspicious of interference, and especially of interference in judicial independence. But there is also potential suspicion that judicial sentiment towards the judicial community plays a role here. During the transition period, judges were often criticized and thus became a more and more closed community full of suspicion about reforms from outside.

The decision on the Special Court and the decision on reforms of the judiciary imply that our Court tends to shape the judiciary, and from this point of view it is a *positive policy-maker*.

*3.4 Positive constitutional interpretation: disputes between constitutional authorities (*organstreit*)*

There are two approaches to judicial review of constitutionality. One group of scholars believes that as many laws as possible should be in conformity with the Constitution. They prefer to see a perfect and consistent legal order. Application of law by individuals is a by-product of this consistency. The opposite approach is based on stressing the constitutional conformity of law, which is frequently applicable against individuals. Hence there is either an accent on laws or an accent on rights.

It was expected that during the early transition years there would be many disputes among constitutional bodies. Consequently, the drafters introduced the competence for the SCC to interpret the Constitution if a real dispute (case and controversy) among constitutional authorities occurred.

Here, interpretation itself is not part of the reasoning of a decision. The interpretation is directly stated in the operative part of the decision. As a result, it is formulated very much like a norm. It is binding not only for the parties, but also generally. It can be overcome only by further proceedings on interpretation or by the constitutional amendment. It is almost a new part of the Constitution. It belongs among the competences where perfect and consistent legal order is cultivated, where stronger accent is put on objective consistency of laws.

Another example of positive constitutional interpretation is the 'investiture controversy.' The Slovak constitution still has elements of a concept of unity of power. For example, there is almost no need to countersign presidential acts.[23] Paradoxically, this helped to balance out the power of the Prime Minister during the tough years of the 1990s. In the famous decision I. ÚS 39/93, the Constitutional Court stated that the President is obliged to take into account the Prime Minister's proposal to appoint a new minister, but s/he is not bound by this proposal. Later this was changed by constitutional amendment.

More recently the Court decided on a highly emotional dispute as to whether or not the President is bound by the proposal of Parliament to appoint the Prosecutor General. The Court stated in the operative part of the decision PL. ÚS 4/2012:

> The President is under obligation to act on a proposal from the National Council for the appointment of the Prosecutor General under Article 102t of the Constitution. If the candidate has been duly selected in accordance with the law, the President is under an obligation within a reasonable time either to appoint the proposed candidate or to inform the National Council that s/he will not appoint the candidate.
>
> The President may decline to appoint the candidate for one of two reasons: either the candidate does not fulfil the legal requirements for appointment, or there are serious factors connected with the candidate's personality which substantially compromise their ability to discharge the office in a manner which does not diminish the status of its constitutional position, or the body itself of which this person is to be the highest representative; or in a manner which is not contrary to the essential purpose of this body, if, as a consequence of the above, the proper functioning of constitutional bodies might be disrupted. The President must state the justifications for the non-appointment so as to make clear that these are not arbitrary.

This interpretation is sophisticated, elegant, and positive legislating. It leaves an open door for rejecting extreme candidates (for example, toxic mafia persons or Communist secret service collaborators); but it is still abstract and open to further interpretation. At the end of the day, it was not welcomed by Parliament (coalition), President and opposition. The SCC did not explicitly mention that rejection of a candidate is reviewable through constitutional complaint. A more serious problem arose when the SCC dealt with a constitutional complaint submitted by the rejected candidates. 'Investiture' problems should not be resolved through human rights protection instruments.

3.5 Positive legislator: 'resuscitator' (1)

The belief in a very consistent, lacunae-free legal order underlies the norm (from the Act on the Constitutional Court) which states that if an amendment is derogated by the Court, then the previous provision becomes effective again.

23 Peter Kresák, 'Government Structure in the New Slovak Republic' (1996) 4 *Tulsa Journal of Comparative and International Law* 15.

This is worthy of consideration: a new law has a provision X. X has never been amended. An older law has a provision Y. Later the provision Y is changed to its new wording Z. According to the Act on the Constitutional Court, if the Court derogates X, then X is just erased from the legal order. However, if the Court derogates Z, then the previous provision is 'resuscitated' and becomes effective again as part of the legal order.[24]

In 2003 the SCC derogated a provision which regulated later payment charges (payment for delay) for debts between health facilities and their suppliers. The Court derogated this provision because the charges were too high (PL. ÚS 38/03). The previous provision became alive again, and unfortunately, the rate according to this newly effective resuscitated provision was even higher than that which was declared as unconstitutional (PLz. ÚS 1/06).[25]

In this way, the SCC sometimes unintentionally becomes a positive legislator. The true legislator (Parliament) expresses the will to change the provision of law, however the previous provision may become effective again because of a decision by the Constitutional Court in combination with the Act on the Constitutional Court. The Court must always be aware of the effects of its decisions derogating amendments. This feature is very much influenced by the accent on written law in our legal culture.

3.6 Positive legislator: 'resuscitator' (2)

The real issue here is the question whether the SCC may review a norm which derogates another norm. An authority with standing may challenge a norm, which has just derogated another norm, arguing that erasing the norm has led to a situation of unconstitutionality. If the Court agrees, then the derogated norm may become alive again after the Court derogates the derogation. The tricky part is that after the original derogation by Parliament, the derogatory norm becomes part of a law, and the result is *nothing – no norm.* From this particular point of view there is nothing for the Court to review, just *no norm* or a missing norm. In case PL. ÚS 103/2011 the Constitutional Court declared that it has competence to review a derogatory norm, but in this particular case the Court considered this derogatory norm as constitutionally acceptable. The SCC nevertheless clarified that an eventually resuscitated norm must make sense and such a norm is again reviewable by the Court.

3.7 Positive legislator – lacunae and 'super-lacunae'

There are cases where the (un) constitutional point (*Sitz der Verfassungswidrigkeit*) lies not in the norm, but in the absence of a norm. There are two possibilities here: (1) An authority with standing thinks that the legal order lacks the norm A2. Around the norm A2 there are norms A1 and A3. Without the norm A2, norms A1 and A3 are unconstitutional. Hence the authority with standing may challenge A1 and A3. If the Court accepts this, it derogates A1 and A3. The result would be 'superlacunae' and Parliament

24 Cf. Article 140.6 of the Austrian Constitution.

25 See subsequent decision III. ÚS 381/06 (CODICES Identification SVK-2007-2-002).

would be under stress to adopt new A1, A2, and A3 as soon as possible; (2) The second possibility is either constitutionally conforming interpretation or an (*obiter dictum)* pressure on Parliament (compare point 29.4 of the recent decision U-I-199/2019 of Croatian Constitutional Court - Same Sex Couples as Foster Parents).

There are two cases where these strategies came to mind in which the derogation of a badly-chosen norm ultimately did not solve the constitutional problem. The requirement for 20000 members for a religious society to be registered (though a high number) was accepted as constitutional (PL. ÚS 10/08). But the problem was not the 20000 members condition for churches with all privileges, but the absence of a less demanding regime for new religions. A similar situation arose due to the absence of a less demanding regime for challenging paternity in family law (PL. ÚS 1/2010).

The Court distinguishes between legislative *nonaction* and legislative *omission.* In legislative *nonaction* Parliament deliberately does not regulate something. Legislative *nonaction* is usually not reviewable by the Court. For example, there are special pensions for state police officers, but not for the communal police (PL. ÚS 10/2012). It is not discriminatory if there is legislative *nonaction* regarding the communal police. On the other hand, legislative *omission* is reviewable. The Court may either derogate norms A1 and A3, generating legal and societal pressure on Parliament, or it may try to express a constitutionally conforming interpretation of A1 and A3.

4 The SCC's law-making activity: view from 'the outside'

Most stakeholders following the SCC's decision making are highly unlikely to operate with such a complex classification of its law-making activity as the one introduced in the previous heading. Nevertheless, these stakeholders, ranging from the public at large to more specialized constituencies – the political elites and the expert community[26] – are essential in shaping the image of the SCC, including its law-making activity, via presenting their views on the decisions and other actions of the Court. This heading provides a rare, albeit brief and selective, assessment of these perceptions, which shows how the nuances of the Court's 'craftsmanship'[27] are frequently sidelined in favour of a few 'grand' cases and their outcomes.

As there is almost a complete lack of empirical research on media and public perceptions of the SCC, only a few observations are provided on the basis of available data. Three major trends deserve attention. Firstly, in terms of general public opinion about the SCC, the first SCC in the 1990s scores best in public trust until 2010.[28] At the same time, other government institutions scored higher in this period as well,[29] so the SCC may have succeeded in this period because the voters of opposition to

26 This includes former SCC judges as well.

27 Herbert M. Kritzer, 'Towards a Theorization of Craft' (2007) 16 *Social & Legal Studies* 321.

28 Public opinion polls ceased to be made after 2010, indicative of the decreased interest in singling out trust levels of specific institutions.

29 Ol'ga Gyárfášová & Marián Velšic, 'Spoločensko-politická klíma (Verejná mienka)' in Miroslav Kollár & Grigorij Mesežnikov (eds.) *Slovensko 2001. Súhrnná správa o stave spoločnosti* (IVO 2001) 253.

Mečiar perceived it more positively due to its challenges to his policies, while the supporters of Mečiar did not perceive it *too negatively*. Secondly, 2001 (the period of the second SCC) was the first time when more individuals distrusted (mildly or substantially) the SCC than trusted it. Thirdly, the trust levels since then have oscillated around 50 per cent, but went down quite sharply after (approximately) the start of the SCC's third term and the decision on the Special Court (see p. 189–90). It is at this time that, according to Slovak public opinion experts, a 'politicized understanding of the institution' has become ingrained among the supporters of most major political parties (see Figure 10.1).[30]

4.1 Media

The media reporting about the SCC's decisions, and about the institution as such and its judges, exhibit two trends. Firstly, they believe in the importance and capacity of the SCC to exert political change, to which some of its landmark rulings have contributed. Secondly, however, they are also generally critical of several of these landmark rulings, giving space to (sometimes extensive) criticisms of the SCC by constitutional experts or political elites. As a result, the SCC, towards the

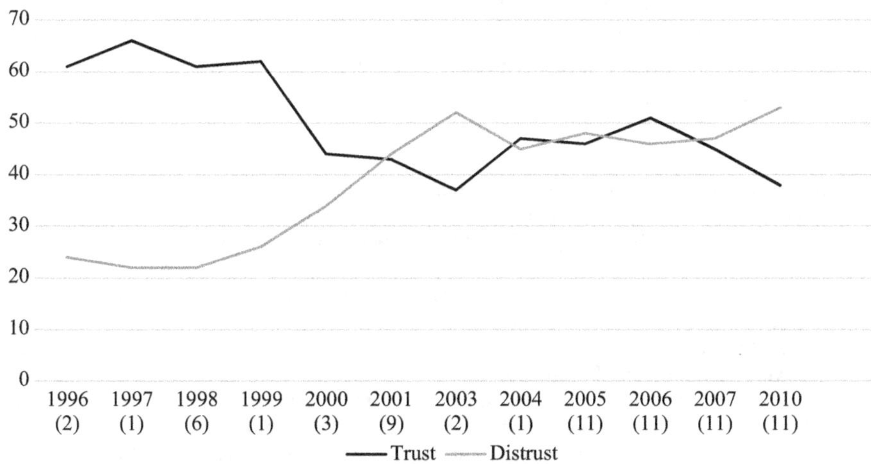

Figure 10.1 (Dis)trust in the SCC as a political institution 1996–2010. Numbers in brackets indicate the month of the data collection.

Source: Darina Malová, 'The Role and Experience of the Slovakian Constitutional Court' in Wojciech Sadurski (ed.) *Constitutional Justice, East and West: Democratic Legitimacy and Constitutional Courts in Post-Communist Europe in a Comparative Perspective* (Springer 2010) 349, and the reports on the state of society in Slovakia published by the Institute of Public Affairs.

30 Zora Bútorová & Ol'ga Gyárfášová, 'Verejná mienka' in Martin Bútora, Miroslav Kollár & Grigorij Mesežnikov (eds.) *Slovensko 2009. Súhrnná správa o stave spoločnosti a trendoch na rok 2010* (IVO 2010) 183.

end of its third term, seems to have reached a general reputation of its majority being supportive of the policies of the executive, in particular the party Smer-SD of Robert Fico. This does not mean that there is notable support for reducing the institution's competences. Rather, there appears to be a demand for landmark decisions that are well justified and cannot be connected with partisan support for Smer-SD's policies.[31]

The SCC's law-making activity was generally met with criticism after the beginning of its third term in 2007. Before that, the overall positive perceptions[32] (although with an occasional critical voice highlighting the 'missed opportunities' for more firm adjudicative foundations)[33] gradually evaporated during the Court's second term, when the lack of expert reflections was coupled with limited public attention to the Court at the time of Slovakia's accession to the European Union. After the ruling on the unconstitutionality of the Special Court,[34] expert attention celebrated a 'comeback.' The diversely formulated positions on partial issues were summarized in the overreaching critique of one of the Court's judges during the 1990s, who argued that the SCC had restricted the possibilities for resolving disputes and protecting rights provided for in the Constitution and adopted an inconsistent approach to the creation of doctrines.[35] The critique was reinforced after the SCC had delivered the interpretation of the presidential powers in (not) appointing the candidate for the attorney general, and subsequently (with rare exceptions)[36] the appointment of constitutional justices.[37] Combined with the Court's procedural approach leaning towards rejecting complaints concerning substantive human rights,[38] the general picture is full of doubts. Yet, most of the doctrinal accounts do not *in principle* oppose the legitimacy and even duty of the SCC to, under certain conditions, engage in law-making activity.

31 An important caveat is that the media perception might omit important judicial decisions as well as elements of the reasoning.

32 Herman Schwartz, *The Struggle for Constitutional Justice in Post-Communist Europe* , op. cit., Chapter 7.

33 Radoslav Procházka, *Mission Accomplished: On Founding Constitutional Adjudication in Central Europe* (CEU Press 2002).

34 Ján Svák & Lucia Berdisová, 'Constitutional Court of the Slovak Republic as Positive Legislator via Application and Interpretation of the Constitution', op. cit., 767, 771, 775; Ivetta Macejková, 'K otázke ústavnosti Špeciálneho súdu v SR' (2010) 149 *Právník* 1193; Tomáš Ľalík, 'Politika a aktivizmus na Ústavnom súde' (2011) 63 *Justičná revue* 691.

35 Ján Drgonec, *Ochrana ústavnosti Ústavným súdom Slovenskej republiky* (EUROKÓDEX 2010).

36 Tomáš Ľalík, 'Born Is the King: The Day When Effective Judicial Review Arrived' *I-CONnect* (2018), http://www.iconnectblog.com/2018/01/symposium-slovak-appointments-case-lalik/.

37 The most notable example here is Ján Drgonec, whose full critical analysis of one of the Court's decisions was published in a respected Slovak daily ('Everything you should know about how constitutional judges ordered Kiska to act' *Denník N* (2017), https://dennikn.sk/972222/vsetko-co-by-ste-mali-vediet-o-tom-ako-ustavni-sudco via-prikazali-kiskovi-konat/).

38 Peter Kresák, 'Reštriktívny formalizmus ako dôvod zužovania ochrany ľudských práv a slobôd v rozhodovacej činnosti Ústavného súdu SR' in Ladislav Orosz & Tomáš Majerčák (eds.) *Ochrana ľudských práv a základných slobôd ústavnými súdmi a medzinárodnými súdnymi orgánmi - III. ústavné dni* (Univerzita P. J. Šafárika 2014) 194.

4.2 Political elites

Political elites have generally obeyed the decisions of the Court, with the notable exception of overruling its judgment against the creation of a special commission of the National Council to review the decisions of the National Security Authority (PL. ÚS 6/04). There, the legislature adopted a constitutional act (254/2006 Coll.) creating a parliamentary committee with very similar competences.[39]

In the third term of the Court (2007–2019), the decisions manipulating the boundaries of presidential powers were met with most resistance from the political elites. Specifically, former President Gašparovič was found to have decided in violation of the SCC's constitutional interpretation when he refused to appoint Professor Jozef Čentéš as attorney general, and swore in another candidate (I. ÚS 397/2014). The fiercest symbolic rejection of the SCC's jurisprudence came a few years later from Gašparovič's successor, Andrej Kiska (advised by the SCC's President between 2000 and 2006, Ján Mazák). In response to the Court mandating the head of state to select from the double number of candidates, the President decided to comply by filling in the three seats, which he had previously resisted to do. Acknowledging the SCC's essential role as 'the most eminent judicial authority that protects the rights and liberties of peoples,' he framed the appointment struggle as a 'value struggle [...] about the mission of the CC,' and identified the opposing parties as either supporting the SCC's role as the 'guardian of the Constitution' (which is stipulated in the Constitution itself) or 'the means to reach selfish goals of the political power.' Kiska then proclaimed the victory of the latter through 'one of the Court's worst decisions [which is] arbitrary, full of formal and substantial mistakes. It is a result of a deep disregard of the Constitution [...], the Court's previous ruling by its own judges, and an example of disrespect towards basic separation of powers in a rule-of-law state.'[40] Here, the SCC found a surprising advocate in the PM, Robert Fico, who himself had supported unconstitutional legislation before. For Fico, disrespecting the SCC marked 'the end of the rule-of-law state,'[41] and the head of state had positioned himself above the court with this 'defamation. [...] No one stands above morality, constitutionality, and this state.'[42] While the boundaries of legitimate distinctions between the criticism of an apex court's particular decisions, as opposed to the court as such, are subject to a legitimate

39 Erik Láštic & Max Steuer, 'The Slovak Constitutional Court: The Third Legislator?' in Kálmán Pócza (ed.) *Constitutional Politics and the Judiciary: Decision-Making in Central and Eastern Europe* (Routledge 2019) 201.

40 'The President will appoint Laššáková, Mamojka and Duriš as constitutional judges' (December 12, 2017), https://www.prezident.sk/article/prezident-vymenuje-na-ustavny-sud-lassakovu-mamojku-a-durisa/.

41 Robert Fico, 'Disrespecting the Constitutional Court is the End of a 'Rule-of-law state' (December 11, 2017), https://www.tyzden.sk/politika/44710/robert-fico-nerespektovanie-ustavneho-sudu-je-koniec-pravneho-statu/.

42 'Fico is Most Concerned with the Style President Kiska Attacked the Constitutional Court' (December 13, 2017), https://www.webnoviny.sk/fica-najviac-ho-trapi-styl-akym-prezident-kiska-zautocil-na-ustavny-sud/.

discussion,[43] in this case the law-making activity of the SCC resulted in the PM (later forced to step down due to allegations of corruption) having been able to position himself as the guardian of the SCC against excessive criticism aimed at undermining its constitutional standing. Hence, to some extent, the SCC became a 'puppet' in partisan rhetorical games about right and wrong constitutional conduct.

4.3 Experts

The expert reception of the SCC's law-making activity has been, with some exceptions, critical, focusing on a few particularly high-profile or otherwise unique cases, rather than on individually less notable, but on the whole significant doctrinal developments, such as the implementation of a robust proportionality analysis in cases concerning the conflict between freedom of speech and other fundamental rights.[44] Probably the first notable expert denouncement of the SCC's law-making activity was concentrated on its invalidation of the Act on the Special Court. This decision split the court into two almost equally large groups, and only some of the members of one of these 'coalitions' have been particularly active in academic discourse (especially judge Orosz and judge Gajdošíková). In addition to them, some of the most notable commentators of the SCC's decisions are former judges as well.[45] Ján Drgonec, an SCC judge during its first term, is also the most prolific constitutional commentator in the country, having authored a commentary of more than 1500 pages[46] in which he adopted a condemning position towards many judgements of the SCC (and which he reflected in a later constitutional law textbook as well).[47] Ján Mazák, who served as President Kiska's legal adviser, took up numerous critical positions towards the court in the media[48] with the potential to reach a much broader audience than constitutional commentaries or textbooks. At the same time, these contributions cannot be seen as 'blindly critical' as they simultaneously praised the dissenting voices on the Court on many occasions, such as dissents by judges Gajdošíková, Orosz, and Mészáros during the constitutional judge appointment cases (their perspective was also backed by the former minister of justice, Lucia Žitňanská).[49]

43 Richard H. Fallon Jr., *Law and Legitimacy in the Supreme Court* (Belknap Press: An Imprint of Harvard University Press 2018).
44 See Darina Malová & Max Steuer, 'Sloboda prejavu v Slovenskej republike: Analýza vybraných súdnych rozhodnutí' (2014) 153 *Právník* 309.
45 As a disclosure, one of the authors of this chapter has also been critical towards the Court in some recent writings – however, these do not reach the level of prominence approximating that of the former SCC judges.
46 Ján Drgonec, *Ústava Slovenskej republiky: Teória a prax* (C. H. Beck 2015) 1462–68. A second edition of the commentary, of almost 1800 pages, has become available in 2019.
47 Ján Drgonec, *Ústavné právo hmotné* (C. H. Beck 2018) 370.
48 Author: Ján Mazák (2019), https://dennikn.sk/autor/jan-mazak/.
49 'The truth of the Constitutional Court' (December 22, 2015), https://dennikn.sk/327154/pravda-ustavneho-sudu/.

Who, then, are the defenders of the Court's decisions which had embodied a form of law-making activity? There are only a few academic elites who formulate staunch arguments in support of the Court.[50] For one, a judge of the second SCC and legal adviser to the Prime Minister for Robert Fico's Smer-SD party, Eduard Bárány, argued in a newspaper that the President put himself 'outside the purview of the Constitution' with his refusal to appoint constitutional judges from the nominees who had been submitted to him.[51] His opinions were mostly presented in popular texts intended for a wider audience. Academic texts on the subject were provided by Tomáš Ľalík, a constitutional lawyer who advocates for a robust role of the Court and has repeatedly supported both its decisions in the appointment-related cases[52] and in the judicial clearance case[53] (the latter against considerable opposition).[54] On the whole, the expert discourse on the SCC as a law-maker is framed primarily through the negative optics of the SCC's concrete decisions with such an element, rather than by identifying decisions where the SCC did not engage in law-making activity despite the existence of plausible arguments for such course of action.[55] An additional consequence of this tendency is a disproportionate focus on a few highly salient and visible decisions, neglecting the development of the Court's doctrine in other areas, especially in protection of specific fundamental rights.

4.4 Summary

The public reflection is overwhelmingly critical of the SCC's law-making activity approached through the lens of a small number of cases. Due to constitutional

50 The debate often follows with a delay after the decision due to the lack of a deadline for the SCC to publish the written decision and justification. See Daniel Krošlák et al., *Ústavné právo* (Wolters Kluwer 2016) 571.

51 'Constitutional lawyer Eduard Bárány: President Finds Himself Outside the Purview of the Constitution' (March 20, 2018), https://spravy.pravda.sk/domace/clanok/463002-ustavny-pravnik-eduard-barany-prezident-sa-nachadza-mimo-ustavy/.

52 Tomáš Ľalík, 'Tretí Ústavný súd: Kontinuita či diskontinuita v rozhodovacej činnosti?' in Tomáš Majerčák (ed.) *Ústavný súd Slovenskej republiky v treťom funkčnom období – VII. ústavné dni* (Univerzita P. J. Šafárika 2019) 141.

53 Tomáš Ľalík, 'Nález PL. ÚS 21/2014 ako nevyhnutný liek na ústavné zákonodarstvo na Slovensku' (2019) 38 *Acta Facultatis Iuridicae Universitatis Comenianae* 274.

54 Marta Breichová Lapčáková, 'Ústava v ohrození – Zopár zamyslení nad jedným nálezom Ústavného súdu Slovenskej republiky (PL. ÚS 21/2014)' (2019) 38 *Acta Facultatis Iuridicae Universitatis Comenianae* 237; Marek Káčer, 'Od ochrany pred hrôzami koncentračných táborov k ochrane "profesionálnej existencie" vydierateľných sudcov' (2019) 38 *Acta Facultatis Iuridicae Universitatis Comenianae* 261.

55 Ján Drgonec does provide a 'middle way' between the two positions by allowing for the possibility of the SCC to rule on unconstitutionality of a constitutional act via a broadly conceived mission of the SCC in defending 'constitutionality' as opposed to 'the Constitution'. Drgonec, *Ústava Slovenskej republiky: Teória a prax*, 1294, 1328–31. The other (collective) constitutional commentary conceives of the SCC's mission more as of a check of the executive and the legislature, therefore, it remains less open for legitimate law-making activity of the Court (Milan Čič (ed.) *Komentár k Ústave Slovenskej republiky* (EUROKÓDEX 2012) 635–38).

lawyers becoming public figures in the debate, the resulting strongest voice is supportive of restraint of the SCC i.e. arguing towards reducing its law-making activity. However, this normative position is not supported by empirical evidence as it is impossible to foresee which constitutional challenges may require the SCC to engage in law-making activity in order to protect the democratic political regime. Hence, the public picture remains skewed by mixing two different dimensions – the Court's approach in specific cases and self-restraint as a 'universal good' in judicial decision making. The result is the sidelining of the Court's more diverse case law in which it had founded new binding legal principles and practices, a process exacerbated by limited specialized journalist coverage of the SCC's regular activities.

5 Conclusion

Slovak judicial review in the last quarter century has been a real ride. *Demokratura* has not been compromised by one single decision, but by a cluster of decisions where the pure declaration that the authoritarian power had violated the Constitution was crucial. The heritage of unity-of-power era implied also in the position of the head of state appears paradoxically positive in extreme constitutional situations. Differentiation between negative and positive legislating is of more symbolic character and not soprecise indeed.

Chronologically, these findings demonstrate that the Court has gradually become bolder in some areas of law-making activity, although its prevalent textualism in the early period of its operation was sufficient to pose a barrier to some anti-democratic tendencies the Slovak government of 1994 to 1998. These tendencies did not go unnoticed in the constitutional discourse and received a mixed reception, with some of the most influential domestic constitutional thinkers recognizing the space for the Court's law-making activity in theory but challenging it when applied in selected cases. While it is not possible to discern precise trends specific for public opinion reception of the 'law-making' decisions of the Court, the available data indicate a shift towards a more 'political' (and occasionally also 'partisan') perception. The new plenum of the Court that began to work in 2019 is hard-pressed to uphold the standards of constitutionality in the face of new as well as recurrent challenges and at the same time win support for its decisions by the scholarly community as well as the broader set of constituencies observing and caring for the Court's rulings.

Part III

European International Courts

11 The Court of Justice of the European Union as a law-maker: enhancing integration or acting ultra vires?

Monika Kawczyńska

1 The Court of Justice of the European Union as a 'hybrid' court

Taking into consideration the autonomous nature of the EU legal order, the Court of Justice of the European Union (CJEU) is perceived as a 'hybrid' court, performing different functions as an international court and the domestic court of the European Union.

As an international court the CJEU is acting as a permanent and independent judicial institution set up by international treaties and deciding the cases on the basis of international law with binding effect on the parties.[1] This is especially apparent in exclusive jurisdiction of the CJEU in disputes between Member States concerning the interpretation or application of the Treaties (Art. 344 TFEU), disputes submitted under a compromise (273 TFEU), and infringement actions adjudicated between Member States (Art. 259 TFEU). It is generally acknowledged that judicial law-making by international courts is creative and that it may have considerable consequences for the regulatory autonomy of states, thus affecting the space for domestic democratic government.[2]

At the same time, the CJEU performs its function as the internal court of the EU and acts in the capacity of a constitutional court, a supreme court, and an administrative court.[3] The main task entrusted to the Court since its origin is to

1 Tobias Lock, *The European Court of Justice and International Courts* (Oxford University Press 2015) 7–8.

2 Armin von Bogdandy, Ingo Venzke, 'Beyond Dispute: International Judicial Institutions as Lawmakers' in Armin von Bogdandy, Ingo Venzke (ed.), *International Judicial Lawmaking. On Public Authority and Democratic Legitimation in Global Governance* (Springer-Verlag Berlin Heidelberg 2012) 4, 7.

3 Koen Lenaerts, 'Some Reflections on the Separation of Powers in the European Community' (1991) Common Market Law Review 28, 32; Vassilios Skouris, The Position of the European Court of Justice in the EU Legal Order and its Relationship with National Constitutional Court (10 November 2019) http://www.us-rs.si/webroot/o-sodiscu/3666/contributions/presentation-by-dr-vassilios-skouris-president-of-the-european-court-of-justice; Francis Jacobs, 'Is the Court of Justice of the European Communities a Constitutional Court?' in Deirdre Curtin, Daniel O'Keeffe (ed.), *Constitutional Adjudication in European Community and National Law* (Butterworth Dublin 1992), 25, 25; Anthony Arnull, 'A Constitutional Court for Europe?' (2003–2004) CYELS (*Cambridge Yearbook of European Legal Studies*) 2; Bo Vesterdorf, 'A Constitutional Court for the EU?' IJCL

DOI: 10.4324/9781003022442-12

'ensure that in the interpretation and application of the Treaties the law is observed' (Art. 19 (2) TUE). Performing its functions as a constitutional court, the CJEU is mainly assessing the validity of the acts of general application adopted by the EU institutions also concerning the horizontal and vertical division of competences (Art. 263 TFEU and Art. 267 TFEU), and adjudicates the infringement actions instituted by the Commission against the Member States (Art. 258 TFEU), including observance by the Member States of the Union values: fundamental rights, democracy, and the rule of law. It also gives its opinion as to whether an international agreement is compatible with the Treaties (Art. 218 (11) TFEU). Acting as the supreme court, the CJEU ensures the uniform application of the EU law among the Member States by preliminary rulings concerning the interpretation of the Treaties and acts of the institutions, bodies, offices or agencies of the Union (Art. 267 TFEU). Performing its function as an administrative court, the CJEU ensures the judicial protection of the private parties against illegal administrative actions and omissions of the EU institutions, organs, and bodies (Art. 263 and 265 TFEU), as well as awarding damages for breach of EU law (Art. 340 (2) TFEU).

Exercising its competence, the CJEU has played a key role as 'a motor' or 'a master' of European integration.[4] Since the 1960s, it has presented a dynamic method of Treaty interpretation and established the foundations of the Union constitutional order. The Court carries out its duties with regard to the values and objectives of the Union enshrined in the Treaty with the view of 'creating an ever closer union among the peoples of Europe' (Art. 1 TEU). Acting within the institutional framework of the Union, the CJEU ensures the consistency, effectiveness, and continuity of the Union policies and actions (Art. 13 (1) TEU). Therefore, it is broadly accepted among the scholars, that the CJEU presents teleological or purposive reasoning, where law is interpreted in the service of an objective that moves European integration forwards.[5] The Court often refers to 'meta-teleological' arguments, referring to the 'thelos' of the entire legal order,

(*International Journal of Constitutional Law*) (2006) 4, 607, 607; Eleanor Sharpston, Geert De Baere, 'The Court of Justice as a Constitutional Adjudicator' in Anthony Arnull et al. (ed.) *A Constitutional Order of States? Essays in EU Law in Honour of Alan Dashwood* (Hart Publishing 2011), 123, 124; Takis Tridimas, 'The European Court of Justice and the Draft Constitution: A Supreme Court for the Union?' in Takis Tridimas, Paolisa Nebbia (eds.) *EU Law for the Twenty-First Century: Re-Thinking the New Legal Order, Volume I* (Hart Publishing 2004) 113, 114. The CJEU also performs minor functions as a labour court in cases relating to disputes between the Union and its servants and as the court of 'arbitration' having jurisdiction to give judgements pursuant to any arbitration clause contained in a contract concluded by or on behalf of the Union.

4 Thomas Horsley, 'Reflections on the role of the Court of Justice as the "motor" of European integration: Legal limits to judicial lawmaking', (2013) *Common Market Law Review* 50, 931, 934; Dorte Sindbjerg Martinsen, *An Ever More Powerful Court? The Political Constraints of Legal Integration in the European Union* (Oxford University Press 2015), 23.

5 Gerard Conway, *The Limits of Legal Reasoning and the European Court of Justice* (Cambridge 2012), 22; Albertina Albors-Llorens, *The European Court of Justice, More than a Teleological Court*, (1999) *Cambridge Yearbook of European Legal Studies* 2, 382.

and the function and consequences of the specific interpretation adopted. In its rulings, the CJEU invokes the effectiveness (*effet utille*), uniformity, legal certainty, and protection of individual rights as meta-purposes of the EU legal order.[6]

2 The binding authority of judgements in the EU legal order

Hans Kelsen distinguished between the work of legislators, which he described as 'creative' and 'positive,' and the work of constitutional judges, which he described as 'negative.' He admitted that the competence to declare legislation unconstitutional is also a law-making, and therefore political, competence.[7] The CJEU assumes both these roles as 'negative' and 'positive' law-maker.

As negative law-maker, the CJEU has the power to declare an EU act invalid in the context of preliminary ruling procedure enshrined in Article 267 TFEU (declaration of invalidity). Moreover, it can declare the act null and void in the action for annulment specified in Article 263 TFUE initiated by individuals, Member States or the EU institutions (declaration of nullity).[8] The judgement declaring invalidity or nullity has an *erga omnes* effect and the contested act may no longer be applied in the EU legal order. As the CJEU underlined in several judgements, the Treaty has established a complete and coherent system of legal remedies and procedures designed to ensure judicial review of the legality of acts of the institutions, and has entrusted such review to the Luxembourg courts.[9]

Positive law-making through adjudication shall be understood as the creation of new legal norms of general application. The creation and development of legal normativity in judicial practice of courts takes place in the context of concrete cases. Judicial decisions settle the particular case between the parties. The court applies relevant norms in the light of the facts and legal interpretations presented to it. At the same time, the court judgement reaches beyond the context of the specific case.[10]

The binding authority of precedent is not an inherent feature of the Union's judicial system. The doctrines of *stare decisis* and precedent do not formally exist in EU law.[11] It applies not only to the horizontal relation of judgements at the level of the Court of Justice or the General Court, but also to so-called 'vertical

6 Jan Komarek, 'Legal Reasoning in EU law' in Anthony Arnull, Damian Chalmers (ed.), *The Oxford Handbook of European Union Law* (Oxford University Press 2017), 46.

7 Hans Kelsen, 'Wesen und Entwicklung der Staatsgerichtsbarkeit'in Veröffentlichungen der Vereinigung der deutschen Staatsrechtslehrer, Heft 5, (Berlin – Leipzig 1929), 56. Alec Stone Sweet, *Governing with Judges: Constitutional Politics in Europe* (Oxford University Press 2002), 35.

8 Koen Lenaerts, Ignace Maselis, and Kathleen Gutman, *EU Procedural Law* (Oxford University Press 2014), 457.

9 Case C-50/00 P, of 25 July 2002 (*Unión de Pequeños Agricultores*), para 40.

10 See von Bogdandy, Venzke (n 2) 12.

11 Daniel Chalmers, Gareth Davies, Giorgio Monti, *European Union Law. Cases and Materials* (Cambridge University Press 2010), 169–170, Trevor Hartley, *The Foundations of European Union Law* (Oxford University Press), 71; Marc Jacob, *Precedents and Case-Based Reasoning in the European Court of Justice: Unfinished Business* (Cambridge University Press 2014) 66.

precedents' where the General Court is not bound by the judgements of the Court of Justice.[12] Historically, this can be explained by the fact that the Community was originally founded by States belonging to the family of continental European civil law systems, with the result that the supranational legal order thereby created has similar characteristics.[13] It is true that the Court of Justice is not bound by its previous decisions, however it is generally acknowledged that in practice it does not often depart from them.[14] Also the General Court often refers to and follows the decisions of the higher court. In practice, judgments of the CJEU are not treated as precedents, related to and interpreted in the context of a specific case, but rather as a set of normative sentences of general validity. In future cases, such normative sentences are applied in a similar way to legal provisions, not limited by the context of the specific case. In its judicial practice the Court extensively uses so-called 'cluster citations' reproducing sentences or entire paragraphs from its own previous judgements.[15]

The judgments of the CJEU having no broader effects would be unacceptable for the development of the Union legal order and uniform application of the EU law. It is beyond doubt, that the judgements of the CJEU delivered in the preliminary ruling procedure, declaring invalidity of the EU act or its certain provisions, have an *erga omnes* effect. They are binding in relation to the national court which made the reference, as well as to other national courts outside the specific dispute in the various Member States.[16] A judgement given by the CJEU under Art. 267 TFEU on interpretation of EU law is binding on the national court hearing the case and all courts and tribunals dealing with the case at a later stage of the proceedings. In accordance with the settled case law, an interpretation which the Court gives of a rule of EU law clarifies and defines the meaning and scope of that rule as it must be or ought to have been understood and applied from the time of its coming into force.[17] Due to declaratory nature of the interpretation given by the Court and necessity of securing uniformity in the application of Union law throughout the Member States, it is widely accepted that also judgements of a preliminary ruling on interpretation extend its binding

12 Kieran Bradley, 'Vertical Precedent at the Court of Justice of the European Union: When Push Comes to Shove' in Kieran Bradley, Noel Travers, Anthony Whelan (ed.), *Of Courts and Constitutions Liber Amicorum in Honour of Nial Fenelly* (Hart Publishing 2014) 47, 65.

13 Opinion C-331/05 P, of 28 March 2007 (*Internationaler Hilfsfonds)* para 85; Takis Tridimas, 'Precedent and the Court of Justice: A Jurisprudence of Doubt?' in Julie Dickson and Pavlos Eleftheriadis (ed.), *Philosophical Foundations of EU Law* (Oxford University Press 2012), 307, 307.

14 Anthony Arnull, 'Owning up to fallibility: Precedent and the Court of Justice', (1993) *Common Market Law Review* 30, 247, 248.

15 Michael Bobek, 'The Court of Justice of The European Union' in Anthony Arnull, Damian Chalmers (ed.), *The Oxford Handbook of European Union Law* (Oxford University Press 2015) 153, 170.

16 See Lenaerts, Maselis, Gutman (n 8), 475.

17 Case 61/79, of 27 March 1980 (*Denkavit)*, para 16; case C-453/00, of 13 January 2004 (*Kühne & Heitz)*, para. 21.

effect outside the specific case.[18] This assumption is further strengthened by the doctrine of *acte éclairé* where the national court may abstain from referring the question under Art. 267 TFEU when the question raised is materially identical with a question which has already been the subject of a preliminary ruling in a similar case.[19] Such is also the case, when the question raised is substantially the same as a question which has already been the subject of a preliminary ruling in the same national proceedings.[20] Also Art. 99 of the Rules of Procedure[21] stipulates that the Court may decide to rule by reasoned order where a question referred for a preliminary ruling is identical to a question on which the Court has already ruled, where the reply to such a question may be clearly deduced from existing case law or where the answer to the question referred for a preliminary ruling admits of no reasonable doubt.

3 The limits to the judicial law-making of the CJEU. The power of constitutional courts to control the CJEU actions as ultra vires

As an institution exercising competences of the EU, the CJEU is bound by the principle of conferral (*principe d'attribution*), laid down in Art. 5 (1) TEU. The second paragraph of the latter provision makes clear that the principle of conferral implies that the EU shall act within the limits of the competences conferred upon it by the Member States, while according to Art. 4 (1) TEU competences not conferred upon the Union in the Treaties remain with the Member States (vertical distribution of competences). Therefore the EU does not dispose of the competence to decide on its own competences (the so-called *Kompetenz-Kompetenz*). At the same time, according to the Art. 13 (1) TEU, the CJEU shall act within the limits of the powers conferred on it in the Treaties, and in conformity with the procedures, conditions, and objectives set out in them (horizontal distribution of competences). In consequence, the dynamic interpretation of the Union law exercised by the CJEU may not lead to extension of the Union competences, as well as its own judicial powers, beyond the limits designated in the Treaties. However, the analysis of the case law confirms the view that the CJEU tends to have an inherent jurisdiction. It is apparent in cases where the Court is responsible for securing the 'complete system of judicial remedies' within the EU legal order and where strict interpretation of legal provisions may lead to denial of justice (*déni de justice*).[22]

18 See Lenaerts, Maselis, Gutman (n 8) 244–246; Rene Barents, 'Remedies and Procedures before the EU Courts' (*Kluwer Law International* 2016), 552; Martin Broberg, Niels Fenger, *Preliminary References to the European Court of Justice* (Oxford University Press 2014) 444.

19 Cases 28/62 to 30/62, of 27 March 1963 (*Da Costa*).

20 Case C-337/95, of 4 November 1997 (*Parfums Christian Dior*), paras 29–30.

21 Rules of Procedure of the Court of Justice of 25 September 2012, OJ L 265, 29.9.2012.

22 Anthony Arnull, 'Does the Court of Justice have Inherent Jurisdiction?' (1990) *Common Market Law Review* 27, 683, 684.

The Constitutional Courts of the EU Member States attempt to set boundaries to judicial activism of the CJEU that may transgress the limits of legal interpretation prescribed by the Treaties. The Federal Constitutional Court in the *Maastricht* judgement,[23] acknowledged its task to review whether EU legal acts remain within the limited competences of the EU and to declare acts that transgress these borders to be ultra vires and hence inapplicable in Germany (ultra vires review).[24] The first occasion to assess whether the action of the CJEU amounted to an ultra vires act was the case *Honeywell*[25] concerning the debateable *Mangold* judgment[26] where the Court found a provision of German labour law to be incompatible with Directive 2000/78/EC and the general principle of non-discrimination on grounds of age. Surprisingly, the Federal Constitutional Court imposed notable limitations on the possibility to declare acts of European institutions inapplicable in the context of an ultra vires control.[27] It held, that 'ultra vires review by the Federal Constitutional Court can only be considered if a breach of competences on the part of the European bodies is sufficiently qualified. This is contingent on the act of the authority of the European Union being manifestly in breach of competences and the impugned act leading to a structurally significant shift to the detriment of the Member States in the structure of competences.' As concerns the CJEU, 'prior to the acceptance of an ultra vires act, it is to be afforded the opportunity to interpret the Treaties, as well as to rule on the validity and interpretation of the acts in question, in the context of preliminary ruling proceedings according to Article 267 TFEU, insofar as it has not yet clarified the questions which have arisen.' Most recently the *Honeywell* conditions have been put to the test in the *Outright Monetary Transactions* reference,[28] where the Second Senate acknowledged for the first time a so-called 'principal ultra vires objection' based on the right to vote. This decision was based on an ultra vires review and constituted the first preliminary reference in the history of the Federal Constitutional Court.[29]

The strong implications of the principle of conferral were also emphasized by constitutional courts of the Member States in the process of ratification of the Lisbon Treaty. The Federal Constitutional Court in the *Lisbon* judgement held that

23 2 BvR 2134/92, 2 BvR 2159/92, of 12 October 1993.

24 Mehrdad Payandeh, 'Constitutional Review of EU law after Honeywell: Contextualizing the Relationship Between the German Constitutional Court and the EU Court of Justice' (2011) *Common Market Law Review* 48, 9, 9. Mattias Kumm, 'Who is the Final Arbiter of Constitutionality in Europe?' (1999) *Common Market Law Review* 36, 351, 364.

25 2 BvR 2661/06, of 6 July 2010.

26 Case C-144/04, of 22 November 2005 (*Mangold*).

27 Anja Wiesbrock 'The Implications of Mangold for Domestic Legal Systems: The Honeywell Case', (2011) *Maastricht Journal of European and Comparative Law* 201, 206–207.

28 Case C-62/14, of 16 June 2015 (*Gauweiler*).

29 Dieter Grimm, Mattias Wendel, Tobias Reinbacher, 'European Constitutionalism and the German Basic Law' in Anneli Albi, Samo Bardutzky (eds.) *National Constitutions in European and Global Governance: Democracy, Rights, the Rule of Law* (T.M.C. Asser Press 2019) 407, 425.

> the Basic Law does not authorise the German state bodies to transfer sovereign powers in such a way that their exercise can independently establish other competences for the European Union. It prohibits the transfer of competence to decide on its own competence (Kompetenz-Kompetenz) (…) The Federal Constitutional Court has already opened up the way of the *ultra vires* review for this, which applies where Community and Union institutions transgress the boundaries of their competences.[30]

Similarly the Constitutional Court of the Czech Republic in two judgements concerning the *Lisbon Treaty* reserved itself a right to review 'whether any act of Union bodies exceeded the powers that the Czech Republic transferred to the European Union,' but only in quite exceptional cases like abandoning the identity of values or exceeding the scope of conferred competences.[31] In a later case *Slovak pensions*,[32] the Czech Constitutional Court for the first time in European history declared the CJEU judgement (in case *Landtová*),[33] as ultra vires. It stated, that 'in that case there were excesses on the part of a European Union body, that a situation occurred in which an act by a European body exceeded the powers that the Czech Republic transferred to the European Union under Art. 10a of the Constitution; this exceeded the scope of the transferred powers, and was ultra vires.'

Correspondingly the Polish Constitutional Tribunal in the *Lisbon* judgement underlined that, 'the States remain the subjects of the integration process, maintain "the competence of competences,"' and set a detailed catalogue of inalienable competences that remain under the prohibition of conferral.[34] The Polish Constitutional Tribunal reserves itself a competence to control EU secondary legislation (normative acts) only where the Constitution explicitly refers to the review of normative acts (i.e. within the framework of a constitutional complaint or questions of law referred by national courts).[35] By virtue of the limitations imposed on the constitutional complaint procedure, the Tribunal would not be able to examine whether a given act was ultra vires, i.e. whether it was within the scope of competence conferred by Poland on the EU. It may only do so, when an ultra vires action resulted in an infringement of Polish constitutional rights and freedoms.[36]

30 2 BvE 2/08 of 30 June 2009, paras. 233 and 240.
31 Pl UŚ 19/80, of 26 November 2008; para 120; Pl. UŚ. 29/09, of 3 November 2009, para 150.
32 Pl. UŚ 5/12, of 31 January 2012; Zdeněk Kühn, 'The Czech Republic: From a Euro-Friendly Approach of the Constitutional Court to Proclaiming a Court of Justice Judgment Ultra Vires' in Anneli Albi, Samo Bardutzky (eds.) *National Constitutions in European and Global Governance: Democracy, Rights, the Rule of Law (T.M.C. Asser Press 2019)* 795, 803.
33 Case C-399/09, of 22 June 2011 (*Landtová*).
34 K 32/09, of 24 November 2010, para. 2.1
35 SK 45/09, of 16 November 2011.
36 Stanisław Biernat, Monika Kawczyńska, 'The Role of the Polish Constitution (Pre-2016): Development of a Liberal Democracy in the European and International Context' in Anneli Albi, Samo Bardutzky (eds.) *National Constitutions in European*

In legal writings one may find a continuing debate whether the CJEU, through the exercise of its interpretative discretion, contributed to the European integration process or rather improperly overstepped the limits of its judicial function by acting ultra vires.[37] This chapter will examine the cases where the CJEU has offered dynamic interpretation of the Treaties presenting its activist approach by creating new legal norms of general application. The cases will be divided into four categories depending on the objectives and the underlining motives of the Court approach.

4 Strengthening the integration

The most vivid example of judicial law-making occurred in the 1960s while the CJEU declared the principle of supremacy. The EEC Treaty contained no provision dealing with the primacy of Community law over national law. Developing the fundamental principle of EU law in the *Costa*[38] case, the Court used a more teleological than textual approach invoking the aims and the spirit of the Treaty. It held that 'the integration into the laws of each Member State of provisions, which derive from the Community, and more generally the terms and the spirit of the Treaty, make it impossible for the States, as a corollary, to accord precedence to a unilateral and subsequent measure over a legal system accepted by them on a basis of reciprocity.' The doctrine of supremacy was founded on the autonomous nature of EU law, resulting from the transfer of competences or limitations of sovereignty by the Member States. According to the Court,

> the transfer by the States from their domestic legal system to the Community legal system of the rights and obligations arising under the Treaty carries with it a permanent limitation of their sovereign rights, against which a subsequent unilateral act incompatible with the concept of the Community cannot prevail.

The doctrine of supremacy was further developed in *Internationale Handelsgesellschaft*,[39] where the Court pointed out that the provisions of the EU secondary law may not be overridden by rules of national law of any character since it would have an adverse effect on the uniformity and efficacy of the EU law. It held that 'the validity of a Community measure or its effect within a Member State cannot be affected by allegations that it runs counter to either fundamental rights as formulated by the constitution of that state or the principles of its constitutional structure.' While the EU Member States were eager to agree on the primacy of EU law over national statutes and executive acts, the constitutional courts of

and Global Governance: Democracy, Rights, the Rule of Law (T.M.C. Asser Press 2019) 745, 756.

37 Paul Craig, 'The ECJ and the ultra vires action: A conceptual analysis', (2011) *Common Market Law Review* 48, 395, 395; See Horsley (n 4) 931; See Conway (n 5) 17.

38 Case 6/64, of 15 July 1964 (*Costa*).

39 Case 11/70, of 17 December 1970 (*Internationale Handelsgesellschaft*).

several Member States have shown reluctance in accepting unconditional and absolute primacy of Union law over national constitutions.[40]

The first attempt to codify the principle of supremacy occurred at the time of drafting the Constitutional Treaty. The Convention proposed a new Art. I-6 TEU that read as follows: 'The Constitution and law adopted by the institutions of the Union in exercising competences conferred on it shall have primacy over the law of the Member States.' The Article on primacy of Union law was not replicated in the Lisbon Treaty, deliberately depriving the TEU and TFEU of any 'constitutional character.'[41] It was replaced by Declaration 17 Concerning Primacy, recalling the well-settled case law of the CJEU that 'the Treaties and the law adopted by the Union on the basis of the Treaties have primacy over the law of Member States.' The Conference has also decided to attach to the Final Act the Opinion of the Council Legal Service of 22 June 2007, declaring that

> primacy of EC law is a cornerstone principle of Community law. According to the Court, this principle is inherent to the specific nature of the European Community. At the time of the first judgment of this established case law (Costa/ENEL) there was no mention of primacy in the treaty. It is still the case today. The fact that the principle of primacy will not be included in the future treaty shall not in any way change the existence of the principle and the existing case-law of the Court of Justice.

The recent research demonstrates that the principle of the primacy of EU law is as absolute and unconditional as it was when it was first developed by the Court in the 1960s and 1970s. The unsuccessful codification in the Constitutional Treaty, the legal relationships between national and European law (constitutional pluralism) as well as the identity clause of Article 4(2) TEU and Article 53 of the Charter, have not essentially altered the principle.[42]

In the 1970s the CJEU developed the doctrine of exclusive implied competence to conclude international agreements by the Community. This is a particularly important legislative activity of the Court, since the doctrine of implied powers deviates from the principle of conferral. At that time the express power to conclude international agreements was provided only in relation to common commercial policy (now Art. 207 TFEU) and association agreements (now Art. 217 TFEU). The judgement in case *ERTA*[43] concerned the question of who had the power to conclude European Agreement on Road Transport, since the competence of the Community to enter into international agreements within the

40 See a review of national legal systems in relation to the principle of primacy, Koen Lenaerts, Piet van Nuffel, *European Union Law* (Sweet & Maxwell 2011), 772–809.

41 European Council Presidency Conclusions – Brussels, 21/22 June 2007, Annex I, para I.3.

42 Monica Claes, 'The Primacy of EU Law in European and National Law' in Anthony Arnull, Damian Chalmers (eds.), *The Oxford Handbook of European Union Law* (Oxford University Press 2015) 178, 211.

43 Case 22/70, of 31 March 1971 (*ERTA*).

sphere of common transport policy was not expressly provided in the Treaty. The Commission argued that since the Council adopted regulation 543/69 on the harmonization of certain social legislation relating to road transport, the Community had the power enter into any agreements with third countries relating to the subject-matter governed by that regulation. The CJEU shared this view and concluded that 'the authority to conclude international agreements arises not only from an express conferment by the Treaty, but may equally flow from other provisions of the Treaty and from measures adopted, within the framework of those provisions, by the community institutions.' In particular when the Community adopts provisions laying down common rules 'the Member States no longer have the right, acting individually or even collectively, to undertake obligations with third countries which affect those rules or alter their scope.'

The doctrine of implied powers was further developed in *Opinion 1/76*.[44] The subject of the case was the legal competence of the Community to enter into an international agreement establishing a European laying-up fund for inland waterway vessels. The aim of the proposed scheme was to eliminate disturbances arising from surplus carrying capacity for goods by inland waterway in the Rhine and Moselle basins. Such a system was an important factor in the common transport policy, the establishment of which was included in the activities of the Community laid down in article 3 of the EEC Treaty. The Court held that

> whenever Community law has created for the institutions of the Community powers within its internal system for the purpose of attaining a specific objective, the Community has authority to enter into the international commitments necessary for the attainment of that objective even in the absence of an express provision in that connection.

The CJEU went further than in *ERTA* since it declared that the Community should exercise its implied competence to enter into international agreements 'in all cases in which internal power has already been used in order to adopt measures which come within the attainment of common policies. It is, however, not limited to that eventuality.'

The doctrine of exclusive implied powers of the EU, developed in the cases described above, was codified in the Lisbon Treaty. According to Art. 3 (2) TFEU, the Union shall also have exclusive competence for the conclusion of an international agreement when its conclusion is provided for in a legislative act of the Union or is *necessary to enable the Union to exercise its internal competence (Opinion 1/76)*, or in so far as its conclusion *may affect common rules or alter their scope (ERTA)*.

5 Safeguarding the powers of Union institutions

The CJEU has dynamically interpreted legal provisions relating to the protection of the powers of EU institutions, either by recognising competences not provided

44 Opinion 1/76, of 26 April 1977 (*Inland waterway vessels*).

for in the Treaties or shielding the decision-making process against the actions of private parties.

The most vivid example of judicial law making activity of the Court is case *Les Verts*,[45] where the members of a political group instituted an action for annulment against two acts adopted by the European Parliament concerning reimbursement of expenditure incurred by participants in the 1984 European elections. At that time the European Parliament was not mentioned as respondent in annulment proceedings. According to former Art. 173 of the Treaty (now Art. 263 TFEU) the Court had only competence to 'review the legality of acts of the Council and the Commission other than recommendations or opinions.' In its judgement the Court held that

> an interpretation of article 173 of the Treaty which excluded measures adopted by the European Parliament from those which could be contested by means of an action for annulment would lead to a result contrary both to the spirit of the Treaty as expressed in article 164 [now Art. 19 (1) first subparagraph TUE] and to its scheme, which is to make a direct action available against all measures adopted by the institutions which are intended to have legal effects.

The Court concluded that 'an action for annulment may lie against measures adopted by the European Parliament intended to have legal effects vis-à-vis third parties.' The possibility of bringing action for annulment against acts of the European Parliament, introduced in case *Les Verts,* was later codified by the Maastricht Treaty as follows 'the Court of Justice shall review the legality of acts adopted jointly by the European Parliament and the Council (…) other than recommendations and opinions, and of acts of the European Parliament intended to produce *legal effects vis-à-vis third parties.*'

The further development of the European Parliament's position in judicial proceedings took place in case *Chernobyl*,[46] concerning the competence of the European Parliament to bring an action for annulment. In 1988 the European Parliament brought an action for annulment against Council Regulation No 3954/87 laying down maximum permitted levels of radioactive contamination of foodstuffs and of feeding stuffs adopted after the nuclear accident that occurred in nuclear power plant in Chernobyl. At that time the competence to bring and action for annulment was provided for in Art. 173 of the Treaty only with regard to Member States, the Council, and the Commission. In *Chernobyl* the Court famously awarded legal standing to the European Parliament in proceedings for annulment against unequivocal wording of the Treaty. The Court held that

45 Case 294/83, of 23 April 1986 (*Les Verts*).
46 Case C-70/88, of 22 May 1990 (*Chernobyl*).

> it would be incompatible with the fundamental interest in the maintenance and observance of the institutional balance (…) to be possible to breach the Parliament's prerogatives without that institution being able, like the other institutions, to have recourse to one of the legal remedies provided for by the Treaties which may be exercised in a certain and effective manner.

At that time the Court was ready to grant a partial *locus standi* to the Parliament in cases when 'the action seeks only to safeguard its prerogatives and that it is founded only on submissions alleging breach of them.' The admissibility of suits from the European Parliament continued to be quite controversial and it was not until 1992 that the institution brought the first action, the admissibility of which was not challenged by a Member State or the Council.[47] In response to the Court case law, the Maastricht Treaty introduced a new third paragraph to Art. 173, that read as follows 'The Court shall have jurisdiction under the same conditions in actions brought by the European Parliament and by the ECB *for the purpose of protecting their prerogatives.*' The full capacity to bring an action for annulment, irrespective of safeguarding the prerogatives, was granted to the European Parliament in 2001 by the Treaty of Nice.

The law-making power of the CJEU was exercised for the purpose of shielding the decision-making process of the EU institutions against the judicial actions instituted by private parties, particularly in cases challenging the acts of general application, such as regulations or directives.

In famous judgement *Plaumann*,[48] the CJEU developed the doctrine of 'individual concern' defining the *locus standi* of the private parties in annulment proceedings. According to former Art. 173 para. 4 of the EC Treaty (now Art. 263 para. 4 TFEU), natural or legal persons were able to institute proceedings against a decision 'which, although in the form of a regulation or a decision addressed to another person, is of direct and individual concern to the former.' The Court held that, 'persons (…) may only claim to be individually concerned if that decision affects them by reason of certain attributes which are peculiar to them or by reason of circumstances in which they are differentiated from all other persons, and by virtue of these factors distinguishes them individually just as in the case of the person addressed.' Due to restrictive interpretation of the individual concern, the possibility of challenging the acts of general application by the individuals was successful only in few cases.[49] The CJEU attitude attracted considerable criticism, since the restrictive conditions set out in *Plaumann* were not expressly provided for in the Treaty and were solely the result of judicial interpretation. The Court has interpreted

47 Margaret McCown, 'The European Parliament before the bench: ECJ precedent and EP litigation strategies', (2003) 10 *Journal of European Public Policy* 974, 977.

48 Case 25/62, of 15 July 1963 (*Plaumann*).

49 Case C-358/89, of 11 June 1992 (*Extramet*); case C-309/89, of 18 May 1994 (*Codorníu*); Anthony Arnull, 'Private Applicants and the Action for Annulment since Codorniu', (2001) 38 *Common Market Law Review* 7, 7.

the provision narrowly, while the lack of definition gave the option of adopting a flexible approach as the Court has done in relation to numerous other Treaty concepts.[50] There was one possibility to open the scope of application of Art. 263 (4) TFUE, where the General Court issued its ruling in case *Jégo-Quéré*.[51] The General Court criticized the restrictive interpretation of the Court and held that 'there is no compelling reason to read into the notion of individual concern (…) a requirement that an individual applicant seeking to challenge a general measure must be differentiated from all others affected by it in the same way as an addressee'. The judges, in order to ensure effective judicial protection proposed a new notion of 'individual concern' of the applicant when 'the measure in question affects his legal position, in a manner which is both definite and immediate, by restricting his rights or by imposing obligations on him'. Regrettably the Court set aside the judgement of the General Court and stated that even in the view of the principle of judicial protection, wide interpretation of Art. 263 (4) TFUE 'cannot have the effect of setting aside the condition in question, expressly laid down in the Treaty. The Community Courts would otherwise go beyond the jurisdiction conferred by the Treaty.'[52] The Treaty of Lisbon has brought some changes to the ability of private applicants to challenge the acts of general application. But even at that time the Court was faced with the duty of binding interpretation of the notion of 'regulatory acts,' mistakenly not mentioned anywhere in the Treaty but in Art. 263 (4) TFUE. The Court interpreted the concept restrictively, covering only non-legislative acts of general application.[53]

The second example of shielding the decision-making powers of the institutions occurred in cases involving action for damages instituted by private parties against the EU. The founders of the Communities left the development of legal conditions applied in cases of non-contractual liability to the judicial activity of the CJEU. Former Art. 215 para. 2 EEC Treaty (now Art. 340 para. 2 TFEU) stipulated that the EU shall make good any damage caused by its institutions or by its servants in the performance of their duties 'in accordance with the general principles common to the laws of the Member States.' In the famous case of *Schöppenstedt*[54] the Court held that 'where legislative action involving choices of economic policy is concerned, the Community does not incur non-contractual liability (…) unless a sufficiently flagrant violation of a superior rule of law for the protection of the individual has occurred.' The restrictive interpretation of the conditions related to non-contractual liability of the EU, for the 30 years of applying the so-called '*Schöppenstedt test*' granted damages to private parties for legislative acts of the institutions only in 14

50 Albertina Albors-Llorens, 'The Standing of Private Parties to Challenge Community Measures: Has the European Court Missed the Boat?' (2003) 62 *The Cambridge Law Journal* 72, 74.
51 Case I-177/01, of 3 May 2002 (*Jégo-Quéré*).
52 Case C-263/02 P, of 1 April 2004 (*Jégo-Quéré*).
53 C-583/11 P, of 3 October 2013 (*Inuit Tapiriit Kanatami*).
54 Case 5/71, of 2 December 1971 (*Aktien-Zuckerfabrik Schöppenstedt*).

cases.[55] The Court applied a less restrictive approach in 2001 in the famous case *Bergaderm*,[56] bringing the conditions of non-contractual liability in line with the conditions of the State liability for infringement of EU law. However, taking into consideration the number of successful claims, the approach of the adjudicating panels have not changed much in favour of the private applicants.

6 Protecting the rights of individuals

One of the most important concepts of EU law created solely by jurisprudence is the direct effect of EU law. The CJEU first articulated its doctrine in 1960s in the famous judgement *Van Gend en Loos*.[57] The Court held that the Community

> constitutes a new legal order of international law for the benefit of which the States have limited their sovereign rights, albeit within limited fields, and the subjects of which comprise not only the Member States but also their nationals. (…) Community law not only imposes obligations on individuals but is also intended to confer upon them rights which become part of their legal heritage.

The Court used its teleological approach and concluded that taking into consideration 'the spirit, the general scheme and the wording of the Treaty,' Art. 12 (now Art. 30 TFEU) must be interpreted as producing direct effects and creating individual rights, which national courts must protect. The doctrine of direct effect applies to legal provisions that are sufficiently clear, precise, and unconditional, closely resembling the concept of 'self-executing' norms in international law. Over the years the CJEU has broadened the catalogue of the Treaty provisions that could be invoked by individuals for the protection of their rights, e.g. prohibition of discrimination based on nationality (Art. 18 TFEU),[58] free movement of EU citizens (Art. 21 TFEU),[59] prohibition of quantitative restrictions and measures having equivalent effect (Art. 34 and 35 TFEU),[60] free movement of workers (Art. 45 TFEU),[61] freedom of establishment (Art. 49 TFEU),[62] freedom to provide services (Art. 56 TFEU),[63] free movement of capital (Art. 63 TFEU),[64] prohibition of concerned practices and abuse of dominant position (Art. 101 and 102 TFEU)[65] or principle of equal pay for male and female workers (Art. 157

55 Monika Kawczyńska, *Pozaumowna odpowiedzialność odszkodowawcza Unii Europejskiej* (Wolters Kluwer Warszawa 2016), 310.
56 Case C-352/98 P, of 4 July 2000 (*Bergaderm*).
57 Case 26/62, of 5 February 1963 (*van Gend & Loos*).
58 Case 293/83, of 13 February 1985 (*Gravier*).
59 Case C-413/99, of 17 September 2002 (*Baumbast*).
60 Case 74/76, of 22 March 1977 (*Iannelli & Volpi*).
61 Case C-281/98, of 6 June 2000 (*Angonese*).
62 Case 2/74, of 21 June 1974 (*Reyners*).
63 Case 33/74, of 3 December 1974 (*van Binsbergen*).
64 Cases C-358/93 and C-416/93, of 23 February 1995 (*Bordessa*).
65 Case 127/73, of 30 January 1974 (*SABAM*).

TFEU).[66] In the light of the effective judicial protection of the individuals the Court accepted the possibility of other EU acts having direct effect, such as regulations,[67] decisions,[68] directives (restricted to vertical relations),[69] and international agreements[70] concluded by the EU.

Another bright example of law-making activity of the CJEU was the concept of the protection of fundamental rights within the Union legal order. The European Communities were originally created as an international organization with an essentially economic scope of action. Neither the Treaty of Paris nor the Treaty of Rome made express reference to the protection of the general principles of law, in particular, fundamental rights. The Constitutional Courts maintained that Community law did not, at that time, ensure a standard of fundamental rights corresponding to their constitutional standards.[71] It was the CJEU who recognized the existence of general principles as important normative limits on EU institutional activity.[72] By comparison to the other EU institutions, the Court has been somewhat of a forerunner, taking the first steps towards a fundamental rights system already in 1969 and contributing in many respects to its further development.[73] In *Stauder*[74] the Court already referred to 'fundamental human rights enshrined in the general principles of Community law and protected by the Court.' In *Internationale Handelsgesellschaft* (see p. 210) it proclaimed that 'respect for fundamental rights forms an integral part of the general principles of law protected by the Court (…). The protection of such rights, whilst inspired by the constitutional traditions common to the member states, must be ensured within the framework of the structure and objectives of the Community.' Later in *Nold*,[75] the Court added that, apart from national constitutional traditions, 'international treaties for the protection of human rights, on which the Member States have collaborated or of which they are signatories, can supply guidelines which should be followed within the framework of Community law.' In *Rutili*,[76] the Court made explicit reference to the European Convention of Human Rights, serving as the inspiration for the development of fundamental rights protected within the EU legal order. The principles established in case law were later codified by the Treaty of Maastricht, where Art. F (2) (now Art. 6 (3) TFEU) stipulated that 'The Union

66 Case 43/75, of 8 April 1976 (*Defrenne*).
67 Case C-253/00, of 17 September 2002 (*Muñoz*).
68 Case 9/70, of 6 October 1970 (*Grad*).
69 Case 41/74, of 4 December 1974 (*van Duyn*).
70 Case C-265/03, of 12 April 2005 (*Simutenkov*).
71 Order of the Second Senate 29 May 1974, 2 BvL 52/71 (*Solange I*), BVerfGE 37, 271; Judgment of Corte Constituzionale of 27 December 1973 (*Frontini*), 18 Giur. Cost. I 2401.
72 Thomas Horsley, *The Court of Justice of the European Union as an Institutional Actor. Judicial Lawmaking and its Limits* (Cambridge University Press 2018), 69–70
73 Allan Rosas, 'The European Union and Fundamental Rights/Human Rights: Vanguard or Villain?' (2017) 7 *Adam Mickiewicz University Law Review* 7, 20.
74 Case 29/69, of 12 November 1969 (*Stauder*).
75 Case 4/73, of 14 May 1974 (*Nold*).
76 Case 36/75, of 28 October 1975 (*Rutili*).

shall respect fundamental rights, as guaranteed by the European Convention for the Protection of Human Rights and Fundamental Freedoms signed in Rome on 4 November 1950 and as they result from the constitutional traditions common to the Member States, as general principles of Community law.'

7 Increasing the effectiveness of Union law through effective judicial protection

The CJEU developed the requirement of effectiveness of EU law, including the principle of effective judicial protection, as a general legal principle. In its jurisprudence the Court continuously held that individuals are entitled to effective judicial protection of the rights they derive from the EU legal order, and the right to such protection is one of the general principles of law stemming from the constitutional traditions common to the Member States.[77] The early case law provided that procedures and remedies for breach of EU law were primarily the matter of the Member States. In *Rewe* delivered in 1976, the Court invoked the principle of loyal cooperation and held that 'it is the national courts which are entrusted with ensuring the legal protection which citizens derive from the direct effect of the provisions of Community law.'[78] Accordingly, the CJEU has developed so-called principle of procedural autonomy declaring that, in the absence of EU rules on the matter, it is for the national legal order of each Member State to designate the courts having jurisdiction and determine the procedural rules on condition, however, that those rules are not less favourable than those governing similar domestic situations (principle of equivalence), and that they do not make it excessively difficult or impossible in practice to exercise the rights conferred by EU law (principle of effectiveness).

The most famous example where the Court ruled that EU law requires national courts to provide a specific form of remedy is *Francovich*,[79] in which the principle of state liability for breach of EU law was introduced. Although not expressly provided in written law, the Court held that, the principle whereby a State must be liable for loss and damage caused to individuals is 'inherent in the system of the Treaty.' In view of the Court 'the full effectiveness of Community rules would be impaired and the protection of the rights which they grant would be weakened if individuals were unable to obtain redress when their rights are infringed by a breach of Community law for which a Member State can be held responsible.' The basis for the obligation of Member States to make good loss and damage was to be found in the principle of sincere cooperation (now Art. 4 (3) TUE). The Court established a set of conditions sufficient to obtain reparation by the individuals in national courts. The principle of state liability was further developed in *Brasserie du Pêcheur*,[80] where the Court clarified the conditions for state liability,

77 Case 222/84, of 15 May 1986 (*Johnston*); case 222/86, of 15 October 1987 (*Heylens*).
78 Case 33/76, of the Court of 16 December 1976 (*Rewe-Zentral*).
79 Case C-6/90 and C-9/90, of 19 November 1991 (*Francovich*).
80 Cases C-46/93 and C-48/93, of 5 March 1996 (*Brasserie du Pêcheur*).

drawing on Art. 215 (2) of the EC Treaty (now Art. 340 (2) TFUE) governing liability for unlawful conduct of the EU institutions. It held that individuals are entitled to reparation, where the rule of EU law breached is intended to confer rights upon them, the breach is sufficiently serious, and there is a direct causal link between the breach and the damage sustained by the individuals. It is beyond doubt that the principle of state liability for breach of EU law is a general principle of EU law, but it has not yet been included in written law. Thus far it is attributed exclusively to the law-making activity of the Court.

In *Unión de Pequeños Agricultores*, the Court made the recapitulation of the existing case law in the field of judicial protection and held that 'it is for the Member States to establish a system of legal remedies and procedures which ensure respect for the right to effective judicial protection.'[81] Such a statement was later codified by the Treaty of Lisbon in Art. 19 (1) second subparagraph TUE stipulating that 'Member States shall provide remedies sufficient to ensure effective legal protection in the fields covered by Union law.'

The CJEU guarantees effective judicial protection in fields covered by Union law in domestic legal order, particularly in the Member States departing from democratic standards. Recent constitutional reforms in Poland and Hungary have demonstrated that a lack of respect for the rule of law and for the fundamental values can become a matter of serious concern.[82] The Member States concerned assert that the organization of the national justice system constitutes a competence reserved exclusively to them, therefore the CJEU transgresses its competences and acts ultra vires. In its jurisprudence, the Court held that although the organization of justice and national procedures falls within the competence of Member States, 'they are required to comply with their obligations deriving from EU law.' In view of the Court 'Member State must, under the second subparagraph of Article 19 (1) TEU, ensure that the bodies which, as courts or tribunals within the meaning of EU law, come within its judicial system in the fields covered by EU law meet the requirements of effective judicial protection.'[83] In fact, the most efficient institution to address systemic threats to the rule of law in countries enforcing illiberal reforms proved to be the CJEU through extensive interpretation of Article 19 (1) TEU.

8 Conclusion

Over the years, the CJEU has been acting as an efficient law-maker, placing itself alongside the EU legislature, in order to enhance the European integration. The influence of the Court in the development of EU law has been essential and in some respects unprecedented in the history of legal systems. Through dynamic

81 Case C-50/00 P, of 25 July 2002 (*Unión de Pequeños Agricultores*).
82 Case C-286/12, 6 November 2012 (*Commission v Hungary*); case C-619/18, of 24 June 2019 (*Commission v Poland*).
83 Case C-64/16, of 27 February 2018 (*Associação Sindical dos Juízes Portugueses*); case C 192/18, of 5 November 2019 (*Commission v Poland*); joined Cases C-585/18, C-624/18 and C-625/18, of 19 November 2019, (*Krajowa Rada Sądownictwa*).

interpretation of the Treaties, it has shaped the distinct constitutional features of EU legal order, in both political and economic spheres.[84] Some of the most important principles of EU law, such as supremacy or direct effect, were developed by the law-making activity of the CJEU, irrespective of the boundaries set by the principle of conferral. It can also be argued that the judiciary has direct influence on European integration, when its considerations and doctrines become incorporated in the policy-making process.[85] In most instances the Court presented a teleological or purposive approach, making reference to the aims or the spirit of the Treaty. As the basis of its legal reasoning, the Court invoked the autonomy of EU legal order, the uniformity of EU law, effectiveness (*effet utille*), legal certainty, and effective judicial protection of individuals.

In acting as an efficient law-maker, the Court has not been immune from the criticism of constitutional courts, raising the objections of transgressing the competences provided for in the Treaties and acting ultra vires. The CJEU has been accused of interpreting the Treaty provisions too broadly, taking actually the form of Treaty amendment. This was predominantly evident where the dynamic interpretation of EU law limited the sovereign powers of the Member States. Whereas most constitutional courts underlined the importance of the principle of conferral, only some reserved a right to review whether EU acts transgress these borders to be ultra vires. Despite the initially sharp tone, the Federal Constitutional Court in *Honeywell* held that ultra vires review can only be considered if a breach of competences on the part of the European bodies is sufficiently qualified. In contrast, the Czech Constitutional Court in *Slovak pensions* declared for the first time in history the EU Court judgement *Landtová* as ultra vires. This does not undermine the role of the CJEU as an institutional actor, being the major force in European integration, at the same time ensuring that in the interpretation and application of the Treaties the law is observed.

84 Takis Tridimas, *The Court of Justice of the European Union* (in:) Robert Schütze, Takis Tridimas (ed.) *Oxford Principles of European Union Law. Volume I: The European Union Legal Order* (Oxford University Press 2018) 581, 581–582.

85 Fabio Wasserfallen, *The Judiciary as Legislator? How the European Court of Justice shapes Policy-Making in the European Union* (2010) 17 *Journal of European Public Policy* 1128, 1129.

12 The European Court of Human Rights and judicial law-making

Krzysztof Wojtyczek

The European Court of Human Rights (ECtHR) interprets and applies the European Convention on Human Rights (ECHR), which contains numerous vague legal terms. In this context, the question arises as to whether the Court applies and concretizes pre-established legal rules or creates new legal rules that were not previously part of the legal system. Law-making through judgements and decisions is not the only way in which the Strasbourg Court creates the law. There are also other ways in which the Strasbourg Court creates the law. Firstly, the Court is empowered to enact its rules. Secondly, the practice of the Court creates legal rules, which complement both the Convention and the rules of the Court. In all three cases, the ECtHR appears to be an important actor of judicial law-making.

The question regarding judicial law-making also arises in the European human rights law in another configuration. The ECtHR expresses certain views concerning judicial law-making at the domestic level. The application and creation of the law by the national courts has become an object of review for the Strasbourg Court when it examines the compatibility of national authorities' acts and omissions with the Convention. In this case, the Strasbourg Court is not a law-making actor but an actor that reviews law-making at the national level.

1 The European Court of Human Rights and judicial law-making at the national level

When addressing the issue of law-making by national courts, it is necessary to briefly present the provisions of the Convention pertaining to the repartition of law-making powers. Article 3 of Protocol No. 1 of the ECHR guarantees the right to free elections to the legislature. The notion of the legislature designates a State body with very broad legislative powers. The wording of this provision suggests that the enactment of legal rules belongs, in principle, to an elected legislature, where law-making by other State organs is an exception that may be justified in cases where detailed rules are required to concretize parliamentary laws or autonomous law-making in limited fields.[1] With this approach, the law-making function

1 Compare the view expressed by the Venice Commission in the 'Opinion on the New Constitution of Hungary', CDL-AD (2011) 016, par. 90.

DOI: 10.4324/9781003022442-13

does not belong to the judiciary. The role of the courts would consist of interpreting and applying the existing legislation and not in creating new legal rules. This interpretation is further supported by the Preamble to the Convention with reference being made to 'effective political democracy' and the 'rule of law.' In an effective political democracy, the law-making function should belong to elected bodies, whereas under the rule of law, State organs should strictly observe the limits of their mandate as defined by the law, act upon the basis of the law, and apply the relevant legal rules.[2] However, the ECtHR does not follow this route when interpreting the Convention and instead leaves the State with broad discretion when dividing law-making powers between the State's bodies. This appears, in particular, in the interpretation of the 'in accordance with law' or 'prescribed by law' clauses in Articles 8 to 11 of the Convention. When read in conjunction with Article 3 of Protocol No. 1, the reserve of the law in these provisions can be understood as the reserve of parliamentary law (*réserve de la loi* in French or *Gesetzesvorbehalt* in German). The Court, however, rejects such an approach and also allows for legal rules emanating from other State bodies.[3] Only exceptionally will the Court require that the domestic law referred to in the Convention should become an Act adopted by the parliament. This is the case when it interprets the clause relating to a 'tribunal established by law' in Article 6 of the Convention. The Court reminds us of this in the following words: 'According to the case law, the object of the term "established by law" in Article 6 of the Convention is to ensure that the judicial organisation in a democratic society [does] not depend on the discretion of the Executive, but that it [is] regulated by law emanating from Parliament.'[4]

In proceedings before international courts, national law is treated as a fact whose content has to be established in the proceedings. The principle *iura novit curia* applies to international law but not to the domestic law of the parties. This is also the approach of the ECtHR.[5] The content of the national law is established on the basis of the submissions of the parties. In particular, the question of the non-exhaustion of domestic remedies is examined only if it is raised by the respondent government, which is required to provide evidence that there is a domestic remedy enabling domestic bodies to examine, in substance, the complaints of the applicant. When establishing the content of domestic law either for the purpose of considering an objection of non-exhaustion of domestic remedies or for the purpose of deciding the merits of the case, the ECtHR takes into account the practice and case law of the domestic courts. Moreover, the Court

2 Compare the dissenting opinions of: Judge Wojtyczek appended to *Firth v. the United Kingdom*, 47784/09 et al.; 12 August 2014; Judges Pejchal and Wojtyczek appended to Orlandi and Others v. Italy, 26431/12 et al., 14 December 2017.

3 See e.g. *Lavents v. Latvia*, 58442/00, 28 November 2002, par. 135.

4 *Coëme and others v. Belgium*, 32492/96 et al, 22 June 2000, par. 98.

5 Dean Spielmann, '*Le fait, le juge et la connaissance: aux confins de la compétence interprétative de la Cour europène des doits de l'homme*' in Pierre d' Argent, Beatrice Bonafè, Jean Combacau (eds.), *Les limites du droit international - Essais en l'honneur de Joe Verhoeven* (Bruylant 2014), 519, 524–525, 530.

accepts that the interpretation of the domestic law belongs to the domestic authorities. In numerous judgements and decisions, the Court reiterates its lack of competence to set forth the correct interpretation of the domestic law.[6] The approach adopted by the Court implies that the domestic law may define the scope of the law-creating powers of the domestic judges when they apply and interpret this law.

On the other hand, the Court recognizes its competence in establishing a qualified error in the application of the domestic law amounting to an arbitrary application of domestic law or to a manifest error in law.[7] Such an error may justify finding that there has been a violation of the domestic law. Moreover, where the Convention refers to domestic law, the Court verifies whether a restriction upon rights has a basis in domestic law.[8] In all such situations, domestic law is not reduced to mere facts, but the Court recognizes its binding force and therefore its normativity.

Concerning judicial law-making at the national level, it is important to stress the following points. First of all, the Court recognizes judicial decisions as a source of law in common-law jurisdictions. At the same time, the Court seems to stress the specificities of the common law. The dicta of the Court seem to convey the idea that different standards are sometimes needed for continental law systems and common-law systems.[9] Common-law systems sometimes require specific standards that accommodate their peculiarities. However, the accommodations made for common-law systems will not be extended to continental systems.

Secondly, as stated on pp. 232–233, the Court establishes the content of national law by taking into account the domestic practice and the case law. For the Court, the relevant domestic law is always law in action. The Court recognizes the importance of case law as a source of law in continental (civil law) jurisdictions.[10]

Thirdly, the established case law may be a source of legitimate expectations protected under different provisions of the Convention.[11] This may be illustrated by the following dicta of the Court in the case of *Pressos v. Belgium*:

> On the basis of the judgments of the Court of Cassation of 5 November 1920, 15 December 1983 and 17 May [...], the applicants could argue that they had a 'legitimate expectation' that their claims deriving from the accidents in question would be determined in accordance with the general law of tort [...][12]

6 See e.g. the *Radomilja and others v. Croatia*, 37685/10 and 22768, 20 March 2018, par. 149.

7 Ibid.

8 See e.g. *Tomaszewscy v. Poland*, 8933/05, 15 April 2014, par. 132–145.

9 See e.g. *A, B, and C v. Ireland*, 25579/05, 16 December 2010, par. 142–43, quoted on.

10 See in particular *Kruslin v. France*, no. 11801/85, 24 April 1990, par. 29: '(...) case-law has traditionally played a major role in Continental countries, to such an extent that whole branches of positive law are largely the outcome of decisions by the courts'.

11 See e.g. *Lecharpemtier v. France*, 67847/01, 14 February 2006, par. 37 and 38.

12 *Pressos Compania Naviera S.A. and others v. Belgium*, 17849/91, 20 November 1995, par. 31.

In other words, when the case law settles an issue concerning certain legal positions, the individuals concerned are entitled to expect that their legal positions will be protected. The existence of settled case law is considered as essential for establishing a legitimate expectation:

> Thus, where a proprietary interest is in the nature of a claim, the person in whom it is vested may be regarded as having a 'legitimate expectation' if there is a sufficient basis for the interest in national law, for example where there is settled case law of the domestic courts confirming its existence.[13]

At the same time, in the absence of settled case law, no legitimate expectation arises: '[W]here the proprietary interest is in the nature of a claim it may be regarded as an "asset" only where it has a sufficient basis in national law, for example where there is settled case law of the domestic courts confirming it.'[14] More generally, a legitimate expectation may stem not only from case law but also from the practice of other State organs:

> It is sufficient in this connection for the Court to refer to the reasons set out above, which led it to conclude that the State authorities had tolerated the applicant's actions [...]. Those reasons are plainly valid in the context of Article 1 of Protocol No. 1 and support the conclusion that the authorities also acknowledged *de facto* that the applicant and his close relatives had a proprietary interest in their dwelling and movable goods.[15]

Fourthly, the established case law of domestic courts may be an important argument in order to conclude that there was a legal basis in domestic law, which was sufficiently clear to enable the applicant to foresee a specific type of interference with his rights. A departure, by a domestic court, from the established case law may justify the conclusion that interference with either rights or possessions was not foreseeable. This is again a clear incitement to follow the previous case law.

Regardless of the conception of the law and its sources that are accepted in a domestic legal system, under the Court's approach previous national case law becomes relevant for deciding subsequent cases.[16] It becomes a source of national law. Even if the Court does not go as far as recognizing the binding force of the previous case law, the approach adopted implies that, in the different fields covered by the protection of the Convention, the national courts should not depart from the established case law without sufficient justification. Such an approach results in introducing at least certain elements of the *stare decisis* principle to the

13 *Özden v. Turkey*, 11841/02, May 2007, par. 27; see also *Geotech Kancev GMBH v. Germany*, 23646/09, 2 June 2016, par. 67.

14 *Kopecky v. Slovakia*, 44912/98, 28 September 2004, par. 52.

15 *Öneryildiz v. Turkey*, 48939/99, 30 November 2004, par. 127.

16 See e.g. *Atanasovski v. the FYRM*, 36815/03, 14 January 2010, par. 38; see also: *Serkov v. Ukraine*, 39766/05, 7 July 2011, par. 35–44; *Petko Petkov v. Bulgaria*, 2834/06, 19 February 2013, par. 32–35.

continental systems. The domestic courts not only have the obligation to take into consideration the previous case law but also to follow it if a departure may infringe on the expectations that are protected under the Convention. This factor plays in favour of the stability of judicial interpretation and sets forth certain limitations upon judicial law-making: a dynamic interpretation of the domestic law may not undermine those legitimate expectations that are protected under the Convention. The limitations are nonetheless relative because the Court does not scrutinize the correctness of initial judicial decisions, which might have been law-creating and, furthermore, a departure from the existing case law may be justified in certain circumstances.

At the same time, it is interesting to note certain dicta in some judgements or decisions, which clearly encourage judicial law-making. The judgement *A, B, and C v. Ireland* contains the following dicta: 'The Court also notes the relevant principles set out at paragraphs 83–85 of its decision in the above-cited *D. v. Ireland* case and, notably, the established principle that in a legal system providing constitutional protection for fundamental rights it is incumbent on the aggrieved individual to test the extent of that protection and, in a common-law system, to allow the domestic courts to develop those rights by way of interpretation.'[17] Interestingly, the reference to common-law systems disappeared later and the approach has been extended to all jurisdictions.[18] The Court clearly proceeds upon the assumption that the dynamic interpretation of domestic law is fully justified and should be encouraged. This general assumption is accepted without any examination of the meta-rules applicable in the relevant legal systems and, in particular, without an examination as to whether and, if so, under which conditions a dynamic interpretation is accepted at the domestic level.

The Court accepts dynamic interpretations even in the field of criminal law:

> [F]or the purposes of Article 7 § 1, however clearly drafted a provision of criminal law may be, in any legal system, there is an inevitable element of judicial interpretation. There will always be a need for elucidation of doubtful points and for adaptation to changing circumstances [...]. Admittedly, that concept applies in principle to the gradual development of case law in a given State subject to the rule of law and under a democratic regime.[19]

The Court tries to reconcile legal certainty with the need for change in law in the following terms: 'case-law development is not, in itself, contrary to the proper administration of justice since a failure to maintain a dynamic and evolutive approach would risk rendering it a bar to reform or improvement. However, it

17 *A, B, and C v. Ireland*, mentioned above, par. 142–43.

18 See e.g. *Vučković and others v. Serbia*, 17153/11 et al., par. 84: 'Indeed, where legal systems provide constitutional protection of fundamental human rights and freedoms, it is in principle incumbent on the aggrieved individual to test the extent of that protection and allow the domestic courts to develop those rights by way of interpretation'.

19 *Streletz, Kessler and Krenz v. Germany*, 34044/96 et al., 22 March 2001, par. 82.

recalls that the existence of an established judicial practice should be taken into account in assessing the extent of the reasoning to be given in a case (…)'[20]

Although – as mentioned above – the Court constantly reiterates that the interpretation of the domestic law belongs to the domestic authorities, the Court sometimes does depart from this approach. In some cases, the Court sets forth clear general directives concerning the implementation of certain Convention provisions, thus guiding domestic case law. Thus, for instance, in *Winterstein v. France*, the Court gave the following guidance to the domestic courts in the States which are parties to the Convention:

> 155. The Court reiterates that the loss of a dwelling is a most extreme form of interference with the right to respect for one's home and that any person at risk of being a victim thereof should in principle be able to have the proportionality of the measure determined by a court. In particular, where relevant arguments concerning the proportionality of the interference have been raised, the domestic courts should examine them in detail and provide adequate reasons (…)
>
> 156. In the present case, the domestic courts ordered the applicants' eviction without having analysed the proportionality of this measure.[21]

In the grand chamber judgement in the case of *Axel Springer v. Germany*, the Court lays down criteria to be applied where the right to freedom of expression is being balanced against the right to respect for private life:

(i) contribution to a debate of general interest,
(ii) how well known is the person concerned and what is the subject of the report,
(iii) prior conduct of the person concerned,
(iv) method of obtaining the information and its veracity,
(v) content, form and consequences of the publication,
(vi) severity of the sanction imposed.[22]

Even though the addressees of these guidelines are not explicitly named, and although nothing prevents the national parliaments from implementing these guidelines through amendments to the relevant legislation, it is clear that the main addressees are the domestic courts. The national judges are clearly expected to adapt their case law and apply the methodology of balancing set forth by the Court without necessarily waiting for any amendments to the legislation.

In some exceptional cases, despite the declared judicial self-restraint in matters of domestic law, the Court inserted dicta criticizing a certain interpretation of

20 *Atanasovski v. the FYRM*, mentioned above., par. 38.
21 *Winterstein and others v. France*, 27013/07, 17 October 201.
22 *Axel Springer AG V. Germany*, 39954/08, 7 February 2012, par. 89–95.

domestic law or suggested a possible understanding of domestic provisions.[23] It is true that even if such dicta are usually couched in cautious terms as mere suggestions for consideration, they tacitly approve a dynamic interpretation of domestic law.

Whatever the stance of the ECtHR is on the question of the interpretation of domestic law, the Strasbourg case law, by its very nature, induces reactions from domestic courts and evolutive interpretations of specific provisions of domestic law in order to ensure compliance with the general standards of the Convention. The necessity of implementing ECtHR judgements is a very strong argument for the acceptance of far-reaching and creative interpretations of domestic law by domestic courts – interpretations that could otherwise have been questioned as departing from the established meta-rules in the domestic legal system. Domestic courts have no other option than to allow, to a growing extent, a dynamic interpretation of domestic law in national legal systems. The international law has increasingly become a moving target. International law evolves quickly and, in particular, the interpretation of human rights treaties evolves quickly. The acceptance of the principle that domestic law should be – to the extent possible under the law – interpreted in accordance with international law, coupled with the evolutive nature of international law, implies that the interpretation of domestic law gains in dynamism and creativity, and increasingly transforms into judicial law-making. The Convention mechanism clearly favours a dynamic interpretation of domestic law and encourages judicial law-making. Moreover, the very idea that the Convention has to be implemented in the process of a judicial dialogue between the ECtHR and the domestic courts presupposes interactions between the judges and thus the dynamic nature of the law to be applied and, implicitly, at least a particular law-making power of the judges at the different levels of the system.

2 The European Court of Human Rights as law-maker

The Convention defines the mandate of the Court in the following terms: '[T]o ensure the observance of the engagements undertaken by the High Contracting Parties in the Convention and the Protocols thereto, there shall be set up a European Court of Human Rights, hereinafter referred to as "the Court."'[24] The reference to 'engagements undertaken by the High Contracting Parties' puts the emphasis on the States as masters of the treaties and their contractual freedom, and implies the existence and stability of legal rules enshrined in the treaty that was concluded. Engagements are, by nature, static rather than evolutive.

23 See e.g.: *Litwa v. Poland*, 26629/95, 4 April 2000, par. 76; *Perlala v. Greece*, 17721/04, 22 February 2007 par. 27; *Apap Bologna v. Malta*, 46931/12, 30 August 2016, par. 84–88; *Portanier v. Malta*, 55747/16, 27 August 2019, par. 47–54. It also worth noting that the Court in *Woś v. Poland, 22860/02*, 8 June 2006, gave guidance to the domestic courts (par. 79 and par. 106); in *Szal v. Poland*, 41285/02, 18 May 2010, the Court commented the response of the Polish courts in the following terms: 'The Court very much welcomes such a positive development in the Supreme Court's case-law, which, at least in part, was prompted by its judgment in the Woś case.' (par. 60).

24 Article 19 of the ECHR.

At the same time, the Preambles to the Convention pose the following relevant principles:

- The aim of the Council of Europe is the achievement of greater unity between its members;
- Effective political democracy;
- A common understanding and observance of *the* human rights;
- A common heritage of political traditions, ideals, freedom and the rule of law; and
- To take the first steps for the collective enforcement of certain of the rights stated in the Universal Declaration.

The Convention is seen as a treaty, which constitutes only the first step for the collective enforcement of certain of the rights stated in the Universal Declaration by States sharing a common understanding of human rights and a common heritage of political traditions, ideals, freedom, and the rule of law. The Court in the judgement in the case of *Golder v. UK* noted that the Convention is a 'selective' instrument granting only certain rights.[25] These rights cannot be preserved without effective political democracy and presupposes broad law-making powers of a parliament elected by universal and direct suffrage as well as a clear separation between the political branches of government and the judicial branch. All these principles invite judicial self-restraint.[26] Nonetheless, certain authors invoke the reference in the Preamble to the 'further realization of human rights' as a mandate for judicial law-making.[27] Such an argument does not seem justified, because the only way for the 'further realization' envisaged here is an international treaty (the Convention) and – by implication – subsequent international treaties, not judicial law-making.

2.1 Law-making through the rules of the Court

Matters concerning the internal organization of the ECtHR are only partly regulated in the Convention. The provisions pertaining to the procedure before the Court are even scarcer. Under Article 25 litera d of the Convention, the plenary court 'shall adopt the rules of the Court.' This provision delegates to the Court a law-making power in the field of internal organization and procedures. The holder of the law-making power is the plenary assembly of the judges that consists of all 47 judges of the Court meeting in camera at administrative plenary assemblies. The Court, acting in the form of a plenary assembly of the judges, is a legislator mandated by the contracting parties to regulate particular fundamental elements

25 *Golder v. Ireland*, 4451/70, 21 February 1975, par. 34.

26 Compare the dissenting opinion of judges Pejchal and Wojtyczek, par. 2, appended to *Orlandi and Others v. Italy*, mentioned above.

27 Jean-Paul Costa, 'On the legitimacy of the European Court of Human Rights' judgments', (2011) 7 *European Constitutional Law Review*, 173, 178–179.

of the Convention's system. One has to note that the rules of the Court are further complemented by several practice directions issued by the President of the Court and which are an important source of procedural law.[28]

The rules of the Court are an example of secondary legislation enacted by international organizations. This legislation regulates inter alia the legal status of the individual vis-à-vis the public power by defining the procedural obligations, and the rights of individuals, and other private parties in relation to the Court. It is obvious that the rules have to be compatible with the Convention. However, given the skeletal nature of the Convention's regulations, the scope of the delegation is very broad. The Convention grants very broad organizational and procedural autonomy to the Court. Moreover, the rules of the Court may not only fill the numerous lacunae in the treaty but may also express a choice between possible interpretations of these treaty provisions, which are susceptible to several interpretations.

The Court has enacted its rules and frequently uses the delegation of the law-making power in order to adopt amendments to the existing rules. Under Rule 116 para. 2, the registrar informs the contracting parties of any proposals by the Court to amend the rules that directly concern the conduct of proceedings before it and invites them to submit written comments on such proposals. The registrar also invites written comments from organizations with experience in representing applicants before the Court as well as from relevant Bar associations.

One has to note that the States may modify the treaty through subsequent practice. In the case of treaties setting up international organizations and bodies, the subsequent practice may not only fill lacunae in the treaty, but it may also depart from the letter of the treaty. It is possible to argue that the practice of international organizations and bodies may modify their constitutive treaties if their State parties acquiesce to it, either explicitly or at least implicitly. From the perspective of the treaty's enactment and the application of the treaty's internal rules on the basis of the treaty, this belongs to the scope of international practice. The long-lasting application of the rules of the Court, acquiesced to by the States, may thus modify the initial meaning of the treaty.

The rules of the Court interpret or modify the treaty. It is possible here to give a few relevant examples. The Convention stipulates in Article 35 in the second sentence that the high contracting parties should undertake not to hinder in any way the effective exercise of the right to lodge an application to the Court, but does not grant the Court the power to apply interim measures. Yet such power was granted in the rules (currently Rule 39). The Court that initially considered that the measures were not binding[29] changed its mind and started to find that there had been violations to Article 35 of the Convention regarding non-compliance with the interim measures that had been applied.[30]

28 See the practice directions listed on the ECHR website: https://www.echr.coe.int/Pages/home.aspx?p=basictexts/rules&c=#n1347877334990_pointer.

29 *Cruz Varas and others v. Sweden*, 15576/8920 March 1991.

30 *Mamatkulov and Askarov v. Turkey*, 46827/99 and 46951/99, 4 February 2005.

Article 43 par. 2 of the Convention is worded as follows: 'A panel of five judges of the Grand Chamber shall accept the request if the case raises a serious question affecting the interpretation or application of the Convention or the Protocols thereto, or a serious issue of general importance.' The reference to 'five judges of the Grand Chamber' implies that these persons are members of the grand chamber for a certain period. However, under the rules of the Court, the panel of five judges of the grand chamber called upon to consider a referral request submitted under Article 43 of the Convention shall be composed of:

- the President of the Court. If the President of the Court is prevented from sitting, he or she shall be replaced by the Vice-President of the Court taking precedence;
- two Presidents of Sections designated by rotation. If the Presidents of the Sections so designated are prevented from sitting, they shall be replaced by the Vice-Presidents of their Sections;
- two judges designated by rotation from among the judges elected by the remaining Sections to serve on the panel for a period of six months;
- at least two substitute judges designated in rotation from among the judges elected by the Sections to serve on the panel for a period of six months.

According to Article 25 litera b of the Convention, the plenary court sets up chambers, constituted for a fixed period of time. Under the rules of the Court, the plenary court sets up sections, whereas specific chambers are designated by the Section President to hear specific cases.

Both examples show that the rules of the Court were the basis of a practice which gave the Convention provisions a completely new meaning.

As a result of the broad delegation of the law-making power to the Court, the procedure before the Court is mainly regulated through the rules of the Court. The obvious advantage of this broad procedural autonomy is the possibility for the Court to constantly adapt the rules of the procedure to the changing external conditions and inflows of new applications and new types of complaints.[31] The Court has an important tool, which enables it to increase its efficiency and promptness in processing an enormous number of incoming applications and adapting the procedure to the requirements of effective case management. The Court has broad discretion in defining the density of its internal rules and thus dividing the norm-making powers between the Court acting in the form of the plenary assembly of the judges and the Court acting as a judicial body establishing internal rules through its practice that complements the written rules.

31 Compare the view expressed by Dean Spielmann 'The European Court of Human Rights: Master of the law but not of the facts?' in Linos-Alexandre Sicilianos et al. (eds) *Intersecting Views on National and International Human Rights, Essays in Honour of Guido Raimondi* (Wolff 2019), 909, 911–913.

2.2 *Law-making through the practice of the Court*

Constituent instruments of international organizations regulate the most important questions concerning their internal functioning, but the regulation therein is never complete. None of the different internal rules adopted by the bodies set forth by the constituent treaties address all the possible legal issues. An important space is left for the practice of the organization.[32]

In international law, the practice of international organizations is recognized as a source of law. The Vienna Convention on the Law of Treaties between States and International Organizations or between International Organizations defines the rules of the organization in the following terms, 'in particular, the constituent instruments, decisions and resolutions adopted in accordance with them, and established practice of the organization' (Article 1 para. 1 litera j).[33] Similarly, the Draft Articles on the Responsibility of International Organizations contain a similar definition in Article 2 litera b: '[The] "rules of the organization" means, in particular, the constituent instruments, decisions, resolutions and other acts of the international organization adopted in accordance with those instruments, and established practice of the organization.'[34] The established practice may entail the creation of customary law that is internal to the organization. The same rule applies to specific international bodies established by international treaties. Although these general principles do not seem to be disputed, their application may be problematic and the identification of specific rules of internal customary law may entail controversies. Especially, the question may arise as to whether a certain practice is sufficiently established. Practice as a source of law may be important not only for the internal functioning of the organization but also for legal subjects who are external to the organization such as States or individuals entering into legal relationships with the bodies of the organization.

One has to note that neither the Convention nor the rules of the Court regulate specific important matters concerning the functioning of the Court or the procedure before it. For instance, neither the Convention nor the rules of the Court decided on the question as to whether the procedure before the Court is based upon the principle of material or formal truth and whether it is guided by the inquisitorial or accusatorial principle. It is not clear whether and to which extent the Court should establish the facts and the domestic law upon the basis of the submissions of the parties and to which extent it may establish particular elements *ex officio*.

32 See Christopher Peters, 'Subsequent Practice and Established Practice of International Organizations: Two Sides of the Same Coin?', (2011) 3 *Goettingen Journal of International Law*, 617 et seq.

33 Vienna Convention on the Law of Treaties between States and International Organizations or between International Organizations Vienna, 21 March 1986, https://treaties.un.org/doc/source/docs/A_CONF.129_15-E.pdf.

34 Report A/CN.4/L.778 adopted by the International Law Commission at its sixty-third session, in 2011, and submitted to the General Assembly as a part of the Commission's report covering the work of that session (A/66/10, para. 87). http://legal.un.org/ilc/texts/instruments/english/draft_articles/9_11_2011.pdf.

In such a context, lacunae in the written rules have to be filled by judicial practice. The constant practice of the Court entails certain expectations among the parties in exactly the same way that citizens base their expectations on the case law of their *domestic* courts. The principles of the protection of legitimate expectations and of a fair trial require that expectations concerning the proceedings stemming from established practice be respected in subsequent practice. In such a context, constant practice clearly has legal consequences and its further observance in the future may be seen as a duty. In this way, judicial practice may lead to the creation of customary legal rules.

One can give a few examples here of the principles or rules developed in the judicial practice of the Strasbourg Court. A judge whose term of office has expired remains in office until his successor takes his office, unless he is not able to remain. The proceedings before the Court are based upon the principle of written proceedings, where the oral hearing is an exception reserved for the grand chamber and very rare chamber cases. Interim measures were initially imposed upon the parties without a legal basis before the practice was finally codified in the rules of the Court.

Article Rule 62 1 para. 1, the first sentence of the rules of the Court is worded as follows: 'Once an application has been declared admissible, the Registrar, acting on the instructions of the Chamber or its President, shall enter into contact with the parties with a view to securing a friendly settlement of the matter in accordance with Article 39 § 1 of the Convention.'

Recently, the Court has started a systematic non-contentious phase for the proceedings aimed at achieving a friendly settlement before the parties without waiting for the application to be declared admissible. One has to explain here that after the adoption of Protocol No. 14, the Court, as a rule, examines the admissibility of an individual application together with the merits. A separate examination of the admissibility of an individual application is now an exception. References to separate admissibility decisions in the rules of the Court have become partly obsolete.

In 2004, the ECtHR introduced the so-called pilot judgement procedure, devised to handle repetitive cases stemming from systemic problems in the national legal systems.[35] With this procedure, the Court selects an individual application, determines whether there has been a violation of the Convention, identifies the systemic problem, and makes recommendations concerning general measures to be taken. The national authorities are invited to adopt the necessary legislative reforms (in particular, to create legal remedies) and other general measures and subsequently to take the individual decisions remedying rights violations. The pilot judgement practice was codified in 2011 in the new Rule 61 of the Rules of the Court.[36]

The role of this practice in international organizations in general and in the Convention in particular resembles, to a certain extent, that of oil in a gear box, enabling smooth articulations between the different cogwheels (legal provisions and institutions), which could otherwise block themselves.

35 *Broniowski v. Poland*, 31443/96, 22 June 2004.

36 ECHR. Press release no. 256, 24.03.2011 https://hudoc.echr.coe.int/app/conversion/pdf?library=ECHR&id=003-3481961-3922418&filename=New%20rule%20on%20pilot%20judgment%20procedure%2023.03.11.pdf.

2.3 Law-making through judgements and decisions

The Convention contains a certain number of highly abstract and vague terms such as 'jurisdiction,' 'degrading treatment,' 'servitude,' 'fair hearing,' 'private life,' 'necessary in a democratic society,' 'public order,' 'discrimination,' and 'public emergency threatening the life of a nation,' which require concretization and detailization in the case law. The application of such terms in specific cases is creative by nature. Moreover, legal certainty requires going beyond an application *a casu ad casum* and setting forth more specific general rules or principles concretizing the application of the vague legal provisions to certain types of repetitive situations. As long as such concretization stays within the limits stemming from the wording of the Convention, the approach, as such, should not be controversial. Controversies may concern the content of specific rules and principles set forth in the case law. More fundamental disputes arise if the court goes beyond the limits stemming from the text of the treaty it applies.

An important period for the interpretation of the Convention was the 1970s when two contrasting views were held among the judges. Most of the judges advocated a dynamic approach going beyond the letter of the treaty, whereas others took a clear stance in favour of a strict application of the rules of the treaty's interpretation. The most prominent representative of this second stream was Sir Maurice Fitzgerald.[37] The advocates of the first approach were in the majority and therefore their view prevailed. One has to add in parentheses that one of the first cases in which the issue of interpretation arose with great acuteness was the case of *Golder v. the United Kingdom*[38] concerning the question as to whether Article 6 guarantees the right of access to a tribunal. The linguistic interpretation of Article 6 clearly gives an affirmative answer to this question. The Court also gave an affirmative reply but stressed that the right in question is not expressly granted by the Convention and relied inter alia upon a functional interpretation, invoking the notion of the 'rule of law' (para. 34) referred to in the Preamble and 'universally "recognised" fundamental principles of law' (para. 35).

There cannot be any doubt that the ECtHR established numerous principles which go beyond the letter of the ECHR and which could not have initially been foreseen by an interpreter relying solely on the applicable rules of the treaty's interpretation. One can name a few examples here:

- The application of the ECHR when a Contracting Party as a consequence of military action – whether lawful or unlawful – exercises effective control of an area outside its national territory;[39]

37 See his in particular his separates opinions appended to: *National Union of Belgian Police v. Belgium*, 4464/70, 27 October 1975 and *Golder v. the United Kingdom*, mentioned above.

38 Mentioned above.

39 *Loizidou v. Turkey* (preliminary objections), 15318/89, 23 March 1995, par. 62; *Cyprus v. Turkey*, 25781/94, 10 May 2001 par. 76–80.

- A procedural obligation to carry out an effective investigation into suspected deaths; this investigation should be prompt, adequate and accessible to the victim's family;[40]
- A procedural obligation to carry out an effective investigation into credible allegations of torture, degrading or inhuman treatment;[41]
- The principle that Article 3 (prohibiting torture and degrading or inhuman treatment) prevents transfer to another jurisdiction if there is serious risk of ill-treatment in this other jurisdiction;[42]
- The right of an accused to have a co-accused summoned and questioned as an element of a fair trial;[43]
- The protection of reputation,[44] ethnic identity[45] or the right for an individual to form and develop relationships with other human beings, including relationships of a professional or business nature[46] as parts of private life; and
- The right to obtain legal recognition of gender re-assignment[47] or to obtain the protection of relationships resulting from same-sex marriages concluded abroad.[48]

Probably the clause which offered the basis for the most far-reaching judicial decisions was Article 8, which, in particular, protects 'private life.' The Court has recently explained the meaning of this notion in the following terms:

> 95. The concept of 'private life' is a broad term not susceptible to exhaustive definition. It covers the physical and psychological integrity of a person. It can therefore embrace multiple aspects of the person's physical and social identity. Article 8 protects in addition a right to personal development, and the right to establish and develop relationships with other human beings and the outside world (...).
>
> 96. Therefore, it would be too restrictive to limit the notion of 'private life' to an 'inner circle' in which the individual may live his own personal life as he chooses and to exclude therefrom entirely the outside world not encompassed within that circle.[49]

As result of the case law, the notion of 'private life' within the Convention turns out to be a bundle of different elements for which it is difficult to find a common denominator. Judge Egidijus Kuris eloquently commented on this issue in the following terms: 'The perspective of examining privacy in terms of the right and

40 *Armani da Silva v. United Kingdom*, 5878/08, 30 March 2016, par. 229–239.
41 *Bouyid v. Belgium*, 23380/09, 28 September 2015, par. 116–123.
42 *Soering v. the United Kingdom*, 14038/88, 7 July 1989, par. 91.
43 *Kuchta v. Poland*, 58683/08, 23 January 2018, par. 44–49.
44 *Pfeifer v. Austria*, 12556/03, 15 November 2007, par. 35.
45 *Aksu v. Turkey*, 4149/04 and 41029/04,15 March 2012, par. 58.
46 *Volkov v. Ukraine*, 21722/11, 9 January 2013, par. 165.
47 *Christine Goodwin v. The United Kingdom*, 28957/95, 11 July 200,2 par. 89–93.
48 *Orlandi and others v. Italy*, mentioned above.
49 *Denisov v. Ukraine*, 76639/11, 25 September 2018.

value protected by Article 8 must be returned to its natural angle. To present it graphically, 8 should indeed be seen as 8 and not – as increasingly tends to be the case – like the sign of infinity: ∞.'[50]

In most cases, the Court presents the applicable substantive rules of the Convention as established in the previous case law and remains silent on the interpretive rules it applies. The principles established in earlier cases are taken as accepted without the necessity of any renewed justification. There are nonetheless numerous judgements in which the Court explicates its views on the interpretation. Such dicta appear mainly if the Court faces a novel or controversial legal issue.

In a certain number of judgements, the Court has stressed that the ECHR should be interpreted under the rules of the treaty's interpretation codified in the Vienna Convention on the Law of the Treaties.[51] The point of departure is therefore the assumption that the ECHR has to be interpreted according to these rules. However, the Court very rarely invokes the specific interpretive rules codified in the Vienna Convention, let alone explains its interpretive choices in terms of them.

The Court resorts to different types of arguments to support the interpretation it chooses. The catalogue of the main arguments used in practice encompasses in particular:

1 A historical interpretation: *travaux préparatoires.*[52]
2 A linguistic interpretation: the text of the Convention and the meaning of the specific words used in French and in English.[53]
3 A systemic interpretation: internal consistency and harmony of Convention provisions;[54] the Preamble to the Convention;[55] relevant rules and principles of international law applicable in relations between the contracting parties[56] including universally recognized principles of law,[57] a 'common heritage of political traditions, ideals, freedom and the rule of law'[58] and the relevant international soft law.[59]
4 A functional interpretation: the aim of the Convention;[60] the purpose of a specific provision;[61] the general principle of the effectiveness of rights;[62]

50 Dissenting opinion appended to *Erményi v. Hungary*, 22254/14, 22 November 2016, par. 4.
51 This principle has been reiterated recently in *Mihalache v. Romania*, 54012/10, 8 July 2019, par. 90.
52 *Maktouf and Damjanović v. Bosnia and Herzegovina*, 2312/08 and 34179/08, par. 72.
53 See e.g. *Mihalache v. Romania*, mentioned above, par. 94.
54 See e.g. Ibid., par. 92 and 113.
55 *Golder v. Ireland*, mentioned above, par. 34.
56 *Saadi v. The United Kingdom*, 13229/03, 28 January 2008, par. 62.
57 *Golder v. Ireland*, mentioned above, par. 35.
58 *Streletz, Kessler and Krenz v. Germany*, mentioned above, par. 83.
59 *Bayatyan v. Armenia*, 23459/03, 7 July 2011, par. 50–70 and par. 105–107; *Baka v. Hungary*, 20261/12, 23 June 2006, par. 72–87 and par. 172.
60 *Coëme and others v. Belgium*, mentioned above, par. 145.
61 *Bayatyan v. Armenia*, mentioned above, par. 100.
62 See, e.g. *Mihalache v. Romania*, mentioned above, par. 91.

changing conditions in contracting States;[63] evolving norms of national and international law[64] including treaties not ratified by the respondent State;[65] and the consensus emerging from specialized international instruments and from the practice of contracting States.[66]

5 The existing case law of the Court.

The Court's case law[67] as legal scholarship[68] points to some further frequently used tools of interpretation – in particular, to the notion of autonomous concepts and the doctrine of a margin of appreciation. In this context, it may be noted that it seems obvious that if the Convention terms have to be interpreted 'in accordance with the ordinary meaning to be given to the terms of the treaty in their context,' which means with their ordinary meaning in English and French, they should not be interpreted through the lenses of the meaning of their equivalents in the different languages used in the domestic legislation of the different contracting parties. The margin of appreciation reflects the general idea that subsisting doubts concerning the meaning of the ECHR and the limitations imposed upon the high contracting parties should be decided in favour of the States.

The Court rarely addresses all the above-mentioned elements, which may be relevant for interpretation in a single judgement. It usually picks up a few arguments freely from the above-presented catalogue. In some judgements, it analyses the letter of the provisions and the *travaux préparatoires*, focusing on the textual arguments and the intent of the parties.[69] This analysis may be coupled with an invocation of the purpose of the treaty. In some cases, the Court interprets the Convention in the light of soft-law instruments, whereas in others no such instruments are invoked. In many judgements, the Court only invokes the idea that the Convention is a living instrument to be interpreted in the light of present-day conditions,[70] without addressing other interpretative directives and issues. This invocation may sometimes be coupled with the analysis of the existence of European consensus and international trends. The interpretive principles established in the case of *Demir ans Baykara* are an excellent example which illustrates the approach adopted by the Court:

> 65. In order to determine the meaning of the terms and phrases used in the Convention, the Court is guided mainly by the rules of interpretation provided for in Articles 31 to 33 of the Vienna Convention [...]. In accordance with the Vienna Convention, the Court is required to ascertain the ordinary

63 *Bayatyan v. Armenia*, mentioned above, par. 102.
64 *Demir and Baykara v. Turkey*, 34503/97, 12 November 2008 par. 68
65 Ibid., par. 78.
66 *Magyar Helsinki Bizottság v. Hungary*, 18030/11, 8 November 2016 par. 124.
67 *Mihalache v. Romania*, mentioned above, par. 91.
68 George Letsas, *A Theory of Interpretation of the European Convention on Human Rights* (Oxford University Press 2007).
69 *S., V. and A. v. Denmark*, 35553/12 et al., 22 October 2018.
70 *Tyrer v. the United Kingdom*, 25 April 1978, 5856/72, par. 31.

> meaning to be given to the words in their context and in the light of the object and purpose of the provision from which they are drawn [...]. Recourse may also be had to supplementary means of interpretation, either to confirm a meaning determined in accordance with the above steps, or to establish the meaning where it would otherwise be ambiguous, obscure, or manifestly absurd or unreasonable [...]
>
> 66. Since the Convention is first and foremost a system for the protection of human rights, the Court must interpret and apply it in a manner which renders its rights practical and effective, not theoretical and illusory. The Convention must also be read as a whole, and interpreted in such a way as to promote internal consistency and harmony between its various provisions [...]
>
> 68. The Court further observes that it has always referred to the 'living' nature of the Convention, which must be interpreted in the light of present-day conditions, and that it has taken account of evolving norms of national and international law in its interpretation of Convention provisions [...][71]

The Court has often stressed the importance of the stability of its case law: 'The Court reiterates that, while it is not formally bound to follow its previous judgments, it is in the interests of legal certainty, foreseeability and equality before the law that it should not depart, without good reason, from precedents laid down in previous cases.'[72] Following previous judgements implies the renouncement of a dynamic interpretation. The principle that the Court should not depart from precedents conflicts to a large extent with the principle of an evolutive interpretation which would then appear circumscribed to situations in which special reasons require an evolution of the case law.

As noted above, the Court is indeed usually very mindful of its case law and tries to follow it or at least to present a new judgement as following the established case law. However, this endeavour only applies to primary rules. It does not apply to the same extent to meta-rules. The dicta on the interpretation do not have the same authority. One may have the impression that they are not often considered as relevant case law, unlike dicta concerning primary rules.

The analysis of the Court's case law leads to the general conclusion that the Court has not established a comprehensive system of rules of interpretation, which would guide interpretations in subsequent cases.

Firstly, the views expressed by the Court concerning the interpretation do not pretend to be exhaustive and they do not encompass all the issues of the Convention's interpretation. The different interpretive rules that have been applied have neither been listed in a comprehensive manner nor systematized and put into a hierarchy through a system of second-degree interpretive rules, although in some

71 *Demir and Baykara v. Turkey*, mentioned above.

72 *Muršić v. Croatia*, 7334/13, 20 October 2016, par. 109; see also inter alia *Chapman v. the United Kingdom*, 27238/95, 18 January 2001 par. 70, as well as *Christine Goodwin v. the United Kingdom*, mentioned above, par. 74, and *Mamatkulov and Askarov v. Turkey*, mentioned above, par. 121.

judgements the Court has addressed this issue by stating that '[i]n the way in which it is presented in the "general rule" in Article 31 of the Vienna Convention, the process of interpretation of a treaty is a unity, a single combined operation; this rule, closely integrated, places on the same footing the various elements enumerated in the four paragraphs of the Article.'[73]

Secondly, as already explained, the approach towards the interpretation of the Convention is very pragmatic and varies from case to case. In particular, the panoply of interpretive directives invoked by the Court and issues addressed vary considerably from judgement to judgement. One judgement may rely on certain interpretive directives, whereas another judgement could rely on a different set of interpretive directives.

A more thorough analysis of the case law shows that the dynamic, law-creating approach is adopted mainly in respect of the most important societal issues dealt with under Article 8 (respect for family and private life). The evolutive approach in this area does not appear to have clearly established legal limits and, in particular, intransgressible limits in the letter of the Convention. The Court determines the pace of the societal evolution and does not hesitate in deciding that some fields are not yet mature enough for evolution.[74] This implies that an important hidden limitation for the creation of the law by the Court may lie in the social acceptability of its case law.

The Court seems much more reluctant to follow the evolutive approach for some other rights. Recent case law highlights a growing number of examples (especially grand chamber judgements adopted by a divided bench) where the Court has rejected a possible interpretation of the Convention, which would either go beyond the established case law or confirm the most recent dynamic case law, even if this interpretation could have been justified by relying on the very letter of the Convention.[75]

In any event, the way the Court applies the rules of interpretation leaves it with a very broad margin of judicial discretion.

As stated on p. 236, one of the elements taken into account in the process of interpretation of the Convention are soft-law instruments.[76] The Court does not necessarily follow the standards established therein – there are cases in which the Court has departed from the recommendations of the soft law.[77] On the other hand, there are examples of cases in which the court has relied on soft-law

73 *Golder v. the United Kingdom*, mentioned above, par. 30; reiterated inter alia in Litwa v. Poland, mentioned above par. 58.

74 See e.g. the dicta in the par. 192 of *Orlandi and others v. Italy*, mentioned above: *The Court reiterates that States are* ***still*** *free …*

75 See e.g. *Correia de Matos v. Portugal*, 56402/12, 4 April 2018, concerning Article 6 of the Convention; see also *S., V. and A. v. Denmark*, mentioned above, concerning Article 5 of the Convention.

76 On this question see in particular Sebastien van Drooghenbroeck, '*Le soft law et la Cour européenne des droits de l'homme*' in Michaela Anca Ailincai (ed.), *Soft law et droits fondamentaux. Actes du colloque du 4 et 5 février 2016*, (Pédone 2016); Charlotte Philippe, '*Le juge de Strasbourg, la lettre de la soft law et l'interprétation*', (2019) 56 *Revue trimestrielle des droits de l'homme*, 579 et seq.

77 See e.g. *Mursic v. Croatia*, mentioned above.

instruments to establish certain standards.[78] Soft law is an important instrument that is taken into consideration in order to give a more precise meaning to some vague clauses. The case law of the Court transforms certain non-binding soft-law standards into Convention standards that are binding to the high contracting parties. These standards are not only binding, but they also become enforceable in judicial proceedings; namely, in the proceedings before the Court. The judicial law-making consists not only of the creation of new legal principles and rules but also of the evolutive transformation of particular soft standards into hard legal rules.

2.4 Reactions to judicial law-making

A judgement of the Court is binding for the respondent State and is implemented in the enforcement mechanism with the participation of the respondent State acting under the supervision of the Committee of Ministers of the Council of Europe.[79] The impact of a judgement extends beyond the respondent State because it establishes or reiterates general principles which the Court follows in other cases; thus, it wins de facto an *erga omnes* effect. The Convention is implemented as interpreted by the Court. It is therefore the case law of the Court that gives the real meaning to the Convention.

The reactions to judicial law-making are mixed. The vast majority of the legal scholarship on international human rights law approves the current practice of the evolutive interpretation of the Convention,[80] thus accepting – at least implicitly – judicial law-making. Some legal scholars who are mostly active in other fields of the legal sciences contest the judicial law-making by the ECtHR.[81] One has to add here that the human rights legal scholarship often rejects the so-called legal dogmatic method (*rechtsdogmatische Methode*) and the defence of judicial law-making is frequently based more on political philosophy arguments rather than on purely legal considerations.

The high contracting parties to the ECHR meeting at diplomatic conferences in recent years have adopted declarations which implicitly express an assessment of the existing case law and their preferences concerning its future development. It is not necessary to determine the legal value of these declarations nor to analyse their

78 See e.g. *Bayatyan v. Armenia*, mentioned above.

79 See Krzysztof Wojtyczek, 'Judicial and Non-Judicial Elements in the Enforcement Mechanism of the European Convention on Human Rights in Paulo Pinto de Albuquerque and Krzysztof Wojtyczek (eds.), *Judicial Power' in a Globalized World, Liber Amicorum Vincent De Gaetano* (Springer Nature Switzerland 2019), 653 et seq.

80 See e.g. Walter Kälin & Jorg Künzli, *The Law of International Human Rights Protection* (Oxford University Press 2009) 38; Letsas (68) passim; Kanstantsin Dzehtsiarou 'European Consensus and the Evolutive Interpretation of the European Convention on Human Rights' (2011) 12 German Law Journal 1730 et seq.

81 See e.g. Jean-Louis Harouel, *Les droits de l'homme contre le peuple* (Desclée De Brouwer 2016); Bertrand Mathieu, *Le droit contre la démocratie?* (LGDJ 2017); see also Marc Bossuyt, 'Des limites à la juridiction de la Cour de Strasbourg?' in Elisabeth Lambert-Abdelgawad et al. (eds.), *L'homme et le droit. En hommage au Professeur de Jean-François Flauss* (Pédone 2014) 117 et seq.; Noel Malcolm, *Human Rights and Political Wrongs* (Policy Exchange 2017).

content in a detailed manner as it suffices here to note that the High Level Conference on the Future of the European Court of Human Rights Brighton Declaration has stressed the importance of the principles of subsidiarity and the margin of appreciation being left to the domestic authorities[82] as well the importance of the consistency of the case law, implicitly inviting the Court to practice judicial self-restraint:

> Judgments of the Court need to be clear and consistent. This promotes legal certainty. It helps national courts apply the Convention more precisely, and helps potential applicants assess whether they have a well-founded application. Clarity and consistency are particularly important when the Court addresses issues of general principle.[83]

The importance of these principles has been restated in 2015 in the Brussels Declaration[84] and in 2018 in the Copenhagen Declaration.[85] At the same time, it is important to note here that the final text of the Copenhagen Declaration accepts that the Court 'interprets the Convention in accordance with relevant norms and principles of public international law, and, in particular, in the light of the Vienna Convention on the Law of Treaties, giving appropriate consideration to present-day conditions.'[86] Moreover, at the same time, the Declarations invite the Court to develop its case law in certain areas (exhaustion of domestic remedies), clearly opting for an evolutive approach, at least if it serves the interests of State sovereignty.

Some States tried to express their criticism of the Court. The initial draft of the Copenhagen Declaration is one of the most telling examples in this respect.[87] On the other hand, there are States which accept judicial law-making in principle.

The interpretation of the Convention established by the ECtHR is not unconditionally accepted by the domestic judges. The legal scholarship provides numerous examples of cases where the domestic judge has refused to implement or fully implement certain judgements of the ECtHR, often invoking principles enshrined in national constitutions.[88]

82 Par. 10–12. https://www.echr.coe.int/Documents/2012_Brighton_FinalDeclaration_ENG.pdf
83 Brighton declaration par. 23.
84 https://www.echr.coe.int/Documents/Brussels_Declaration_ENG.pdf
85 https://www.echr.coe.int/Documents/Copenhagen_Declaration_ENG.pdf
86 Par. 26.
87 https://menneskeret.dk/sites/menneskeret.dk/files/media/dokumenter/nyheder/draft_copenhagen_declaration_05.02.18.pdf
88 P.-F. Laval, '*Les limites les limites constitutionnelles à l'exécution des arrêts de la cour européenne des droits de l'homme à la lumière de la jurisprudence nationale comparée*', (2017) 121 *Revue générale de droit international public*, 661 et seq.; see also Lord Sumption, The Limits of Law, the 27 Sultan Azlan Shah Lecture, Kuala Lumpur, 20 November 2013 https://www.supremecourt.uk/docs/speech-131120.pdf which criticizes the judicial law-making by the ECtHR from the perspective of a national judge.

3 Concluding remarks

Over the years, the Court has developed a very rich case law setting the minimum human rights protection standards for Europe. The scope and importance of the case law are highlighted by the fact that it is simply impossible to understand the Convention by studying and reading its provisions in the light of the Vienna Convention on the Law of the Treaties. The available commentaries on the Convention, unlike many domestic commentaries on legislation, do not aim so much at establishing the 'correct' interpretation of the Convention read under the applicable rules of interpretation, but rather at presenting the very rich case law in a more or less systematic and synthetic manner.

The interpretation of the Convention is a very complicated and delicate exercise. Under the Convention, with its very general and vague clauses, judicial law-making explicating the meaning of such provisions is unavoidable. The question is not whether the ECtHR can or should avoid creating the law, but whether its law-making case law remains within the scope of its mandate, as defined by the Convention read under the applicable rules of treaty interpretation. To formulate the problem more precisely, the main question is whether the case law respects the impassable barrier stemming from the text of the instrument which is applied.

It has been argued that the dynamic approach developed by the ECtHR and justified by changing social conditions entails certain costs. It diminishes the decision capacity of national parliaments in respect of important societal issues.[89] It does not contribute to the creation of a coherent and comprehensive system of interpretive rules applicable to the Convention.[90] It may also enhance the perception of human rights as inherently variable and relative and not as universal, invariable, and timeless barriers for public power.

In this context, it is also legitimate to ask the question as to whether the ECHR is an autonomous legal regime with its own meta-rules and especially its own rules of interpretation, or just a field-specific set of rules belonging to the general international law. References to the Vienna Convention on the Law of the Treaties and, in particular, to the rules of interpretation codified therein, as well as references to other rules of international law, underline that the Convention system has not proclaimed its own autonomy from general international law. At the same time, the Convention system has developed a certain number of specificities. It increasingly appears to be a very specific sub-system of international law, governed not only by general rules of international law but also by a certain number of specific rules developed through judicial law-making, including a certain number of rules and interpretive tools which enhance the dynamics of the whole system and encourage further law-making by judges.

89 Compare the dissenting opinion of judge Wojtyczek appended to Firth v. the United Kingdom, mentioned above.

90 See the views expressed by judges De Gaetano and Wojtyczek in dissenting opinion appended to *S., V. and A. v. Denmark.*

Part IV

Comparative Analysis

13 European constitutional courts as law-makers: research synthesis

Monika Florczak-Wątor

1 The evolution of European constitutional courts

The first constitutional courts (CCs) appeared in Europe precisely 100 years ago. These CCs were established in 1920 in Austria[1] and Czechoslovakia.[2] However, at the beginning of the 1930s, these two CCs actually stopped operating.[3] Therefore, the beginnings of the CC system in Europe could not be considered successful, especially as, after the Second World War, of the above two CCs, only one (the Austrian CC) resumed operations. However, from a theoretical point of view, the interwar period was particularly important for the development of the centralized judicial review model. This is because it was then that Hans Kelsen – a prominent representative of the Vienna School of Jurisprudence and one of the co-creators of the Austrian CC – formulated the basic assumptions for this model. Most CCs, which started to form in Europe after the Second World War, were established mainly on the basis of this Kelsenian model with the role of interpreting and applying the Constitution to preserve its supremacy by controlling the constitutionality of laws to ensure the prevalence of the democratic principle and of fundamental rights, and to adapt the Constitution when social changes and the times demanded such a task.[4] Although currently the basic assumption of the Kelsenian model – namely, that the CC is only a 'negative law-maker' – seems to be disputable, the thesis that the CC is not entitled to create *ex novo* any pieces of legislation still has many supporters.

In this collection of studies, two CC categories that were established and developed after the Second World War are analysed. The first includes those CCs functioning in European countries as constitutional bodies. Among them are those

1 The Austrian CC was established under the Act of 25 January 1919 and the Constitution of the Federal Republic of Austria of 1 October 1920.

2 The CC of the First Czechoslovak Republic was established by the Czechoslovakian Constitution of 1920.

3 See Leszek Garlicki, 'Ewolucja podstaw kontroli konstytucyjności w Austrii', in Janusz Łętowski, Wojciech Sokolewicz (eds.), *Państwo, prawo, obywatel. Zbiór studiów dla uczczenia 60-lecia urodzin i 40-lecia pracy naukowej profesora Adama Łopatki* (Zakład Narodowy im. Ossolińskich 1989) 289, 289–298.

4 Allan R. Brewer-Carías, *Constitutional Courts as Positive Legislators. A Comparative Law Study* (Cambridge University Press 2011) 889.

DOI: 10.4324/9781003022442-14

CCs that were created in Western Europe in response to the negative experiences of the period of Nazism and fascism, as well as CCs that originated in Central and Eastern Europe after the fall of communism. The second category of CCs includes European courts of an international nature; namely, the European Court of Human Rights (ECtHR) and the Court of Justice of the European Union (CJEU). These bodies not only ensure that the Member States of the Council of Europe and the EU, respectively, comply with the obligations arising from the European Convention on Human Rights (ECHR) and EU Treaties, but also, in the case of countries that are moving away from democratic standards, that they are taking over the tasks of national CCs regarding the protection of democratic standards.[5] This is because the standards of the ECHR and EU Treaties are comparable to the constitutional standards of the Member States of the Council of Europe and the EU as they originate from the common constitutional traditions of those countries.

Within the first category, the authors of this book analysed ten European CCs created at different times and under different circumstances. The German and Italian CCs were established in the 1950s as the guardians of the new democratic constitutions adopted in those countries immediately after the end of the Second World War. The Spanish CC was established almost 30 years later as a factor stabilizing the democratic system after the fall of General Francisco Franco's regime. Different reasons constituted the basis for the establishment of the French Constitutional Council in 1958. Its original task was to protect the legislative powers of the parliament arising from the Constitution of the Fifth French Republic. In contrast with the first CCs mentioned above, the Council did not have the power to repeal unconstitutional laws, but purely the competence to issue decisions on them before they became a part of the legal system. It was only at the beginning of the 1970s that the Council started to transform into a 'regular' CC, protecting democracy and human rights.[6] The process of this transformation was finalized following the Constitutional Council being awarded the power to examine the constitutionality of laws in response to the priority preliminary rulings on the issue of constitutionality (QPC).[7]

5 See Francis Jacobs, '*Is the Court of Justice of the European Communities a Constitutional Court?*' in Deirdre Curtin, Daniel O'Keeffe (ed.), Constitutional Adjudication in European Community and National Law (Butterworth Dublin 1992), 25, 25; Anthony Arnull, '*A Constitutional Court for Europe?*' (2003–2004) CYELS (Cambridge Yearbook of European Legal Studies) 2; Bo Vesterdorf, *A constitutional court for the EU?*, IJCL (International Journal of Constitutional Law) (2006) 4, 607, 607; Lukas Bauer, *Der Europäische Gerichtshof als Verfassungsgericht?* (Nomos 2008) 160–161.

6 See Decision 71–44 DC, of 16 July 1971. See also Alec Stone Sweet, 'The Juridical Coup d'État and the Problem of Authority' (2007) 10 *German Law Journal* 915, 915–928.

7 The mechanism of the 'priority' question on constitutionality was introduced on 1 March 2010 by organic act No. 2009–1523 of 10 December 2009. See Xavier Philippe, 'Constitutional Review in France: The Extended Role of the Conseil Constitutionnel through the New Priority Preliminary Rulings Procedure (QPC)' (2012) 53 Annales Universitatis Scientiarum Budapestinensis de Rolando Eötvös Nominatae. Sectio iuridica 65, 66.

In Central and Eastern Europe, the first CCs were established shortly after the fall of communism to become the guardians of the new democratic constitutions adopted at the beginning of the 1990s. In this study collection, this group is represented by the CCs of Hungary, Bulgaria, the Czech Republic, and the Slovak Republic. In Latvia, which was also included in the research, the CC was established as late as 1996, and in addition, in that country, unlike many other countries from that region, a new constitution had not been adopted, whereas the one passed in 1922 was upheld. In all these post-communist countries, CCs were one of the main achievements of the political transitions. Only the Polish CC was created under completely different circumstances. It was established in the mid-1980s by way of an amendment to the 1952 Communist Constitution that was in force at that time.[8] Therefore, the CC appeared in the Polish legal order before the start of the political transition and, therefore, for obvious reasons, it could not initially be seen as a guarantor of democracy and the rule of law. It had limited powers and was formally subordinated to the parliament, which at that time held the overriding position in the system of State authorities. Every CC ruling on the unconstitutionality of laws could have been rejected by the parliament. However, the position of the CC and the scope of its competences evolved together with the change in the political system. The introduction in 1989 of the principle of a democratic law-governed state into the 1952 Constitution was of key importance to its further functioning. From that moment onwards, the CC actively engaged in the process of the democratization of the State by inferring from the principle of a democratic law-governed state further important constitutional principles, as well as the rights and freedoms of individuals, which were omitted from the Communist Constitution. Ultimately, the Polish CC received its current status as an independent authority, while its rulings became final as late as 1999, which was ten years after the political transformation started and two years after the new democratic Constitution entered into force.

The further evolution of the CC system currently being observed in specific Central and Eastern European countries is a consequence of power being taken over in those countries by populist governments that are moving away from the idea of democracy and the rule of law. This trend has been especially visible in Hungary since 2010 and in Poland since 2015. The CCs in these two countries have become politicized in recent years, whereby the ruling parliamentary majorities have filled them with 'their own' judges. The main task of these 'new' CCs has become the legalization of constitutionally doubtful pieces of legislation that have been adopted by the parliamentary majority. Instead of controlling the activities of the parliament, the CCs in Poland and Hungary have started to execute its

8 This was the Constitution of the People's Republic of Poland adopted on 22 July 1952, which only lost its full force when the Constitution of the Republic of Poland entered into force in 1997. On the narrative of discontinuity versus the continuity of the 'constitutional environment' see Aleksandra Kustra-Rogatka, 'The Polish Constitutional Court and Political "Revolution" after 1989: Between the Continuity and Discontinuity of the Constitutional Narrative' (2016) 6 Wrocław Review of Law, Administration & Economics 62, 66 et seq.

political decisions. This type of CC 'activism' poses a serious threat to the democratic constitutional order and its underlying axiology.[9]

In this situation, the role of the CCs in the countries affected by constitutional crises started to be taken over by the international courts; namely, the ECtHR and the CJEU. The citizens of these countries and their judges have begun to address the complaints to the ECtHR and preliminary references to the CJEU in matters, that would otherwise have been resolved by the Hungarian and Polish CCs. As an example, there was the case on Polish legislation concerning the lowering of the retirement age of Supreme Court judges, where the CJEU held that the application of this legislation to the judges in post within that court is not justified by a legitimate objective and undermines the principle of the irremovability of judges, that principle being essential to their independence.[10] This group of cases includes also the case before the ECtHR concerning the premature termination of the President of the Hungarian Supreme Court's mandate on account of his criticisms of legislative reforms, which was contrary to the Convention.[11]

2 The law-making activity of constitutional courts

Law-making (understood as the process of abrogating, modifying, and supplementing laws) in cases where the CCs act as positive legislators can be analysed in many different ways and from different perspectives. The authors who have studied this problem to date have been mostly trying to distinguish between the different types of judicial law-making undertaken by CCs. Allan R. Brewer-Carías, in his report on CCs as positive legislators in comparative law, identified four main trends regarding such types of activity.[12] The first trend he described concerned CCs interfering with the Constituent Power by enacting constitutional rules and even mutating the Constitution. The second trend is related to CCs interfering with existing legislation by complementing statutes, adding new provisions to

9 See Leszek Garlicki, 'Disabling the Constitutional Court in Poland?' in Andrzej Szmyt & Bogusław Banaszak, (eds.), *Transformation of Law Systems in Central, Eastern and Southeastern Europe in 1989–2015.* Liber Amicorum in Honorem Prof. dr. dres. H. C. Rainer Arnold (Gdańsk University Press 2016) 63, 63–69; Tomasz Tadeusz Koncewicz, 'Polish Judiciary in Times of Constitutional Reckoning, of Fidelities, Doubts, Boats and … a Journey' (2017) 38 *Gdańskie Studia Prawnicze* 292, 292–306; Wojciech Sadurski, 'Polish Constitutional Tribunal Under PiS: From an Activist Court, to a Paralysed Tribunal, to a Governmental Enabler' (2019) 11 *Hague Journal on the Rule Law* 63, 63–84.

10 C-619/18, of 24 June 2019 (*Commission v. Poland*). See also Jakub Jaraczewski, Age is the limit? Background of the CJEU case C-619/18 *Commission v Poland*, VerfBlog (26.11.2019), https://verfassungsblog.de/age-is-the-limit-background-of-the-cjeu-case-c-619-18-commission-v-poland.

11 Case 20261/12, of 23 June 2016 (*Baka v. Hungary*). See also: Attila Vincze, 'Dismissal of the President of the Hungarian Supreme Court: ECtHR *Judgement Baka v Hungary*' (2015) 21 *European Public Law* 445, 445–456; David Kosař & Katarina Šipulová, 'The Strasbourg Court Meets Abusive Constitutionalism: Baka v. Hungary and the Rule of Law' (2018) 10 *Hague Journal on the Rule of Law* 83, 83–110.

12 Brewer-Carías (n 4) 893.

them and determining the temporal effects of legislation. The third trend is defined as CCs interfering with an absence of legislation due to absolute or relative legislative omissions. Finally, he identified the fourth trend as the role of CCs as legislators on matters of judicial review. In turn, Anna Gamper, in her paper, distinguished between six different types of CC law-making; namely, negative legislation, positive legislation as entailed by negative legislation, legislative proposals, substitute and mandated legislation, and legislation through interpretation.[13] These are only two examples of the different approaches that can be adopted by those examining the issue of the law-making activity of CCs.

In this book, the law-making activity of CCs was simultaneously analysed at the constitutional level as well as at the sub-constitutional (mainly statutory) level. In both cases the authors of specific chapters were trying to identify the different types of positive (even creative) influence that CCs have on the legal order. They distinguished law-making through the creative interpretation of laws as well as through shaping the content of the law due to various legal effects arising from CC judgements. The authors also tackled the issue of legislative omissions and the question of whether CCs can, in some cases, supplement legislation, or event substitute for the legislator. Finally, they analysed the power of CCs to create procedural rules on judicial review and to formulate legislative recommendations for the law-making authorities.

One of the purposes of the book, as mentioned in the Introduction, was the establishment of the relationship between the law-making activity of national CCs on the one hand and the ECtHR and CJEU on the other hand. Therefore, this issue was also analysed in some chapters. As Krzysztof Wojtyczek explained in his chapter, the law-making activity of the CCs can be an object of review for the ECtHR when its examines the compatibility of national authorities' acts and omissions with the ECHR. Moreover, the established case law may be a source of legitimate expectations protected under the Convention.

3 Law-making at the level of constitutional regulations

3.1 Determining the scope of admissible constitutional changes

The main task of the CC is to preserve the supremacy of the Constitution. However, the CC is not merely a guardian of the wording of the Constitution, but is first and foremost a guarantor of its spirit and axiology. Therefore, although only some European countries such as Germany, France, Italy, and the Czech Republic have constitutions containing unchangeable provisions, CCs from other countries also consider themselves as having the competence to protect the inviolability of those constitutional principles that determine the 'identity of the Constitution' and that constitute the 'constitutional core.' However, in cases where explicit

13 Anna Gamper, 'Constitutional Courts and Judicial Law-Making: Why Democratic Legitimacy Matters' (2015) 4 *Cambridge Journal of International and Comparative Law* 423, 424–434.

constitutional decisions on the 'eternity clauses' are lacking, the CC adjudicates which constitutional provisions cannot be amended. Therefore, the Italian CC defines the constitutional core as the set of fundamental principles of the legal order and human rights,[14] while the Slovak CC, as Ján Štiavnický and Max Steuer explained in their chapter, perceives the material core of the Constitution as containing all the principles of the rule of law including the principle of independence of the judiciary. In turn, the Hungarian CC uses the concept of constitutional identity,[15] which is currently even the legal term, as in 2018 it was introduced into the text of the Hungarian Constitution. This term of 'constitutional identity' also appears in the judgements of the Polish CC, although it has not yet been positivized.

CCs applying these concepts consider themselves as having the competence to assess whether EU law is in breach of this constitutional core or the constitutional identity of the given State.[16] The Czech CC has increased its ability to assess the constitutionally acceptable degree of State interference in the process of European integration by increasing the scope of the 'constitutional order' from the point of view of which such an assessment is made. Using the so-called Euro-amendment to the Constitution adopted in 2001, the Czech CC arrived at the conclusion that the notion of the constitutional order includes also various types of international treaties protecting human rights, e.g. the ECHR and the International Covenant on Civil and Political Rights (ICCPR).[17] The effect of this ruling involved, on the one hand, the addition of new constitutional patterns of control in the process of examining the constitutionality of laws and, on the other, the obligation of the ordinary judges to refer the control of the compliance of laws with human rights treaties to the Czech CC. The Court simultaneously emphasized that the impassable limits of State intervention in the processes of European integration are set by the principle of a democratic law-governed state. This is because it acknowledged that the transfer of EU competencies would only be consistent with the constitutional order understood in this way if it respected the basic attributes of the rule of law principle that must not be breached.[18]

By determining the scope of admissible constitutional changes, CCs thus place themselves de facto above the Constituent bodies. Moreover, by specifying the impassable limits – from the constitutional point of view – of European integration, the CCs may even affect the activity of the State in the international arena.

14 See cases: 183/1974; 1146/1988; 105/14; 24/17.

15 Decision 22/2016, of 5 December 2016.

16 However, this is not the case in the Slovak Republic as the Slovak CC acknowledged the dominance of EU law over domestic law and showed no preference for constitutional pluralism. See Max Steuer, 'Constitutional pluralism and the Slovak Constitutional Court: the Challenge of European Union Law' (2018) 8 *The Lawyer Quarterly* 108, 127.

17 Pl. ÚS 36/01, of 25 June 2002.

18 Pl. ÚS 50/04, of 8 March 2006.

3.2 Determining the constitutionality of constitutional amendments

In practice, the provisions of the Constitution are rarely subject to CC examination, as they are most frequently a pattern for examining provisions positioned lower in the hierarchy of the sources of law. It is also disputable as to whether the CCs can examine the constitutionality of an amendment to the Constitution. Their competence in examining the constitutionality of the procedure for amending the Constitution is questioned less frequently. However, some of the CCs analysed in this book not only considered themselves as competent at conducting a substantive examination of amendments to the Constitution, but they even found amendments to the Constitution to be unconstitutional as a result of such an examination. This applies, as asserted by Martin Belov and Aleksandar Tsekov in their chapter, to the Bulgarian CC, which declared an amendment to the Constitution awarding the President of Bulgaria the power to dismiss the Chairman of the Supreme Court of Cassation, the Chairman of the Supreme Administrative Court, and the State Prosecutor General, as unconstitutional.[19] This was also the case with the Czech CC, which annulled Constitutional Act No. 195/2009 Coll. (on the Prorogation of the Fifth Term of Office of the Chamber of Deputies), as affirmed by Jan Malíř and Jana Ondřejková.[20] However, the most illuminating example of this type of law-making activity is the Slovak case, mentioned by Ján Štiavnický and Max Steuer in their chapter. In January 2019, the Slovak CC derogated a part of the Constitution concerning one-time screening of active judges as this regulation was found to violate the material core of the Constitution.[21]

These types of CC rulings essentially restrict the freedom of the Constitution-makers and therefore they should only be issued in the form of preventive controls, as the *ex post* elimination of an unconstitutional amendment to the Constitution can seriously destabilize the functioning of the State. Therefore, in such cases, control of the constitutionality of the constitutional amendments should be exercised before the amendment has been enacted through a popular vote, when required.[22]

3.3 Law-making through constitutional interpretation

The interpretation of the Constitution is essentially creative, mainly because its provisions are formulated in a highly general way and leave room for various understanding.[23] Undoubtedly, in many countries, such a mode of constitutional regulation is also the effect of a constitutional compromise and of attempts to

19 Case 6/2006, of 13 September 2006.
20 Pl. ÚS 27/09, of 10 September 2010.
21 See Marek Domin, 'A Part of the Constitution Is Unconstitutional, the Slovak Constitutional Court has Ruled' Verfassungsblog (8 February 2019), https://verfassungsblog.de/a-part-of-the-constitution-is-unconstitutional-the-slovak-constitutional-court-has-ruled/.
22 Brewer-Carías (n 4) 895.
23 See e.g. Jeffrey Goldsworthy, 'Constitutional Interpretation' in Michel Rosenfeld & András Sajó (eds.), *The Oxford Handbook of Comparative Constitutional Law* (Oxford University Press 2012), 689, 689–690; Lino A. Graglia, 'Creative Constitutional

address the most contentious and controversial issues in the Constitution without prejudging them clearly and unequivocally. However, the task of the CC is not only to concretize the constitutional provisions, but also to develop them and to adapt them to changing social conditions, and even to supplement them with new rules whenever such supplementation has occurred and has been seen to be necessary. Although the intensity of these kinds of law-making activity through constitutional interpretation differs among the CCs that have been examined, one can point out that in some countries the informal amendments to the Constitution through its creative interpretation take place quite often. The Hungarian CC, as affirmed by Zoltán Pozsár-Szentmiklósy in his chapter, has made twelve such constitutional changes to date. Some of them were accepted by the Constitution-maker implicitly *post factum* (by not taking any legislative action), while others were 'legalized' (by amending the Constitution and introducing into its content a norm formulated via CC interpretation),[24] or successfully rejected (by introducing a norm into the Constitution, which differs from and supersedes the one formulated by the CC).

The creative interpretation of the Constitution by the CC is sometimes necessary as the Constitution is a living instrument functioning in a perpetually changing social reality. A good example of this is the ruling of the Spanish CC on same-sex marriages, as mentioned by Covadonga Ferrer Martín de Vidales in her chapter. There is no doubt that when preparing the text of the Spanish Constitution in the 1970s, the authors did not have in mind same-sex marriage, so it cannot be assumed that they either allowed them or that they ruled them out. It was only in this ruling that the Spanish CC decided that when regulating the institution of same-sex marriages, the law-makers exercised legislative freedom within the limits set by the Constitution.

The creative interpretation of the Constitution by the CC can also touch on more concrete, or even technical, constitutional provisions. As Jan Malíř and Jana Ondřejková explained in their chapter, the Czech CC applied such an interpretation for determining the method of calculating the deadline for the President of the Republic to veto a bill, as prescribed by the Constitution. A creative interpretation of this kind is also applied by the CJEU, for instance, in matters on the safeguarding the powers of EU institutions.[25]

The constitutional review of the law requires the CC to reconstruct the normative content of the constitutional provisions using various methods of

Interpretation as Justification for Rule by the Supreme Court' (2019) 51 *Arizona State Law Journal* 109, 109–111.

24 See e.g., Article 9 paras. 6–7 of the Hungarian Fundamental Law, which 'legalized' the earlier CC decisions granting to the President of the State the power to refuse to appoint some state officials and to refuse to award prizes in the name of the state (CC decisions: 8/1992, of 30 January 1992; 36/1992, of 10 June 1992 and 47/2007, of 3 July 2007).

25 See e.g., cases regarding the competence of the European Parliament: 294/83, of 23 April 1986 (Les Verts); C-70/88, of 22 May 1990 (Chernobyl); Case 25/62, of 15 July 1963 (Plaumann); Case 5/71, of 2 December 1971 (Schöppenstedt).

interpretation. Some of those methods support the law-making activity of the CC (in particular, the functional, teleological, and systemic interpretations), while, in contrast, others limit this type of CC activity (e.g. historical or linguistic interpretations). CCs also take into account the wording of the norms of the ECHR and EU legislation in the process of interpreting the Constitution (a pro-convention and pro-EU law interpretation, known also as an ECHR and EU law-friendly approach). However, some CCs set clear boundaries for the application of this type of interpretation. This is the case of the Polish CC stating that an interpretation that is friendly to European law must not lead to results that are in conflict with the explicit wording of the provisions of the Constitution and must not destroy the Constitution's implementation of its basic guarantee function. As the Polish CC emphasized in the judgement regarding the constitutionality of the Accession Treaty,[26] the provisions of the Constitution regarding the rights and freedoms of an individual set a minimum and unsurpassable threshold that cannot be lowered or challenged as a result of the introduction of Community regulations.[27]

3.4 Developing constitutional rights and principles

The most creative interpretations of the Constitution take place regarding constitutional principles, and the rights and freedoms of an individual.

Various examples of constitutional principles can be given, the actual content of which were determined not by the way in which they were expressed in the Constitution, but by the way in which they were understood and applied in the CCs' rulings. The best example of this is the principle of a democratic law-governed state. Its basic elements were formulated by the German FCC and they were later derived and developed by other CCs, especially those from Central and Eastern Europe. The Polish CC, as Piotr Czarny and Bogumił Naleziński mentioned in their chapter, inferred from the principle of a democratic law-governed state such principles as the principle of the protection of trust in the State and the law, the principle of the protection of acquired rights and legitimate expectation, the principle of the protection of pending interests, the principle of contractual freedom, and the principle of proper legislation. None of these principles has been formulated *expressis verbis* in the text of the Constitution of the Republic of Poland to this day, although all of them are treated by the legal doctrine as constitutional principles. However, the creative interpretation of the Constitution by CCs also covers principles that are explicitly expressed in the Constitution. This applies to the Spanish CC, which formulated in its jurisprudence, as Covadonga Ferrer Martín de Vidales mentioned in her chapter, the basic elements of the

26 K 18/04, of 11 May 2015.

27 See Justyna Holocher & Bogumił Naleziński, 'Konstytucyjne determinanty stosowania prawa Unii Europejskiej przez organy władzy sądowniczej w Rzeczypospolitej Polskiej' (2018) 4 Rocznik Administracji Publicznej 47, 52; Aleksandra Kustra, 'The Polish Constitutional Tribunal and the Judicial Europeanization of the Constitution' 35 (2015) *Polish Yearbook of International Law* 193, 215.

principle of the regional State.[28] This is also true of the Latvian CC, which specified the content of the principle of the continuation of the Latvian State, the principle of the separation of powers, as well as the principles of good legislation, justice, and proportionality, as expressed by Anita Rodina and Alla Spale in their chapter.

The creative interpretation of the principles is especially essential in the case law of the European international courts. The rules arising from the judgement of the CJEU are even recognized as general principles of the Union's law being part of primary EU law. Although some of these principles still exist outside the wording of the treaties, the EU Member States do not question their legality. The latter remark should be emphasized because all the countries covered by our research have adopted the civil law system, in which court rulings do not, in principle, constitute a separate category of sources of law. Among the examples of general principles arising from the CJEU case law that were provided by Monika Kawczyńska in her chapter, the principle of the supremacy of EU law and the principle of the exclusive implied competence of the Union to conclude international agreements were examined. The first of these principles was formulated in the ruling in the Costa case[29] and was later developed in the ruling Internationale Handelsgesellschaft.[30] This principle has been operating outside the treaties for over half a century, although there was an attempt to codify it. In turn, the second principle was formulated in the ruling in the ERTA case,[31] developed in Opinion 1/76,[32] and codified as late as in the Lisbon Treaty.[33]

The second domain of constitutional regulation that is particularly susceptible to creative interpretation by the CCs is that of the provisions on the rights and freedoms of an individual. Interpretations in this area are creative *sensu stricto* since CCs supplement the Constitution with new individual rights and freedoms that are not explicitly stated in its provisions. Before 1997, the Polish CC inferred from the principle of a democratic law-governed state such rights as the right to privacy, the right to life, and the right to a fair trial, although in the Communist Constitution in force at that time these rights were not guaranteed *expressis verbis.* Similarly, the German FCC, as Ruth Weber mentioned in her chapter, has added new types of rights to the catalogue of constitutional rights; namely, the right to informational self-determination, and the right to the confidentiality and integrity of information technology systems.

The law-making approach that has the purpose of strengthening the rights of the individuals is also noticeable, as asserted by Monika Kawczyńska in her chapter, in the case law of the Luxembourg courts. The CJEU in the Van Gend en Loos case has established the principle of the direct effect of EU law, that could be invoked by individuals for the protection of their rights. Moreover, the CJEU

28 STC 114/2017, of 2 February 1981, para. 3.
29 Case 6/64, of 15 July 1964 (Costa).
30 Case 11/70, of 17 December 1970 (Internationale Handelsgesellschaft).
31 Case 22/70, of 31 March 1971 (AETR/ERTA).
32 Opinion 1/76, of 26 April 1977 (Inland waterway vessels).
33 Case 26/62, of 5 February 1963 (van Gend & Loos).

derived the fundamental rights, as part of general principles of the Union's law, from constitutional traditions common to the Member States and international human rights treaties, in particular the ECHR. Currently the principle of protection of fundamental rights within the EU legal order is expressed in Article 6 TFEU. In a similar manner, the CJEU formulated the principle of effective judicial protection of the individual, referring to the principle of effectiveness derived from the principle of sincere cooperation (Article 4 (3) TEU) and common constitutional traditions. The obligation of the state authority to provide remedies sufficient to ensure effective legal protection of the individuals in the fields covered by Union law is now foreseen in Article 19 (2) TEU.

4 Law-making at the level of statutory regulations

CC rulings can apply not only to statutes, but also to other legal acts. However, within the group of acts examined, statutes hold a special place. They are adopted by parliament with its strong democratic legitimacy to act on behalf of the sovereign. None of the CCs have the normative power to create new pieces of legislation.[34] Therefore, when examining the statutes passed by parliament, CCs should act with restraint, treating a ruling on the lack of constitutionality as an *ultima ratio.* CCs should also respect the freedom of the parliamentary majority to implement its own vision of the policy as long as it falls within the constitutional framework set by the constituent body.[35] The examination of the constitutionality of a statute by the CC gives rise to specific dilemmas regarding the division of powers and the limits of the judicial review of legislation. Therefore, the law-making activity of the CC at the statute level has far more significant effects from both the theoretical and the practical point of view than at the level of sub-statutory legal regulations. Consequently, the chapters of this book have been more closely analysed at CC law-making level than at the statutory level.

4.1 Preventing the emergence of a dysfunctional legal gap as a result of constitutional court rulings

The CC rulings on the lack of constitutionality of a statute result in negative effects; namely, an unconstitutional statute (its provision) is repealed and ceases to be a part of the legal system. Such a situation may create a legal gap (lacuna) that involves a lack of regulation of a matter that should be encompassed by legislation. A legal gap of this kind may be more unconstitutional than the regulation that was removed from the legal system by the CC. Therefore, CCs have developed

34 As the French Constitutional Council emphasizes, 'the Constitution does not confer on the Constitutional Court a general power of discretion and decision identical to that of Parliament.' See decisions: 74–54, of 15 January 1975; 80–127, of 20 January 1981; 86–218, of 18 November 1986.

35 In Italy, Art. 28 of Law No. 87/1953 on the Rules on the Establishment and Functioning of the Constitutional Court explicitly forbade the CC from examining how parliament exercises its discretionary authority.

different instruments for preventing the emergence of a dysfunctional legal gap as a result of their rulings. Two situations should be distinguished in this respect.

The first is when the matter regulated by the legal norm that was removed by the CC due to its unconstitutionality can be covered by the scope of the regulation of another legal norm. This situation happens quite frequently as the law is a system of connected vessels and the change in one of these vessels frequently affects all other vessels. Therefore, the removal of one norm from the legal system usually results in 'filling' its scope of regulation with another norm that still remains in the system. In this way, a negative CC ruling simultaneously gives rise to positive effects, modifying the scope of the regulation of the provisions that were not even examined in proceedings before the CC. A statutory norm that has been removed from the legal system can be replaced by another statutory norm or by a constitutional norm that is concrete and suitable for direct application. A constitutional norm may, in such a situation, be applied either independently or jointly with a statutory norm, and then the former may supplement the shortcomings of the latter. The co-application of the Constitution and a statute is also a type of direct application of the Constitution.[36]

The second situation, which should be distinguished in this regard, is one where the matter at hand cannot be encompassed by a statutory regulation and thus the direct application of the Constitution is impossible. Thus, to avoid the emergence of a dysfunctional legal gap, the CC may use various methods of postponing the derogation effect of its ruling. The most frequently encountered situations include the deferred entry into force of the CC ruling or a delay in issuing the CC ruling on the unconstitutionality of the law.

If the CC defers the entry into force of the ruling on the unconstitutionality of a provision, until the moment stipulated in the operative part arrives, the provision found to be unconstitutional temporarily remains in force and, as a consequence, prima facie should be applied by all public authorities during that time. In some countries, such as Poland, the maximum deferral period is set by the Constitution,[37] while in others (such as, Latvia) the CC has broad discretion to specify the length of the deferral period.[38] Deferral is always a result of a certain axiological compromise, as it is used when the CC concludes that the need to protect certain

36 As Leszek Garlicki noted, 'the direct application of the Constitution (of its provisions on fundamental rights) is present in the decisions of all the courts and judges. The Constitutional Court, while preserving the last word if a controversy arises, no longer claims a monopoly over application of the Constitution but, rather, acts as a coordinator of that process'. See Leszek Garlicki, 'Constitutional courts versus supreme courts' (2007) 5 *International Journal of Constitutional* 44, 52.

37 In accordance with Article 190, para. 3 of the Polish Constitution, the Polish CC may specify another date for the end of the binding force of a normative act. Such time period may not exceed 18 months in relation to a statute or 12 months in relation to any other normative act.

38 In Latvia, the period of the deferral is not specified in the Constitution, so the CC has broad discretion to determine the length of this period (most frequently deferral is for 6 months).

values or interests requires that the unconstitutional law remains in force for a limited period of time.

The CC may also defer issuing a ruling on the unconstitutionality of a provision, leaving the law-makers with time to amend it. Various types of decisions on 'expected unconstitutionality' are intended to prevent a gap from arising in the law by appealing to the parliament to immediately amend the unconstitutional provision under the pain of issuing a ruling on its unconstitutionality. These decisions involving non-compulsory judicial recommendations may take various forms. The Italian CC, as mentioned by Nausica Palazzo in her chapter, uses so-called exhortative judgements to force a legislative reaction on the parliament within the deadline set for it.[39] This type of threat involves striking down an unconstitutional provision if the legislator fails to execute the CC's recommendations. Similarly, as asserted by Julien Mouchette in his chapter, the French Constitutional Council issues so-called decisions of appeal to the legislator, in which it requests the law-makers to amend the provision, sometimes even within a deadline it has set on its own. The Council also formulates specific guidelines about the content of the future legal regulation and so it is pointed out that this is a form of 'close dialogue' between the Council and parliament.

The group of rulings that prevent the emergence of a dysfunctional legal gap also includes a declaration of unconstitutionality, which is used by the German FCC, as Ruth Weber mentioned in her chapter, to temporarily leave an unconstitutional regulation in force, the immediate removal of which from the legal order would be detrimental to the public interest. Likewise, as Covadonga Ferrer Martín de Vidales noted in her chapter, the Spanish CC also applies 'unconstitutionality without nullity' in its rulings, limiting itself to declaring the unconstitutionality of the legal regulation that it examined and leaving the law-makers to consider the matter of correcting it.

Rulings through which the CC restores the previous (pre-amendment) wording of the provision, when it finds that the provision amending the regulations being examined is unconstitutional, also constitute a way of avoiding a legal gap and, simultaneously, they are an obvious manifestation of judicial law-making. The power to restore the previous wording of the provision is used by the Polish and Latvian CCs. The Polish legal doctrine refers to such CC decisions as resuscitation decisions because they cause 'the revival' of a provision that has lost its binding force and has ceased to be part of the applicable legal order.[40] The Latvian CC, as Anita Rodina and Alla Spale noted in their chapter, emphasizes the temporary and provisional nature of this institution, indicating that the restoration of the provision is a remedy for a legal gap arising from a ruling on unconstitutionality that

39 See ruling 207/2018 regarding criminal liability for assistance in euthanasia by DJ Fabo.

40 Andrzej Grabowski, Bogumił Naleziński, 'Kłopoty z obowiązywaniem. Uwagi na tle orzecznictwa Trybunału Konstytucyjnego' in Jerzy Stelmach (ed.), *Studia z filozofii prawa* (Wydawnictwo Uniwersytetu Jagiellońskiego 2001), 219, 251–257; Monika Florczak-Wątor, *Orzeczenia Trybunału Konstytucyjnego i ich skutki prawne* (Ars boni et aequi 2006) 142–145.

will disappear when the law-makers pass a new legal regulation. Also, the Bulgarian CC and the Slovak CC apply the institution of the revival of a repealed provision.

4.2 Partial unconstitutionality and its effect

Contemporary CCs increasingly rarely state that the provisions being examined are entirely unconstitutional and increasingly frequently hold that they are partially unconstitutional. The reason for adopting such an adjudication strategy is the conviction that moderation is required with respect to interference with the parliament's legislative powers. Contrary to appearances, however, a ruling that a provision is partially unconstitutional can have more far-reaching effects than a ruling that the same provision is unconstitutional in its entirety. This is because a provision that is declared partially unconstitutional continues to operate in the legal system to the extent to which it is amended by the CC. The wording of this provision can therefore significantly distort the intentions that guided the law-makers at the time of its establishment. It can also be completely differently understood and applied in practice due to the amended normative content. The amended provision can also affect the way in which other provisions are understood and applied in its normative environment. However, primarily, the main problem with partial rulings is that they modify the normative content of a provision while keeping its wording unchanged. This, in turn, gives rise to difficulties related to establishing the actual scope of the normative change arising from this type of ruling. Consequently, until the legislator adjusts the wording of the provision to designate its new normative content, there will be a discrepancy between the wording of the provision and its normative content. This is a major problem for all authorities applying this regulation, including the courts.

To avoid discrepancies in applying the regulations after the ruling regarding their partial unconstitutionality, the indication given by the CC on the correct interpretation of the regulation is taken into account. This interpretation has different levels of significance depending on which parts of the CC's ruling are given guidelines. If the guidelines are found in the justification of the ruling, they are often treated by the courts as being the recommended – and not simply the 'correct' – method of interpretation. In contrast with the operative part, the justification does not generally have binding force. However, CCs sometimes include this desirable way of interpreting an examined provision in the operative part of their judgement, which is referred to as an interpretative judgement.[41] An interpretation of this kind is binding on all addressees of the CC's judgement. The inclusion of the recommended interpretation of a provision in the operative part of a positive ruling means that the provision is in compliance with the Constitution, provided that it is applied in the manner specified by the CC. Therefore, this is a form of conditional constitutionality, as it assumes that the provision will be left in the legal system under the condition that it will be understood and applied in a

41 See e.g. Piotr Tuleja, *Wyroki interpretacyjne Trybunału Konstytucyjnego* (Ars boni et aequi 2016); Brewer-Carías (n 4) 74–78; Florczak-Wątor (n40) 93–102.

specific way. In practice, if this type of adjudicative activity by the CC is respected by the courts, it can lead to the harmonization of the interpretation applied in the courts of various levels. However, the problem is that the supreme courts exercise supervision over ordinary courts regarding judgements. Therefore, the imposition by the CCs of a particular type of interpretation of a law is frequently treated by the supreme courts as interfering in their powers.[42] CCs also use the negative variant of interpretative rulings, indicating in the operative part of the ruling the unconstitutional understanding of the provision under review. The aim of such decisions is to eliminate unconstitutional interpretations, although, in order to avoid a dispute with the highest courts, as a rule, the CCs emphasize that the interpretation itself is not subject to review, while the CCs only examine the result of this interpretation in the form of a specific meaning of the provision. However, it should be noted that these interpretative rulings are also a source of conflict in relations between CCs and the highest courts, which is demonstrated, if only, by the example of Poland.

The concept of interpretive judgements has been especially developed in the case law of the Italian CC, both as so-called interpretative judgements of acceptance and so-called interpretative judgements of dismissal. However, the most extreme form of law-making constitutes 'manipulative judgements,' because, as their name implies, they manipulate the text of the statute and give it a meaning that can give rise to serious doubts. The Latvian CC and the Czech CC most frequently use the positive variant of interpretative rulings, which is less invasive because it enables the provision being examined to be kept in the legal order when its constitutional understanding exists. Additionally, the Bulgarian CC uses the so-called conformity interpretation as an intermediate solution between a ruling on the constitutionality of a provision that is being examined and a ruling on its unconstitutionality, as confirmed by Martin Belov and Aleksandar Tsekov in their chapter. In turn, positive and negative interpretative rulings can be found in the case law of the Spanish CC.[43] The Hungarian CC uses the concept of 'constitutional requirements' in a similar sense, which was reflected, for instance, in the ruling on punishing the homeless for occupying public space, as analysed by Zoltán Pozsár-Szentmiklósy in his chapter. Finally, the technique of interpretative reservations used by the French Constitutional Council is also worth mentioning. It involves declaring a provision to be compatible with the Constitution, with the reservation that it will be understood and applied in a strictly defined manner. Three types of reservations have developed in the jurisprudence

42 This is the situation, e.g. in Poland, where interpretative rulings are not respected by the courts because the Supreme Court questions the competence of the CC to issue them. On this matter see Rafał Mańko, '"War of Courts" as a Clash of Legal Cultures: Rethinking the Conflict between the Polish Constitutional Tribunal and the Supreme Court Over "Interpretive Judgments"' in Michael Hein et al. (eds.), *Law, Politics, and the Constitution: New Perspectives from Legal and Political Theory* (Peter Lang 2014) 79, 79–94; Florczak-Wątor (n 40) 204–206.

43 See Leo Brust, 'The interpretation according to the constitution and the manipulative sentences' (2009) 2 *Rev. direito GV* [online] 134, 135–136.

of the Constitutional Council, as explained by Julien Mouchette in his chapter; namely, neutralizing reservations (eliminating an unconstitutional interpretation), directive reservations (attributing liability to the law-makers for applying the law), and constructive reservations (adding a specific norm to the wording of a provision in order to make it compliant with the Constitution). This latter type of reservation gives rise to the greatest doubts because it can lead to the situation in which the law, in its new shape given by a decision of the Constitutional Council, will be in conflict with the original intention of the law-makers.

4.3 Referring to the application of a provision that is found to be unconstitutional

The inclusion in the operative part of the CC ruling of a decision referring not to the content of a provision but to its application is also a form of judicial law-making. In fact, such a decision contains a kind of intertemporal norm prejudging either how to apply a provision that is held to be unconstitutional after a CC ruling or how to apply a CC ruling, which held that this provision is unconstitutional. In the first case, the CC specifies the moment from which the provision is considered unconstitutional, and similarly introduces a state of 'unconstitutionality divided in time,' because it assumes that, up to that moment, the provision will be considered constitutional.[44] Examples of such rulings include the Polish case regarding the inheritance of agricultural farms, in which the CC held that the contested provisions are compliant with the Constitution to the extent to which they apply to inheritances that were opened before the date of the publication of the CC judgement and are unconstitutional to the extent to which they apply to inheritances opened since the date on which the CC's ruling became effective.[45] Examples of judgements from the second category are those in which the intertemporal norm contained in the operative part of the CC ruling specifies the method of applying this judgement in practice, especially on matters regarding citizens. In the Polish legal doctrine, such decisions are called applicative rulings,[46] examples of which are the rulings of the Polish CC in which it was stated that various types of fees paid on the basis of a provision subsequently recognized as unconstitutional are not refundable, although, in accordance with Article 190, para. 4 of the Constitution, a citizen is

44 On the concept of 'unconstitutionality divided in time' see Jan Podkowik, *Niekonstytucyjność prawa i jej skutki cywilnoprawne* (Wydawnictwo Naukowe Scholar 2019) 197–207.

45 P 4/99, of 31 January 2001. For more on this ruling and the effects of its entry into force, see Monika Florczak-Wątor, 'Zasady dziedziczenia gospodarstw rolnych. Komentarz' in Leszek Garlicki et al. (eds.), *Na straży państwa prawa. Trzydzieści lat orzecznictwa Trybunału Konstytucyjnego* (Wolters Kluwer 2016) 354, 367.

46 See Justyna Holocher, Urszula Kosielińska-Grabowska, 'Dolce Vita? O wpływie wyroków aplikacyjnych Trybunału Konstytucyjnego na orzecznictwo sądowe' in Aleksandra Samonek (ed.), *Teoria prawa: między nowoczesnością a ponowoczesnością* (Wydawnictwo Uniwersytetu Jagiellońskiego 2012) 233, 233–242; Florczak-Wątor (n 40) 114–116.

entitled to a refund of these fees.[47] Another example of such a ruling is the decision of the Slovak CC on the unconstitutionality of the provisions constituting the 'Special Court,' as analysed by Ján Štiavnický and Max Steuer in their chapter. In this case, the CC held that its ruling has no influence on the validity of the judgements issued by this Court and does not give them the right to reopen proceedings in cases that have ended in a final and binding manner.

The most obvious manifestation of judicial law-making involves the CC filling existing legal gaps via various methods of interpretation, especially with functional and teleological interpretations. Examples of these types of law-making activities appeared in the rulings of all CCs analysed in this study collection. Some of them, such as the Polish and Latvian CCs, clearly emphasize the difference between absolute legislative omissions and relative legislative omissions, recognizing that they only have the competence to examine the latter. An absolute legislative omission, and therefore those situations in which the law-makers decided not to resolve a given issue, is not subject to control by the CC, as it cannot declare the unconstitutionality of something that has not yet been regulated by parliament. However, a relative legislative omission applies to a legal regulation, which is considered defectively formed due to the defects appearing in it. The Czech CC approached the problem of examining legislative omissions more comprehensively, as affirmed by Jan Malíř and Jana Ondřejková in their chapter. The Czech CC enables the examination of absolute legislative omissions, including those involving the failure to publish a statute that the citizens were counting on.[48]

The problematic nature of the legal consequences of rulings in which the CC declares the unconstitutionality of a relative legislative omission should be highlighted. The Polish CC is of the opinion that judgements of this kind do not cause changes in the legal system (in particular, they do not add an accidentally omitted element to an existing legal regulation), but only obligate the law-makers to take legislative action to improve the existing legal regulation. However, in other cases the Polish CC took a different stance, stating that such a type of ruling has a self-executing effect and corrects the unproper piece of legislation by adding the missing legal norm. Similarly, in Italy, it is accepted that rulings in which the CC declares the unconstitutionality of a relative legislative omission are of a legislative nature. Furthermore, they are referred to as 'additive judgements,' distinguishing – as explained by Nausica Palazzo in her chapter – their two categories; namely, those adding guarantees or services and those adding legal principles.

A separate category of CC judgements concerns those which are issued in the form of a preventive control and therefore apply to the problem of the constitutionality of statutes before their introduction into the legal system. Preventive control is used not only in France but also in other European countries. A

47 See e.g. P 7/00, of 6 March 2002; P 6/02, of 10 December 2002; K 24/03, of 27 April 2004.

48 See ruling Pl.ÚS 9/07, of 1 July 2010, in which the Czech CC held that the parliament's failure to pass the act on the settlement of the historical property of churches and religious communities is unconstitutional, including, as a result, breaching the principle of the protection of a legitimate expectation.

provision that is considered unconstitutional does not become part of the applicable legal order, while the result of a CC ruling may either be the end of the legislative process without the introduction of the statute (or its unconstitutional provision) into the legal system or the referral by the president of the statute for further parliamentary work intended to correct it. The French Constitutional Council – as explained by Julien Mouchette in his chapter – can additionally correct the title of a statute if the content of the statute is amended as a result of its ruling.[49] However, such interference by the Constitutional Council cannot mean a substantive amendment to the statute. It is only a form of editorial revision of the particular piece of legislation.[50]

5 Guidelines for the law-makers

Very often, CC rulings contain various directives, guidelines, and recommendations for the law-making authorities indicating the necessity of adopting specific legislative regulations. If formulated in the justification of the CC's ruling, these directives, guidelines, and recommendations are not of a binding nature and the law-making authority is not liable for not taking them into account. However, they doubtlessly constitute a certain form of interference in the legislative autonomy of the law-making authorities. This is because, as a rule, the CC does not usually restrict itself to stating that it is reasonable to regulate a specific issue, but also frequently indicates the optimal method of regulating it or even the content of the optimal regulation. The more detailed the directives, guidelines, and recommendations are, the greater the probability that they will determine the content of the future legal regulations. Such detailed guidelines may appear, for instance, in cases where the CC finds an absolute legislative omission and therefore a lack of jurisdiction for adjudicating the case. It then frequently makes various appeals to the law-makers and requests them to issue the legal regulation that they had omitted. This also applies to provisions that were not examined by the CC, when their defectiveness (not necessarily their unconstitutionality) was discovered while examining another (contested) regulation, or in a factual context in the light of which a constitutional complaint or legal question was issued. These types of guidelines have a signalling nature and their main purpose is to improve the quality of the law and remove existing legal gaps or conflicts.[51] These statements frequently assume the form of a request addressed to the law-makers to pass specific regulations or to correct an existing regulation.[52] They are not formally

49 Which is referred to as the 'rectification of the law by consequence'. See Pl ÚS 63/06, of 29 January 2008.

50 See e.g., the replacement of a comma with a hyphen. See Decision No. 2012–250 QPC, of 8 June 2012.

51 On the signalization in the Polish CC case law see Marek Safjan, *Poland. The Constitutional Court as a Positive Legislator* in Brewer-Carías (n 4) 717–718.

52 See e.g., the Polish CC request addressed to the parliament to comprehensively regulate the protection of consumers against the bankruptcy of property developers (S 3/10, of 2 August 2010).

binding, but, as already mentioned, such guidelines can constitute a form of warning sent to the law-makers by the CC that the provision will be removed from the legal system if it is not corrected.

However, the directives, guidelines, and recommendations that are closely related to the decision itself, which are contained in the operative part of the CC judgement, are much more important. This applies to cases in which the CC finds the partial unconstitutionality of a provision, as a consequence of which the provision remains in the legal system but needs to be corrected by the law-makers because its wording does not reflect its new (corrected by the CC) normative content. Rulings of this type, as previously mentioned, are called partial rulings. Very detailed directives on what, to what extent, as well as how (in which direction) to correct a regulation are frequently formulated in the CC's justification. These directives may be considered binding on the law-makers because they supplement the operative part of the CC's judgement in a situation where the decision contained in it must be executed. The directives contained in the justification of a ruling on the unconstitutionality of a provision, which is left in force by the CC so that the law-makers have time to amend it, are similarly binding. The obligation to amend the provision arising from the operative part of such a ruling is valid, while a lack of amendment to the prescribed extent is treated as a failure to perform the CC's ruling.

In practice, the extent of the CC's control over the freedom of the law-makers is constantly increasing. A good example in this respect is the so-called review of the manifest error of assessment used in the jurisprudence of the French Constitutional Council. Although, as it emphasizes in its rulings, the Constitutional Council does not examine the aims set by the law-makers, it still assigns itself with powers of limited control over the means used to achieve them.[53] If the Constitutional Council find these means to be manifestly irrelevant to achieving the aim of a legal act, it considers itself as entitled to declare them unconstitutional. In some cases, as Julien Mouchette mentioned, a review of a manifest error of assessment of this type can lead to the assessment made by the parliament being replaced by a different assessment made by the Constitutional Council. In recent rulings, this control assumed the nature of proportionality control or, in other words, control of what is 'manifestly disproportionate.'

6 Regulatory powers of the constitutional courts

CCs covered by the research have among their competences those of a legislative nature *sensu stricto* because they are entitled to issue their internal rules. They are issued on the basis of the authorizations contained in the law, within the regulatory autonomy awarded to the CC as a guarantee of its independence and

53 This method of control was applied in Decision 2004–508, of 16 December 2004. On the same method see also Andrzej Grabowski & Tomasz Gizber-Studnicki, 'Normy programowe w Konstytucji' in Janusz Trzciński (ed.), *Charakter i struktura norm konstytucji* (Wydawnictwo Sejmowe 1997) 95, 109–111.

impartiality. As a rule, such internal regulations adopted by the CC either repeat the constitutional and statutory regulations or specify them in greater detail. However, they sometimes enter the sphere of the rights and freedoms of the individual, specifying, for instance, the principles of their participation in hearings, access to case files or the effects of exceeding the instructional deadlines. Even then, it can generally be said that from the point of view of the impact on the applicable legal order, legal acts arising from the CCs' use of the statutory powers conferred on them are of marginal significance. For this reason, they were not of any great interest to the authors of the specific chapters.

However, the above-mentioned internal rules adopted by international courts are of greater importance. Neither the ECHR nor the EU Treaties regulate in detail the organization and principles of operation of the ECtHR and the CJEU, respectively. These acts make reference to internal rules, which are not only established by the ECtHR and the CJEU, but are also developed by those bodies involved in the practice of applying them. As Krzysztof Wojtyczek mentioned in his chapter, the ECtHR has broad discretion in defining the density of its internal rules and thus dividing the norm-making powers between the situation when it acts in the form of the plenary assembly of judges and the situation when it acts as a judicial body establishing internal rules through its practice that complements the written rules.

7 Conclusions

The examination of the rulings of the European CCs covered by this book leads to the conclusion that their influence on the applicable legal order at the level of both the Constitution and the statutes is significant and undoubted. The rulings of these courts no longer fall within the framework of the concept of the negative law-maker described by Hans Kelsen. This is because contemporary CCs do not restrict themselves to reviewing the constitutionality of statutes and possibly repealing those considered unconstitutional, but they also correct, supplement, and develop the wording of statutes as a result of the creative interpretation applied and the appropriate formulation of the operative part of issued rulings and their legal effects. Additionally, they indicate to parliaments the need to change the law, thereby initiating further processes for its correction, supplementation, and development.

The law-making activity of CCs is manifested at the level of both the provisions of the Constitution as well as statutory norms. In the first case, the CCs do not so much protect the wording of the Constitution (although this also happens, especially in cases where the Constitution contains above-mentioned unchangeable clauses), as its spirit and axiology. The CCs limit the freedom of the Constitution-makers to the extent to which it is possible to amend the Constitution, guaranteeing the immutability of its provisions, which constitute the so-called core of the Constitution or the constitutional identity. In this way, some CCs also specify constitutionally acceptable limits of State involvement in the processes of European integration. On the other hand, CCs creatively develop and supplement the Constitution, especially in the parts in which it stipulates the constitutional principles and the rights and freedoms of an individual. In short, the CCs are real creators of the rigid Constitutions. At the statutory level, however, the law-making abilities of the CCs are especially manifested in the partial and interpretative rulings that it issues, as well as in its rulings confirming the unconstitutionality of legislative omissions. CCs also create intertemporal norms to defer either the effectiveness of their ruling or the deprival of the effectiveness of a provision acknowledged in that ruling as being unconstitutional. Additionally, CCs frequently include very detailed signalling guidelines in the justifications of their rulings that can determine the content of future statutory regulations adopted by parliament.

Index

For Product Safety Concerns and Information please contact our EU
representative GPSR@taylorandfrancis.com
Taylor & Francis Verlag GmbH, Kaufingerstraße 24, 80331 München, Germany

www.ingramcontent.com/pod-product-compliance
Lightning Source LLC
LaVergne TN
LVHW011120300926
849160LV00008B/450

9781032187990